THE GREAT WINE BOOK

THE GREAT WINE BOOK

Jancis Robinson

William Morrow and Company, Inc
New York 1982

To Nick,
my husband, taskmaster,
chauffeur and constant companion
during the extensive travelling this
book involved, only rarely in body
but always in spirit

First published in Great Britain in 1982
by Sidgwick and Jackson Limited

First published in the United States in 1982
by William Morrow and Company, Inc.

Produced, edited and designed by
Shuckburgh Reynolds Limited,
8 Northumberland Place,
London W2 5BS

Designed by Roger Pring
Assistant designer: Dinah Lone
Photography by: Bob Davis, Patrick Eagar, Jean-Paul
Ferrero, Judy Goldhill, Michael Kuh, Michael Lister, Colin
Maher, Edward Piper, Roger Pring, Tessa Traeger, Nik
Wheeler and Jon Wyand.

Illustrations by: Robert Chapman, Sharon Finmark, Dinah
Lone, David Mallott, Janos Marffy, Andrew Popkiewicz,
Timothy Rowe and Gill Wren.

Typesetting by: SX Composing Ltd, Randall Typographic
Ltd and Filmoset Ltd

Colour origination by: Lithospeed Ltd

Inquiries should be addressed to
William Morrow and Company, Inc.,
105 Madison Avenue, New York, N.Y. 10016.

Library of Congress Cataloging in Publication Data

Robinson, Jancis.
    The great wine book

    Includes index.
    1.   Wine and wine making.   I. Title.
TP548.R645   641.2'22   82-6427
ISBN 0-688-00727-9   AACR2

Printed and bound in Spain by
Printer Industria Grafica, Barcelona
DLB 20345 – 1982

First Edition
1 2 3 4 5 6 7 8 9 10

CONTENTS

INTRODUCTION

There is something almost absurd about the concept of greatness applied to an agricultural commodity, which is what wine at its most mundane level is. Imagine potatoes being the subject of august professional tastings, the bestselling World Atlas of Beetroot, or evening classes in citrus appreciation. Other crops are capable of giving enormous physical pleasure, as any gastronome knows, and some (usually illegal) can even enhance perceptions and gladden the spirit. But only the vine, a pretty but unremarkable plant that grows both wild and cultivated over huge tracts of land all over the world, is capable of producing a liquid that can achieve, in so many subtle and different ways, such excellence. Great wine inspires, impresses, invigorates and, perhaps most significantly of all, intrigues.

As any wine student knows, there are many complex factors that combine to make wine great, but it is impossible to define great wine. Wine is above all subjective, which is the source of its appeal. When two or three are gathered together at the tasting or dining table, you may be sure there will be as many opinions on each wine as there are tasters.

Although an enormous amount of work has been done in recent years on the scientific analysis of wine, it remains impossible to formulate a set of analytical criteria to characterise greatness. We know roughly that acidity, alcohol and sugar levels should fall between certain desirable maxima and minima; but each wine's character is formed by the combination of so many tiny elements that "the 'great' formula" promises to be tiresomely elusive for many years yet.

There are some objective pointers to quality, however. Price seems the most obvious one, but it is of course only a fairly crude measurement. Hype, saleroom hysteria, fashion and sheer marketing bravado can all play a part in boosting a wine's price above its inherent quality – while a very obvious lack of any of these elements means that a wine like Gaston Huet's Vouvray may be wildly undervalued. In some of the world's more traditional fine wine regions, those in search of the greats may be helped by an official classification, such as those that have carved up the Médoc into league divisions and delineated *"grands crus"* in appellations as dissimilar as Gevrey-Chambertin and Savennières. Different owners and winemakers come and go, however, making these rankings only a general guideline rather than a specific guarantee of the best. Attempts at even more dogmatic identification of what is greatest in wine tend to be even more temporary in their relevance. As long as wine exists, so will the temptation to compare one with another in the context of competition. Throughout the wine world there are individual wines that are gold medal-winners, whether in Los Angeles, Sydney, Stuttgart or Llubjana (although a first growth claret would not dream of subjecting itself to such competitive analysis).

This book is concerned with enterprises with a track record of excellence. They say in Australia, where "wine shows" assume an importance unparalleled elsewhere, that with a bit

of craft anyone can make a medal-winner that will dazzle on the day of the judging itself. In this collection are winemakers whose cellars should be stocked with previous vintages as inspiring as the wines they are currently producing. An important factor in the selection process has been the wines' potential for longevity and development. There are all sorts of conscientious and fascinating producers in wine regions such as Beaujolais and Sancerre where wines are designed to be drunk in their youth. They have been eliminated from this collection of superpowers in the world of wine, though they deserve to re-emerge in another volume on another occasion.

Never before has man (and, increasingly, woman) played such an important part in the making of great wine. One of its very special features is that, as in no other field of connoisseurship except perhaps that of the greatest architecture, human ingenuity is combined with optimum natural conditions. The exact balance of these two elements varies considerably, of course. In the classic fine wine regions, history has tended to prove the local theory that geography and climate determines all and that man is a mere instrument through which the goodness meted out by the soil and weather can be turned into wine. Even in a region as traditional as Bordeaux, however, the whims of Mammon and human intervention can be seen to have a profound effect, even on such bastions as the first growths. Some disappointing vintages in the 1970s from Châteaux Margaux and Ausone served to prove the point. And all over the world in less well-established wine regions there are individuals determined to prove that *they*, rather than any particular patch of earth, can make top-class wine. Attempts to master nature are being made as never before, especially in California and by the better-heeled of Australia's wine producers.

Shorts and T-shirts may be *de rigueur* at Mondavi in California, but just a little more formality is required at Burgundian banquets.

This is a very exciting time for wine. In the old days there were the established greats, enjoyed by one tiny and privileged slice of consumers, most of whom could choose from only a narrow range of different wines. The wine world has shrunk dramatically in the last twenty years so that communications between producers and their peers and customers have improved enormously.

One of the most fascinating insights this book has provided has been into the relations between different winemakers all over the world. There are still one or two who continue to produce great wine apparently in a vacuum. Jacques Reynaud of Château Rayas leads an almost hermit-like existence in the old family *mas* above Châteauneuf-du-Pape, while Jesus Anadon of Vega Sicilia in Central Spain is hundreds of miles from any other wine producer of note, and made only one (admittedly important) wine trip in his life.

Most of the winemakers in this book are very much more aware of developments in the vineyards and cellars of others than their fathers would have been, however, and some – such as Robert Mondavi, Jean Hugel, Gérard Jaboulet, Robert Drouhin, Madame Bize-Leroy and Miguel Torres – see travel as an essential part of their work. Even those concerned with the lofty first growths of the Médoc are now packing their bags occasionally in order to take a good look at what is going on elsewhere, particularly on the other side of the Atlantic. California has been the recipient of the ultimate accolade from Bordeaux: investment. Both Baron Philippe de Rothschild of Château Mouton-Rothschild and the Dewavrin-Woltners of Château La Mission-Haut-Brion have a direct stake in the Napa Valley, and are just two of the most famous names involved in what one well-known California winemaker calls this "unfortunate but inevitable" French financial interest in his territory. The Baron's Californian partner Robert Mondavi has further international connections, with the Western Australia Leeuwin Estate (though not so close that he always knows how to spell it), while Australia's own most colourful wine man, Len Evans, has made forays into both Bordeaux (two properties) and California (one vineyard).

Equipment as well as people hurtle around the world. The trans-Atlantic trade in oak casks has flourished as long as serious winemaking in Rioja, but received a boost in the opposite direction when California winemakers realised that to produce wines of Bordelais quality they would have to import their barrels from France. All sorts of more modern and complicated wine hardware has crossed the Atlantic, for Californians with an eye to quality have not been deterred by a detail such as cost – they are sometimes struck on their travels through Europe by the almost prehistoric charm of some of the equipment they see used there. Even bottles are transported round the world to satisfy the desires of the more cosmetically-minded wine producers. Mondavi (again) imports proper old-fashioned Bordeaux bottles for his Reserve Cabernets; the Tyrrells have white burgundy bottles shipped over to Australia from France; while the people at California's Chateau St Jean find it cheaper to get theirs from New Zealand (it sounds as though they should tell Murray Tyrrell). But, of all this traffic, that in knowledge and information is the most valuable. For workers in what is after all an industry, winemakers are extraordinarily generous with their professional secrets.

Improved communications have brought changes to those who buy wine as well as those who make it. The market has expanded dramatically. Wine is no longer the sole domain of the landed gentry – indeed such people are "drinking down" all the time. Wine is now a perfectly respectable and extremely popular interest among all sorts of men and women. The fortunes on which today's cellars are built might raise many an aristocratic eyebrow – and so much the better, perhaps, for today's wine-lovers match their thirst for wine with a thirst for knowledge about it. The myriad publications on wine provide a natural incentive for winemakers everywhere to do their best and the rewards are great for those prepared to strive for top quality. The auction houses too have done a great deal to create a connoisseurs' market for wine – and have thereby reaped their own reward, as well as providing a natural focus for the attentions of the wine world.

This curious world is so rich in human quirkiness that it seems extraordinary how little has been written about wine *people*. This book largely ignores the historical aspects which have already been covered so well, and concentrates on the personalities behind the world's greatest wines. For the character of a wine and, especially, the will to produce really fine wine, is inextricably bound up with the personality,

Some of the characters, *opposite*, in the wine world's *dramatis personae*.
Top row, *l. to r.*:
Jean Hugel, Robert Mondavi and Baron Philippe de Rothschild.
Middle row:
Robert Drouhin, Madame Laura Mentzelopoulos and Graf Matuschka von Greiffenclau.
Bottom row:
Murray Tyrrell, Jesus Anadon and Walter Schug.

Even in ultra-traditional Vouvray, as here at Huet, old oak vats have given way to shiny stainless steel tanks for white wine fermentation – though there is a move back to oak ageing for some grape varieties.

psychology and philosophy of its maker.

The men and women in this book have reached their present position as makers and/or proprietors of great wines by a variety of routes. A high proportion simply followed the family tradition, with Marchese Piero Antinori commanding a leading position in this inimitable commodity. Even among these congenital winemakers there are the rebels. Had Miguel Torres not been the sort of man who kicked against having to join the family firm, he would probably not be the innovative winemaker he now is. And were Graf Matuschka-Greiffenclau a less ambitious man, without a successful business career already, he might not have formulated his unique plan for selling German wines with noticeably less residual sugar than most of us are used to. There is no shortage of contrasts and unexpected parallels among the characters in this book. These are highlighted on pages 12 and 13.

Despite traditional wine lore, man's influence on wine affects every factor in its production, except for the soil in which the grapes are planted and the weather during the year leading up to the vintage. As with all good rules, there are exceptions even to the immutable nature of these two basic elements. Thanks to fertilisers, bulldozing and all manner of wind and spray machines, some winemakers even try to influence what in the past was always regarded as God-given. But for most wines, their makers' influence starts with the choice of the vine.

There is still surprising and vigorous disagreement between winemakers in the "ancient" and "modern" wine regions about the importance of soil, with Californians virtually discounting the factor on which France's main tenet, and the *appellation contrôlée* system, rest. There is no such dispute about grape varieties,

however. Most of the wines included in this book are made from a remarkably small collection of vines: Cabernet Sauvignon, Merlot, Pinot Noir, Syrah (alias Shiraz or Hermitage in Australia) in reds and Riesling and Chardonnay in whites. If, like the author, you feel there is a danger that in the twenty-first century we may be growing too limited a range of grapes, you will be particularly interested in those wines which manage stunning quality even though made from a grape rarely encountered outside its home. Italy has the Sangiovese and the Nebbiolo, both of which are capable of great things, while Spain specialises in blends of local grapes that have not yet had many ampelographical links established with other major vine types. Their Garnacha is of course related to the Grenache, a grape laughed at in some regions but responsible for the wonderfully concentrated Château Rayas in the southern Rhône. And Chenin Blanc, although grown all over the world, seems to reach greatness only in the middle Loire, especially in Vouvray.

It now seems to be accepted wisdom in California and Australia – and has been known in Bordeaux for centuries – that Cabernet Sauvignon is best softened by a bit of Merlot; but in these newer regions it is taking time to sort out which grape variety is best suited to which vineyard and micro-climate, and vice versa. It is tempting for the lateral thinker to suppose that there could still be considerable profitable experimentation with grape varieties even in the established regions. He is usually thwarted by the news that behind each traditional combination is a solid bank of experiment and established fact.

The decision when to pick is the most crucial one in the winemaker's year, and here again there is disparity. In the cooler areas, the benefits of extra ripeness are set against the risk of a ruined crop (though each year the Bordelais and even the Burgundians are getting better and better at compensating for climatological disaster). In the hotter vineyards of California and Australia, there is a tendency to produce wines that too faithfully portray the enormous amounts of sunshine allowed to ripen the grape before they were picked. We can expect to see rather less "Brix worship" here in the years to come, although in hot climates they have to keep the grapes in the vineyard long enough to give them sufficient complexity if they are to be wines of quality.

Still in the vineyard, the question of yields is perhaps the most contentious. The Germans argue that high yields are perfectly possible, even for top quality wine, provided the vines are healthy. Most of the rest of the world disagrees, although there is little doubt that a surprisingly high proportion of the vines responsible even for the best wines in the world could do with a medical check-up.

In the winery there is probably even more variation in method among the makers of fine wine. Wood is one of the most explosive issues. Even within the commune of Pauillac there is intense disagreement about the advisability of fermenting in oak versus stainless steel vats, as outlined on page 16. Every year seems to bring new thinking, in California at least and even to a certain extent in Burgundy, about which sort of oak is best for maturation.

Opinion on each side of the Atlantic varies considerably about ideal fermentation temperatures, with the French gently dropping theirs as more recent additions to the ranks of the world's best winemakers admit that they have perhaps chilled too assiduously in the past. The enthusiastic coolers tend to be fanatical about winery hygiene too, with some of the newer wineries looking positively space-age. This contrasts intriguingly with the rather less savoury aspect of a down-home winery such as Château Rayas, or with the comparatively ancient equipment still in use even at some of Burgundy's most admired properties.

Behind many of these arguments lies the fundamental dichotomy: technology or tradition? A surprising number of the traditional properties are gently adopting technical innovation, and showing no ill-effects whatsoever. Christian Moueix, for instance, is able to put his Davis, California training into effect when making what the Australians call "the world's most expensive dry red," Château Pétrus – particularly by controlling the malo-lactic fermentation. Paul Draper at Ridge, on the other hand, designs winery equipment specifically inspired by Bordeaux catalogues of the nineteenth century.

The wine world is changing. This book attempts to chart some of those changes, and in particular to put wine into the very human context in which it belongs.

About this selection. The great wines and winemakers in this book, listed on pages 12 and 13, are not an arbitrary collection, but an attempt to present the very best the world's vineyards have to offer. Sustained quality has been all-important, with the only additional criterion to assemble an interesting and varied collection of people. In Chablis, for instance, there were several contenders other than Louis Michel, but as a peasant smallholder, with an uninterrupted tradition of working the land in top class Chardonnay, he is particularly and delightfully typical of the region.

In the introductions to each region there is some indication of the most obvious "also-rans". The following listings suggest those properties or producers that would have been included if this book could have been twice or three times its present length, together with a few names that would find their way into any selection that did not demand longevity as a prerequisite for greatness in wine.

Bordeaux
Château Ducru-Beaucaillou, St Julien
Château Pichon-Lalande, Pauillac
Château Figeac, St Emilion

Burgundy
The list is endless, but constantly changing and open to criticism – such are the vagaries of this complicated region. Many of the most likely candidates are those strange-sounding pygmies we call "small growers."

Robert et Michel Ampeau, Meursault
Marquis d'Angerville, Volnay
Domaine Bonneau de Martray, Pernand-Vergelesses
Domaine Clair-Daü, Marsannay-la-Côte
Domaine Dujac, Morey-St-Denis
Henri Gouges, Nuits-St-Georges
Domaine Leflaive, Puligny-Montrachet
Domaine Armand Rousseau, Gevrey-Chambertin

Beaujolais
Georges Duboeuf
Château des Jacques, Thorin

Rhône
Chapoutier, Hermitage
Gérard Chave, Hermitage
Vidal-Fleury, Côte Rôtie

Château des Fines Roches, Châteauneuf-du-Pape
Domaine de Mont Redon, Châteauneuf-du-Pape

Provence
Château Vignelaure
Domaines Ott *(for fame, at least)*

Loire
Château du Nozet/Ladoucette, Pouilly-sur-Loire
Marquis de Goulaine, Muscadet
Moulin Touchais, Anjou *(for intrigue)*

Alsace
Trimbach

Germany
Bischöflichen Weingüter, Trier
Friedrich-Wilhelm-Gymnasium, Trier
Vereinigte Hospitien, Trier
Egon Müller, Scharzhof

A. Anheuser, Nahe

Schloss Eltz, Eltville
Schloss Reinhartshausen, Erbach
Schloss Schönborn, Hattenheim

Italy
Aldo Conterno, Barolo
Gaja, Barbaresco
Renato Ratti, Barolo
Pio Cesare, Barolo

Biondi Santi, Brunello di Montalcino
A host of Chianti Classico estates

Spain
Sherry as a subject is the most obvious omission here.

La Rioja Alta, Rioja
Marques de Caceres, Rioja

Portugal
The country's great fortified wines, port and madeira, deserve a section all to themselves – and the table wines the port shippers bring up to drink themselves are among the best Portugal has to offer.

Ferreirinha's Barca Velha
Palacio de Brejoeira, Vinho Verde *(for curiosity value)*

Hungary
State Wine Cellars, Tokay

USSR
Institute Magarach, Crimea

Lebanon
Château Musar

South Africa
Meerlust
Nederburg *(for Edelkeur)*
Twee Jongegezellen

The United States
Chateau Montelena, Napa
Heitz Cellars, Napa
Stag's Leap Wine Cellars, Napa

The Eyrie Vineyards, Oregon

Australia
Brown Brothers, Milawa, Victoria
Leeuwin Estate, Margaret River, Western Australia
Lindemans *(for Leo Buring Rieslings and old Hunter wines)*
Mount Mary, Yarra Valley, Victoria

New Zealand
Nobilo's

Comparisons
a table of facts and figures

Property, location and administrative address	Principal owner(s) and senior winemaker[1]	Vineyard area planted[2] and % of own needs supplied	Average annual production (cases) and approx. number of different wines made	Greatest wine[3] and selling price[4]	Open to casual visitors
BORDEAUX					
Château Lafite-Rothschild, Pauillac, Médoc 33250 Pauillac	Eric de Rothschild[5] Jean Crété[6]	90ha. 100%	28,000 2	Château Lafite-Rothschild 1961 £100, *$180*	No
Château Latour, Pauillac, Médoc 33250 Pauillac	Pearson Group, UK Jean-Paul Gardère	60ha. 100%	20,000 2	Château Latour 1961 £80, *$144*	No
Château Margaux, Margaux, Médoc 33460 Margaux	Mme. Laura Mentzelopoulos Jean Grangerou[6]	85ha. 100%	25,000[7] 3	Château Margaux 1961 £70, *$126*	No
Château Mouton-Rothschild, Pauillac, Médoc 33250 Pauillac	Baron Philippe de Rothschild Lucien Sionneau	75ha. 100%	20,000 1	Château Mouton-Rothschild 1961 £90, *$162*	Yes, esp. Museum
Château Haut-Brion, Pessac, Graves 33602 Pessac	Joan, Duchesse de Mouchy Jean Delmas	44ha. 100%	13,000 3	Château Haut-Brion 1961 £70, *$126*	No
Château La Mission Haut-Brion, Talence, Graves 33400 Talence	M. & Mme. Francis Dewavrin Henri Lagardère	26ha. 100%	8,000 3	Château Laville-Haut-Brion 1961 £50, *$90*	No
Château Palmer, Margaux, Médoc 33460 Margaux	Peter Sichel[8] Yves Chardon	40ha. 100%	11,000 1	Château Palmer 1961 £75, *$135*	No
Château Léoville Las Cases, St Julien, Médoc 33250 Pauillac	Michel Delon[5] Michel Rolland[6]	80ha. 100%	33,000 2	Château Léoville Las Cases 1961 £30, *$54*	Yes
Château Ausone, St. Emilion 33330 St. Emilion	Mme. Dubois-Challon Pascal Delbeck	7ha. 100%	2,000 1	Château Ausone 1964 £40, *$72*	Yes
Château Cheval Blanc, St. Emilion 33330 St. Emilion	Héritiers Fourcaud-Laussac Jacques Hébrard	35ha. 100%	12,000 1	Château Cheval Blanc 1961 £60, *$108*	Yes
Château Pétrus, Pomerol 33500 Libourne	J. P. Moueix Christian Moueix	12.5ha. 100%	3,000 1	Château Pétrus 1961 £170, *$306*	No
Château d'Yquem, Sauternes 33210 Langon	Comte Alexandre de Lur-Saluces	82ha. 100%	6,000 2	Château d'Yquem 1967 £40, *$72*	Yes
BURGUNDY					
Comte Georges de Vogüé, Chambolle-Musigny, Côte de Nuits 21770 Chambolle-Musigny	Comte Georges de Vogüé Alain Roumier	12.5ha. 100%	4,500 6	Le Musigny 1966 £40, *$72*	No
Domaine de la Romanée-Conti, Vosne-Romanée, Côte de Nuits 21670 Vosne-Romanée	Mme. Bize-Leroy & Aubert de Villaine, André Noblet[9]	22ha. 100%	8,000 7	Romanée-Conti 1966 £80, *$144*	No
Marquis de Laguiche (Drouhin), Montrachet, Côte de Beaune 7 rue d'Enfer, 21200 Beaune	Robert Drouhin[5] Robert Drouhin	2ha. 100%	650 1	Le Montrachet 1976 £35, *$63*	Yes
Louis Michel, Chablis Boulevard des Ferrières 89800 Chablis	Louis Michel Louis Michel	18ha. 100%	7,000 8	Chablis Grand Cru 1976 £10, *$18*	Yes
RHONE					
Paul Jaboulet Aîné, Tain l'Hermitage, North Rhône 26600 Tain l'Hermitage	Jaboulet family Gérard Jaboulet	100ha. 25%	125,000 30	Hermitage la Chapelle 1961 £22, *$40*	No
Château Rayas, Châteauneuf-du-Pape, South Rhône 84230 Châteauneuf-du-Pape	Jacques Reynaud Jacques Reynaud	22ha. 100%	2,500 6	Château Rayas rouge 1969 £22, *$40*	No
LOIRE					
Gaston Huet, Vouvray, Loire Le Haut-Lieu, 37210 Vouvray	Gaston Huet Gaston Huet	32ha. 100%	10,000 18	Le Mont Moelleux 1976 £5, *$9*	Yes
CHAMPAGNE					
Krug, Rheims, Champagne 5 rue Coquebert, 51100 Reims	Krug family[10] Henri Krug	16ha. 20%	40,000 2	Grande Cuvée £21, *$38*	No
ALSACE					
Hugel, Riquewihr, Alsace 68340 Riquewihr	Hugel family Jean Hugel	25ha. 25%	80,000 20	Sélection de Grains Nobles 1976 £20, *$36*	Yes

THE TABLE ON THESE TWO PAGES illustrates in graphic form some of the most fascinating contrasts between the different enterprises responsible for the finest wines in the world. It has been assembled with as much accuracy as the vagaries of an international collection of winemaking geniuses will allow. The odd half-hectare may be wanting, each vintage varies enormously in the amount of wine it produces, but the general picture is here for all to see. The great Bordeaux châteaux concentrate in stately singlemindedness on what they know they make best: their Grand Vin Rouge, occasionally supplemented by a "second" red wine and, in the case of the revitalised Château Margaux and the two Graves greats, a small quantity of mouthwatering white. This is at complete variance with the German, Alsace and Vouvray winemaker's preoccupation with small quantities of wines of many different qualities, or the tendency in California and Australia to try to offer customers the full range of all possible wine types. Look carefully too at the varied proportions of grapes under the complete control of those who make the resultant wine, and compare the quite dissimilar amounts produced by each enterprise. CUNE in Rioja and Robert Mondavi in the Napa Valley manage to turn out more than one hundred times as much wine each year as the two smallest Bordeaux properties and the quirky Châteauneuf-du-Pape property in this intriguing collection of greatness.

Property, location and administrative address	Principal owner(s) and senior winemaker[1]	Vineyard area planted[2] and % of own needs supplied	Average annual production (cases) and approx. number of different wines made	Greatest wine[3] and selling price[4]	Open to casual visitors?
GERMANY					
State Cellars, Eltville, Eltville, Rheingau 56-62 Schwalbacher Strasse, 6228 Eltville	German State Hans Ambrosi	193ha. 100%	125,000 200	Rauenthaler Baiken 1976 TBA £55, *$99*	Yes[11]
Schloss Vollrads, Oestrich-Winkel, Rheingau 6227 Oestrich-Winkel	Graf Matuschka-Greiffenclau Georg Senft	62ha.[12] 100%	40,000 20	Schloss Vollrads 1976 BA £20, *$36*	No
Von Bassermann-Jordan, Deidesheim, Rheinpfalz 6705 Deidesheim	Dr. Ludwig von Bassermann-Jordan[9]	65ha. 100%	60,000 20	Forster Jesuitengarten 1976 Aus £10, *$18*	No
Bürklin-Wolf, Wachenheim, Rheinpfalz 6706 Wachenheim	Frau Bürklin-Wolf Georg Raquet	100ha. 100%	100,000 30	Wachenheimer Gerümpel 1976 Aus, £10, *$18*	Yes
Joh. Jos. Prüm, Wehlen, Mosel Uferallee 19, 5550 Bernkastel-Wehlen	Dr. Manfred Prüm Dr. Manfred Prüm	13.5ha. 100%	10,000 25	Wehlener Sonnenuhr 1976 BA £55, *$99*	No
ITALY					
Tignanello (Antinori) Santa Cristina, Chianti Classico f.b. Piazza degli Antinori 3, 50123 Firenze	Marchese L. & P. Antinori Giacomo Tachis	12ha.+ 100%	12,000 1	Tignanello 1977 £8, *$14*	No
SPAIN					
Torres, Vilafranca del Penedes Aptdo 13, Vilafranca del Penedes (Barcelona)	Torres family Miguel Torres	400ha. 50%	1,000,000[13] 15	Gran Coronas Black Label 1971 £12, *$22*	Yes
CUNE, Haro, Rioja Alta Haro, Rioja Alta	Vallejo family Basilio Izquirdo	380ha. 50%	300,000 10	Imperial Reserva 1970 £7, *$13*	No
Vega Sicilia, Peñafiel, Valladolid Finca Vega Sicilia, Peñafiel, Valladolid	Neumann family Jesus Anadon	120ha. 100%	16,500[7] 3	Vega Sicilia 1964 £14, *$25*	No
UNITED STATES					
Robert Mondavi Winery, Oakville, Napa 7801 St. Helena Highway, Oakville 94562 CA	Robert Mondavi Tim Mondavi	1,100a.[14] 70%	300,000[15] 15	Reserve Cabernet Sauvignon 1975 £20, *$36*	Yes
Chateau St. Jean, Kenwood, Sonoma 8555 Sonoma Highway, Kenwood, 95452 CA	R. & E. Merzoian & K. Sheffield Richard Arrowood[9]	120a. 30%	100,000 25	Robert Young Chardonnay 1979 £15, *$27*	Yes
Joseph Phelps Vineyards, St. Helena, Napa 200 Taplin Road, St. Helena, 94574 CA	Joseph Phelps Walter Schug	230a. 75%	50,000 15	Selected Late Harvest Johannisberg Riesling 1979 £17, *$31*	No
Ridge Vineyards, Cupertino, Santa Cruz Mountains 17100 Monte Bello Road, Cupertino 95015 CA	Brainy consortium Paul Draper	50a. 25%	45,000 15	York Creek Zinfandel 1979 £8, *$14*	Yes, if you can find it
AUSTRALIA					
Tyrrell's, Pokolbin, Hunter Valley Pokolbin, N.S.W. 2321	Murray Tyrrell Murray Tyrrell	110a. 95%	50,000 15	Chardonnay Vat 47 1978 £6, *$11*	Yes
Penfold's Grange Hermitage, Nuriootpa, Barossa Valley, PO Box 96, Magill, South Australia 5072	Large public company Max Schubert	200a. 100%	100,000 50	Grange Hermitage 1975 £20, *$36*	Yes
Petaluma, Piccadilly, Adelaide Foothills PO Box 34, Crafers, Adelaide Foothills, S. Australia	B. Croser[9], L. Evans & D. Horgan	Embryonic 40%[7]	22,000[7] 3	Chardonnay 1978 £16, *$29*	No

Footnotes

1. As near as possible, the man who makes the crucial decisions.
2. In current production. 1 hectare (ha.) = 2.47 acres 1 acre (a.) = 0.4 hectares
3. The wine which chiefly justified inclusion in this book. 1976 has been chosen as a representative fine vintage for European whites, but most wines are still far from their peak. (Aus – Auslese; BA – Beerenauslese; TBA – Trockenbeerenauslese.) The Californian and Australian vintages chosen are still mostly youthful, like their makers.
4. Price in 1982 in pounds sterling and US dollars of one bottle from a good vintage that is ready, or nearly ready, to drink. This is probably the most approximate figure in this book!
5. Administrator
6. Advised by Prof. Emile Peynaud.
7. Projected figure.
8. Together with the Mähler-Besse and Miailhe families.
9. Winemaker.
10. Sales controlled by Remy Martin.
11. At Kloster Eberbach only.
12. Including 15ha. at Fürst Lowenstein.
13. Including brandy (about 50%).
14. Controlled eventually.
15. Napa Valley only.

OFFICIAL CLASSIFICATIONS

Only those as foolish as wine writers or the most well-heeled collectors of fine wines dare to venture qualitative ratings of individual wine producers. The newer wine regions have their own State Fairs and medal-giving bonanzas to rank particular bottles, but are decades away from formulating a classification of vineyard land. This tricky exercise has been attempted so far only by the French and, to a less useful extent, by the Italians and Spanish.

The nearest we have to an official ranking of individual properties in any wine region are the famous classifications of Bordeaux châteaux, the longest-established of which is the 1855 classification of the Médoc and Graves.

RED WINES	Appellation
Premiers Crus	Contrôlée
Château Lafite	*Pauillac*
Château Latour	*Pauillac*
Château Margaux	*Margaux*
Château Haut-Brion	*Graves*
Château Mouton-Rothschild[1]	*Pauillac*
Seconds Crus	
Château Rausan-Ségla	*Margaux*
Château Rauzan-Gassies	*Margaux*
Château Léoville Las Cases	*St Julien*
Château Léoville-Poyferré	*St Julien*
Château Léoville-Barton	*St Julien*
Château Durfort-Vivens	*Margaux*
Château Lascombes	*Margaux*
Château Gruaud-Larose	*St Julien*
Château Brane-Cantenac	*Margaux*
Château Pichon-Longueville	*Pauillac*
Château Pichon-Lalande	*Pauillac*
Château Ducru-Beaucaillou	*St Julien*
Château Cos d'Estournel	*St Estèphe*
Château Montrose	*St Estèphe*
Troisièmes Crus	
Château Kirwan	*Margaux*
Château d'Issan	*Margaux*
Château Lagrange	*St Julien*
Château Langoa	*St Julien*
Château Giscours	*Margaux*
Château Malescot-St-Exupéry	*Margaux*
Château Cantenac-Brown	*Margaux*
Château Palmer	*Margaux*
Château La Lagune	*Haut-Médoc*
Château Desmirail[2]	*Margaux*
Château Calon-Ségur	*St Estèphe*
Château Ferrière[3]	*Margaux*
Château Marquis d'Alesme-Becker	
	Margaux
Château Boyd-Cantenac	*Margaux*
Quatrièmes Crus	
Château St-Pierre-Sevaistre	*St Julien*
Château St-Pierre-Bontemps	*St Julien*
Château Branaire-Ducru	*St Julien*
Château Talbot	*St Julien*
Château Duhart-Milon	*Pauillac*
Château Pouget	*Margaux*
Château La Tour-Carnet	*Haut-Médoc*
Château Lafon-Rochet	*St Estèphe*
Château Beychevelle	*St Julien*
Château Prieuré-Lichine	*Margaux*
Château Marquis-de-Terme	*Margaux*
Cinquièmes Crus	
Château Pontet-Canet	*Pauillac*
Château Batailley	*Pauillac*
Château Haut-Batailley	*Pauillac*
Château Grande-Puy-Lacoste	*Pauillac*
Château Grande-Puy-Ducasse	*Pauillac*
Château Lynch-Bages	*Pauillac*

continued

Château Lynch-Moussas	*Pauillac*
Château Dauzac	*Margaux*
Château Mouton-Baronne-Philippe[4]	*Pauillac*
Château du Tertre	*Margaux*
Château Haut-Bages-Libéral	*Pauillac*
Château Pédesclaux	*Pauillac*
Château Belgrave	*Haut-Médoc*
Château Camensac	*Haut-Médoc*
Château Cos Labory	*St Estèphe*
Château Clerc-Milon	*Pauillac*
Château Croizet-Bages	*Pauillac*
Château Cantemerle	*Haut-Médoc*

1. Elevated to Premier Cru by Presidential decree in 1973.
2. Château Desmirail was acquired by Château Palmer long ago and is no longer made as a separate entity.
3. Château Ferrière, when made, is made in tiny quantity at Château Lascombes.
4. Château Mouton-Baronne-Philippe was formerly known as Château Mouton-Baron-Philippe, and before that as Château (Mouton) d'Armailhacq.

In the same year, and for the same great Paris Exhibition, the brokers of Bordeaux came up with this classification of the sweet white wines of Sauternes which were then so much in demand. Château d'Yquem was elevated one rank above even the top red wine properties.

WHITE WINES	
Premier Grand Cru	
Château d'Yquem	*Sauternes*
Premiers Crus	
Château Climens	*Barsac & Sauternes*
Château Coutet	*Barsac & Sauternes*
Château de Rayne-Vigneau	*Sauternes*
Château de Suduiraut	*Sauternes*
Château Guiraud	*Sauternes*
Clos Haut-Peyraguey	*Sauternes*
Château Lafaurie-Peyraguey	*Sauternes*
Château La Tour-Blanche	*Sauternes*
Château Rabaud-Promis	*Sauternes*
Château Rieussec	*Sauternes*
Château Sigalas-Rabaud	*Sauternes*
Seconds Crus	
Château Broustet	*Barsac & Sauternes*
Château Caillou	*Barsac & Sauternes*
Château d'Arche	*Sauternes*
Château de Malle	*Sauternes*
Château de Myrat[5]	*Barsac & Sauternes*
Château Doisy-Daëne	*Barsac & Sauternes*
Château Doisy-Védrines	*Barsac & Sauternes*
Château Filhot	*Sauternes*
Château Lamothe	*Sauternes*
Château Nairac	*Barsac & Sauternes*
Château Romer	*Sauternes*
Château Suau	*Barsac & Sauternes*

5. Château de Myrat ceased production in the late 1970s, "a sad comment on Sauternes's problems," as Edmund Penning-Rowsell has pointed out.

A century later, the St Emilionais came up with their own first classification of the many tiny properties in their region. They took the exalted-sounding rank of Grand Cru Classé as their most basic designation, including more than sixty properties at this level. The classification is open to regular revision, but there have been no alterations to the top designation, Premier Grand Cru Classé, given here.

Appellation St Emilion Premier Grand Cru Classé A Contrôlée
Château Ausone
Château Cheval Blanc

Appellation St Emilion Premier Grand Cru Classé B Contrôlée
Château Beauséjour
continued

Château Belair
Château Canon
Château Figeac
Clos Fourtet
Château La Gaffelière
Château Magdelaine
Château Pavie
Château Trottevieille

Four years later the following red and white wines of the Graves region were officially classified as superior to the rest.

RED WINES
Appellation Graves Contrôlée

Château Bouscaut	Château Malartic-Lagravière
Château Carbonnieux	
Domaine de Chevalier	Château Olivier
Château Fieuzal	Château Pape-Clément
Château Haut-Bailly	Château Smith-Haut-Lafitte
Château Haut-Brion	
Château La Mission-Haut-Brion	
Château La Tour-Haut-Brion	
Château La Tour-Martillac	

WHITE WINES
Appellation Graves Contrôlée

Château Bouscaut	Château La Tour-Martillac
Château Carbonnieux	Château Laville-Haut-Brion
Domaine de Chevalier	Château Malartic-Lagravière
Château Couhins	Château Olivier

It is only because individual properties in Bordeaux coincide so neatly with individual plots of land that the classifications above give us such a neat picture. Burgundy has its own classification of Grand Cru land, although each vineyard tends to be shared among a score or more different owners. The Côte d'Or Grands Crus are given here to illuminate the picture painted in this book of various Domaines' vineyard holdings.

Côte de Nuits
Gevrey-Chambertin

Chambertin	Griotte-Chambertin
Chambertin-Clos-de-Bèze	Latricières-Chambertin
	Mazis-Chambertin
Chapelle-Chambertin	Mazoyères-Chambertin
Charmes-Chambertin	Ruchottes-Chambertin

Morey-St-Denis
Bonnes-Mares (also in Chambolle-Musigny)
Clos-de-la-Roche
Clos-de-Tart (also in Chambolle-Musigny)
Clos-St-Denis
Chambolle-Musigny
Bonnes-Mares (also in Morey-St-Denis)
Clos-de-Tart (also in Morey-St-Denis)
Musigny (including a little white wine)
Vougeot
Clos-de-Vougeot
Vosne-Romanée

Echézeaux	Richebourg
Grands-Echézeaux	Romanée-Conti
La Tâche	Romanée-St-Vivant

Côte de Beaune
Aloxe-Corton
Charlemagne
Corton (red wine and some white)
Corton-Charlemagne (white wine only)
Puligny-Montrachet & Chassagne-Montrachet (white wines only)
Bâtard-Montrachet
Bienvenues-Bâtard-Montrachet
Chevalier-Montrachet
Criots-Bâtard-Montrachet
Montrachet

FRANCE
Bordeaux, Burgundy, Chablis, Rhône, Loire, Champagne and Alsace

BORDEAUX

As every serious wine lover knows, the often unremarkable vineyards of the Gironde department constitute the greatest concentration of quality anywhere in the world, with the average size of individual properties high relative to those precious strips of Côte d'Or land, or the favoured pockets of the right micro-climate in the newer wine regions. Bordeaux has been established as fine wine territory at least since the eighteenth century, and has operated as such continuously since then. This means that there has been plenty of time to put everything in order. Not for Bordeaux the reputations made and broken with each new vintage as in the frenetic *arriviste* regions. A joy for anyone attempting such a task as compiling this collection, Bordeaux has its own well-defined classifications of quality, with "first growths" proclaimed for all to see from as far back as 1855 in the most important case. (The 1855 classification of the Médoc and Graves appears on page 14.)

Of course there is nothing absolute about these rankings, and the 1855 classification in particular has its severe critics. It is argued that the geographical shape of some of the properties classified has changed so much in the last century and a quarter that their ranking is no longer valid. Some prefer the hard commercial reality of the saleroom as an indicator of quality; and it is certainly here that Château Palmer can be seen to be appreciated with a fervour that puts its prices way above its third-growth status and only just below the rank of first growth.

The striking facet of claret terrain is, as Bordeaux's gratefully-hailed historian Pijassou has pointed out, that tiny nuances of geology have played the major role in determining which properties produce the best wine. Château Lafite is flanked by vineyards of considerably more lowly rank, and by some land that is not suitable for vine-growing at all. The sometimes quite staggering prices that such first growth wines can command allow their makers to afford to continue to keep their *chais* in the manner to which they had become accustomed. Making wine with aspirations to top quality is an expensive business; the decision to use only new oak each vintage can never be taken lightly. It is easy, therefore, to see how only a first growth can really afford to produce first growth wine. But the fact remains that, in general, methods are remarkably similar from *chai* to *chai* and it is the soil and the *encépagement* that mould the wildly and fascinatingly different characters of the wines produced even on adjacent properties.

Perhaps the only really obvious distinguishing mark of a Bordeaux cellar is whether the fermentation vats are made of traditional oak, more new-fangled glass-lined cement, or spanking new stainless steel (now twenty years old at Château Latour!). There seems to be no clear-cut case for any of these, but one of the strongest arguments in favour of continuing with expensive wood can sometimes seem to be based more on sentiment than on quality. As the *maître-de-chai* of a very highly-regarded property where wood still reigns confessed, *"It's a little bit of tradition, but why not believe in it?"*

"Establishment" is a word that seems particularly apt for Bordeaux. It is so well-established that there is already an enormous wealth

The twentieth century has brought so much traffic to Château La Mission-Haut Brion in Bordeaux that it has outgrown its original gateway.

of written data about it – much of it either historical or gustatory. This book tries to concentrate on the people and the places – to provide a backcloth to the excitement to be found in so many bottles and glasses. Then there is the Bordeaux Establishment, the close-knit ranks of proprietors, brokers, merchants and buyers which have grown up over the centuries to give Bordeaux social life a structure almost unknown elsewhere. Protocol and etiquette are still important features in the salons and dining rooms of the wine châteaux and the *négoçiants*. *"You must remember that you are now a first, and be careful whom you entertain,"* Laura Mentzelopoulos was instructed when she became *châtelaine* at Château Margaux.

Everything here is restrained and well-

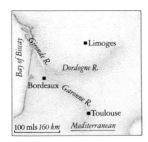

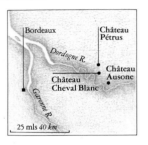

ordered. Those looking for something akin to Burgundian rumbustiousness will be disappointed. Only a handful of Bordelais, such as the admirably energetic Pierre Coste of Langon and some of the wine farmers closest to their *paysan* origins, employ the "let's crack open another bottle" technique – and then more out of the spirit of enquiry than indulgence. The typical Bordeaux host counts his decanters carefully in advance, such is the decorous way things are done in this region of formal entertaining. A famous actress was heard to complain somewhat testily in the private apartments of one of the first growth proprietors, "I've never seen anyone actually *drunk* in Bordeaux."

Orgueil is another important abstract noun in the Gironde. For a century and more there has been inter-property rivalry stimulated by enormous pride in possession, with the opening price of each year's new vintage a good indicator of current self-esteem. Towards the end of the 1970s, however, the Bordelais found themselves united against a common adversary. Because it is so well-established, Bordeaux has been accustomed to being used as a model by those attempting good things with Cabernet Sauvignon and Merlot, not always consciously, but graciously at least. Now California seemed to threaten to overstep the bounds of respectful imitation by making exalted claims for the quality of Cabernets from some of the state's most precious wineries. It is taking time for the world's wine connoisseurs and, more importantly, the amorphous group we call "the media," to calm down on this issue of mid-Atlantic agonising and to realise that California and Bordeaux have different styles of wine to offer. In the mean time, the Bordelais have not been able to remain aloof about this new "threat," but *salon* gossip is unanimous that, with all that sun, Californians will never be able to achieve the subtlety to which Bordeaux has always laid claim.

Most of those who have been appreciating fine wine for a long time would agree, although they are occasionally frustrated by the doggedly smug attitude of the winemakers of Bordeaux. In contrast to their counterparts in the newer wine regions who are constantly in search of techniques that will improve their product, the Bordelais regard experimentation with horror. This may be dangerous in the long term, although Bordeaux's own technical fairy godmother, Professor Emile Peynaud of Bordeaux University, who is consulted widely as the oracle

on winemaking and tasting, is healthily aware of the most recent developments.

Even within the Gironde there are enormous contrasts. The observations above refer most directly to the Médoc, the most aristocratic and extensive of the vineyard areas, and by no means exciting as a tourist attraction with its flat, almost bleak aspect enlivened only by châteaux that can be rather oppressively nineteenth-century in inspiration. The Graves region, apart from the intensely urban section described on pages 45-55, is similar but becomes prettier and greener as it spreads southeast to join the gentle Sauternes described on page 77. On the right bank across the "Deux Mers," the Garonne and Dordogne, St Emilion and Pomerol are quite different again. Much less formal, the wine life of these right bank properties centres on simple farms and much smaller properties than those crowned by noble buildings on the left bank. Proprietors here tend to live on the premises. The absentee landlord based in Paris or even London is a left bank phenomenon.

The choice of properties in this section is hardly contentious. There are the five first growths of the Médoc and Graves, supplemented by Château La Mission-Haut-Brion where that wonderful and unique dry white Château Laville-Haut-Brion is made and, of course, by the great sweet white of the world, Château d'Yquem. Also included from the Médoc are accounts of two highly-respected properties from slightly lower down the ranks: Château Palmer, whose best wines fetch such dizzy prices, and which has in recent years determinedly established a reputation for very high standards, (just as Jean-Eugène Borie at Ducru-Beaucaillou has); and Château Léoville Las Cases. From the other side of the Gironde the selection of the two top properties of St Emilion, Châteaux Ausone and Cheval Blanc, and that international superstar Château Pétrus, should provoke little disagreement. From each of these estates come wines which have wonderful depth of flavour and enormous attraction for the range of complex sensations and even emotions they can provoke. Bordeaux has won itself the reputation of producing the majority of the world's longest-living wines. Let us hope this continues to be cherished.

Château Lafite-Rothschild

Château Lafite was known as the *"premier des premiers"* a century before the French banking branch of the many-tendrilled Rothschild family acquired it, at a great price, in 1868. Its pre-eminence, the fact that there seems to be an uncommon number of venerable bottles available to the collector, and its sheer quality have combined to make it the most sought-after claret in the world. Men of all ages and nationalities bring fortunes old and new to the auction houses in the hope of starting or augmenting their own stake in this famous name. Five-figure sums are paid with delight for early nineteenth-century vintages. Restaurants, especially in the United States, pride themselves on their Château Lafite-Rothschild collections, with the Forge Restaurant in Miami outdoing them all with its 200 bottles carrying dates between 1825 and 1899. What is more, they manage to sell them to their customers.

This is not to say that Château Lafite produces a wine infinitely superior to the other first growths every vintage; there is no shortage of years in which Lafite has to struggle to justify its reputation. But when it succeeds, it manages to combine a mouth-watering range of different taste elements with lightness of touch. There is a certain "silkiness" to its texture – whereas Latour, made of sterner stuff, might be brocade, Mouton-Rothschild velvet and Margaux lace, if such fanciful analogies may be allowed. Lafite manages to be very complex and harmonious without being heavy; the horribly vague word "elegance" is a constant theme in tasting notes.

The man in charge of this great and much-contested reputation is young Eric de Rothschild. Tall, slim and blond, he is a Paris-based cosmopolite whose uniform is the well-cut suit of an important *cadre* of the family enterprise (headquarters in the rue Laffitte, Paris 9ème). Eric's particular responsibilities lie in the important shipping and transport division, trading within Africa where he travels regularly; but he spends "at least four days a month" at Château Lafite, as well as about half a day a week on the overall administration of it from Paris. *"It's so difficult to separate work from play when it comes to my wine interests,"* he says enthusiastically, and admits that whenever he entertains African friends at the Château, *"we always have very jolly times."*

His is the sort of ultra-polite, rather Wode-housean English that is spoken only by exceedingly well-educated Frenchmen. An additional delight is that, unlike his predecessor, Eric is so obviously very eager to please. In 1974 he took over from his uncle, the redoubtable Baron Elie de Rothschild (whose rivalry with Mouton's Baron Philippe the press loved to dramatise), representing his father Alain's holding in the

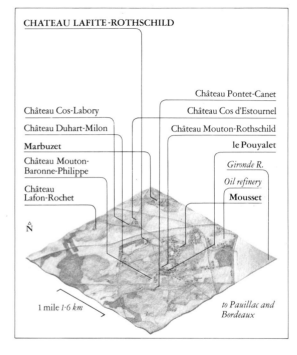

CHATEAU LAFITE-ROTHSCHILD

Château Cos-Labory
Château Duhart-Milon
Marbuzet
Château Mouton-Baronne-Philippe
Château Lafon-Rochet

Château Pontet-Canet
Château Cos d'Estournel
Château Mouton-Rothschild
le Pouyalet
Gironde R.
Oil refinery
Mousset

N

1 mile 1·6 km

to Pauillac and Bordeaux

wine property. The three other co-proprietors are Mrs James de Rothschild, and Guy and Edmond de Rothschild, the latter now said to be much pre-occupied with the renovation of the modest Médoc property Château Clarke.

It is doubtful whether the two wine Barons Elie and Philippe were ever quite such antagonists as it was amusing to pretend, but certainly today relations between all five *premiers* are very amicable indeed. Eric and Baron Philippe's daughter Philippine see a great deal of each other in Paris, and the five now meet regularly round the dinner table to discuss their mutual problems and concerns, over a meal conventionally encompassing a wine from each first growth!

At this well-charged table, Baron Philippe will be the one who, through fifty years' experience, will have the greatest *connaissance du vin*; but only Eric can claim any formal training

Lafite's special elegance may be partly because it is at the northern boundary of Pauillac. The oriental tower in the distance belongs to Château Cos d'Estournel, already in the commune of St Estèphe.

Régisseur Jean Crété runs things day to day when no representative from the rue Laffitte is in residence.

in wine. As soon as it was decided that his was the job of guiding the fortunes of the family's dabble in the wine market, he enrolled for a course of studies at the Institut d'oenologie at Bordeaux under the famous Professor Peynaud, and completed it. *"I found it very, very interesting,"* is his comment, and doubtless that of many of his more lowly fellow-students. *"It has given me the capacity to discuss all aspects of wine production and to be a kind of sounding board for the people who work at Lafite."* He finds the actual making and drinking of the wine a good deal more interesting than the public relations bubble that necessarily surrounds a first growth property of the Médoc.

"My job is keeping the men who work there happy," is his view of his own role. *"I try to give them the confidence necessary to try experimenting with new ideas. If I didn't go down there and listen to them every now and again, they might not have the confidence to try something new. I'm trying to put more imagination into the property."*

One such detail to which attention has been paid recently is the development of a proper selection programme for replantings of Merlot, the vine that many argue plays the definitive part in determining Lafite's special charm. On Lafite's 90 planted hectares the soft Merlot now represents almost 20 per cent, with a little bit of Cabernet Franc; but the Cabernet Sauvignon still predominates here as elsewhere. This, and the very variable yields of Merlot, means that the proportion of Merlot-based wine in the blend can be anything from 5 to perhaps 30 per cent, depending on the exact weather conditions of the vintage. Because they are not happy with the overall Merlot performance, at Château Lafite they have started to mark the consistently good *pieds*, for both quality and quantity, among their Merlot vines and are replanting only with cuttings from them.

Another new idea, which has been implemented *"because someone could say they'd talked to Monsieur Le Patron about it,"* is taking visible shape in the *tonnellerie* at Lafite, the only first-growth which still relies entirely on casks from its own coopers. The custom previously had been for the *régisseur* to select and buy the necessary wood from Illats near Langon, and leave it to dry at Lafite for only a year before making it up into the classic Bordeaux *barrique* of 225 litres. This, it was felt, resulted in oak that imparted a tannin element to the flavour that was

just too raw, and so the wood is now being bought two years ahead instead.

In charge of the cellars on a day-to-day basis are the third generation *maître-de-chai* Robert Revelle, tiny, moustachioed and sharp as his responsibilities require, and Jean Crété who arrived at Lafite from North Africa via a four-year stint as *régisseur* at Château Léoville Las Cases, a property for whose wines he still has enormous respect (page 60). Jean Crété took over from André Portet, whose sons Bernard and Dominique are now managing, respectively, the Clos du Val winery in California and Taltarni in Australia (both of these properties making wines to a concentration that most of their neighbours find difficult to understand). The vacation of *"l'appartement de Portet"* has enabled a fourth member of the team, Yves Le Canu, based in Paris and responsible for the commercial aspects of Château Lafite, to establish a second home in Pauillac. Another of Peynaud's ex-students, Monsieur Le Canu was chosen for this attractive job from his post as accountant in a quite unrelated part of the Rothschild empire ("I thought he would like a change, and liked the fact that he played the cello and so on," is Eric's explanation) at about the same time as Jean Crété arrived; but he now seems thoroughly at home in the somewhat daunting atmosphere of Château Lafite-Rothschild itself.

The turreted Château stands on the same plateau as Château Mouton-Rothschild about two miles north of Pauillac, determinedly facing a quite different direction and with a good view of the ornately crenellated Château Cos d'Estournel just over the stream that separates the commune of Pauillac from that of St Estèphe. Unlike Mouton, Lafite does not welcome the visitor, who might well find it difficult to find signs of human life there at all. In the meadowy dip between the Château and the road there is a fruit and vegetable garden that is clearly well-tended (by Madame Crété). But the wistaria-hung Château building itself will usually look decidedly empty.

And, so it is, unless Yves Le Canu or Eric de Rothschild are on one of their brief visits from Paris, or "there are some cousins who want a few days to have some fun, write a book or something," as Eric so charmingly puts it. Inside, it is a wonderful period piece. Still in very good condition (it was earmarked for Goering apparently), it nevertheless looks remarkably as one expects the original purchaser Baron James de Rothschild would like to have seen it – with the addition of the odd signed photograph of more recent British royalty on the ormolu mantelpiece in the green brocaded study.

The drawing room is lined with crimson brocade, its windows swathed in heavily-bunched lace curtains, and its dizzily-patterned carpet dotted with artful little chairs and studded, curvy sofas. In the pretty green and white dining room, as seems de rigueur in first growth dining rooms, lighting is low: long, cream candles are the only source of light once the heavy shutters have been closed. Warmed by the flickering candelabra and an "introductory" wine, the diner may be offered "first growth asparagus" in season, a worthy tribute to the green fingers of Madame Crété, who has reared not a few cuttings from the Oxfordshire garden of one of Lafite's more avid students, Edmund Penning-Rowsell.

Most of the serious work at Lafite takes place on the other side of the courtyard, however, in the exceptionally well-placed *chais* from which the wines have undoubtedly benefited over the years. The vintage is fermented in the *cuverie*, a long, low tunnel of a room with little spare for anything other than the 27 magnificent oak *cuves*, each with a capacity of about 170 hectolitres. As he did at Château Léoville Las Cases down the road, Monsieur Crété is super-

vising an all-oak fermentation here, in which he thinks "*le parfum du chêne*" plays an important part. The keen-eyed visitor will spot a couple of small stainless steel vats lurking among the oak, but "*these are only for small work.*" The fermentation lasts about twelve days and is followed by a period of up to eight days' further *cuvaison* for full extraction of colour and flavour from the skins. They aim for a temperature of about 27°C (81°F) and pump through a serpent to cool the must when necessary, just as the *remontage* of must over skins is done by pump. Because they have a *cuverie* whose temperature is particularly easy to control, the malo-lactic fermentation can usually be relied upon to take place within the first month after the alcoholic fermentation at Château Lafite.

This early "malo" means that the *cuves* are ready for critical assessment by Christmas, so that one of the most important events of the year can take place just afterwards. One morning in late December Eric de Rothschild, Messrs Le Canu, Crété and Revelle and, most significantly, Professor Emile Peynaud as consultant and mentor, gather in the rather cramped first-floor bureau above the courtyard to assess samples from each of the different *cuves* from the vintage just over. Overlooked by the family portraits which seem to line most rooms at Lafite, the tasters have to make the potentially painful financial decision as to which *cuves* are worthy of the little Lafite label, with its pretty black and white engraving of the Château that has not been changed since 1868.

The beautifully delicate Lafite label to scale, one of the smallest labels in Bordeaux.

MIS EN BOUTEILLES AU CHATEAU

CHATEAU LAFITE-ROTHSCHILD
1975
APPELLATION PAUILLAC CONTRÔLÉE

PRODUCE OF FRANCE

73cl

DÉPOSÉ   SOCIÉTÉ CIVILE DU CHATEAU LAFITE-ROTHSCHILD, PROPRIÉTAIRE A PAUILLAC (GIRONDE)

The "second wine" of Lafite is called Moulin des Carruades after the local name for the plateau shared by Lafite and Mouton vines, and has been made since 1974 – although in a vintage as good but small as 1975 there was none, as all the wine was deemed up to full Lafite standard. The commercial man Le Canu points out dolefully that this is an expensive exercise: *"We sell the first wine at perhaps 100 francs a bottle, but the second wine at only about 25. In 1979 the equivalent of 90,000 bottles of wine were rejected from the first wine, which meant the loss of about seven million francs. It wouldn't happen if there were a lot of different owners who wanted to live off their earnings from this property, you know."* Moulin des Carruades is therefore determined by taste rather than by provenance or age of the vines, and is designed to have something of Lafite's character about it, but with considerably less concentration of colour and flavour.

The wine from the *cuves* approved for *"le vrai Lafite"* is now sanctioned for a two-year stint in new wood, in one of the 1,000 to 2,000 *barriques* made each year at the Château, which will later be used either for Moulin des Carruades of a subsequent vintage, or for the associated fourth growth Château Duhart-Mouton-Rothschild. Both first- and second-year *chais* are admirably cool, the second one built into the slope and with a natural earth floor which keeps the humidity up and the temperature regular, and provides a convenient spittoon. The luxury of such a suitable second-year *chai* has been only a relatively recent one at most other first growth châteaux.

Also underground, behind bars and lit as for a horror movie set, is Château Lafite's *vinothèque*, probably the best collection of ancient Médoc in the world (though with a mere 60,000 bottles, smaller than the one at Mouton). Even the most serious *cache* across the Atlantic is but a droplet compared to this deeply-enviable lake of fine wine. The equivalent of a *barrique*, 300 bottles, of each vintage since the Rothschilds took over has been stored here, augmented by additional bottles going back to 1797.

Messrs Le Canu and Crété are slightly bemused by the Rothschilds' fascination for ancient vintages, their joint favourite being the 1959. They stalwartly supply the bottles as asked, however, and Yves Le Canu describes a dinner at the Château for Baron Elie at which the 1940 (not very pleasant) and the 1840 (pleasant

but strange, disappearing in five minutes) were called for. They followed avidly the 1979 tasting in Texas conducted by that generous man Marvin C. Overton at which were served Lafites back to 1799 (still a wine, but a cloud of a wine).

The cellist is a great one for musical analogies. To Monsieur Le Canu, Lafite is reminiscent of Schubert or even Vivaldi, depending on the year, but definitely delicate, while Latour may be more like Brahms and Mouton brings to mind Schumann. As for California, their wines are pure Wagner.

This wonderful hoard of ancient bottles has given Robert Revelle great skill in the operation of recorking, which traditionally should be done about every thirty years. Alone among the first growths, Château Lafite generously initiated a programme of despatching Monsieur Revelle,

The ancient Second Empire furnishings inside the château, *left,* would have been installed almost a century after the oldest bottle was laid down in the famous *vinothèque* above.

Madame Crété's carefully-tended garden, on land that is so wet it would produce *"vin du Midi"* if planted with vines.

with his equally diminutive mate "Marc the chauffeur," to various staging posts where they recork older bottles of the Château's wine. They go regularly to Paris and elsewhere, and in May 1981 ("a quiet time in the cellar") they even ventured across the Channel to recork several hundred bottles of pre-1954 Lafite in British cellars. Monsieur Revelle, who had never been quite so far afield, persevered with his Berlitz English classes, but in the end Madame Crété drove over with them and their Heath Robinson recorking equipment to act as interpreter between them and the anxious owners. By advertising this admirable after-sales service in advance, several important collections of Lafite were unearthed: one in Yorkshire and one built up by a London barrister that included no fewer than 44 bottles and two magnums of wine made in the last century and 113 bottles from the great 1945 vintage. It is planned to offer the same service to Americans who have similarly indulged their Lafite fantasies, and Monsieur Revelle will presumably take his stock of new corks over the Atlantic for a tour of each of those wonderful American collections. *"In a way this service we offer is terribly easy,"* says Eric de Rothschild magnanimously. *"And cheap. It costs virtually nothing to send someone to the United States and if we make all that effort to produce the wine, it's surely too silly to have it spoilt by not having a good enough cork."*

The commercial man, Monsieur Le Canu, is much struck by the Lafite riches he knows of across the Atlantic. Does he think there are such treasure troves in France? He smiles enigmatically. *"Oh, the American people you know, they always talk about it if they are rich. But the French, they don't say a word!"* He knows very well that there are avid buyers for the world's best-known claret in France as anywhere else and is concerned, in a helpless sort of way, about the impact of this on wine prices and the wine market. *"Every time a customer asks for an old vintage of Lafite, I ask him why he wants it and I am always told some story about a son or a daughter's birthday or something. But I have my suspicions, and I know that it is probably really for speculative purposes. Although I am against it, it's impossible to stop speculation in wine, especially Château Lafite-Rothschild."*

Château Latour

To London commuters the Millbank Tower office block just across the Thames from Southern Region's main rail artery is a familiar sight. But very few of them probably realise that one of France's top five wine châteaux is controlled from its seventeenth floor. The Hon Clive Gibson is in the enviable position of dividing his time between these offices, a 6,000-acre farm and Elizabethan mansion in Sussex, and Château Latour.

The Gibsons are, by marriage, part of the Pearson family, who took over control of this famous *grand cru* in 1963. It had been in the hands of the Marquis de Ségur and his descendants the de Beaumonts for three centuries, an unusually long term of Médocain ownership, but in 1962 the de Beaumonts were finally forced to go to Lazards and ask them to sell it. *"It was no longer financially sexy, if you like,"* is how Château Latour's bright young current President puts it. *"Lazards told them they thought only the Pearson family would be crazy enough to buy it. At that time we were still a family business, you see, and interested much more in assets than highly-taxed profits. And we like quality. We bought Crown Derby because that's the best china. We bought* The Financial Times *because it's the best newspaper. And we bought Lazards because it's the best bank. We also have an agricultural bias because of being landowners. We're men of the soil in a way."*

Clive Gibson is a quick-witted, lively fellow whose days at Eton and Magdalen seem far less than a decade behind him and whose easy impish charm doubtless allows him many an undetected leg-pull.

"The de Beaumonts kept 15 per cent or so. They're absolutely divine. Comte Philippe de Beaumont is still on the board and has the best manners I know. It was all sort of Brideshead Revisited French-style, not having changed hands for centuries and all that. And because we didn't really know anything about wine, we invited Harveys, which were still independent then, to take 24 per cent and through them Harry Waugh has played a very big part. Then David Pollock, who was our family lawyer, said he'd loved wine all his life and would love to run it, which he did superbly until I took over as President in 1976." Running such a revered French property as an Englishman cannot be easy; indeed it was only with great difficulty that the English family acquired Latour (*"It is almost impossible to exaggerate the importance of a*

The Hon Clive Gibson has to overcome two disadvantages in overseeing the hallowed vineyards and cellars of Latour: his youth and his nationality. Having a French wife helps.

Château Latour is
notoriously stately in its
development. Even the 1971
should still be magnificent in
2000.

his wedding and was now 42, took over in time to
make the 1963 vintage. David Pollock was determined to do two things: to improve the living
quarters for the workers on the estate, most of
which were in a pretty spartan state, and to give
the new team as much money, support and
advice as they needed to make the best possible
wine. This policy of allowing the chosen
managers almost complete autonomy continues
today at Latour. *"I would never dream of inter-
fering,"* says Clive Gibson. *"We discuss the vinification of course, but the selection of the cuves is
done entirely by Jean-Paul Gardère."*

Just as at Château Margaux when the
Mentzelopouloses took over, Latour's fabric
was in a sorry state when the new English regime
arrived. *"The cuves were in a very bad way – in
fact one exploded altogether during the 1963 harvest – so we had to decide how to replace them
and whether to have oak or stainless steel. Martin
and Gardère said they wanted stainless steel right
from the start. They wanted the neutrality of
taste, just grapes and juice, to begin with. And
they wanted the ease of control. But back in 1964
this was unheard of for a* premier cru. *There was*

premier cru *in France. We had to go all the way
up to de Gaulle to get an answer".*) Clive has the
great advantage in French eyes, however, of
having a French wife Anne, who is a connection
of the Marquis de Ségur to boot. This man is
brilliant!

"The régisseur *in those days was 82, lived in
Bordeaux and only came out to the Château once
a week. It didn't stop him making great wine
though. Think of the '59, the '61. It's so humbl-
ing. However well you think you're doing things,
you can always look back at what they did in the
past.*

*"Lots of Bordeaux people told us we must
get a man called Henri Martin, you know of
Château Gloria; he agreed on condition that he
brought his friend Jean-Paul Gardère, who is a
very extraordinary man. He came from very
simple origins, his father was a* vigneron, *and in
the teeth of opposition from all the Bordeaux
grandees, he had become a very successful and
highly respected* courtier *based in his native
Pauillac. He started with nothing more than a
bike and a typewriter, going round every little
village in the Médoc knowing exactly who was
idle and who was efficient, always having access
to* des vins sérieux *for his customers."*

So Henri Martin, aged 67, with his protégé
Jean-Paul Gardère, who had been altar-boy at

The twin forces behind
Latour: native cunning from
Jean-Paul Gardère, *top*, is
backed up by scientific
theory from his assistant
Jean-Louis Mandrau, *below*.

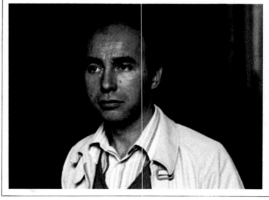

much discussion. The decision went to the highest level, and the expected outcry came; people said the English were turning Latour into a dairy. As it was, 1964 was our first vintage with steel cuves and our 1964 was by far the best in the Médoc.

"Over the next 10 years the property was gradually restored. We dug out a new second-year chai, restored the roofs, rebuilt walls, and built up a track record of what we had achieved. I'm passionate about it but not at all technically qualified. I had been acting as David's understudy for three years before I took over as Président, and a year later Henri Martin retired and Jean-Paul Gardère has been gérant since 1977. He found and took on Jean-Louis Mandrau who is his assistant and complete opposite. Jean-Paul is a peasant and does things by instinct. Jean-Louis has every diploma you can imagine, and his approach is terrifically technical. He has a little laboratory and analyses every cuve. He gets a computer print-out from the Méteo while Jean-Paul simply looks out of the window. They work terribly well together because they always reach the same conclusion but by different routes. It's great fun to watch them."

Gardère and his highly-qualified right-hand man (one of the few making *premier cru* wine who has formal training) sit facing each other in a small, very smoky office overlooking the vineyards and the church of St Julien. Through the glass door that gives them such a good view may come the smiling, bespectacled Henri Martin, for this great old man of the Médoc and Château Gloria still keeps in close touch with his old property.

It is Jean-Paul Gardère, with his strange combination of grey crewcut and ever-active thick dark eyebrows, who is the boss now however. For him, talking about wine is clearly as much of a joy as tasting it. *"Man feels something special about wine, a bit like racehorses,"* he will pronounce vehemently, taking a quick puff before continuing his theory. *"We don't care nearly as much about, say, turnips and pigs. And like the racehorse owner, we are always working for the future; with a wine like our 1975 we have to think of what will happen in 50 years time."*

Bordeaux is known for the longevity of its best wines, but no château has a wine-style destined so determinedly for the decades hence as Latour. It is impossible to see the bottom of the glass even through relatively small tasting samples of the most youthful vintages of the "Grand Vin de Château Latour," and the same is

usually true even of the "second wine" introduced in 1966, Les Forts de Latour. When young (and, since all things are relative, "young" for Latour can sometimes mean well into its second decade), the wines are so enormously tannic, so doggedly dry and austere, that it can be difficult to make out even the most blurred shape of what is obviously lurking under there. Latour is perhaps the epitome of the claret man's claret. Just as it is difficult to develop but impossible to lose a love of claret, the same is true of Château Latour, only more concentratedly so.

At Latour, the *encépagement*, that most vital of statistics for students of Bordeaux, includes well under 10 per cent Merlot, 10 per cent Cabernet Franc, 5 per cent of the hard Petit Verdot and the great majority Cabernet Sauvignon at what Jean-Paul Gardère reckons is the maximum possible level for the Grand Vin. But according to one who has spent two decades studying the property, it is the soil that makes Latour produce such very distinctive wines. Although in the same commune as Lafite and Mouton, Latour is quite a way south of them, and very much closer to the Gironde. As Jean-Paul boasts, Latour is the only *premier* within sight of the wide, grey estuary, and not only does this add interest to the view from the Château itself, but the misty-moist atmosphere saves the

When young, Latour has an unrivalled concentration of colour. This is the relatively light 1980 vintage.

vineyards from many a spring frost.

Almost exactly the same methods are used at each of the first growths, and the soil at each is alluvial, of almost exactly the same age, and equally well-drained; but because Latour's vineyards are so close to the water, they have a noticeably high clay and water content in the subsoil under the gravel topsoil that is so characteristic of the Médoc. Jean-Paul Gardère points out that in terms of soil structure Latour is closest to those consistently exciting Châteaux Léoville Las Cases and Pichon-Lalande, but that the further away from the estuary are the vineyards, the higher the sand content in the subsoil and the lower the quality.

The vineyards at Latour are meticulously kept, with rosebushes at the end of each row, and their total of 60 hectares make Latour the smallest of the Médoc first growths. Only 49 hectares are responsible for the Grand Vin, the plateau of vines that skirt the Château and cellars at an altitude of a few metres above sea level. The rest are the "Pinada" and "Petit Batailley," patches on the other side of the road into Pauillac, where the soil is slightly less worthy. *"The Grand Vin must come from the land between the road and the Gironde."*

Les Forts is made from a blend of wine from the vines near the Pichons and Châteaux Léoville-Poyferré and Batailley, and younger vines on the main plateau, according to the quality of each *cuve*. Les Forts constituted an average of almost 40 per cent of the estate's total production and can be a remarkable wine, with the very definite Latour stamp, but it is slightly more accommodating to the impatient.

There is usually no shortage of young vine material from the plateau, as Gardère insists that only vines of eight years and older be used for the Grand Vin. The average age of the vines is perhaps 30 years, and here they still practise painstaking vine-by-vine replanting so that there is always a high proportion of ancient vines in the blend.

Vintage and winemaking is the all-absorbing event that it is at any serious wine property. For the last few vintages Clive and Anne Gibson have installed themselves in the neat, four-square Château and taken an active role in the social round that accompanies the grape harvest in certain circles. With croquet on the lawn, a Union Jack fluttering in the breeze, and the rooms impeccably decorated by Colefax and Fowler to look like we wish all English country

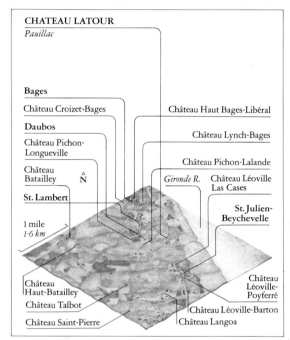

CHATEAU LATOUR
Pauillac

Bages
Château Croizet-Bages
Daubos
Château Pichon-Longueville
Château Batailley
St. Lambert

1 mile
1·6 km

Château Haut-Batailley
Château Talbot
Château Saint-Pierre

Château Haut Bages-Libéral
Château Lynch-Bages
Château Pichon-Lalande
Gironde R. Château Léoville Las Cases
St. Julien-Beychevelle
Château Léoville-Poyferré
Château Léoville-Barton
Château Langoa

houses did, Château Latour must provide a much-appreciated contrast to the rather more formal French style of setting and entertainment. There are beautiful fresh flowers everywhere, 18th-century English prints and books such as *An Illustrated History of Gardening* and *Life in the English Country House* lying expectantly on the coffee tables. Everything is small and cosy rather than imposing and grand, but that does not curtail the Gibsons' part as hosts in the "social vintage."

Just back from Bordeaux in late October 1981, Clive Gibson could reel off the following guests of the previous weeks without a second's thought: *"the Harry Waughs, Norman Parkinson, Lord and Lady Lever, Philippe de Rothschild, Guy Schÿler, the Préfet of Aquitaine, Daniel Lawton, the Cruses, Alexis Lichine, the chairman of Knopf, de Casteja, Edmund Penning-Rowsell, Ribéreau-Gayon, Laura Mentzelopoulos, the brother of Président Mitterand, the Michael Broadbents, Eric de Rothschild of Lafite, the Duc et Duchesse de Mouchy of Haut-Brion, the Lur-Saluces of Yquem . . ."*

When they entertain visitors to a cup of coffee or freshly-squeezed orange juice in the Château's pretty drawing room overlooking the lawn and the Gironde, Messrs Gardère and Mandrau are just slightly uneasy. They are most at home in the handsome and much-renovated

Opposite, not the original eponymous tower, but a later addition in 1640 with the even later Château behind, where all that entertaining takes place.

The famous, and contentious, stainless steel *cuviers* precede ultra-traditional treatment for each new vintage, as during *soutirage*.

cellars, the long, low *chai* so clearly visible from the road beside the squat, domed little tower that was built in 1640 to glorify the Château's name from the stones of the original fortress.

They follow the grapes as they are rigorously sorted before going to those contentious stainless steel vats for a *cuvaison* of about three weeks, including a week's temperature-controlled fermentation. They press the pulp again twice, usually adding all of the first gentle press, and waiting until the *assemblage* in July to decide how much of the *vin de presse* proper to add according to the vintage character. This tough second press wine is seen as necessary seasoning in some years by Gardère, who likens it to "pepper in cooking." The rest of the wine, which must surely be the world's toughest, is served to the staff for everyday drinking with meals. They must have strong constitutions.

Following the finest of Bordeaux traditions, the Grand Vin is put into new oak, while Les Forts goes into half new and half used oak. *"It is shock treatment to put young vines' wine into new oak,"* explains Gardère, who administers one of Bordeaux's most fastidious cellars with what must be extreme attention to detail, and a certain modesty. *"It's not more difficult to make Latour than other wines,"* he says. *"We shouldn't have a swollen head. It is all God's work."* He is quick to admit that great wines are made all over the world, even volunteering that contentious word "California" himself, and generously allows that among the *grand crus* there is no difference in quality level, simply one of styles. However, *"Je suis obligatoirement partiel; Latour est systématiquement le meilleur."*

There are many Britons who would agree with him, and thanks to their tireless ambassador Harry Waugh (or "Arry Vog" as the French call him), Latour's following in the United States is great too. Whatever their personal favourites among the first growths, most connoisseurs have to applaud Latour for the quality of the wines they make in "off" vintages. In 1965, 1967 and 1968 the Grand Vin was of very high quality, and subsequent vintages seem likely to continue to justify this reputation – which Gardère attributes to that wonderful soil.

The trouble with Latour is that it demands such patience. According to Gardère in 1981, the 1964 (the first vintage produced under fully British auspices) is the youngest drinkable vintage of the Grand Vin, and great years such as 1961 and 1975 will only start to reach their peak

when they are about 30 years old.

In contrast to the Grand Vin, of which up to 200,000 bottles are sold every year, usually to sit in cellars and accrue value, Les Forts is put on the market only when it is ready to drink. The sales office moved from the 1973 to the 1976 vintage early in 1982, for instance. This can also be a remarkably good wine in lesser years, with the 1967, 1969 and 1972 all good examples.

Jean-Paul Gardère shakes his head over some of these great vintages of Grand Vin and laments that they will be ready for drinking "only when I'm shaking with senility." It is difficult to imagine this man being anything other than his present dynamic self, but he has certainly chosen an eminent successor in the smiling, young academic Mandrau. His path from his parents' property in the Entre-Deux-Mers region took him to agricultural studies in Nancy, thence to Montpellier and back to the University of Bordeaux. He has travelled wider, though, as befits any curious student, including backpacking through Yosemite.

Gardère is no great traveller – to know one small region better than anyone seems to be his *métier* – but Clive Gibson is enthusiastic about a project for the two of them to go and nose round California together. *"I know very little about other areas,"* he confesses apologetically, but *"the most incredible cellar left by my grandfather"* makes sure he is well-versed in Bordeaux and Oporto at least. *"I'm very keen on California wines, but it can be difficult to find them. And I love white Bordeaux. I think they're vastly underrated, and adore Domaine de Chevalier as well as Sauternes. We have great fun in Bordeaux because there are quite a lot of us who are relatively young – the Lur-Saluces, Eric de Rothschild – we all get on terribly well. And of course in Bordeaux at least if you're British you're not thought of as too much of a foreigner. When we bought Latour they all said 'Au moins, c'était pas des Parisiens'."*

Gibson freely admits he is no expert in winemaking, but he is clearly thrilled to the last sandy eyelash to be able to direct the fortunes of a property such as Latour. *"The charm and seductive power of those vineyards is such that I find it totally absorbing,"* he enthuses at his smart desk in Millbank Tower. *"It's like having a runner in the Derby every year, and the friendly rivalry between the premiers is as though we all did. And of course it's better not to nobble others' reputations, because the better the wines we produce, the better the race."*

Eighty per cent of both the Grand Vin and the "second wine" Les Forts de Latour is sold abroad – especially in Britain and the United States.

Château Margaux

I n the world of wine, things are supposed to happen at a very sedate pace, and in the exalted realm of great wine the process of evolution is usually even more stately. At Château Margaux, however, the only first growth with a truly first class Château architecturally, changes have been taking place at a dizzy rate. In the last six years, the vineyard, cellars and Château have been swept through with a new broom more vigorous than any previously allowed at such an elevated level. There have been two *châtelains*, one of them non-French; and now, for the first time, a *premier cru* is under the direction of a *châtelaine*.

The Greek-born financier André Mentzelopoulos finally bought the property in 1977 from the Ginestet family, who simply could not afford to keep the vines, the cellars and the beautiful Palladian villa up to scratch. This occurred after a generous bid from the American giant National Distillers had been vetoed by the French government on the grounds that it would be unseemly for one of their most glorious wines to come from the same stable as the likes of Almadén Mountain White Chablis. During the week he was busy with his Félix Potin grocery and property empire in Paris, but at weekends he and his Toulousaine wife Laura would commute to Bordeaux to supervise comprehensive refurbishment and renovation at this very special jewel in the Médoc crown. He died suddenly at the end of 1980 just as his substantial improvements were starting to take effect, but his widow has continued his work with enormous energy and dedication – almost, one suspects, as a monument to him.

Many were the mutterings in the *salons* of Bordeaux and Paris when the Mentzelopouloses took over. After all, as Laura is quite ready to confess, *"my husband knew nothing about wine, but he always wanted only the best, and he knew that*

Margaux could be one of the best." When restored, the villa and its garden would make a very pretty country establishment for well-heeled Parisians, and there were many who suspected that the Mentzelopouloses' ambitions might be confined to the social and cosmetic aspects of ownership. They underestimated the astuteness of a man who had managed to build up a fortune via grain and Pakistan and to develop it so successfully in his wife's native land. André Mentzelopoulos fully realised that his first priority must be to re-establish the pre-eminence of Château Margaux as a wine.

From about 1968 until the Mentzelopouloses took over, the Ginestets' lack of cash showed in the wine produced, causing its price to fall behind those of the other first growths. But for André Mentzelopoulos there was little point in owning a first growth unless it produced first growth wine, and he therefore instituted a rigorous programme throughout vineyards and cellar (to coincide, it must be admitted, with one as generous to the Château building itself) which is now in the evidently capable hands of his widow.

"Glamorous" and "vivacious" are the words most often written about the new *châtelaine*, with perhaps "blonde" thrown in for good measure, just in case you don't get the picture. She is, there is no doubt about it, all of these things. She is also extremely chic, dressing in the wonderfully modish clothes Parisians call "classic." Luckily for the wine, the ultra-conservative Bordelais are currently being taught an important feminist lesson: that it is possible to be utterly beguiling in the most feminine way at the same time as caring deeply about and supervising carefully the making of great wine. Château Margaux

The Médoc's most glamorous proprietaire, *right,* with her PR lady, elder daughter Marie-Christine.

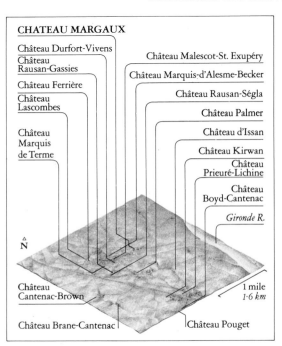

CHATEAU MARGAUX

Château Durfort-Vivens
Château Rausan-Gassies
Château Ferrière
Château Lascombes
Château Marquis de Terme
Château Cantenac-Brown
Château Brane-Cantenac

Château Malescot-St. Exupéry
Château Marquis-d'Alesme-Becker
Château Rausan-Ségla
Château Palmer
Château d'Issan
Château Kirwan
Château Prieuré-Lichine
Château Boyd-Cantenac
Gironde R.
Château Pouget

N

1 mile
1·6 km

The Palladian villa that is Château Margaux, now restored to its original glory both inside and out. Only the housekeeper, Josette, remains from the Ginestet régime.

La Bégorce

Town of Margaux

This bird's eye view shows clearly how Margaux's wide avenue leading up to the château itself provides that famous view. The outbuildings on the right of the château are the newly renovated *chais*, including the completely new second-year *chai*. On the left of the avenue in the *Cour d'artisans* there is still a cooperage as well as workers' quarters which are currently being subjected to the same remodelling treatment as the château.

1978 and 1979 have been received enthusiastically by those who have already been lucky enough to taste them, and even as early as Easter 1981, the first anniversary of the Mentzelopouloses' inaugural meal at the Château, Laura Mentzelopoulos could say with satisfaction: *"Now I know I can claim to be among the best in the world."*

The Mentzelopoulos secret has not been in taking intensive courses in oenology themselves, nor in simply flailing about with a fat chequebook. They used instead that eminently sound business principle of recruiting the very best adviser, in this case the apparently ubiquitous Professor Emile Peynaud. To an idle observer it might look potentially dangerous to have the same man advising at so many properties in one region, particularly when he is already such a major influence at another *premier cru*, Château Lafite-Rothschild, only 15 miles away at Pauillac. That is to underestimate not only the integrity of the man but also the variety of the Médoc, where even contiguous plots of land can produce wines of a completely different character. Although traditionally Margaux and Lafite have always been grouped together among the first growths as producing more "feminine" wines, they are very distinct, with Margaux usually more ample or *"corsé,"* as Professor Peynaud puts it, while Lafite might be very

subtle but more austere at first.

When it attains its full splendour, as in vintages like 1953 and 1961, Château Margaux is noted for its intensely seductive perfume. Perhaps more than any other first growth wine, it is totally absorbing and intriguing long before the taster has had the chance to take any liquid into the mouth. There is a suppleness and balance in its flavour once tasted, rather like tasting rubies, but that complex fragrance comes back again at the back of the mouth once it has been swallowed or, perish the thought, spat out. The 1978 was proudly showing this immense charm on the nose in April 1981, surprisingly open and welcoming already, while the 1979 was showing primarily a wonderfully deep colour and a dry, firm character with the promise of things to come. Even the 1980 tasted at the same time was already appealing, having surprising richness so that it was almost chocolatey, but with some hint of the violets so many find in the bouquet. Third-generation *maître-de-chai* Jean Grangerou points out that the *"éloges"* for this wine are due to *"le Professeur."* Was it perhaps difficult for him, the established winemaker at the Château, to accept this important new director of operations? *"Absolument pas,"* says Monsieur Grangerou vehemently, adding with conviction how lucky he thinks they are to have the services of such an authority.

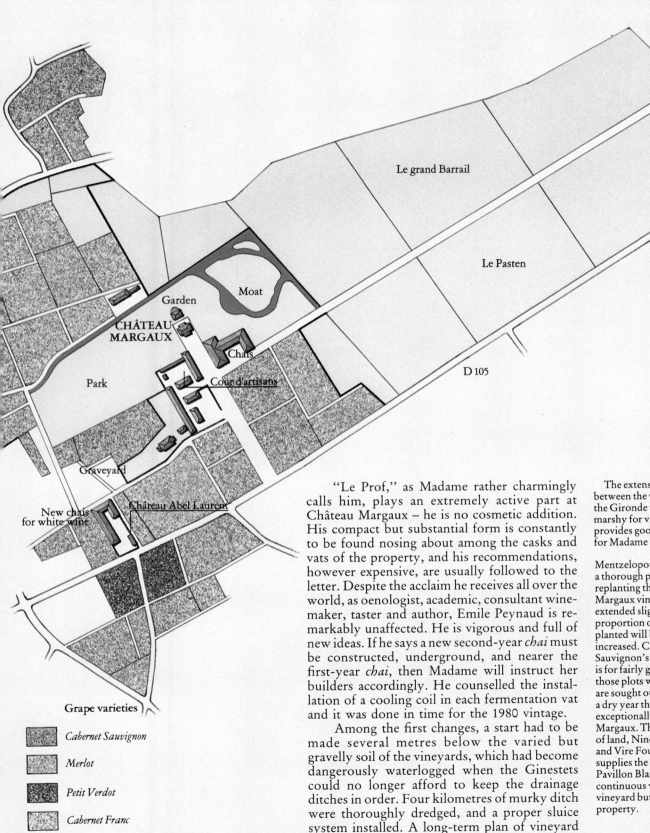

Le grand Barrail

Le Pasten

Moat

Garden

CHÂTEAU MARGAUX

Chais

Cour d'artisans

Park

D 105

Graveyard

New chais for white wine

Château Abel Laurent

Grape varieties

Cabernet Sauvignon

Merlot

Petit Verdot

Cabernet Franc

100 yards

100 metres

"Le Prof," as Madame rather charmingly calls him, plays an extremely active part at Château Margaux – he is no cosmetic addition. His compact but substantial form is constantly to be found nosing about among the casks and vats of the property, and his recommendations, however expensive, are usually followed to the letter. Despite the acclaim he receives all over the world, as oenologist, academic, consultant wine-maker, taster and author, Emile Peynaud is re-markably unaffected. He is vigorous and full of new ideas. If he says a new second-year *chai* must be constructed, underground, and nearer the first-year *chai*, then Madame will instruct her builders accordingly. He counselled the instal-lation of a cooling coil in each fermentation vat and it was done in time for the 1980 vintage.

Among the first changes, a start had to be made several metres below the varied but gravelly soil of the vineyards, which had become dangerously waterlogged when the Ginestets could no longer afford to keep the drainage ditches in order. Four kilometres of murky ditch were thoroughly dredged, and a proper sluice system installed. A long-term plan of vineyard replanting was drawn up so that 75 hectares are now under vine for red wine – though not all of them producing yet – and the proportion of Merlot, which had declined, will eventually be restored to approximately one quarter with al-

The extensive parkland between the vineyards and the Gironde would be too marshy for vines but provides good grazing land for Madame

Mentzelopoulos's cattle. In a thorough programme of replanting the Château Margaux vineyard is being extended slightly and the proportion of Merlot planted will be marginally increased. Cabernet Sauvignon's natural affinity is for fairly gravelly soil, but those plots with some clay are sought out for Merlot. In a dry year the Merlot gives exceptionally good results at Margaux. Three more plots of land, Ninotte, Chigarray and Vire Fougasse (which supplies the Sauvignon for Pavillon Blanc), are not continuous with the main vineyard but are part of the property.

most all of the balance made up of Cabernet Sauvignon. The plan is for great scrupulousness in the vineyard, leaving the land fallow and untreated by fertiliser for all of five years between *arrachage* and replanting. Also in production are nearly 10 hectares of Sauvignon for one of Château Margaux's unique features, the dry white Pavillon Blanc of which Madame has, probably quite rightly, great hopes. The white Sauvignon vines have been planted on superb gravelly soil that is, unfortunately, prone to May frosts. But no matter, Madame will install a sprinkler or propellor system to obviate this little hazard of nature. The aim is to produce an average of about 250 *tonneaux* of wine in total on the property eventually.

One of Madame's chief preoccupations has been even more prosaic: manure. She is determined to make the property as self-sufficient as possible (in the old days there was even a Château Margaux bakery in the workers' quarters), and sees the purchase of a lovely but deserted farm between Margaux and the Gironde and two hundred head of cattle to go with it as one very important means towards this end. "*I don't want to make money from them, vous comprenez, I just want to make sure we get the right sort of manure for Margaux.*"

Meticulous upkeep on Margaux's gravelly soil.

Vineyard work is now carried out to the most exacting standards in each of the little plots which go to make up the property, on the same gentle hillock just east of Margaux village as Château Palmer, whose wines have on occasion been known to fetch higher prices in the saleroom than those of its much higher-ranking neighbour. Grangerou argues that his wine has more finesse and bouquet than its neighbour because of the variety afforded by the predominantly gravelly soil of Château Margaux, whereas Château Palmer is more powerful because of the limestone and clay in the soil of its particular plot of land. He claims too that at Margaux selection is even more rigorous.

His opposite number at Château Palmer might well dispute this, but *triage* of the "almost overripe" grapes which are harvested each year at Château Margaux is certainly rigorous. This policy, combined with very strict pruning, keeps the average yield down to about 28 hectolitres per hectare, the low norm for a first growth.

Since the installation of the cooling system in Margaux's *cuverie*, fermentation can be a noisy business, with alarm bells ringing on the control panel if any of the *cuves'* temperature rises above 28°C (82°F). In many rather larger and more technologically advanced wineries, a cooling system would be switched on automatically, but here Jean Grangerou or Professor Peynaud are in control – or still required to make decisions, depending on your point of view. Château Margaux is still an all-oak property in terms of its red wine fermentation, although perhaps slightly less vehemently than some of its peers: when asked what he thought wood's advantages were in this respect, one high-ranking employee answered "visual."

A twelve-day *cuvaison* follows the eight-day fermentation, and they have expressly refashioned the *cuverie* in order to hasten along the malo-lactic fermentation, as at Château Lafite. For the moment, however, the Professor has to content himself with a two-month wait between the tasting and *assemblage* at Lafite and its counterpart at Margaux. By the middle of March, therefore, he has decided of which *cuves* the previous vintage's Château Margaux will be made up. Madame is not heavily involved in this process, which Jean Grangerou thinks is just as it should be, so that quality should not be affected by proprietorial anxiety. Unless there has been some dreadful mistake, the *cuves* rejected for the Grand Vin will be blended to make up Pavillon Rouge, a label revived by the Ginestets in 1974 just as Moulin des Carruades was brought forth by Château Lafite to take up some of the slack of this large but unexciting vintage. Like Les Forts de Latour, Pavillon Rouge is to be sold only when ready to drink and at the same price as a second growth. Madame is confident that by the time the new vines come into production there will be Pavillon Rouge available in good quantity and quality.

It is on Pavillon Blanc, however, that the enterprising and commercially astute new *châtelaine* has put great emphasis and spent much money in the last year or so. Knowing that her red wines are of necessity going to be slow to reveal themselves to the public, and that in this full-bodied dry white she has something unique in the Médoc, she has been anxious to make the very best wine possible and to launch it as a suitable herald of what is to come from the new ownership at Château Margaux.

In the past, Pavillon Blanc has been no more exciting, and perhaps less so, than other Médoc whites such as Caillou Blanc from Château Talbot and Château Loudenne Blanc – so rare now, although some white grapes used often to be grown on most Médoc properties, either to make a little white wine for the proprietor or to lighten the "red" wine. Clever Laura, however, has seen how well an investment in making a stunning Pavillon Blanc could pay off, and has accordingly invested.

Throughout 1978 and 1979 Professor Peynaud considered carefully the conditions in which Pavillon Blanc could best be made, and was able to propose that a small adjoining property whose label is no longer used, should be turned over to white wine production. The 1980 vintage was the first Laura was allowed to market herself under the terms of their agreement with the Ginestets. By the time it was being gathered in the new *chai* had been equipped with two new Vaslin presses, three brand-new stainless steel tanks for the *débourbage* ("for 24 hours only – *c'est fou!*" Laura exclaims delightedly when showing visitors round her new treasure), and about 80 *barriques*, one third of them brand new, ready for fermentation. The combination of this ultra-clean free-run juice and the wood, in which the wine rests for six months before bottling, results in a wine with enormous richness and power, with an almost Sémillon-like lemoniness, even though it is made from 100 per cent Sauvignon, Madame has even constructed a special cool room – a great luxury in France – so much does she care about this new wine.

By dint of great powers of persuasion on her part and delicate bargaining, she has managed to persuade even such an experienced *courtier* as Daniel Lawton that she is quite right to be charging more for Pavillon Blanc 1980 than for Pavillon Rouge 1974 – 60 francs a bottle in 1981 –

and this for a wine that is entitled only to the appellation Bordeaux Blanc! When Madame Mentzelopoulos feels something strongly, she knows how to get her way, by a combination of vehemence and arch use of her sugary voice. "*I know my Pavillon Blanc is good,*" she cooed. "*You could always arrange a blind tasting of all the top whites of Bordeaux to prove it.*"

Although she puts in long hours at the offices of "*le 'olding*" Félix Potin when in Paris, she tries to spend at least every weekend at her darling Château. This is clearly her major preoccupation, even though she is ostensibly merely holding the reins until her daughter Corinne, currently also working for "*le 'olding,*" is ready to take over. In addition to the enormous amount of work she has done here herself, she reckons she will end by putting in at least as much as the purchase price, 72 million francs, on renovation.

It must be hard to sustain this effort alone and as an outsider (although the Parisian social round had brought her into contact with some of the other first growth proprietors before the purchase), and sometimes she feels that progress is unbearably slow. "*All we have done these last three years has been underground, not very visible at all,*" she sighs, wrapping her cashmere shawl a little tighter round her elegant frame as she peers approvingly into a short stretch of

The wine that put Château Margaux on the map again.

Madame's bathroom –
complete with fitments
specially treated to look
ancien.

de-clogged ditch. Whether the local villagers, still dazzled by the newly-scrubbed pale stone exterior of the lovely classical Château, would agree is doubtful, but Madame is much readier to recall the horrors of renewing the antique plumbing.

Visitors allowed inside the Château will be even more unconvinced by Laura's claim that all her improvements are invisible. Her apricot and white alcoved entrance hall, cleared of clutter to show the dangerously shiny black and white marble floor, is there for all to see, as is her carefully-marbled dining room with specially-commissioned vine-leaf frieze, and her newly-papered library with books bought specially from Paris. With the help of Paris's top interior designer, she has swept the Château clean of its previous Napoleon III heaviness and restored the interior furnishings to what she calls "*Om-peer*" to match the period of construction. The only exceptions to this rule are her mauve bedroom which is Charles X, "*pour changer un peu*," and the red and pink salon which looks like Rousseau out of Colefax and Fowler. It is by the fire that she feels most at home, and is the most charming and warm hostess, laughing at herself for her ineptitude with the new locks and internal telephone system, taking childlike delight in the control panel by which she can light up any point in her domain, even including Margaux church, at the press of a button.

She is always anxious to seek advice – and Alexis Lichine whose Château Prieuré-Lichine is just down the road has been a help here – but is guided overall by a strong core of good sense and the determination to "*make my wine the best.*" This can only be good news for lovers of great wine.

Château Mouton-Rothschild

The French wine world claimed to have been taken by surprise when, late in 1979, the news was first leaked that Baron Philippe de Rothschild was to go into partnership with Robert Mondavi to produce a great, long-lived, Cabernet-based counterpart to his Château Mouton-Rothschild – in the Napa Valley. They should not have been. What could have been a more logical next episode in the high jinks of this grand old *enfant terrible* who, since he arrived at Mouton on 22 October 1922 at the age of 20, initiated château-bottling, turned the property from run-down farm to tourist haunt complete with Michelin-starred museum, developed the world-famous Mouton-Cadet brand, and – an unparalleled feat – managed to get his property officially upgraded from second to first growth?

Mondavi, the most voluble and most talked-about winemaker of that very publicity-conscious wine region California, is the most obvious trans-Atlantic answer to "the Baron." But even his remarkable achievements pale into

insignificance compared with the extraordinary scope of Philippe de Rothschild's escapades. It is those outlined above that are most familiar to wine-lovers, but Philippe de Rothschild, unusually for the wine world, has not been content to confine himself to a single discipline. Well-published poet, translator of Marlowe and Fry's tricky comedies, conceptualiser and director of the Théâtre Pigalle, he has made his mark on the arts as both executor and patron. He also has his daredevil side, game in his time for any way of getting up speed. Visitors to the unique Musée du Vin at Mouton are shown a model of the Bugatti in which he took part in the 24-hour race at Le Mans in 1929, as well as a photograph of a grinning Philippe, his distinguished nose clearly recognisable under the goggles and leather skullcap.

A sense of drama and theatre has shaped the Baron's life. Without it, the Château would doubtless be producing exactly the same sort of wine – powerful, almost aggressive *cassis* when

Sensibly ignoring research that shows the derivation of Mouton as "a little hill," the Baron has installed sheep and lamb imagery everywhere. This bejewelled object is a snuff box, made for a Scottish regiment in the early 19th century.

Drama is all with Baron Philippe and his daughter Philippine, who benefit from (and pay the price for) having no board of co-owners.

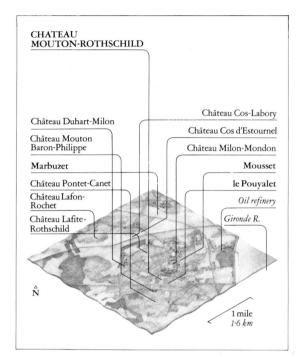

CHATEAU
MOUTON-ROTHSCHILD

Château Duhart-Milon

Château Mouton
Baron-Philippe

Marbuzet

Château Pontet-Canet

Château Lafon-Rochet

Château Lafite-Rothschild

Château Cos-Labory

Château Cos d'Estournel

Château Milon-Mondon

Mousset

le Pouyalet

Oil refinery

Gironde R.

N

1 mile
1·6 km

young, maturing eventually to great opulence with a dry, firm finish. Philippe's great passions have involved not the details of the winemaking process, but the trappings that surround it. The trappings are particularly obvious to the visitor, whose route is carefully devised so as to give him a dramatic first aspect of the property from the three-dimensional gold Star of David mounted on a stone plinth in an enclave in the Château Pontet-Canet vineyard. He cannot fail to be impressed by the view up the lovely, neat gravelled avenue through the specially-landscaped park that the Baron was able to have constructed after buying the fifth growth Château next door (named first d'Armailhacq, then Mouton d'Armailhacq, then Mouton-Baron-Philippe, then Mouton-Baronne-Philippe since its absorption into the Mouton estate in 1933). The visitor will then be guided into the car park, constantly being expanded to accommodate an annual total of visitors that has been known to reach 100,000 – in an area where in general tourism is little known. He will next be ushered into the reception centre where he is given the opportunity to buy all sorts of well-designed mementoes, and probably shown into a waiting room known as "Le Club" and given the chance to see a skilful, moody film about Mouton. Not a trick is missed (although it must be said that Latour managed

to trump the last card with their own film by Snowdon).

Now past 80, seeming a youthful 50, the Baron has a good life which, by dint of his own creative direction, is still dramatic and thoroughly entertaining. *"I love life, good wine, and good company."* He divides his time between a large cottage of a house in Paris, Edward Heath's old Albany quarters in London, the odd trip to the United States and sometimes four months a year in his exotic apartment at Mouton. The story of how he and his beloved, much-missed American designer second wife Pauline converted the old stables and cowsheds on one side of the courtyard into inventive and idiosyncratic first-floor living quarters (a sort of European Hearst's Castle), and those on another into the famous museum, is well-documented.

Today the Baron works in his vast bedroom overlooking those who daily swab down the light stone terrace as though it were a ship's deck. His enormous canopied bed is flanked by telephones, specially-aimed reading lights, neat piles of manuscript, books galore and always, at the foot, his two dogs – Radjah on the right and Tati on the left. Towards 10 o'clock he is brought fried eggs and a litre mug of tea, lime and honey, kept warm by a precariously-balanced pewter dish, while he works throughout the morning on

The Baron's *coup de théâtre* in commissioning well-known artists to design each vintage's label has since been copied widely.

a great board mounted on his knees. (Robert Mondavi was very struck by the bedroom business, but to get away with it in California you would surely have to be far more eccentric than Baron Philippe.)

Later in the day, he will probably have some journalist or camera to satisfy, an important visitor to receive or new scheme to devise or administer. He employs a full-time architect to keep the many artifacts skilfully dotted around the whole property up to scratch, and in a dimly-lit *atelier* opening on to the courtyard beneath his bedroom an artist will usually be hard at work executing some new improvement dreamt up by the Baron. *"He's always fiddling with the lighting,"* said one of his artistic retinue rather testily, continuing with many a tale of the hardships endured holding umbrellas in the rain and spotlights in the dark. One is surprised *not* to hear that the Baron has a special whitening programme for the famous doves that wheel in the courtyard.

Everything at Mouton is done with great, but always unconventional, style. Heaven knows what the Queen Mother thought of her three-day stay there in 1977 (another great coup for the Baron). Being a good sport, she was presumably much amused by everything, from the falsely marbled balustraded staircase circling tightly up to the two main reception rooms; the long, half-empty salon overlooking the vineyard with Renaissance model horse, fur-bestrewn sofas and deliberately half-finished spiky gold and cerulean frieze; and the library so obviously an ex-stable with its sloping roof and open rafters and little brass study lamps turned to brighten the walls of books.

Feasts at Mouton are doubly moveable. Baron Philippe approves the medieval idea of taking your dining table where you want to go, and duly gives instructions each day where he wishes to eat that evening. The timing has to be fairly flexible too, especially if his ebullient actress daughter Philippine is in residence. Philippe has always been larger than life, but Philippine's dramatic whirlwind manner makes her father seem positively sedate. Delighted by being dubbed "the bubbling Baroness" by the press when she went to the United States to represent her papa in 1981, she is the sort who can induce a feeling of limp inadequacy within seconds, and is one of those rare women who can get away with wearing jewellery the size of a fist. Her eldest son Philippe (of course) is currently at

university in Paris but is already getting involved with the family property, especially during the holidays spent with the family at Petit Mouton, the compact Napoleon III *"petit château"* squeezed into the middle of the courtyard inhabited by the Baron until his more enterprising new quarters, "Grand Mouton," were ready in the 1960s. (Philippine's wedding inaugurated the library in 1961 with a feast attended by "the other Rothschilds" from that much more reserved property just over the Carruades plateau of vines.)

A meal at Mouton nowadays is preceded by the Baron's own special champagne, vintage of course, produced under a unique agreement linking Champagne and Bordeaux by Henriot. During dinner, served on a series of fascinating and totally unrelated sets of china, conversation will be lively, often literary, sometimes scurrilous, rarely vinous – unless you count father and daughter's dispute as to whether it's Cheval Blanc or Haut-Brion in the first decanter. And then as to whether the 1900 is really past it. The wine-minded visitor will probably be charmed by the Mouton tradition of knotting a claret-coloured kerchief round the top of the swanlike necks of the Mouton decanters (apparently this stems from a time of severe rationing when the Baron's butler couldn't get hold of soap with which to clean tablecloths of the drops his master was liable to spill). He may be less enthusiastic about the way in which the Baron has his habitual Yquem served, chilled so fiercely that precious Sauternes ice chips clink in the bottom of the wine glass.

The wine-minded visitor could by this stage be forgiven for wondering when he is to be allowed to get to the winemaking heart of Château Mouton-Rothschild. This is an exceedingly difficult business, even for the most determinedly curious. Just as some of the better-organised cruise ships are said to have one captain who actually sails the craft and another who satisfies passengers' curiosity and desire to dine with someone suitably bronzed and knowledgeable, so at Mouton the job of making wine and talking about it is divided. On the one hand, there is a team of great professionals headed by Lucien Sionneau who, with the affable Philippe Cottin on the commercial side, took over from the famous Monsieur Marjary three decades ago; and on the other the energetic Raoul Blondin.

This is not to suggest that Raoul Blondin is a mere PR agent; his father and grandfather worked at Mouton and, as guardian of the Baron's private cellar, no one has a better knowledge of the different vintages in his charge. He shows visitors round expertly, allowing them time to gasp in awe at the specially-lit, immacu-

lately-kept hall in which the new first-year *barriques* are stored. Then he may give honoured guests a taste of the current vintages in cask before leading them, carrying a dripping candle on a long wand, down to the treasures below – 100,000 bottles from many different properties all over Bordeaux, with a specially thick coating of wax drips on some of the more enviable bottles such as the 1870 *impériale* of Château Latour or, the oldest bottle, Château Mouton (no Rothschild then) 1853.

Like the Baron, Raoul Blondin is very demonstrative, although he is liable to substitute a vice-like grip on your arm for his master's more gentle caress. He loves pronouncing on different vintages, and can get extremely excited by the whole business. *"The 1978 and 1979 are both great, but whereas 1978 has finesse the 1979 has body. The 1976 hasn't really got the constitution of most of our wines for a very long life; I am enjoying it already. The 1978 will need another 25 years, the 1975 another 40 and the 1970 another 30. The wonderful 1945 is still not ready – though it's perfect in halves – and you may have to wait until the middle of the next century for it."* He will tap your shoulder knowingly, before advising that the 1910 and 1887 are showing beautifully at the moment. Like that other great showperson across France in Burgundy, Lalou Bize-Leroy, Raoul Blondin preaches the gospel of patience for those with bottles from lesser vintages. *"We never make bad wines. It's just a question of choosing the right moment to open them. You should never judge too soon; our wines ripen in bottle."* He is, of course, very proud of Mouton's very special style – one that distinguishes it from more "typically Pauillac" wines such as Lynch-Bages, Latour and the Baron's own Clerc-Milon.

One of Blondin's most important tasks is to present the Baron with his wines for each meal, and if you catch sight of his hunched blue-clad figure hopping like a merry goblin across the courtyard, he is probably on his way to put some baronial instructions into effect. The pair are great friends, and have had fifty years to become so. Such is the affection that has grown up between them that there is now a dimly lit chamber, called by Blondin *"mon décantoir,"* which has been done out like an extremely smart school science laboratory in order to give Raoul Blondin a suitably stylish setting in which to prepare the wines for service. *"C'est le Baron qui m'a fait ça,"* he says proudly.

The much-photographed Raoul Blondin at work in his *"décantoir."*

After sixty years of directing Château Mouton-Rothschild, Moutonne-Baronne-Philippe, Clerc-Milon and a highly-successful *négoçiant* business called La Bergerie whose pride, joy and mainstay is Mouton-Cadet, the Baron must at times feel that he has had his say on the subject of wine. Many is the film camera-man or newspaper interviewer who returns from Mouton disappointed that, however hard they tried, they could not get the Baron to talk in anything other than generalities, and none but the generalities *he* chose. For those who wish for a closer look at the winemaking itself, things can be difficult. Once in the courtyard at harvest-time, it is possible to see the grapes being hoisted up in the great pale blue carriers to the upper level of the traditional *cuverie*. However, you will have to penetrate the defences of the pretty blonde guide if you wish to see inside the *cuverie* itself and admire how the Baron has even managed to adorn the plain whitewashed walls with artfully-placed old vine skeletons.

An army of pickers is responsible for getting the very ripe grapes from Mouton's 75 planted hectares in under fine conditions. One of the most important factors in Mouton's distinctive flavour is the high proportion of Cabernet Sauvignon, which all disagree on but some put as high as 90 per cent. There is certainly extremely little Merlot, and the richness of Mouton comes mainly from the maturity of the grapes on the well-tended vine. Such is the strong blackcurrant aroma of many of the wines when youthful that they are even vaguely reminiscent of the "Cassis du Maître-de-Chai de Mouton" made from local blackcurrant bushes and served alongside the Château's own *prune* and *fine* at the end of meals at Mouton. What is extraordinary is that, even though the Mouton vineyards border on those of "rival" Lafite to the north, there is such a marked difference between the two wines. This must be one of the most exciting mysteries of the wine world.

At Mouton there is perhaps an even longer period of vatting. Prolonged maceration after the week-long alcoholic fermentation usually lasts for at least another three weeks, and the wine will usually stay in the *cuverie* until the malo-lactic fermentation is over. It will doubtless surprise few to learn that the Baron is of the oak *cuve* school. Trusty Blondin has a homespun analogy to explain it, which revolves around how much longer he will live breathing Médoc air than he would if he were domiciled in Paris. *"Stainless steel, just like mechanical harvesters, will never come in my working lifetime – nor that of the Baron."*

After the *assemblage*, which usually involves the addition of at least some press wine, the wine is put into the impressive ranks of new casks in Monsieur Blondin's first port of call on his tour, the "cask hall" that is half the size of a football pitch. Each cask has its crimson belt round the middle and the arms of Mouton sten-cilled with care on the ends.

Unlike the other first growths, Château

Contrary to some tourists' impression, the first-year *chai* does function as a workplace as well as a "sight," complete with tantalising bottles of the product.

At Mouton gravel-raking is a serious, and daily, business.

Mouton-Rothschild does not have a recherché little "second label" under which those *cuves* rejected for the first wine can be sold. Its only equivalent is the best-selling Mouton-Cadet, offered not at the price of a second growth like Les Forts de Latour or Pavillon Rouge de Château Margaux but at a price that befits a heavily advertised Bordeaux Rouge. It is said that rejected *cuves* from Château Mouton-Rothschild find their way into the blend for this superwine, dreamed up by the Baron in the 1930s. If so, it must constitute a very small proportion of the blend! The name, by the way, is not unrelated to the fact that the Baron is the youngest or "cadet" of his family.

He is by any standards an amazing man, and one suspects that his apparent insouciance hides a deep concern with every detail of his many enterprises. It was a wonder to watch his beautifully-timed entrance and exit during a typical day at Mouton, when a party of British retailers were being rewarded in an ante-room to the museum for having taken part in the *vendange*, by lunch cooked by the Baron's (second) chef. He waited until the visitors were just about to be served and in their most receptive state before padding in, a striking character in brown espadrilles, extraordinary orange-and-turquoise patterned loose brocade jacket, cowboy cord tie, flapping checked trousers and a benevolently apologetic expression beneath his heavily-hooded eyes and wispy long grey locks. "*Gentlemen,*" he rallied them in his low, gravelly voice, "*I'm so sorry I can't lunch with you. I have to go to Bordeaux for some terribly boring meeting this afternoon. It is my great sorrow. However, I would like to thank you very much indeed for coming.*" Pause for extended shrug and then, on his exit: "*Be confident. Your food will come!*" And off he shuffled, managing to wave a dignified farewell in his clown's clothing.

There are those who, with varying degrees of approbation and envy, argue that Château Mouton-Rothschild is a circus. One thing is certain: the Baron is no fool.

Château Haut-Brion

Perhaps more than any other first growth, Château Haut-Brion is in the hands of a single man, Jean Delmas. A good-looking 46-year-old with bouffant grey hair, trimly-carved light suit and strong Eau Sauvage bouquet, he could well be taken for a successful nightclub owner rather than an extremely *sérieux* administrator who, unusually for Bordeaux, is carefully looking as far ahead as he looks back. The present Director Joan, Duchesse de Mouchy and granddaughter of American banker Clarence Dillon who rescued the estate in 1935, visits from Paris every month or so, but decision-making is left largely to the thoughtful Monsieur Delmas.

"We believe that the grands crus *did not grow up by chance,"* he says sternly from his enormous desk in an office well-guarded by the female part of the cohesive team at the property.

"They evolved because the people behind them had both money and passion. If you look at the historian Pijassou you see that they were really empassioned by what they were doing. They would experiment with different plots of land and then ended up with the best parcels. This phenomenon is very typical of Bordeaux, and what particularly fascinates me about its history is why we ended up making wines designed for such longevity."

Château Haut-Brion may be the oldest of the *grands crus*, but it is a tribute to the importance the French, and particularly the Bordelais, attach to wine that it and its close neighbour Château La Mission-Haut-Brion, across the road and even more enmeshed in the suburban tangle of Bordeaux, have managed to survive at all.

The de Mouchys, twenty-fifth propriétaires since the château was built in 1550, stay here on their occasional visits.

CHATEAU HAUT BRION

1975

Premier Grand Cru Classé
Appellation Graves Contrôlée

Mis en bouteilles au Château   Domaine Clarence Dillon s.a. Pessac, Gironde

G. CHARIOL - BORDEAUX   **73 CL**   PRODUCE OF FRANCE   MARQUE ET BOUTEILLE DÉPOSÉES

The British writer and Bordeauxphile Edmund Penning-Rowsell played a part in reinstituting this fine engraving on Haut-Brion's label in 1974.

Neither great wine property is much more than a mile from the centre of the city, on land that developers would presumably dearly like to get their hands on. It is difficult to think of anywhere else in the world where vines are grown in such an urban setting – but presumably once those special parcels of vineyard are found, those who dedicate their lives to making great wine are loath to see them become prey to the bulldozer.

Château Haut-Brion has about 44 hectares of Graves land, gravelly topsoil but with a rich mix of sand and clay beneath, just into the Pessac commune with the major part of it, on the Haut-Brion side of the road, facing south-east. Monsieur Delmas clearly sees the Médoc, onto whose classification his property was so flatteringly grafted in 1855, as *terra* almost *incognita*. Yes, the soil may be pretty similar there, he is not too sure. He has noticed with some satisfaction, however, that at those properties where some enlargement has been attempted by buying additional land it has been found that in general the new land has not been able to produce such good wine as the old. *"There is a limit to quality,"* he says, knowingly surveying his own perimeter so uncompromisingly defined by the encroachment of suburbia.

Compared with most Médoc first growths, Haut-Brion has a relatively low proportion of Cabernet Sauvignon, 55 per cent, with 25 per

cent Merlot and 20 per cent Cabernet Franc, *"which can make great wine in certain spots,"* according to Monsieur Delmas. It and, particularly, Merlot are much more sensitive to the exact composition of the soil in which they are planted, and he has noted with some amusement the difficulties most Californians have experienced with these two varietals. This is not to say that Jean Delmas is anti-California, however. He is fascinated by the region and its wines and has been there twice recently, completely of his own choosing. *"On a loué les motor homes en famille."*

But Jean Delmas has more than a generously open-minded attitude to the "newcomers" on the other side of the Atlantic; almost alone in Bordeaux he is painstakingly putting into practice the sophisticated technique of clonal selection. This method of choosing only the best-performing and healthiest vines for replanting is already *de rigueur* in some of the newer wine regions, and is also well-established in Germany, as outlined on page 140. In the Gironde, however, it is so little-known that a dear lady proprietor on the opposite bank to Haut-Brion was able to say with quite genuine curiosity in 1981, *"'Clone' – qu'est-ce que ça veut dire?"* And even Jean-Paul Gardère of Château Latour, when asked for his policy statement on clonal selection, admitted cautiously that it *could* be useful, but then dismissed it with a shrug because *"it takes a hundred years to see its value."*

Delmas simply says: *"It's my speciality, and with it I hope to make Haut-Brion even better eventually."* He is well aware of how great a task he has taken on, and has enlisted the support of INRA, the official agricultural research institute. *"It is not a new phenomenon,"* he explains patiently, clearly used to an extremely sceptical reception. *"We are the only Château in Bordeaux using it, but INRA started their programme in 1955, getting their first results in the early 1960s. Because I was particularly interested I asked INRA to make a special selection for Haut-Brion, not for the quantity produced or the typicality of the resultant wine, which is what INRA tend to be most interested in, but for the quality and concentration of the wine at Haut-Brion. These were planted in 1972 and we subsequently marked 150 plants of INRA which we are observing, together with some special selections from Haut-Brion. We planted them here in 1977 and so 1981 was the first time we were able to see which give the best personality for great wine*

Years of hard work lie ahead
in the château's unusual
project of clonal selection.

Jean Delmas, the man behind
the project and his desk.

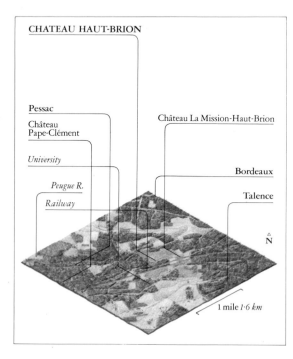

CHATEAU HAUT-BRION

Pessac

Château
Pape-Clément

University

Peugue R.

Railway

Château La Mission-Haut-Brion

Bordeaux

Talence

N

1 mile *1·6 km*

made from our soil. The idea is to have not just one but a complex collection of different clones.''

For each of these clones Monsieur Delmas keeps a bulky and detailed record for each year's performance: how it flowered, how many bunches, what weight of grapes were harvested, as well as full analyses of the resultant wine. When he has sufficient data, he will be able to earmark the very best clones that will eventually be responsible for vintages of Haut-Brion towards the end of this century. He stresses that his methods do not involve importation of new vines into the region, merely selection of the best that currently exist. *"This is in line with the genetic rule that if you isolate a group, such as vines making great wine, they develop marked characteristics.''*

Surprisingly few of his peers even know what Jean Delmas is up to, or perhaps they once knew, didn't fully understand, and forgot. *"It doesn't seem as though the Bordeaux people are very interested,''* he says a little sadly. *"It is very complex and of course part of the difficulty is that there is very little advanced technology around to help solve the problem.''* Monsieur Delmas himself has to make do with a tiny lab behind his office; and in 1981 he was looking for a small computer to help sort out his results, still in bulky ledgers on sheets covered with mini-

scule figures.

He and his staff do a "micro-vinification" from each of his now 300 clones and a tasting of the 1980 and 1978s, still from very young vines, was a revelation. The samples were served from Haut-Brion half-bottles, with the same distinctive squared-off shape as the usual bottle; the 1980s were presented at one table and then we moved, as at Oporto's Factory House, to an identical table for the next course, the 1978s. The wines had been made without any chaptalisation, so most were less than 10°. The extraordinary thing about the tasting was the difference between the different clones, and this from a group that had already been pre-selected. Jean Delmas clearly has enormous scope in this new and wide-open field.

He launched into the project almost as soon as he took over from his father, after having been brought up on the estate and studying oenology at the university close by. His father's own particular innovation can be seen on the other side of the courtyard from the offices, in the well-lit pretty *chai* modelled in pale stone. In 1961, four years before Château Latour, Père Delmas had stainless steel *cuves* installed, automatically temperature-controlled externally by water.

Of course this attracted enormous criticism, but as Edmund Penning-Rowsell has pointed out in his classic *The Wines of Bordeaux: "After nearly twenty years at Haut-Brion and not much less at Latour it would be hard to argue that the quality of these wines had deteriorated or that they are less likely to enjoy a long life.''* This noted English Bordeaux authority played an important part, incidentally, in bringing about the restitution of the original engraving of the Château itself which has been used on the labels since the 1974 vintage. His remarks about the rather coarser image used before this were so derogatory that they eventually wore down the resistance of both the de Mouchys and Delmas.

The fermentation takes about eight days and is allowed to reach temperatures of 32°C (90°F) – rather higher than at most comparable properties, but then Monsieur Delmas is aiming for a typical taste that is "almost burnt." After a further two to three weeks with frequent *remontage* over the skins, the skins are pressed and some *vin de presse* usually added back. Delmas himself does the *assemblage*, as one might expect, and the second wine of the Château is sold, when ready to drink, as the non-vintage Château Bahans-

Haut-Brion. A good half of the 1980 vintage went into one-year-old wood because of the lightness of the vintage. *"In the old days, you needed new wood to keep the wine healthy,"* is his claim, *"but today you have to be very careful about the structure of the wine. Frequent racking is most important, and it oxidises the wine very, very slightly, which can be a good thing."*

A tasting at Haut-Brion is a wonderful ritual. As you descend to the obliquely-lit second-year *chai* you may catch sight of a black-and-white-uniformed maid scurrying about with a tray of glistening glasses. She will be on hand later as you approach the black marble tasting table in a smart alcove of the cellars to light the candles in their ornate gilt candlesticks, adding to the feeling that you are tasting in a side-chapel of some rather liberal cathedral. She will solicitously hand round the small squares of *croque-monsieur* that constitute the solid part of this act of communion.

Jean Delmas likes to discuss wines as well as taste them, and at home tries to drink widely *"so as not to get used to my own faults."* Latour 1928, Margaux 1953 and Richebourg 1937 are seen as high points in his experience. His "extra-mural" tasting may include Château La Mission-Haut-Brion, but not his drinking; for there is still a certain rivalry between these two châteaux, fostered by all those comparative tastings held by British and American connoisseurs. Delmas feels that his red wines are characterised by harmony and finesse, whereas those of La Mission will usually be more tannic (perhaps due to the slightly higher proportion of Cabernet Sauvignon).

Both of these great Graves properties make some full-bodied dry white wine, Haut-Brion Blanc and Château Laville-Haut-Brion. Haut-Brion have even less land devoted to this precious rarity, a mere three hectares divided equally between Sémillon and Sauvignon, which in a good year gives Monsieur Delmas 600 cases of white wine as *"un petit amusement."* *"Petit"* does not strike the outsider as a suitable word to describe the style of either of these wines, which have a special richness which develops only after several years in bottle. Jean Delmas reckons that the different soils on which the two white wines are produced gives them a quite different structure, but over the road they also have a different grape variety make-up with more Sémillon in Laville-Haut-Brion. The Sémillon that is most suitable for dry white wines is, according to Monsieur Delmas the vine enthusiast, a different

clone to the easily-rottable Sémillon that is so useful for sweet wines.

Haut-Brion Blanc can be a pretty, ripe thing in youth and a great waxy number after six years or so, but it is clearly in red winemaking that Monsieur Delmas has most interest. He is particularly enthusiastic about his 1979 and 1975 which he feels were especially typical of Haut-Brion, as opposed to the 1976 and 1978 – which is not to say that he is ashamed of these last two vintages. Far from it. There are all sorts of fruits in the 1976 already, and although the 1978 will take time to show itself, it is already suggesting ripe prunes lurking down there in the mulberry-coloured depths. One characteristic of Haut-Brion is this very intense colour, as well as a certain earthiness of texture (which is perhaps all that it has in common with the average Graves

Gardens unusually informal for Bordeaux, just two or three miles from the city centre.

Press wine for Haut-Brion's manly constitution dyed these mats, seen here drying in the welcome autumn sun.

wine). The 1979 which Monsieur Delmas thinks so typical of his beloved property has enormous scent and lots of fruit; it is almost sweet it's so rich, and an easy-to-appreciate wine that is clearly made from very ripe fruit.

About 1970 in general he is unusually reserved. Jean Delmas is not a great enthusiast for this much-acclaimed vintage, believing that "you never find great quality with quantity" and that therefore the 1970s will never round out and be ready. *"It is merely an ego-trip to make wines that will not be ready for 50 years,"* he says, adding that 1961, the first vintage with the *"inox cuves,"* is the one of which he has been most proud.

Château Haut-Brion tends to be overlooked. This is partly because its production is smaller than that of the other properties classified as *premiers* in the 1855 line-up, typically making just 12,000 cases of red wine each year. It

is also perhaps because geographically "the two Haut-Brions" are not set in touristically exciting country – and presumably many of the visitors who do manage to spot the entrance to the property on the Route de Pessac think that the rather run-down building they see before them in the middle of the vineyards is the Château itself. This in fact houses three families of vineyard workers; while the cellars and offices and the pretty Château itself with a nicely informal wooded park complete with bronze lions are well hidden behind the wall of the property.

For years Haut-Brion has been exceptional in Bordeaux in being the only Graves property included in the famous official classification of the Gironde. Perhaps in years to come it will be thought of as exceptional in Bordeaux in being the only property whose vines have been chosen with exacting rigour according to one of modern viticulture's most painstaking techniques.

Château La Mission-Haut-Brion

Even closer to the city centre of Bordeaux, and just across the Route de Pessac from Château Haut-Brion, is Château La Mission-Haut-Brion. This property, whose main buildings are as ecclesiastical as the name suggests, was not included in the 1855 classification and does not enjoy quite the elevated status of its rather larger neighbour. Thanks to the energy and devotion of the Woltner family, under whose auspices it has been run since early this century, however, the estate is acknowledged as producing claret of first-class quality.

Since the death of the brothers Henri and Fernand Woltner in the 1970s, the estate has been run by Fernand's daughter Françoise and her entrepreneurial husband Francis Dewavrin whose many business interests already included a wine warehouse outside Paris and a *négoçiant* enterprise in Bordeaux before he took on this new responsibility. In 1981 he announced a holding he and his wife had taken in the Napa winery Conn Creek, as well as the establishment of a vineyard high above the Valley where they hope eventually to make a major contribution to the range of fruit quality currently available in California.

Francis Dewavrin travels as only a thoroughly modern businessman can and will, but tries to make time for a visit to Bordeaux every two months or so. The bedrooms and living rooms of the Château are therefore kept in readiness and the whole property, unlike some of its counterparts, has no air of being either neglected or deserted. The buildings, originally a seventeenth-century Lazarite mission, are built round three sides of a pleasantly cluttered courtyard, and look out on to part of the ornately fantastic gardens, complete with working dovecote, small colonnade, classical pool and *Alice Through the Looking Glass*-like trellising. In the ivy-hung guest quarters all is very pre-Raphaelite, lots of midnight-blue wallpaper with gold fleur-de-lys, studded doors and gothic arches. Across the way is the carefully-decorated salon, looking as though the twentieth-century Woltners made no decorative changes at all other than hanging the odd family portrait. On a summer's day one sits here at peace, thinking with satisfaction of how little the place has been touched by the ravages of time – until suddenly jolted out of this naïve reverie by the roar of an express train less than thirty yards away.

The Château has been split from a major

Françoise and Francis Dewavrin at La Mission. They now live part of the year in the Napa Valley, where the servant problem is rather more acute.

CHATEAU LA MISSION-HAUT-BRION

Château Pape-Clément

University

Peugue R.

Pessac

Château Haut-Brion

Bordeaux

Talence

Railway

N

1 mile *1·6 km*

CHÂTEAU
LAVILLE HAUT BRION
APPELLATION GRAVES CONTRÔLÉE
Grand Cru classé
1966
SOCIÉTÉ CIVILE DES DOMAINES WOLTNER
PROPRIÉTAIRE
BORDEAUX
FRANCE
MIS EN BOUTEILLE AU CHÂTEAU

The original "Mission" was Lazarite and 17th-century. Today the Lazarite cross is everywhere: on the label, *above*, on all agricultural equipment, on the grape-pickers' hods and by the old corking machine, *below opposite*.

part of its vineyards by the main railway route from Bordeaux to Spain – in effect the main railway route from northern Europe, which therefore makes its presence felt. Perhaps a third of La Mission's tiny total of 26 hectares of vineyard lie neatly between the tracks and the busy Pessac road, bisected by the handsome drive from the gothic main gates, kept permanently closed since 1977 because they are dangerously narrow. The alternative entrance round the back of the Talence *abattoir* now has to be found, a task made no easier by the Château's neighbours' apparent obliviousness to the riches next door to them.

From this back gate runs the railway bridge which must be crossed by Henri Lagardère and his team every time they want to reach the main part of the vineyards. Monsieur Lagardère, his name confusingly similar to his counterpart at Château Latour, needs no encouragement to go into his vineyards, for he is still, after 25 years at La Mission, terrifically enthusiastic about every aspect of his domain. A bumpy tour round the vineyard in his Renault 16 will involve many a stop and an instructive stomp around the rows of vines.

Lesson One: *"Regardez, regardez! L'osier, c'est tout à fait naturel, vous savez."* As at the most meticulous châteaux, only wicker is used to tie up the vines so as not to damage them. Lesson Two: this vine cutting snaps easily so it must be

Cabernet Sauvignon. Lesson Three: see how the small buds are starting to appear out of the third leaf? If they come from the fourth or fifth, it will be an especially good vintage. Lesson Four: rose-bushes are planted at the end of each row of vines, not only for ornament, but because they are more sensitive to oïdium than vines and will therefore signal the need to spray against it. And so on and so on. A substantial and kindly-looking chap, his black locks sleeked back, Henri Lagardère seems as positive as one would expect of someone much younger: *"There are several things that I like – order, cleanliness, human contact, and improving the quality of the wine. With me it's a passion.*

"Oh, if only Monsieur Woltner had followed my advice," sighs this usually happy man as he tours the outer extremities of the vineyard looking at the neat front gardens of the Talence bungalows. *"I remember when all of this was covered with vines. I told him to buy more land, but he hesitated too long and now look!"* One of the most important encroachers on La Mission's borders has been the University of Bordeaux, with part of the largest campus in Europe overlooking these famous vines. This has its advantages. There can be no harm in having one of the world's foremost oenological faculties yards away; for Henri's son Michel it was a short commute to his studies under Peynaud; and the University provides La Mission with a ready supply of pickers each vintage-time.

To the east of the vineyards lies an area which was originally a separate property, Château La Tour-Haut-Brion, whose building still stands in pretty parkland, and is now let off as a home for retired Bordelais. In recent years there has been even fiercer determination to make a Château La Mission-Haut-Brion only of the highest quality, and Château La Tour-Haut-Brion is now treated as a general label for wine of a different style from La Mission rather than as a separate property in its own right. Henri Lagardère likens La Tour-Haut-Brion to a farm-horse while La Mission is a racehorse. La Mission has more lift and finesse while La Tour, still predominantly from the heavier soils of the original property, together with other *cuves* thought unsuitable for La Mission, is a weightier specimen.

The *encépagement* for the 21 hectares of red vines is classic left bank – Cabernet Sauvignon 60 per cent, Merlot 30 per cent and Cabernet Franc 10 per cent – which is why it is surprising how

Henri Lagardère and his son Michel, who trained at Bordeaux University just next door to the property.

Pomerol-like some of these rich Graves can become after many years in the bottle. The Merlot in La Mission's vineyards is planted in the lower, damper parts of the vineyard because the Merlot bunches, being less tightly packed than those of Cabernet, dry out faster and leave the grapes less prone to rot. The red vines are planted on La Mission's best soils where in places the gravel is as deep as 15 metres – leaving the vines to burrow deep for moisture and making the resultant wine all the more intriguing and, literally in this case, minerally.

In the far south-eastern corner of the vineyard (which also includes a parcel called "Le Residu" inside the Château Haut-Brion vineyard) is a small plot, almost five hectares, of low-lying, much richer soil. The story goes that Frédérick Woltner originally planted this land with white grapes in the 1920s in order to discourage his sons Henri and Fernand from trying to make red wine on this unsuitable land.

Whatever the reason, a white wine was first made at La Mission in 1928, first called Château Laville-Haut-Brion in 1931, and its quality to this day continues to stagger those lucky enough to taste it. The white vines cope admirably with the rather richer soil here, and are planted in the proportions of about 60 per cent Sémillon, 35 per cent Sauvignon and 5 per cent of the traditional Sauternes aroma-donor Muscadelle. Henri Lagardère is not completely satisfied with this formula, believing that the Muscadelle is too perfumed and should therefore be dropped and that the Sauvignon proportion should be increased to 50 per cent so as to give the dry white sufficient *"nervosité"* and keep it from being too weighty through too much Sémillon. *"Seventy or eighty per cent Sauvignon would be too much,"* he believes, *"because you need Sémillon for richness, length and longevity."*

In future vintages, then, Château Laville-Haut-Brion is likely to become just a little lighter, but its present fans must hope that it will not lose its lovely depth of flavour and full, lanolin character. In its youth, the wine still carries a distinct Sauvignon character on the nose, and only the weight apparent in the mouth and in the languid lines of glycerine on the sides of the glass betray what might develop in fifteen years or so. For an evening meal in 1981 Monsieur Lagardère chose two vintages of Laville-Haut-Brion, but would not allow broaching of either the 1970 or 1971, classics as they are, because they would still be far too rich. The 1969 had a wonderful lemony

nose, but so rich it had to be lemon cheese, and great vibrancy. The 1966 was so full that, like a great white Burgundy, it (wrongly) suggested there was some residual sugar there. This vintage seemed to be just coming into its own.

The style of Laville is such as to suggest extremely ripe grapes, but in fact the team at La Mission is instructed to gather these white grapes first of all, in late September usually, to avoid any incidence of overripeness or rot. The pickers go out with their hods – like every other piece of equipment, as well as every label, covered with the Lazarist cross – and the grapes are brought in to allow the must to settle for twenty-four hours before being decanted into small oak, rarely new, for a fermentation that can go on for three weeks – which may be the norm in Australia, but is exceptionally long for Bordeaux. This little patch of vineyard has had half a century to develop its own yeasts, and Monsieur Lagardère rarely uses any special cultures or even any external heat to get the fermentation of whites going. He reports that fermentation temperatures for whites can reach 32°C (90°F), but is very proud of his converted milk cooler (a reminder of Australia again) which he uses to cool the red must in some years when it shows signs of going above 30°C (86°F) in his unique (for Bordeaux) vitrified glass-lined enamel fermentation vats.

The cooling process for the whites comes after the newly-fermented wine has been racked off into clean *barriques*, which are then put into a specially cooled chamber (as at Château Margaux, its uniqueness in France is claimed) for precipitation of the tartrates. Monsieur Lagardère is disapproving of quicker refrigeration techniques. *"Our way takes weeks, not hours,"* he says proudly. When he is satisfied with progress in this giant icebox, his team of cellarmen put on as many warm clothes as they·can and enter the chamber to rack the wine again, at –5°C, before allowing the temperature gradually to reach a more normal level. And this, apart from a basic filtration, is the only treatment the white is given. In thirty years, there have been experiments to find the ideal bottling time, everything from six to thirty months after the vintage. The prescribed time is now eight to ten months afterwards, giving the wine time for just a little development in the cask.

There is certainly no trace of oak as such in the taste of Laville, but one would be very surprised indeed to find the richness in old age evident in a wine that had seen no wood. In some vintages there is little to choose between Haut-Brion Blanc and its counterpart made just over the road; in others Laville scores for its ability to develop. This is partly, of course, because there is more Château Laville-Haut-Brion made, about 1,000 cases (as opposed to 1,500 cases of Château La Tour-Haut-Brion and 5,500 cases of the Grand Vin rouge), and therefore more of it reaches the point at which it can give most in terms of interest.

Moreover, Monsieur Lagardère is so clearly enthusiastic about this special product of his vineyards. *"I am really empassioned by it,"* he beams. *"It's one of those very rare dry white wines that you can keep, that you should keep, for a very long time without it showing the least sign of maderising. Even after 30 years it will still be in excellent health. The 1961 and the 1937 were probably the finest two vintages we ever made, and both are still tasting wonderfully."* For years Château Laville-Haut-Brion was sold at a price considerably below that of the estate's top red wine (partly, it is said, because Henri Woltner was such a fan of white burgundy that he tended to undervalue his own answer to it), but the dry white wine is now put on the market for at least the same price as Château La Mission-Haut-Brion and, because so little is made, it manages to command these prices quite happily.

Henri Lagardère makes some effort to keep up with wines produced elsewhere. His brother has lived in California since 1952, and so when his son Michel, who now works with his father from a nearby house he built himself, went there

on holiday back in 1967, he brought back a case or two of samples. *"Yes, I tasted them,"* allows Lagardère seriously. *"I thought some of them were very good. They may not have had the finesse or race of our wines, but they are definitely getting there."*

Yet, quite apart from the lovely golden liquid that trickles out of La Mission each year, Monsieur Lagardère clearly draws satisfaction from knowing that there is nothing like it anywhere else in the world. An Haut-Brion Blanc or a well-aged white from Domaine de Chevalier may perhaps come close to it, as may possibly one or two of the Hunter Valley's best Semillons (a mature Lindeman's?) – although they would probably be betrayed by their slight lack of vibrancy. Château Laville-Haut-Brion is extremely special, and even today a well-kept secret among its devotees.

The scale is relatively tiny at La Mission, as for these traditional red wine presses.

Château Palmer

Dutch, French and British flags hint at the château's complicated ownership.

It is appropriate that this impressive property, established by that English oenophile General Palmer after his occupation of the Médoc in the Napoleonic Wars, should now be in the hands of another Englishman passionately concerned about wine, Peter Sichel. Since the Mähler-Besse and Miailhe family trusts were distributed to their beneficiaries in 1979, the quiet Englishman has been left with the major shareholding of 31 per cent, *négociant* Henri Mähler-Besse himself having 13 per cent and the remaining 56 per cent split between six local ladies. Let us hope that "Peter Allan" (called thus to distinguish him from his more flamboyant cousin "Peter Max" Sichel of New York) has better financial luck than his Anglo-Saxon predecessor. As Edmund Penning-Rowsell reports, General Palmer went bust in 1849, without even having got round to building a château.

More important in the long term, however, the enthusiastic General worked hard to promote the quality of his wine, with the result that in the famous 1855 classification Château Palmer appears, quite respectably, in the third division. More recently, and particularly in the second half of this century, the wines of this next-door neighbour to Château Margaux have been so outstanding that they have been sold at prices well above those of second growths – and its famous 1961 has managed to fetch higher prices than either Margaux or Haut-Brion of the same vintage. In most respects first growth standards are employed at Palmer (or "Palmaire," as the French call it), and in some practices they are even stricter.

The absence of a handsome château building was corrected in 1856 by the Paris banking family, the Pereires, who followed the vinously acquisitive lead of the Rothschilds by acquiring Palmer. Today the distinguished turreted building can be seen through disconcertingly urban iron railings as visitors to the Médoc speed through the hamlet of Issan just south of Margaux proper. Peter Sichel lives just down the road at the bourgeois property Château d'Angludet, and Château Palmer is empty, although there are dinners and meetings of the shareholders there. In summer the Château will be enlivened by the flying of the red, white and blue flags of Britain, the Netherlands (for the Mähler-Besse faction) and France on the masts high up on the steep grey-slated roof, and the Château also appears on one of Bordeaux's most distinctive labels – the gold gravure on midnight blue, or is it black?

The man in charge of putting the share-holders' wishes into practice is the *gérant*, Bertrand Bouteiller, an efficient suit-and-tie sort who administers the 40 hectares of land, in ten different parcels as far apart as Margaux and Cantenac – two whole kilometres! In the past there has been a certain amount of exchange of vines with the Lurtons of Château Brane-Cantenac, as well as the absorption of Château Desmirail, which was originally classified as a third growth. Thirty-seven hectares are currently in production, and all are cultivated in the traditional manner with vines planted a metre apart and strict pruning. *Maître-de-chai* Yves Chardon, whose father Pierre and brother Claude still work at Palmer, maintains that the average yield at Palmer is only about 25 hectolitres per hectare, with the figure of 36 achieved in 1979 being the highest ever. An important factor here is the high proportion of old vines in the Palmer vineyards which may produce yields of only 10 or 12; and Merlot is an even more feeble bearer in old age than Cabernet. *"On ne force pas la vigne,"* says Chardon with satisfaction.

The main parcel of vines belonging to Château Palmer is on the plateau of high ground between Issan and Margaux and is shared by Palmer and what its *maître-de-chai* calls "the best bit of Château Margaux." There is only a cart-track between the two properties, yet they produce two very different wines. The richer soil and the higher proportion of Merlot make Palmer a rather more robust wine than most vintages of Château Margaux, though it will be interesting to monitor comparisons between these two properties now that there is a new regime at Château Margaux, and they are increasing Merlot plantings there. Château Palmer in a good year such as 1961, 1976 and 1978 has enormous character as well as great finesse and charm.

For a great wine, Château Palmer is ready to drink remarkably soon – after only eight or ten years according to the *maître-de-chai*, who was already enjoying the 1976 in 1981 (though Peter Sichel was then enjoying the 1962, 1967 and 1966!). *"Margaux as a commune makes supple wines anyway,"* he says, *"but at Château Palmer this is even more true because we have so much Merlot."* With 40 per cent (it used to be even more) Palmer has more Merlot than any other wine of great reputation on the left bank of the Gironde – not that there is much to recall St Emilion or Pomerol in the style of its wines.

The label that connoisseurs have come to associate with quality that can take on the first growths in vintages such as 1961.

Cabernets make up most of the rest, Sauvignon taking 40 per cent of the vineyard and Franc a further 10 per cent, with Petit Verdot (according to Monsieur Chardon) accounting for the remaining 10 per cent and, with its high tannin, acidity and extract, balancing some of the softening effect of Merlot. Merlot has its problems, being so prone to *coulure* and spring frosts, but then the main Palmer patch is usually high enough to escape danger. *"It's awful for the village at frost time,"* moans Yves Chardon, all of whose family live within a few hundred yards of the Château where they work. *"The burners are terribly smutty. You can't hang anything out on the washing line."*

Cabernet Sauvignon adds the bouquet which Palmer develops so enticingly, and as for Cabernet Franc, *"Il ne donne pas grande chose,"* admits Monsieur Chardon. The different *cépages*, planted in different parcels, are kept separate until the time for *assemblage* in February or March, as is the Bordeaux rule.

At vintage time, Palmer becomes a popular tourist attraction, as the only place where it is possible to see old-fashioned destalking of the grapes by hand on a big wooden tray, with seven men in long crimson purple-stained aprons and rubber boots carefully routing out any grapes that are not fully ripe and healthy. Then there's

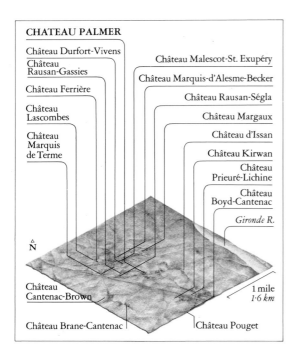

CHATEAU PALMER

Château Durfort-Vivens
Château Rausan-Gassies
Château Ferrière
Château Lascombes
Château Marquis de Terme
Château Malescot-St. Exupéry
Château Marquis-d'Alesme-Becker
Château Rausan-Ségla
Château Margaux
Château d'Issan
Château Kirwan
Château Prieuré-Lichine
Château Boyd-Cantenac
Gironde R.
Château Cantenac-Brown
Château Brane-Cantenac
Château Pouget

N

1 mile
1·6 km

At Palmer traditions die hard, as in the manual destalking (unique in the Médoc) and scented oak *cuviers, right,* although a Willmes press has recently snuck in to provide a background, *opposite left,* for good old-fashioned racking.

the week-long fermentation and further two-week *cuvaison* in the wooden *cuves* that run down the long whitewashed *cuverie*, imparting a lovely vanilla smell.

The disastrous 1963 vintage brought a change in policy for the crucial *assemblage* at Palmer. In the past it was left to the *maître-de-chai*, but since then the proprietors have taken a first-hand interest in the commercially vital question as to which *cuves* should pass muster for the Château, and today Messrs Bouteiller, Mähler-Besse and Sichel all contribute to the decision. Chardon describes his peers as unusually courageous to continue to reject unsatisfactory *cuves*, despite the financial loss involved, though this surely is what great winemaking is all about.

In 1963 all the wine was sold as common-or-garden AC Margaux (not, as some have it, as Château Desmirail, a name that has not appeared since 1938 according to Monsieur Chardon); and in 1965 only one *cuve* was deemed fit to be sold as Château Palmer. More recently, the 1973 vintage produced one *cuve* that had too much young-vine character to warrant the Grand Vin label (and indeed the "proper 1973" did not excite many), and a *cuve* was rejected in 1980 too.

In Monsieur Chardon's much-photographed first-year *chai* with a suitably saintly-looking bishop at the end, the wine is stored and topped up twice a week at first (losses by evaporation are calculated here to account for 15 per cent of total production), about one-third of the wine going into new oak. One tradition Yves Chardon feels passionately about is that filtering at any stage is A Bad Thing. *"The wine is just too pretty when it comes out of the filter,"* he says, railing at some of his counterparts who practise this modern habit. *"If you compare our wines with theirs, you will see that ours has a nice deposit after about 10 years – and that's after the wine has left about five litres of deposit in each cask."*

He sums up his own view of the reason why Palmer manages to make great wine. First, it enjoys some very well-sited vineyards. Secondly, they don't push their vines to high yields,

even though some of their neighbours can get 60 hectolitres from some of their hectares. And thirdly, the proprietors are prepared to make commercially unattractive but qualitatively admirable decisions. Peter Sichel on the other hand maintains: *"The most remarkable aspect of Palmer to me consists of the qualities of the Chardon family who are now in their fourth generation at Palmer, and the fact that the property was bought for almost nothing as recently as 1938. I remember the days in the early 1950s when I was travelling around Britain and came back very proud if I managed to sell a hogshead (24 dozen) in bulk at almost exactly the same price at which we now ration out a single case. The wine was being made with the same care then as now, although, of course, better prices have brought the possibility of using more new casks, eliminating inadequate vats and so on."*

Peter Sichel is brutally realistic. *"There is no doubt that success is not only a question of quality but also of the tastes and fashions of the time. What we are trying to do there is quite simply to enjoy the ego trip of trying to produce the best wine in the Médoc, and hoping that the economic conditions will allow the trip to be a long one."*

Pierre Chardon, *centre above*, with his two sons Claude and Yves. All three work or have worked at the Château Palmer and still live no more than a stone's throw away. Peter Sichel, *top*, lives on his own property, Château d'Angludet, just down the road.

Château Léoville Las Cases

As Michael Broadbent comments before awarding four stars to the 1971 vintage of Château Léoville Las Cases in his *Great Vintage Wine Book*, *"The owner of this big estate quietly gets on with making excellent wine. Like Ducru, he can be relied upon to make the best of the material available."* Yes, Michel Delon's way of doing things is to "quietly get on" with them. No fanfares will be heard rallying press and public to the unique walled vineyard on the northern fringes of St Julien. He rarely travels further than his second office in Bordeaux. With his grey suit and deliberately correct manners, he is thorough and determined; and one of the things he is determined to do thoroughly is make great wine. Another is to make sure that you realise it.

Imagine the scene. You are in Bordeaux, lying low, with no idea anyone other than the hotel receptionist knows of your whereabouts, much less this courteous Monsieur Delon who has just telephoned you and will call for you tomorrow morning to take you out to Château Léoville Las Cases, in which he happens to think you will be very interested. Before you are out of the commercial sprawl of Blanquefort he has told you that he was at the estimable Château Pichon-Lalande between 1975 and 1977, but since then has been looking after this property that belongs in a most complicated way to his family. By the time you reach Château La Lagune he has enquired with the utmost politeness and tact whether the foie gras and *filet* he has ordered for lunch will suit you, and is already discussing the vintages you would most like to taste with them. Long before Margaux is reached you find out that he knows exactly where you have been in the last few days and, even more disconcertingly admirable, exactly which wines you have tasted. It would be impossible to work for Michel Delon and not be a perfectionist yourself.

Château Léoville Las Cases is almost as big as that other St Julien giant, Château Gruaud-Larose, with more than 70 hectares planted, nearly 50 of them in the impressive Clos de Léoville Las Cases, whose handsome gateway is one of the best-known landmarks on the road to Pauillac. It is a Château without a château, in that the Léoville estate is now split into three wine properties, Barton, Las Cases and Poyferré, with not enough proper château buildings to go round. Las Cases shares Poyferré's U-shaped single-storey building round a courtyard just off the main road through the village. Here Monsieur Delon has an elegant office ("I like beautiful things") lined with plates for the châteaux whose wines or personnel he particularly admires (these include Chasse-Spleen, Ducru-Beaucaillou and Grand-Puy-Lacoste), and with a desk whose left side opens up to reveal his own personal short-term cellar. It is admirable that from this office Monsieur Delon manages to make such consistently exciting wine on such a large scale, with average yields that are high compared to most properties associated with such high quality, and without being able to afford more than about one-third new oak for each vintage of *barriques*.

Monsieur Delon is happy to be able to say that *"austerity and longevity are the keynotes for Léoville Las Cases."* *"It's barely drinkable at less than 10 years,"* he adds happily, although he makes an exception for vintages such as 1973 and 1976. There is lots of fruit and ripeness, but all the wines finish very dry with an interesting "texture" to the flavour that is vaguely reminiscent of a fine red Graves. These are elegant, aristocratic wines. The 1961 was a wonderful herald of the good things to come (Michel Delon is the first to admit that before 1959 the Château was not producing wines of the current excitement).

Perhaps it is the scrupulous care of the grapes as they are brought in that plays an important part here. Monsieur Delon says rather contemptuously of the process that involves rejection of *cuves* before *assemblage* that it is a sign that not enough trouble was taken during the vintage and vinification. At Léoville Las Cases the policy is to vary the speed of reception into the crusher-destemmer according to the *cépage* and age of the vine, to maximise the quality and health of the must. They have about 65 per cent Cabernet Sauvignon, 17 per cent Merlot, a tiny amount of Petit Verdot and just over 15 per cent

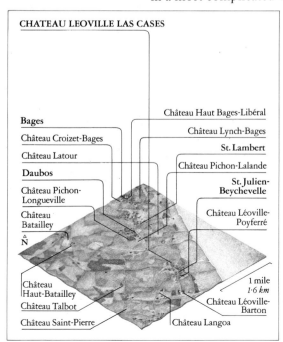

CHATEAU LEOVILLE LAS CASES

Château Haut Bages-Libéral

Bages

Château Lynch-Bages

Château Croizet-Bages

St. Lambert

Château Latour

Château Pichon-Lalande

Daubos

St. Julien-Beychevelle

Château Pichon-Longueville

Château Léoville-Poyferré

Château Batailley

N

Château Haut-Batailley

1 mile
1·6 km

Château Talbot

Château Léoville-Barton

Château Saint-Pierre

Château Langoa

That side of the Léoville building, shared with Poyferré, that is designated Las Cases houses one of the Médoc's most efficiently kept *cuveries, left,* where Michel Delon, *above,* persists with wood mainly for aesthetic reasons – and admits it.

Cabernet Franc; and they try to keep the different generations segregated, a subtlety that is made easier by the size of their *vignoble.*

All this is dictated by a control panel, rather out-of-place in the beautifully-maintained traditional *cuverie.* He is very frank about his wooden *cuves,* which cost about 50,000 francs apiece as compared with less than 30,000 for ones of stainless steel or cement. He admits that *"inox"* is marvellous for good wine, "really a pleasure to vinify with;" but he chooses wood for the beauty of the building – and also because no one knows yet how long stainless steel vats will last. They have been in the Médoc for less than twenty years, whereas wooden *cuves* are known to last for up to fifty. When it is proved which method is the more satisfactory, you can be sure that Michel Delon will be one of the first to act on it.

Next door is a cement *cuverie,* complete with stove, in which the malo-lactic is encouraged to occur within fifteen days of the two-week *cuvaison.* Even in late years, thanks to this room, they are able to decide on the *assemblage* by Christmas, together with friend Peynaud who must spend the week between Christmas and New Year comparing notes on the likely outcomes at this property and Lafite, his other concern just up the road. No doubt Jean Crété of Lafite, late of Las Cases, is interested in his ruminations too.

The alternatives at Léoville Las Cases, since Monsieur Delon refuses to acknowledge the possibility of rejecting a *cuve* altogether, is to classify it as a definite Léoville Las Cases, a possible Léoville Las Cases, or a definite *cuve* for the second label, Clos du Marquis. The final decision is not taken until just before or just after the following vintage, when the wine will be moved over the road from the first to the second year *chai* (a much more workmanlike building where things are run with almost German rigour and

efficiency). Clos du Marquis usually accounts for about a tenth of the average production of Château Léoville Las Cases, and is sold at a price that comes somewhere between Château Chasse-Spleen and Gloria, says Monsieur Delon, not without pride. *"I have great confidence in Clos du Marquis; it is as good as many crus classés."* The 1978 vintage, for instance, might be sold at 60 francs a bottle as compared with 85 for a bottle of Château Léoville Las Cases.

An average of about two-thirds of each vintage goes into oak that has been used at least once. The efficient Monsieur Delon offers a taste of his 1980 vintage in both new oak, older oak and *"assemblé."* There was much more attack and life in the new oak sample than the old, but a very noble scent from the blended version. Do not expect much more from a youthful sample of Léoville Las Cases than you would from one of Château Latour.

After a decade, the St Julien wine will reveal much more than the Latour, but Monsieur Delon's are still reticent wines, without always displaying the overall class and weight of a first growth. But they are dependable and excellent examples of a very conscientious approach to winemaking.

Maître-de-chai Michel Rolland and assistant rack a new wine that is doggedly austere, concentrated and slow to mature.

Château Ausone

It took exactly a century after the drawing-up of the 1855 classification of the Médoc before St-Emilion had its own, and then on a very different basis. There was a long list of "Grands Cru Classés," a relatively lowly rank open to revision every ten years, with twelve "Premiers Grands Crus Classés" of which ten were designated somewhat inelegantly "B" and just two, Châteaux Ausone and Cheval Blanc, "A".

Despite this elevated status, Ausone has languished in some disfavour for many a vintage, with those who pride themselves on their collections and comparative tastings of "the firsts" being careful to graft Cheval Blanc and Pétrus on to the Médoc and Graves five, but rarely bothering to include Ausone. It is therefore cheering to be able to report that, as at Château Margaux, there has been a sharp upturn in the quality of wine being produced and the care exerted in the vineyard and cellar.

This is a direct consequence of a brave decision taken in 1975 by the charming Madame Dubois-Challon to take on a scarcely-trained but exceedingly keen 21-year-old as director of operations. Pascal Delbeck is a serious youth, the studious and impenetrable thick black beard enlivened by the highly perceptive gleam in the eyes above it. Under his direction and nursemaid's care, the Château has produced wines in 1976, 1978 and 1979 that have already won acclaim, and the 1980 when tasted in cask showed an excitement decidedly rare for that vintage.

Pascal Delbeck is modest about his achievements, in which he has been able to rely on advice from the Moueix family's highly respected oenologist Jean-Claude Berrouet. *"Our 1976 was good, but that was not me, it was the year,"* he smiles (one thinks) beneath the beard. *"Madame Dubois-Challon was very good to take me on so young, which is a most unusual thing to do here. No, I didn't go to the Uni-*

Château Ausone, perched on St-Emilion's limestone escarpment.

versity. I couldn't afford it. When I came here I had eighteen people to manage, so I immediately set to work learning a bit about everything that has to be done."

"I know that there has been a lot of criticism of Ausone and some of it, by no means all of it, has been justified. Some of the vines were simply too old perhaps, and in some cases there were instances of the wine not being looked after quite as carefully as it might be. It was simply a question of age. People grew old and perhaps became a little bit too relaxed about the quality, so it declined slightly. But underneath the quality was always the same. It was only the extra elements that were lacking. Even our 1970, for instance, was a little lacking in body."

The young Delbeck lives at Château Belair, the property wholly owned by the generous Madame D-C and closely associated with Château Ausone. The best-known photograph of Ausone shows a carthorse pulling a plough along the skyline above the entrance to the Château's cellars, which are dug into the rock on

Back on form again with this stunning vintage.

which St Emilion town is built. These sixteenth-century cellars are reminiscent of the chalk *crayères* of Champagne, except that they are even more *"humide"* and therefore seem even colder. In this grotto, with a high, naturally vaulted roof and ghostly suspended neon lights, the slightly gnomic Delbeck works his spells.

The contrast between this *chai* and its grand counterparts in the Médoc, or even at the larger and more-visited properties on the right bank, is, shall we say, marked. There is none of that careful working of the scarlet wine into the middle band of each *barrique* to give the look of a neat ham sandwich, nor any artful lighting to make the tourist gasp. But then that does not matter, for Ausone is not a property for tourists. Relatively few visitors, even ones intimately concerned with the world of wine, find their way down the rickety lane that leads off one of the St Emilion plateau's more obscure country roads to the pretty country house in which Madame Dubois-Challon lives. Even among those who could find Château Ausone, there must be writers and merchants who have so denigrated or spurned it in the past that they feel wary of imposing themselves now.

They should feel confident of Madame's naturally warm welcome, however, as well as of an interesting interlude with her modest new *régisseur*. He has made some significant changes in his short period working below that old cemetery now planted with vines (including the installation of a computer in his office – technological sophistication of the highest level for Bordeaux). One of his most resourceful moves has been the improvisation of a corner of the cellars into a small temperature-controlled chamber in which are fitted into the irregular rock shapes, with some ingenuity, seven stainless steel *cuves* in which the malo-lactic fermentation can be persuaded to take place at a conveniently early point. This chamber, in use since the 1980 vintage, can also be used for blending and bottling.

Seven seems to be the magic number at Ausone, and delineates very clearly its tiny capacity. With a mere seven hectares of planted vineyard, this is the smallest property in this book – smaller even than the illustrious international star down the road at Pomerol. Because of its very special position, however, these seven hectares include a fine range of varied soil components so that the wine is able to draw on all sorts of underground elements for its make-up. The huddle of old stone that is the small town

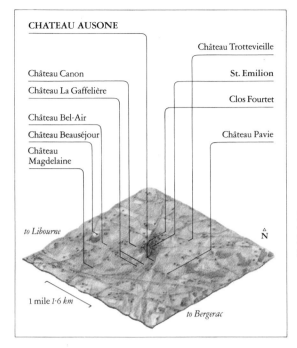

CHATEAU AUSONE

Château Trottevieille

Château Canon

St. Emilion

Château La Gaffelière

Clos Fourtet

Château Bel-Air

Château Beauséjour

Château Pavie

Château Magdelaine

to Libourne

N

1 mile 1·6 *km*

to Bergerac

of St Emilion, which provides one of the few obvious tourist attractions of the Gironde with its steep winding cobbled streets, ancient church and cloisters, is built on and up against a limestone escarpment, steeply sloping away down to the rural valley below. It is on this ridge, just on the southern fringes of the town, that the Château and cellars of Ausone are built, with a breath-taking view down to the road below over the steep vineyards of the property. If you look up at the vineyards from this lower road, you will see the windmill in the middle that is used to pump water; and you may hazard correctly that at Ausone there is that prerequisite for top quality – good drainage.

Because of this dizzy angle at the edge of the plateau, the Ausone vineyards span each of the three specific St Emilion soil characteristics. The property is chiefly a good mix of limestone and clay, which has to be continually banked up and vineyard walls built against erosion. The height of at least the top portion of the vineyards gives them good protection against frost, so that even

People behind the label – the charming Madame Dubois-Challon and her protégé Pascal Delbeck in his office, *bottom*, complete with *le high-tech. Maître-de-chai* Monsieur Lanan looks after the contents of the cellars hewn out of the St Emilion rock, *below left.*

that disastrous winter of 1956 was followed by a vintage in which the average yield was almost 20 hectolitres per hectare. Yields normally average between 25 and 30, with very strict pruning and a regime of treatments such as manuring.

On this side of the Gironde, the Merlot grape reigns, and any Cabernet encountered is much more likely to be Cabernet Franc than the great grape of the Médoc. Pascal Delbeck explains that at Ausone, at least, what little Cabernet Sauvignon there is (about two per cent at most) hardly ever fully ripens. This is because

These few scrubby acres have supplied a host of treasures for Ausone's enviable private reserve.

the limestone soil demands a late-ripening rootstock, and once the late-ripening Cabernet Sauvignon is grafted on, its ripening date will be even later than usual. He saw his Cabernet Sauvignon ripen in the particularly hot summer of 1976, but has not seen the phenomenon since.

These few Cabernet Sauvignon vines apart, the *encépagement* at Ausone is almost equally divided between Merlot and Cabernet Franc. The vines are in general extremely ancient, some of them as many as 80 years old and on average at least 50 (and average yields are only 20 to 25 hectolitres per hectare). This is presumably because, on a property of just seven hectares, there is great reluctance to uproot a single vine. Pascal Delbeck is now trying, piece by piece, to establish long-term renovation of the vineyard, but this can only happen very slowly.

At vintage time, this must be one of the few wine properties where grapes have to be carried *up* the steep vineyard slopes to the cellars. In the Mosel and the Rhône Valley, gravity at least is on the winemaker's side! One advantage of this small vineyard area at least is that the vintage can be achieved in a very short time, with minimal risk-taking once the decision to pick has been

A set for Tutankhamun, plus those controversial new casks.

made. The fermentation takes place in wooden 50-hectolitre *cuves*, of which there are (of course) seven, although to Pascal Delbeck's knowledge the seventh has never been filled. Because his aim is to make a relatively austere wine, there follows a lengthy *cuvaison*, up to three weeks, before the wine is moved to the new temperature-controlled chamber for malo-lactic fermentation so that early decisions may be taken on *assemblage*.

There is no "second wine" at Ausone. As the young *régisseur* says somewhat gloomily, with seven hectares everything is either all good or all bad. In 1963, 1965 and 1968 for instance, there was no wine sold with the Château Ausone label; and it is thought that even over a couple of decades the property only just breaks even. As the younger vines come into production, their wine tends to be sold off in bulk separately, although in 1979 it was added to the main wine as its quality justified it, according to Monsieur Delbeck, and this certainly seems to have done it no harm.

After *assemblage* the new wine now goes into 100 per cent new wood, as it always has, "despite what has been written," Delbeck adds darkly. He seems to feel that poor old Château Ausone has come in for quite unwarranted criticism in the past, and is determined to rout this phenomenon. What with this "cause" to fight for and another property in his very varied domain to look after, he is a very busy man, for Pascal Delbeck is also responsible for the bigger vineyard at Château Belair, the charming farmhouse where he lives just along the ridge from Château Ausone. During the autumn "busy season," he is always dashing off to one of his cellars in the middle of the night just to check that all is proceeding as it should. Some argue that Belair is so like Ausone that, at its much lower prices, it is the bargain. It should be remembered, however, that its higher limestone content makes a much lighter wine.

Pascal Delbeck keeps a respectful distance from his vivacious employer and she lives her own very separate life in the Château, but she is clearly highly appreciative of this new enthusiasm in her cellars next door. Madame Dubois-Challon is perhaps an unlikely proprietor for a first growth property. Bird-like in her appearance and movements, she is a thoughtful and generous hostess, but seems to treat her vinous treasures with no more interest than she does her victuals, bought in from the best *traiteur* that Libourne can offer. This may of course simply be because she has so many vinous treasures. Her private reserve kept in the damp cellars behind iron gates includes bottles of Château Ausone back to 1831, as well as a good collection of Château Belair, built up since her family acquired the property in 1916.

Lunch with her, the youthful Fourniers of Canon and a bottle of Château Ausone 1849 was more like pantomime than a dramatic tribute to a great wine. Chattering or giggling incessantly, shaking her gold locks occasionally and scolding her ancient maid regularly, she led us through the meal – in her high-ceilinged salon, decorated like the rest of the Château with great enthusiasm and obviously very much lived-in – to the venerable bottle. It was in wonderful condition. Its chief attribute was its texture, almost jewel-like in its smoothness; and yet, amazingly, it still had structure: a beginning, a middle and an end. The tawny colour masked an extremely elegant bouquet and great life on the palate with a neat, positive finish. We sat and marvelled at this lively survivor from the years of revolution, somewhat stunned. We came round to hear Madame's commentary continuing unabated. *"Yes, it's not bad, is it? Most of these nineteenth-century wines have a jolly nice perfume, even the 1832, as I recall. . . . "* Our head-shaking over our glasses, still sending distinctly unspiritual messages back from the nineteenth century, was interrupted by the sight of Madame reaching up to the dangling flex above the table, her line of communication with the old retainer in the kitchen. *"Now, let's see what's happened to that* bombe!"

Pascal Delbeck's aim is to restore Château Ausone's wines to their rightful place, as "the Latour of St-Emilion." He wants to make wines that can last longer than any other wines in this rather "carefree" region; and he is looking for a style that is both classic and noticeably dry, to provide a contrast to the rather riper charms of Château Cheval Blanc, St Emilion's traditionally more-acclaimed Premier Grand Cru Classé "A". It may well be that, once a new track record has been established for Château Ausone, it will be known as one of the most lean and Médocain of the St Emilion properties.

Château Cheval Blanc

Ausone may be enjoying a renaissance, but there is no doubt that, until it has a decade of dazzling new vintages in the sepulchral private reserve cellar, Château Cheval Blanc will continue to be thought of as the very finest St Emilion property. In almost every way, Cheval Blanc is exceptional, both in St Emilion and in general.

The typical château in St Emilion is a low farm building surrounded by just a few hectares of vineyard on the "Côtes," the large central area made up chiefly of clay and chalk with a bit of limestone. It makes ripe, almost peppery wines that are ready to drink as soon as two years after the vintage and are extremely charming when young, but tend to tire and fade early. The cluttered map entitled "Juridiction de Saint-Emilion" shows more than three hundred such properties in an area well under 10 square miles.

Cheval Blanc is large – about 35 hectares are planted at present, out of a total of 41 – but, more importantly for the quality of its wine, it is situated at the very edge of the St Emilion limits, in the small, higher sub-region Graves-St-Emilion. As its name suggests, the vineyards here are much more gravelly than those of the Côtes, which gives texture to the wines of the leading Graves-St-Emilion properties Château Cheval Blanc and Figeac. Cheval Blanc is even more

unusual, however, in being almost an outcrop into Pomerol territory. With Pomerol properties La Conseillante and L'Evangile (two comforting neighbours) at its boundary, Cheval Blanc has the same sort of plummy richness – what the taster has to call sweet, for want of a more flattering word – as a great Pomerol.

The property is also unusually grand for its district, with its properly gracious driveway, and a handsome sweep by the cellars towards the very respectable Château inhabited by the current guardians of the estate, Monsieur et Madame Jacques Hébrard.

Madame is a Fourcaud-Laussac, one of the many cousins who represent the Héritiers Fourcaud-Laussac featured, along with a rather dubious pair of medals, on Cheval Blanc's somewhat plain label. Monsieur is a phlegmatic gentleman of almost frightening height who, until ten years ago, ran rubber and cocoa plantations in lands as distant and now as altered as Vietnam and the Belgian Congo. Jacques Hébrard's father had an even more exotic and unlikely occupation, being one of the early trans-Atlantic pilots, and his elder son is also a professional man of the air. The other son, Dominic, is engaged in more earthly and homely pursuits, however, and may follow his father at Cheval Blanc after studying commerce and oenology in Bordeaux.

If he seems an unlikely incumbent at Cheval Blanc, this is not to suggest that Jacques Hébrard is at all an unsuitable one. It may be extremely difficult to persuade him to talk with passion about his wines and the way in which they are made, but he has some very clear ideas about his role. *"My aim is to make wines that will age well."*

What puts Cheval Blanc way ahead of its neighbours in so many vintages (although Château Figeac can rival it occasionally) is that its structure is so clearly designed for a long life. When so many St Emilions might be starting to taste tired and hollow, Cheval Blanc is just starting to come into its own – seductive, ripe, powerful and with a backbone that makes its flavour a complete experience. Vintages such as 1921, 1934 and 1947 have made its reputation, but there are many subsequent ones that will sustain it. There is a certain "gaminess" in the wine that brings to mind something a little exotic – something very slightly suggestive of those curiously similar wines Vega Sicilia of Spain and Grange Hermitage of Australia (although this comparison

Unusual grandeur and scale for St Emilion.

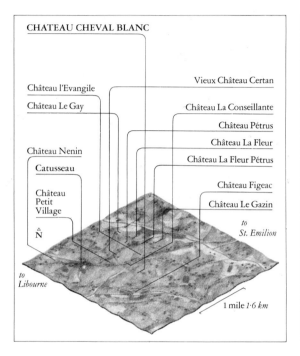

One of the world's favourites, *above,* the only great wine produced principally from Cabernet Franc.

would doubtless horrify any self-respecting Bordelais). Monsieur Hébrard himself admits that some of the Bordeaux *négoçiants* used to remark on a curious flavour in Cheval Blanc, reminiscent of a sort of banana jam, something almost burnt about it. This was attributable, says Monsieur, to the fact that until 1945, all the way from 1890, Cheval Blanc was the only property in this intensively-farmed neighbourhood to have proper drainage ditches. And its rich mix of soils played some part too.

The *encépagement* at Cheval Blanc is another distinctive feature. It is one of the few providers of world-class wine based predominantly on Cabernet Franc (known here as Bouchet). This variety, dismissed as a rather flimsy thing on the left bank of the Gironde, makes up about two-thirds of the vineyard, with almost all of the rest being planted with the usually more prolific Merlot. There is still a very little of what Monsieur Hébrard calls "Vieux Malbec," although these old vines are now being pulled up – along with the small plot of Cabernet Sauvignon that was planted some years ago but further proved the point that this variety will rarely ripen here. *"I am not in favour of everyone growing Cabernet Sauvignon,"* he pronounces. *"We'd all end up producing exactly the same sort of wine that way."* He is a great fan of Merlot and points out with some satisfaction that at Château Latour, whose wines he admires tremendously in their own way, the Merlot plantings have recently been increased. Merlot is traditionally planted in the most gravelly bits of the estate.

Even here, where Cabernet Franc covers such a large area, it is difficult to get a precise description of its characteristics. Monsieur Hébrard is extremely reluctant to elaborate, maintaining sagely that *"the most important thing is to make a good wine."* It is certainly difficult to see how at Cheval Blanc they can make so rich a wine relying so heavily on a grape that many feel is rather puny. One must assume that, here on the Pomerol-St-Emilion boundary, it reaches its apogee.

As in general on the right bank, the 1956 winter frosts did terrible damage to the vines, and to the amount of Cheval Blanc available in the late 1950s. *"It disrupted everything, and there had to be an extensive plan of pulling up, not necessarily those vines that were the oldest, but those which were incapable of producing wine any longer."* The average age of vines on the property is still thirty-seven years. Today the parcels which are to be replanted are left fallow for a full two years before the young vines are put in, and their produce is not allowed into the Grand Vin for at least four years.

The "Héritiers Fourcaud-Laussac," Monsieur and Madame Jacques Hébrard, and a dining room that has seen not a few mouth-watering vintages of Cheval Blanc.

The vintage here can last two weeks, and a team of about seventy-five pickers will be hired every October to supplement the permanent staff of fewer than twenty people. The Merlot is, as usual, picked first and taken to the distinctly unpicturesque *cuvier*. This is very much a working area, with concrete *cuves* closely packed together. Each *cuve* is in use for perhaps twenty days a year and the wine gets some of that backbone from the addition of the first press wine, and even perhaps the second as well, depending on the vintage. *"The press wine is a good test of the vintage,"* Jacques Hébrard believes. *"If the press wine is good, the vintage will be good too, because it's like the essence of the vintage."* After the tasting and selection of the *cuves*, with the second wine being sold as straight St Emilion, the young wine is put into new wood in the rather smarter *chai*, where everything is kept in extremely good order. Just above this is the recent extension, containing a large *salle des réunions*

(useful for the local Jurade) and a flat roof terrace from which one may survey the Cheval Blanc property as well as parts of its most famous Pomerol neighbour, Château Pétrus.

In an average year between 110 and 120 *tonneaux* of Cheval Blanc will be produced, but in years such as 1963, 1965 and 1968 there was none, or very, very little. The costly but admirable philosophy of putting the label only on wine that earns it, is followed stringently here. This is not to say that the Hébrard policy is to let nature dictate exactly what will be what each year. One of his favourite vintages, for instance, is 1980 ("much better than 1979"), because this was a difficult year in which human intervention played the most important role in making something exciting from it. He keeps well abreast of what is going on in the cellars of his distinguished colleagues across the Gironde, and was an early admirer of the "revived Margaux" vintages of 1978 and 1979, and a great fan of Médoc first growths in general, *"though I can take great pleasure in a well-made* petit vin *too, you know, even a Beaujolais Nouveau so long as it is a good one."* His standard beverages may be water and the wine of young Cheval Blanc vines, but he clearly loves the chance to take part in comparative tastings – such as the famous one organised by Jean Delmas of Haut-Brion at which everyone failed to spot their own first growth.

Wearing another hat, Monsieur Hébrard is also a chancellor of L'Académie du Vin de Bordeaux. And what, I asked innocently, does that entail? *"We decide on the quality of books about Bordeaux,"* he smiled grimly.

Château Pétrus

For years Pétrus, and indeed the whole of Pomerol, was regarded as nothing more than a provider of attractive, easy, soft wines that could give wine-lovers a foretaste of a vintage while they were waiting for the "proper" clarets (from the Médoc and Graves) to mature. Thanks largely to the efforts of the indomitable Madame Loubat who controlled Château Pétrus in the 1940s and 1950s, and was determined that its wine should be sold for not a *sou* less than she thought fit, this property and the whole of Pomerol in its shadow rose in public esteem, so that today Pétrus can command higher prices than any other wine. As much as 40 per cent of the vineyard's tiny production of 3,000 cases (its paucity is a not unimportant factor in its value) is now shipped across the Atlantic to wow American wine lovers; if a Texas oil sheik wants to impress, he will do it with "Pet*roos*."

Since 1961 the property has been part of the extremely powerful Moueix empire. Today it encompasses two highly successful *négociant* businesses and controls fourteen châteaux from the simple Château Canon in Fronsac to Pétrus itself, all from businesslike headquarters in Libourne. Jean-Pierre Moueix is the taciturn patriarch of the family, and he oversees all these activities from his office on the quayside of this small market town. His eldest son Jean-François looks after the fine wine business Duclot, and it is his other son Christian who is charged with the overall responsibility for the family's most famous wine estate.

Unlike his father, who seems to enjoy his rather Hitchcockian role of private authority and public silence, Christian is highly articulate and keenly conscious of the world outside Libourne, outside Bordeaux and even outside France. Wine encourages loquaciousness, and there are many who will happily talk about wine for as long as Christian Moueix; but there are few who exhibit such demonstrable proof that they actually *think* about the subject as well. Still in his mid-thirties and youthfully lanky, Christian has charm and exquisite manners, and is good at being teased. One imagines he has learned this last skill from his playful and vivacious wife Marie-Laure, probably the only woman in the world who waves aside a second glass of Pétrus with a *"No thank you, I can drink it any day."* They are a deeply enviable couple in more respects than this, he with his precious wine, she with her own *haute couture* boutique in Bordeaux, both with their little Edouard et Charlotte in their sizeable chalet-château decorated with skill by Marie-Laure, ex-interior

The simple farm building, an unlikely Mecca for lovers of great wine, houses a smart little salon but no successor to the formidable Madame Loubat.

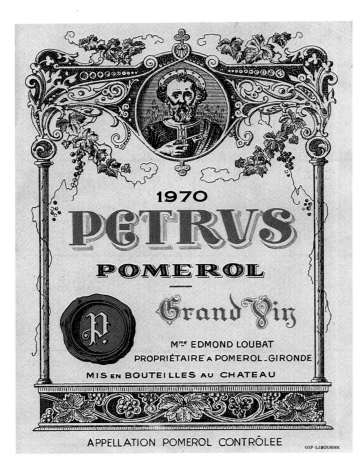

The glamorous Christian Moueix, *above right,* is intelligent enough to realise how lucky he is to be in charge of the most sought-after wine in the world.

designer, and set in its own small park on the peaceful Dordogne just outside Libourne. *"There is no need for a vacation,"* he says simply.

That word "vacation" (as opposed to holiday) comes from Christian's years doing his Master's at Davis, a wonderful complement to his training as an agricultural engineer in Paris. He still has many friends in California and was, in particular, the supplier of Merlot cuttings to that great Wild West pioneer of Merlot, Ric Forman. An enthusiast for the best of California, Christian Moueix is no chauvinist, and particularly enjoys the frankness and openness between winemakers there. This must contrast sharply with more traditional life back on his particular farm, Château Pétrus. In fact, the Château itself is hardly more than, perhaps even less than, a farm. This undistinguished two-storey building with its turquoise shutters has not been lived in since the pre-Loubat days. It has no kitchen, and was refurbished in 1980 only so that visitors could decently be invited in to sign the visitors' book. Those pilgrims, mainly American, whom Christian finds mounting a vigil of up to a day hoping to see someone, just anyone, connected with this wine shrine must be disappointed by the reality of the bricks and mortar.

Visitors who wish to do more than sit hopefully on the Château steps are seen, understandably, by appointment only, and Christian will whisk them immediately into the middle of the vineyard. *"We can all buy impressive cellars,"* he snorts somewhat contemptuously, *"but there is only one soil like Pétrus's."* Of Pomerol's 2,000 acres (Christian Moueix must be the only wine guide in the world who switches with ease from hectare to acre according to his audience), only 600 are the best, plateau land, and only 30 of those, about 12 hectares, are "the bump in the middle of the plateau" that is Pétrus. The wine property is surrounded by others, for Pomerol is a one-crop region, and Cheval Blanc on the western edge of St Emilion is easily within sight of its famous Pomerol rival. Christian points out the various buildings and copses on the skyline – Figeac, Cheval Blanc, Vieux Château Certan, Gazin, La Fleur-Pétrus (another Moueix property) – all on the same strip of gravel that encircles Pétrus. *"But Pétrus, and especially the central part of the vineyard, is almost pure clay. Not the sort of damp clay you find near rivers that gives such coarse wine, but a very special sort of clay, brown not red on top, and streaked with blue, because of the iron content, about two feet below the surface. Soil makes 80 per cent of every great wine, and it is because our soil is so very special – even La Fleur-Pétrus only a few hundred yards away has white, gravelly soil that is quite dif-*

ferent – that our wine is so very special. There is no difference between our microclimate, for instance, and that of our neighbours."

There are only very few tiny bits of gravel in Pétrus's clay, and the vineyard has to rely largely on its height for that essential of good drainage. Soon after Christian took over in 1970 he had drainage ditches made so that the land would not get too muddy for tractors to work the vines, but even they could not have compensated much for the three weeks' continuous downpour in the early summer of that year when the mud made usual spraying methods impossible and helicopters had to be drafted in. This would presumably have been prohibitively expensive for Pétrus's 12 hectares alone, and highlights just one way in which the property is able to benefit from its kinship with other Moueix properties.

Christian believes that, after the composition of the soil, the age of the vines is the next most important, but often overlooked, factor. The average age at Pétrus is 35 years. Like Cheval Blanc, Pétrus was hit particularly badly by the hard winter of 1956, but Madame Loubat was not daunted by this cruel hiccup of nature. She scrabbled about in the vineyard and found a number of roots that were still alive and grafted on younger vines, so that even today there are vines aged about 25 years whose roots are 60 and 70 years old. Their yield is lower than if their roots were younger, but they are in part responsible for the quality of Pétrus. About one-third of all the Pétrus vines are by any standards grand old men, but there are a few vines that have barely reached 10 years, the minimum for inclusion in the great wine itself – a stricter standard than at any other property discussed in this book.

The aim is to replant parcel by parcel every eight to ten years, each newly-treated plot being just one hectare. Christian, believe it or not, has a precise replantation programme that takes the property, if not him, up to the year 2055. He is at odds with his friend Jean-Paul Gardère of Château Latour on the relative merits of his own programme and vine by vine replanting, and they have "discussed" this subject. The Latour habit of having the young vines among the old marked with special ribbon and picked first is seen as a luxury by the Moueixes, who merely leave a memorial space in the row for any vine that dies before an ancient parcel is pulled up.

Early training of the vine is seen as vital at Pétrus and is explained with much human

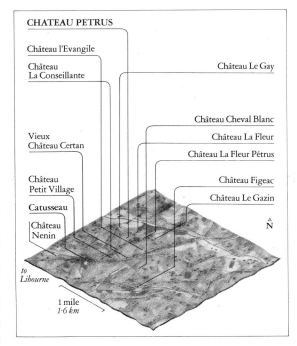

metaphor. The young vines are brought up extremely strictly, through severe pruning being forced to dig deep and extend a solid root system that will stand them in good stead for the decades of useful work expected of them. *"Instead of pruning them so that they will produce a lot of wine early, we never allow them more than eight buds and they are well-equipped to struggle for perhaps 60 or 80 years,"* explains Christian. *"If we allowed ten buds, we could increase the yield by 25 per cent, but we would no longer be producing Pétrus.*

"We use only natural fertilisers at Pétrus, and the best fertiliser is that," he points at a patch of rippling green in one corner of the vineyard, a mixture of oats and deep-rooting vetches that he has found to be ideal after years of researching the right crop to plant in the fallow vineyard. *"The vetches need the oats to make them stand up, and the oats give the soil some fibre. In 10 years you'll see this mixture will be used all over Bordeaux. We have had a monoculture here in Pomerol for centuries, so we should really leave our land fallow for six or seven years before replanting, but no-one can afford to; so here we use chemicals to disinfect the ground after resting the land for a summer and then adding the necessary minerals and planting my mixture as a spring crop before the new vines go in."* The time during

The Moueix oenologist Jean-Claude Berrouet, *above*, is one of Bordeaux's new highly-trained breed. Wise patriarch Jean-Pierre Moueix, seen here under the chestnuts in front of his empire's Libourne headquarters, would see to that.

which the precious land is not planted with vines is thus reduced to two years.

Christian Moueix is unusual in his ability to sustain an argument or theme of a lecture while guiding you over rough terrain. An hour after advancing his soil theory, followed up by his observations on the importance of the age of the vine, he will suddenly address you: *"And the third factor is the balance of different grape varieties, one of the few areas in which we have a free choice."* It is widely thought that only Merlot is planted at Pétrus, and indeed Christian Moueix himself is a great fan of this underrated grape, believing it to be chiefly responsible for the great popularity of Pomerols in general. Two of Pétrus's 30 acres, however, are planted with Cabernet Franc (Bouchet), which in some years can make quite a significant contribution to the make-up of Pétrus. In other years, however, its yield can be so small that the wine is practically 100 per cent Merlot. The little two-acre patch was planted in 1957 and is not scheduled for replanting till 2030 on Christian's master plan; so, as he points out with satisfaction, there is plenty of time for discussion of its merits and demerits before then.

He feels strongly that it would be inappropriate to plant Cabernet Sauvignon – and in particular the rot-resistant but low-alcohol Cabernet Sauvignon that was sanctioned by the authorities in the early 1970s in the wake of the disastrous 1968 vintage. *"It was an awful time when in theory you couldn't plant what you*

wanted," he shudders. *"I prefer to have a year like 1976 when the grapes are very ripe and there is perhaps 10 per cent rot, rather than to risk having low-alcohol grapes every year. With our very strict training and sap coming through only an extremely small vein, we tend to harvest grapes with between 12.5° and 13° alcohol without difficulty."* Thanks to this careful long-term planning, and the situation of the vineyards, Pétrus tend to harvest very ripe, very healthy grapes even in vintages which are generally thought of as mediocre – their 1980, for instance, had wonderful life and depth when tasted in cask the following summer. Even frost is rarely a problem because of their extra height – although they took the precaution of buying smudge pots in the spring of 1980. Sprinkling on this clay would be out of the question, for it would simply clog up the vineyard.

Christian's fourth and final ingredient in determining the quality of Pétrus's precious liquid is the all-important "human factor," which he sums up with the stern motto: *"Things have to be done the day they have to be done."* This of course is the advantage of having under 13 hectares to control, and then only as part of a group of properties for which labour and machinery are needed anyway. Ploughing at Pétrus can take just two fine days, for instance, when five of the Moueix tractors are put on the job; and the system really comes into its own when that crucial decision in every winemaker's calendar – when to pick – has to be made. The Moueixes employ the same troop of 180 pickers from northern France every year. They are moved around the different properties according to geography and ripeness, but when the day comes for Pétrus to be picked, all other priorities are set on one side. During vintage time, Christian, the busy Moueix oenologist Jean-Claude Berrouet and the determined young *régisseur* at Pétrus consult together every morning at seven. By 7.10 the decision has been taken where to pick that day, and the whole of Pétrus is picked on two or three clear afternoons taking a total of just 10 hours. *"We could usually vintage on any of up to 20 days,"* says Christian, *"but we look for afternoons – always afternoons so that the grapes are quite dry and we can ferment at a higher temperature – that look set fair and guarantee us maximum ripeness. So far we have never made a mistake, although we once finished picking at 5.00, just fifteen minutes before the start of a storm."*

Château Pétrus is clearly nurtured in every detail even before the grapes reach the unspectacular cellars attached to the small Château; and it is hardly surprising therefore that the wine so consistently has this "ultra-ripe" taste. Christian himself admits: *"It is a supple, sweet wine, but we want it to last 50 years and we want to be certain of its structure, so we give it an education in the winery for a long life. Like straightening the back of a child, we give it tannin by putting in between 15 and 20 per cent of the stalks, and we have increased the time we allow the must to macerate on the skins from about 14 days to sometimes as much as 25 days. The lighter the year, the longer the fermentation process."*

The grapes are so ripe and warm when they come in that there is rarely any need to heat, and a fermentation that is hot by most other standards is usually well underway by the second day. They like the fermentation to take place at between 29° and 32°C (84°-90°F), cooling if necessary by external serpent, in distinctly unglamorous concrete *cuves*, of which they fill between five and seven most years.

The press wine, wine from the first and only pressing, is added back straight away. Christian takes a typically unusual stance on this, maintaining: *"I think it's a false problem, the question of how much press wine to add. If you add it all immediately then it ages with the Grand Vin and therefore softens and develops as the whole, not as a separate entity. If you do otherwise, the press wine can take on a bitter taste. Yes, I think I am alone in this thinking."* This last observation is added with no trace of boastfulness, but certainly not a shadow of doubt. Perhaps there is just a trace of pride in his explanation of Pétrus policy on malo-lactic, as well there might be. *"We try to achieve the malo-lactic fermentation at the same time as the alcoholic fermentation by adding lactic bacteria. This is a technique which I studied at Davis and I believe it will eventually be adopted everywhere."* (Tim Mondavi takes the same view.)

The next important event in the cellars at Pétrus, so tiny even after the recent addition of a smart second-year *chai* in comparison with their equivalents across the Gironde, takes place as soon as Moueix Senior gets back from his January vacation. Each *cuve* is then tasted blind by those few vitally concerned with the property. *"Usually the blend of all cuves tastes better than any single cuve,"* points out Christian. *"In 1980 we chose to include each of the three cuves made, but in a big, variable year we may reject several cuves. The age of the vines is the major criterion, for our grapes are almost always healthy. We don't have a "second label" under which these cuves can be sold, and I am very against that idea. Il y a un Pétrus. Point à la ligne."*

"Le" Pétrus rests in immaculately-maintained casks, made specially for Moueix by their coopers in Libourne, until the precise day on which the bottling "has to be done." The flexibility of approach now adopted at Pétrus is another recent development designed to maximise quality. *"In the old days, wine used to be bottled according to the calendar, but now it happens according to the wine. Our '79, for instance, slowed down in development in cask quite suddenly, so we put back the bottling date, and may bottle as late as the end of November."*

When he manages to drag himself away

Attention to detail is minute on Pétrus's tiny plot of very special clay.

The reputation, and price, of Pétrus was built up by this determined lady, Madame Loubat, in the 1940s and 1950s.

from the day-to-day running of Pétrus, his own Pomerol property Château La Grave Trigant de Boisset and the commercial aspects of the Moueix business with which he is charged, Christian Moueix makes a wonderful ambassador. He exudes an air that is very rare, very cosmopolitan and very fresh for Bordeaux. The very fact that, as a Bordelais – sorry, Libournais – he was so keen to go to Davis speaks volumes. And now at Pétrus he is not trying to revolutionize the processes that have consistently made a wine of awe-inspiring quality, but to put into practice the lessons he has learned elsewhere only if appropriate.

"On n'est pas obsédé par Pétrus," he will maintain with a cautionary wag of the finger over a beautifully-served lunch on his *terrasse* overlooking the gentle river. We are treated to Pétruses 1971 and 1952, wines of very differing stages but both of such enormous intensity that there is really no need for food alongside; but we are told it is rare to enjoy such an exclusive selection of wines (to follow just a little Bollinger RD as *apéritif*). They drink lots of white Burgundy, for instance, a sure sign of open-mindedness on this side of France, and Christian manages to keep more in touch with developments elsewhere in the wine world than almost any other inhabitant of the Gironde *département*. He was the only one, for instance, to exhibit any curiosity about his "bookfellows" in this collection, his curiosity being so strong as to threaten research into his own entry.

Christian Moueix is a thinker, and keenly aware of his exact and privileged position. Over coffee, sitting in a carefully-chosen cane chair under one of his plane trees he presented a personal philosophy which one could hardly accept as self-sacrificing in this setting, but which is certainly totally dedicated: *"I have been allowed to inherit a tiny patch of earth that is capable of producing great wine. If I am given this opportunity, then it is natural that I give my life for it. My sole purpose is that no-one should ever be disappointed in a bottle of Pétrus. I know how much people are paying for this wine, and I believe that the name Pétrus must never be given to anything that could conceivably disappoint. I am very conscious of the fact that we have one of the best soils of the world, and I have nothing to add to that."*

Château d'Yquem

The lush green countryside of the Sauternes area is quite unlike the bleaker wastes of the Médoc in terms both of aspect and of time. With its small farmhouses in weathered stone, horses and peasants working deliberately through the fields, and no thoroughfare more sophisticated than the lanes that wind their way through small copses and skirt the gentle hills, Bordeaux's sweet white wine country seems decades behind that responsible for its most famous reds. This is the land of which jigsaw puzzles and chocolate-box lids are made.

In some senses the time-warp is not one of decades but of centuries; there is something distinctly medieval about Château d'Yquem. The Château itself dominates the Sauternais plain from the brow of an outcrop, and to get to it you must first have a Michelin map or ask any local (the signs went down in 1980 and they *still* have 10,000 visitors a year). You will then ascend through vineyards worked, you learn later, by the same families as have worked them for 300 years, to what amounts to a fortified, crenellated farm, built round an echoing pale stone courtyard, and redolent not of Médoc grandeur and nine-teenth-century wealth but of tradition.

The current in-cumbent is the Comte Alexandre de Lur-Saluces in whose family's hands the Château has been since 1785. He sees himself as a medieval knight guarding an almost-forgotten treasure when at home, and seems to feel in his travels that he has been entrusted with a crusade. *"I feel terribly strongly that I must carry on the old traditions because they, after all, are our most important asset."* The Count, who succeeded his famous uncle Bertrand in 1968, lives half an hour up the new autoroute in Bordeaux, leaving the Château empty and cold. Today it is rarely used, although in it visitors are shown the film *"Le Risque d'Yquem"* which Alexandre had made in the mid-1970s, and about which he feels passionate-ly. *"People said it was extravagant,"* he confides as Julian Bream plays to the opening credits, *"but the decline of Sauternes has been due to distrust and ignorance. If only we can show everyone how difficult it is to make our wines, and how expensive they* have *to be."* He is deeply distressed by the world's apparent disregard for the greatness of Sauternes, and even nominates certain well-known Bordeaux authorities who he feels show scant regard for Yquem in com-parison with their enthusiasm for the great red

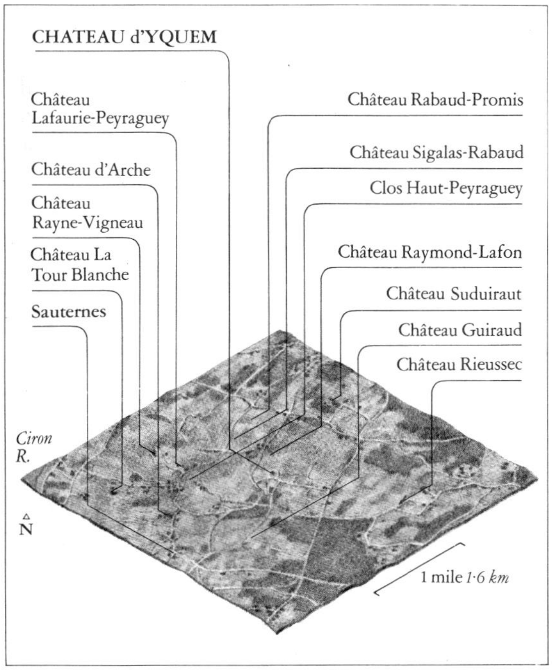

CHATEAU d'YQUEM

Château Lafaurie-Peyraguey
Château d'Arche
Château Rayne-Vigneau
Château La Tour Blanche
Sauternes
Château Rabaud-Promis
Château Sigalas-Rabaud
Clos Haut-Peyraguey
Château Raymond-Lafon
Château Suduiraut
Château Guiraud
Château Rieussec

Ciron R.

N

1 mile 1·6 km

Yquem owes its lusciousness to this strange fungus, *pourriture noble*, already concentrating Sémillon juice in the autumn sunshine that the Sauternais hope for each year.

Château d'Yquem

Lur-Saluces

— 1976 —

wine properties. Sauternes and its inner commune Barsac are, as Nicholas Faith and Robert Freson showed so poignantly in *The Sunday Times* in 1978, being passed by in the twentieth century. Many vine-farmers have been finding it hard to earn a living making wines that are so unfashionably sweet, and there is little encouragement to continue even for the very top properties. Yquem was the only property to be classified as both "premier" and "grand" in 1855 when it was in its heyday, with rapturous customers in the prosperous courts of Tsarist Russia. Today its pre-eminence remains unquestioned, and its wines can easily command the same price as a Médoc first growth. Yet this is hardly enough to make sufficient return on all the effort that goes into making such a handcrafted wine, and the *réclame* of this single estate alone is hardly enough to keep the whole region in a healthy wine-producing state. When Alexandre de Lur-Saluces says that he is convinced that "very soon" Sauternes will be "modish" again, one feels this is more of a desperate invocation than a confident prediction.

There can be no other wine in the world (other possibly than the best of those "made again" wines, champagne, port and sherry) made quite so laboriously. Each vine at Yquem produces an average of just a glassful of wine a year. Then there is the total number of permanent staff, a good indication of effort: 48 to produce barely 6,000 cases of wine annually, as compared with 75 at Château Lafite, for example, where in most years five times as much wine as this is made. Perhaps the all-important picking process provides the most revealing insight into meticulousness here, with the pickers going as many as eleven times through the same vines each year in order that the grapes are picked only at the optimum time.

Even at the most basic level there is great selectiveness: 102 of the 173 hectares which comprise the Yquem estate satisfy the Appellation Contrôlée authorities of their suitability, but only about 82 are currently producing wine up to the standards required for Yquem. And when the *régisseur* Pierre Meslier decides a parcel of vines need uprooting, he will allow the land the luxury of lying fallow for a full three years before replanting, not using the fruit for Yquem until the fifth year after that.

The heavily-scented Muscadelle grape is spurned at Yquem, where the *encépagement* is the classic 80 per cent Sémillon and 20 per cent

Sauvignon, the two varieties now planted in separate parcels rather than the old method of planting "four and one" along the row. This modern arrangement allows them to treat the vines separately for the different maladies to which they are prone, and match them to the appropriate soil.

The greatness of Yquem, and indeed of any well-made sweet wine whether from Sauternes, Monbazillac, the Loire, Rhine or Mosel, is the result of that curious fungus which must look to any casual observer like a dreadful malady of the vine: noble rot, *botrytis cinerea, pourriture noble* and *Edelfäule* it may be called in various parts of the world, but its effects are just the same. Nowhere, however, thanks to the soil, vines and microclimate, does it produce wines of quite such unctuousness as at Yquem. The Sémillon of Sauternes is a particularly rich waxy grape wherever it is planted, and in the soil of Yquem, gravel and sand on a thick layer of water-retaining clay, it produces wine of even greater liquorousness.

The lie of the land at Yquem, some of the highest vineyards of the region, is perfect for just the sort of weather that encourages *botrytis.* Indeed, Alexandre de Lur-Saluces tells the story of how he was discussing the problems of making sweet wine with that great German Graf Matuschka-Greiffenclau, and made the mistake of bemoaning the fact that at Yquem they failed completely every ten years or so. "We manage to *succeed* once every ten years," the German count told him gently. The late-ripening grapes of Yquem manage to escape frosts and hail most years and remain intact and healthy for a high incidence of autumn mist, clearing during the morning to sunny afternoons – the ideal *botrytis* conditions.

As the fungus attacks a ripe grape, its colour turns first a pinky-red; the grape then starts to shrivel, for the fungus starts to cut off communications with the moisture-giving vine, and the grape is covered with a revolting grey-brown, thick, cobwebby powder. The sugar content of the grape will actually decline during this process, a fact not often appreciated, for the fungus is a great consumer of sugar. The water loss is even greater, however – usually about 50 per cent – so that the overall effect is one of concentration, sometimes up to a potential alcohol level of about 20°. *Botrytis* also reduces the acidity level in the grapes as it eats up tartaric acid at the same time as the sugar, meanwhile producing about four times as much glycerol as is nor-

The property's altitude gives it a wonderful view, *opposite,* and its wines a special finesse – even in such ultra-rich vintages as 1976.

Maître-de-chai Latrille, *left,* has a countenance ripened by all that golden treasure in his cellar, while that of *régisseur* Meslier has been worn by years of expensive decision-making at vintage time.

mally found in ripe grapes. This can later be seen in thick trickles down the side of any glass that has held Yquem.

Another important effect of the busy *botrytis* is that it tends to destroy the natural aroma of the grape, substituting for it that wonderful "burnt golden syrup" smell of the rot itself, thereby making it particularly important to look at the weight and palate of a sweet wine as well as the "nose" when trying to identify it. This is not disastrous for Sémillon which is not naturally a very aromatic grape, and the Sauvignon, whose fresh tartness can add an important element to the flavour of a great Sauternes, will usually be picked much earlier than Sémillon – partly to retain this aroma characteristic and partly because it is not so prone to *botrytis* as Sémillon in any case.

The vital concentrating of the Sémillon grapes can happen relatively fast. In the wonderful year of 1967 there were scarcely eight days between the time the *botrytis* first attacked and the day it had completed its work. In some years the pickers at Yquem might have to wait for weeks until the last grapes have been properly affected by the fungus, however, thus prolonging the risk of rain and the appearance of the distinctly less savoury grey rot.

It is clear that the selection of bunches that are affected by the right sort of rot and ready to pick is a highly skilled task, and Monsieur Meslier (who is also *régisseur* at Château de Fargues as well as having what he calls *"mon propre petit château à côté,"* Château Raymond-Lafon) would not dream of taking on any casual pickers for the vintage, as happens elsewhere. The team can comprise as many as a hundred pickers, most of them having worked on the same patch for many years. Each has his or her own role, which does not change from year to year, and the Comte says he finds his women pickers much more meticulous. There are some elderly gentlemen, and a few young women being trained, but the bulk of the harvesting team is made up of comfortable middle-aged Sauternaises, in old wide-brimmed straw hats and determinedly sensible footwear. Bunch-by-bunch picking requires great dexterity. Fingers, all sorts of secateurs and even long-handled instruments that look like castrating irons are used by the ladies, who sometimes work for six weeks through until the end of November. They are paid by the day, but may have to wait until 1.30 in the afternoon before the mists clear and they can go to it, collecting the grapes into ancient wooden baskets and then emptying them, amid clouds of noble rot dust, into Yquem's special small two-handled hods, which are carried reverentially and rather like a sedan chair.

The thousands of visitors that come to nose around the Château and cellars of Yquem each year are often disappointed by the apparently small scale of operations there. In the long white-washed shed where the grapes are received and finally checked to make sure they are all of the right quality, there are just three small basket presses – tiny things that look as though they'd take the *surplus* production of any decent-sized property in a big year. The reason for this, Alexandre de Lur-Saluces explains patiently, is that the harvest is usually so lengthy that they never receive a very high proportion of the total vintage in any one day. They usually press enough grapes to fill only 20 *barriques* a day, and if they need to process more grapes, as in 1967 and 1976, they simply work a 20-hour day, presumably reckoning that the benefits of such a good vintage outweigh this temporary discomfort.

Using ancient hydraulic presses, the grapes are pressed first, to produce 80 per cent of the must, before two further pressings, producing fifteen and five per cent respectively and becoming progressively more concentrated with sugar. The two grape varieties are kept separate throughout fermentation, which takes place in new barrels made of dense Slovenian oak, each marked with the exact date of harvest. The neat cellar may have to be heated to get fermentation going if the harvest was late and the temperatures correspondingly low. The yeasts then get to work on the enormous amount of sugar present

in the must. It would take superyeast and more to convert all of this sugar to alcohol, but so potent are the Sauternes yeasts (as compared say, to those in Germany) that they stagger on up to between 13° and 14°, sometimes leaving six degrees of potential alcohol's worth of unconverted sugar. This gives the wine a wonderful richness. The wine is racked after fermentation, and then again every three months or so for the next three years as it gradually attains ripeness and clarity and is put into bottle.

During this time the wine is carefully assessed and a high proportion of *barriques* rejected as being unsuitable for Yquem. Even in a year as good as 1967, only 80 per cent of the wine was kept to be sold as Yquem, whereas in wholly unsatisfactory years such as 1972 and 1974 there was no Yquem at all.

The wine rejected for Yquem might well be sold off in bulk to be blended under some AC Sauternes label, but in some years it is kept as an ingredient for the dry wine "Y" (Ygrec in French) which first appeared from the cellars of Château d'Yquem in 1959. The Comte is very keen that this should not be seen as a sort of "Yquem *manqué*". It is true that if one of the *barriques* manages an alcohol level of only 12°, together perhaps with a further two degrees of unfermented sugar, then this would make it an ideal candidate for *Ygrec*, but the style of the dry wine is such that Sauvignon plays an important part, as one would expect.

The *maître-de-chai* Guy Latrille wants the same sort of 50-50 balance between the two grape varieties in his dry Ygrec as his counterparts at Châteaux La Mission Haut-Brion and Haut-Brion want for their great dry white Graves. Those years when the Sauvignon bears more generously than the Sémillon are ideal for

the production of Ygrec therefore, and in the 1970s for instance this dry wine, sold at about one third the price of Yquem, was made in 1979, 1978, 1977, 1973, 1972 and 1971. Ygrec gets less than two years in wood usually, and the Comte thinks it is best drunk as soon after this as possible. It is an enormously rich wine, still with about six grams of sugar per litre and tasting even heavier than any Graves, presumably because of the rich soil and extensive wood-ageing.

The pneumatic press lurking in the corner of the Yquem cellars is used for Ygrec-bound Sauvignon, according to the Comte, who is somewhat furtive in his allusions to this, as to an equally modern phenomenon at Yquem, an automatic bottling line.

There is no bottle-ageing policy at Yquem, but then whenever a new vintage is launched on the wine-drinking public, through the Bordeaux *négociant* network, there seems to be no shortage of willing buyers, whatever the price. Far and away Comte Alexandre de Lur-Saluces' most enthusiastic customers are Americans – in fact he can be even more specific than that and nominate medical enclaves in San Francisco and Dallas as being responsible for the most impressive sales of his precious wine. He has clearly enjoyed his travels in the United States, although he tells with horror the story of how he was relaxing with a fellow-countryman over a bottle of champagne after an exhausting day in San Francisco and saw a bottle of what was clearly very venerable Château d'Yquem whizz past them to a nearby table. It then made the journey back to the *sommelier*'s lair, the *sommelier* clearly much chagrined. The Frenchmen asked if they could taste it. It tasted absolutely wonderful, but had been sent back because of the lovely tawny colour that mature Yquem takes on!

The size of the presses gives some idea of scale at this château, where each vintage is measured in individual *barriques* rather than *tonneaux,* and men are still much more important than machinery.

This is no tourist stunt, but still the normal way of doing things in Sauternes. Average yields are below 10 hectolitres per hectare, although 25 is allowed.

The second most enthusiastic customers are the Japanese, and by the look of the visitors' book in the archway leading to the cellars the Château is a regular stop-off point on Japanese tours of Europe. Yquem is seen as the ultimate gift bottle in this country where gifts are such an important part of life. Even the Benelux countries buy more Yquem than either the French or the British. This may be simply a question of amounts of disposable income, but there is also the question of fashion. It is strange that in Britain at least, supposedly the land of the great connoisseur, there is relatively little appreciation of one of the greatest wines (and certainly one that is least copied) in the world.

Comte Alexandre de Lur-Saluces believes that the tag "dessert wine" is a great disadvantage here. *"I struggle against this. It is so dangerous to treat our wine as a sort of sweet lemonade."* He is opposed to the matching of Yquem with most sweet dishes and hearty puddings. *"Frangipane and other almond-based pastries perhaps, and Yquem is delicious with melon and other simple fruits. But I serve it with foie gras, homard, langoustes, even turbot mousseline. It can be delicious with roquefort too – although of course it's all a question of selection and contrast, and it would be stupid to drink Château Margaux with such a strong cheese, for instance."*

When asked to nominate his favourite wines other than those he made himself, the Comte thought immediately of other Sauternes, preferably 1955 Château Rayne-Vigneau or Suduiraut. *("I admire Trockenbeerenauslesen, but I find them more of an essence than a wine.")*

Perhaps his continuing appetite for the rich wines of Château d'Yquem wines which he must taste every day, is proof enough of their continuing interest and uncloying nature. Of course they share the characteristic of any good sweet wine, that of being high in sugar with sufficient acidity to keep them in balance; but Yquem has a special breadth of flavour, a taste that really does suggest a liquid version of the lovely golden colour of the wine when young, mellowing with age to great, rich tawniness, unsullied by maderisation despite this fast browning.

How dreadful it must be when the Comte hears that familiar cry: *"No, thank you. I don't like sweet wines."*

BURGUNDY

For a misguided author trying to choose "the greatest," Burgundy poses more problems than any other wine region. In place of the order and discipline that characterize Bordeaux, Burgundy offers complication and diffusion. "Aha, no! That's *another* exception to the rule" is the delighted cry of the Burgundian explaining his region's wines to the visitor.

Even the area included in the region is confusing. To some, the prolific vineyards of the Beaujolais region, way to the south, should not be considered part of "Burgundy proper." The Mâconnais, the Côte Chalonnaise and, on its own up in the north, Chablis all have their claims to an individual existence. Only on the Côte d'Or, the pathetically narrow pelmet of magnificent vineyards squeezed up against the mountain ridge running down from Dijon to Chagny, do the locals talk about *"nous Bourguignons"* with suitably Burgundian conviction.

Clos de Vougeot – one of Burgundy's most parcellated vineyards.

Burgundy is above all else a jolly region, with little pretensions to anything other than local pride. The typical Burgundian is straightforward and welcoming. An enthusiastic trencherman, he is always ready to call forth just one more bottle, and can eat his way with relish through feasts as gargantuan as the famous Paulée de Meursault that brings to an end the weekend of the Trois Glorieuses which coincides with the Hospices de Beaune sale. There are comfortable clusters of relatively prosperous farmhouses, but few grand buildings. This is the region of the proud peasant, who expects to work hard at his widely-scattered rows of vines but also expects to do well from them.

The division of Burgundian vineyards between a multiplicity of owners is notorious. One man's Meursault may even taste like another man's Mâcon Blanc (Jean Thevenet's for example), so vineyard names alone cannot be taken as a guarantee of style, let alone quality. Different men can make two quite different wines from two adjacent rows of vines, but then no one can be relied upon to produce wines of a consistent style no matter what the vineyard and vintage. In France's most northerly fine (still) wine region, there is enormous vintage variation, amounting sometimes almost to vintage deprivation when a freak hailstorm, for instance, devastates the vines of an entire commune.

The situation is further confused by the important role played by *négociants* in Burgundy. Much more than in Bordeaux, they are makers of fine wines as well as of basic generic appellations. Some of the region's most dependable fine wines come from the small group of houses who care desperately about their reputation. But these may not always come from vineyards owned or controlled by them, thereby putting them out of court for the elusive epithet "great."

On the other hand, there are some wonderful winemakers in Burgundy who do not happen to have holdings in the finest vineyards. There

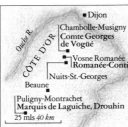

are those who make dazzling wine some years, but are not consistent. And then there are wines carrying great vineyard names, but that have not been especially well-made.

Beaujolais, delicious though it is, must be ruled out of a book of this sort on rather the same grounds as Sancerre and Pouilly-Fumé are: almost all of the wine is made for early drinking. Admittedly there are more exceptions to this rule in Beaujolais than on the Central Loire vineyards. Every now and then someone, perhaps Thorin at the Château des Jacques, makes a Moulin-à-Vent of an exceptionally good year that eventually takes on the characteristics and stature of a good red burgundy, but this does not happen often enough to counteract Beaujolais' main function – to keep us all in lovely, easy, gulpable wines that need cause us no intellectual strain of appreciation. As a character, however, *"le* (self-appointed) *prince de Beaujolais"* Georges Duboeuf perhaps deserves a chapter for the extent to which he has raised beaujolais to the level of a sophisticated international wine.

The Mâconnais into which Beaujolais merges northwards must be excluded for much the same reasons. Even the best Pouilly-Fuissé can hardly be called "great"; this is a lighthearted wine that is sometimes sold at rather serious prices. On the Côte Chalonnaise there are one or two more serious contenders for inclusion – Antonin Rodet of Mercurey and Delorme of Rully can make very appetising wines – but in terms of sheer quality (although not value) this southern patch of vineyards will always be overshadowed by the Côte d'Or.

It is up on "the golden slope" that Burgundy's true greats are to be found, in great number so that it is not easy choosing just three (which when complemented by one Chablis is in just proportion to the Bordeaux selection in terms of the amount of fine wine produced). The logic in the resulting selection was governed by the fact that the Domaine de la Romanée-Conti can still command higher prices than any other wine estate in the world. Besides, Madame Bize-Leroy ("Lalou" to her friends) is one of the great characters in the French wine world.

Enormous red Côte de Nuits of Grand Cru level is thus accounted for, but there is also room for a detailed look at another impeccable Côte de Nuits property whose wines have thrilled amateurs the world over. Le Musigny, red and white, from the largest owner in that vineyard, the Comte Georges de Vogüé, shows the other

face of the northern half of the Côte d'Or. The Comte's tiny production of wines manages great delicacy and intrigue as well as depth of flavour and longevity.

Of course white burgundy deserves a spotlight all to itself. There are other great red wines, but very, very few dry whites which are capable of great development into something anywhere near as complex and interesting as white burgundy, of which Le Montrachet must represent the pinnacle. There are just a handful of owners of this undistinguished-looking patch of vines at the southern end of the Côte de Beaune. The Domaine de la Romanée-Conti produces a little Montrachet from its small holding, and rather more substantial holdings are owned by the highly reputable *négociant* Bouchard Père et Fils and the Domaine Baron Thenard. The greatest single owner, however, is the Marquis de Laguiche, whose wines and vines are in the complete control of one of Burgundy's more energetic spokesmen, Robert Drouhin. Because of this special relationship, and because he is turning out some wonderful wines from the Grand Cru vineyards of his own family firm Joseph Drouhin, this winning combination of vineyard, owner and *négociant* (a title which he repudiates in favour of *propriétaire-viticulteur*) has also been included. There are almost as strong arguments for including Bouchard Père et Fils or Louis Latour, on the basis of the excellent wines they make from their own domaines; and a fourth Beaune *négociant* Louis Jadot is also responsible for some great bottles.

An obvious omission in this selection is a fine producer of Le Chambertin, in a traditional sense perhaps Burgundy's most famous red wine. The Domaine Clair-Daü, Armand Rousseau and Trapet are all eminently trustworthy names here, as is the Domaine Dujac a little further south. On the Côte de Beaune some wonderful whites, notably Corton Charlemagne, are made by Bonneau de Martray, while Robert Ampeau is probably the most consistent Meursault grower. Perhaps in no other wine region is the excellent so difficult to sort out from the mediocre. A Bordeaux château is a homogeneous entity, but in Burgundy only the vineyards have been classified, and there are some very indifferent wines sold under the label of a Grand or Premier Cru. A classification of producers would doubtless rate small but careful producers such as Tollot-Beaut, Matrot and Marquis d'Angerville highly.

These well-merited claims to "greatness" make Burgundy the most fascinating hunting ground for lovers of really fine wine. But this is a region that gives itself few airs and graces. Typical of the unlikely confrontation between preconception and reality for the visitor is the daily scene in La Cuverie, a tiny village *café* round the back of Vosne-Romanée, a few miles out of Nuits-St-Georges. This is the sort of place that serves a set lunch of *soupe de légumes*, ragout, cheese and fruit (for all of 30 francs) to the same band of working men every day. They lay a place for each of them along the trestle tables covered with paper tablecloths: knife, fork, spoon and prosaic tumbler.

In the tourist season, however, they keep a few places on the rather more respectable side of the dining room free for the tourists who are inevitably driven in by lunchtime hunger-pangs, withdrawal symptoms from the morning indulgence in milky coffee and croissants. These outsiders will usually be wine pilgrims, international travellers who have crossed the Atlantic, or at least the English Channel, to worship at the shrine of the Domaine de la Romanée-Conti just around the corner. They will be disappointed if they expect to experience anything more closely connected with fine wine than possibly sharing the fruit basket with one of the Domaine's cellar workers. The grandest liquid they will be offered is a Bourgogne Rouge "Réserve" of dubious provenance. Everyone else will be happily, and with typical Burgundian gusto, swigging supermarket litre stuff.

To catch a whiff of the reverential atmosphere that Burgundy's best wines deserve, it is necessary to go to the great restaurants of Paris, Geneva and New York.

Beaune's much-photographed Hospices. The wine auction each November still makes a major contribution to its finances.

Domaine Comte Georges de Vogüé

One morning every month, an elegant gentleman in his eighties travels ten miles down the N74 from his home in Dijon for a detailed meeting with the manager of his wine estate in Chambolle-Musigny. His name, Comte Georges de Vogüé, is known throughout the serious wine-drinking world as the provider of great Le Musigny, a wine that combines the definition of fine Côte de Nuits red with elegance and deeply-intriguing subtlety, and whose Musigny Blanc is thought by some to be the finest white burgundy. The 12½-hectare Domaine is one of the oldest in Burgundy, dating from about one generation before Columbus reached America, although it has been under the sway of the de Vogüé family only since 1766. The present Count is the fifth to be involved with this highly-respected property. He has one daughter who lives in Argentina, is related in a fairly contorted way to the de Vogüés of Moët & Chandon and Veuve Clicquot as well as to the Ladoucette family of Pouilly (Fumé), and is giving nothing away about his future plans for the estate.

The count is still intimately concerned with the intricacies of his much-loved wine property. He has the mind and manner of the *Ancien École Militaire Française* – extremely polite but putting efficiency and method above all else. With an annual production so tiny, it needs a military mind governed by precision, loyalty and a sense of *le fair play* to allocate his treasures: *"So many boxes of Bonnes Mares for mon ami Reynier de Londres; so many for nos amis Dreyfus à New York . . ."* He speaks the most wonderful Edwardian English, a nicely-dated memento from his days at the Knightsbridge Barracks after Dunkirk during the Second World War.

The man who calls this nobleman "le patron" is Alain Roumier, 27 years his junior, born and raised in the little village of Chambolle-Musigny (twinned, in a surprisingly enterprising manner, with Sonoma in California) and totally at home in his role. The Roumier family have their own Domaine just down the village street, where Alain's brother Jean-Marie makes good but rather less aristocratic wines from much the same appellation as the de Vogüé domain.

A word of warning: do not visit Alain Roumier if you are feeling remotely delicate. For someone approximately five feet tall, he makes an extraordinary amount of noise – not in a steady thunder, but in a wearing storm of guffaws, doom-laden grunts, well-judged raspberries and frequent roars of laughter. His expressive face and shoulders, red-veined cheeks and quizzical look make his proud claim *"Je suis un homme de terrain"* superfluous. It comes as no surprise to learn that his father and grand-

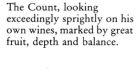

The Count, looking exceedingly sprightly on his own wines, marked by great fruit, depth and balance.

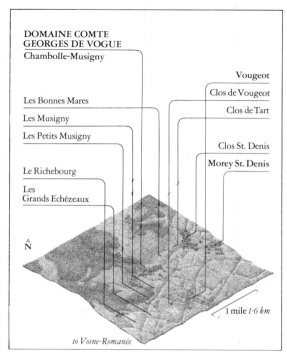

DOMAINE COMTE
GEORGES DE VOGUE
Chambolle-Musigny

Les Bonnes Mares

Les Musigny

Les Petits Musigny

Le Richebourg

Les
Grands Echézeaux

Vougeot

Clos de Vougeot

Clos de Tart

Clos St. Denis

Morey St. Denis

N

1 mile 1·6 km

to Vosne-Romanée

The traditional courtyard is still the centre of activity.

Much-treasured vineyards press right up against the hillsides that are virtually worthless as sites for top quality vines.

Alain Roumier with his 60-year-old vines producing some of the world's most prized red wine just a stone's throw from scrubland.

father also carried out this important job at the Domaine Comte Georges de Vogüé, nor that his own viticultural studies were based just up the road in Dijon. On the face of it, he should be in his element, responsible for some of the finest wines in the world, in a village and vineyards he has known all his life. But things are not as simple as that in present-day France. *"Nowadays it is not enough to understand vines and to understand wines,"* he rises to a hysterical crescendo. *"I must understand all the detail of administration, personnel, taxes, official forms. The bureaucracy is unimaginable! We have* ten *people working here!"* He waves deliriously at the outer chamber to his efficient-looking office in one corner of the beautiful old Burgundian courtyard. One suspects he really would have been happier in an earlier generation. His passion is wine, not the cumbersome documentary web wound round it by the authorities, nowhere thicker than in Burgundy.

Yet he is not insular in his outlook. *"Nous Bourguignons ne sommes pas chauvins, vous savez,"* he rattles away admonishingly, explaining how his son Hervé, currently working his way round the cellars under his father's tutelage, did a *stage* at Carneros Creek where he saw some of Napa's best Pinot Noir being made. In his office the only bottles visible are Pinot Noirs from that winery and Calera, and a Chardonnay from Mount Eden Vineyards. Roumier Senior has been twice to the United States himself, although all that bureaucracy leaves him little time for travel.

Alain Roumier is clearly keenly concerned with his property's image abroad. The United States, Britain, Belgium and Switzerland are his most important customers outside France. *"We have sent no Chambolle Musigny, Les Amoureuses at all to America since 1974,"* he says with pride. *"We have only young vines there since we replanted, you see."* And while he cherishes his American customers for their fastidiousness, he is prepared to nurture his British ones in another respect: *"We have not increased our UK prices as much as for other countries. We understand what difficulties you are in."*

The Domaine encompasses just half a hectare of Chambolle Musigny, Les Amoureuses; nearly two hectares of Premier Cru Chambolle Musigny vineyard; nearly three hectares of Bonnes Mares; and, the real treasure, nearly three-quarters of the entire 10.7 hectare Grand Cru vineyard Le Musigny, the one that gave the little village of Chambolle its important suffix. This gives them an average annual production of only about 400 hectolitres, perhaps 4,500 cases, of which 1,500 will be of Le Musigny in a good year. Alain Roumier shrugs his ever-mobile shoulders and sticks out his lower lip and palms as if to catch any free-falling drop of wine. *"A bad year like 1981 poses great problems for us. We have certain rules – a determination to stay in the first division, like football. Or like tennis. You don't play against McEnroe if you have the 'flu. Our best player, our Bjorn Borg, is the best Musigny. But what can we do in a year like this when even Le Musigny will have to be declassified to Bourgogne?"*

On 31 August 1981 there was a localised but disastrous hailstorm aimed, as if by an enemy bomber pilot, directly at the best vineyards around Chambolle-Musigny. It was clearly very demoralising for men like Alain Roumier. He is a strong supporter of the pan-Côte d'Or anti-hail guard, a team of pilots and suitably-equipped planes on constant standby during the dangerous late summer months. Or at least he *was* just after seeing the hail damage in 1981. (Others felt that the fees imposed, perhaps 500 francs a hectare, are not justified by the results, and that 1981 should be the final year of the compulsory operation of the scheme.)

M Roumier clearly takes the damage to his precious Musigny vines extremely personally. More than half the vines are of very advanced years, between 40 and 60. The wine from this very special ancient stock is sold separately as Le Musigny Vieilles Vignes, or as he calls it "the quintessence of Musigny." It is considerably more expensive than the already-very-special

Before fermentation, a yeast starter culture may be added, while during it the array of implements *below* is used to push down the cap of skins for maximum colour extraction.

Musigny, and is appreciated particularly by the Swiss. Vines on this precious plot of land, pressed up against one of the steeper slopes of the hills that make the Côte d'Or a Côte, are pulled up in tiny parcels as is judged timely.

The Burgundians may not yet have found a solution to their greatest climatological problem, but even a traditionalist like Alain Roumier admits what an enormous difference the use of anti-rot preparations now makes. He was particularly beguiled by the way the 1980 vintage was saved, in terms of quality at least. *"It was a miracle, and the wines are surprisingly attractive and supple."*

The vintage usually starts towards the end of September and by mid-October the delicate grapes will be in Monsieur Roumier's wooden fermentation vats. No *"inox"* for him. *"Other people are trying to get rid of these,"* he waves an expansive hand around his row of vanilla-scented vats, *"but they don't realise they are quite irreplaceable."* And what sort of wood does he use for this and his small ageing barrels? Another shrug. *"On dit Tronçais."* They are chosen by "the professionals," not by him. Along the walls are hung a wonderfully inventive array of tools, some especially designed to punch down the cap of Pinot skins during fermentation in the most effective way. Fermentation lasts for 10 to 15 days, and in good years a bit of (gentle) press wine is added. In poor years like 1974 and 1975 hardly any will go in. *"I can't give you a formula, you know,"* bellows Alain Roumier. *"Making wine is like good cooking. There's no recipe."*

He is even less dogmatic about the tiny amount of white wine he makes from a small patch of Le Musigny. *"Whites are very difficult. You need a lab really, and there can be all sorts of worries. Our Musigny is very vulnerable because*

Picking in the rain can be as dismal as the wine resulting from it, but de Vogüé tries to put his name only on bottles of some quality. With the savage effects of hail as shown above, 1981 was a difficult year for the property.

Fermentation vats carry a record of morning and evening progress chalked on the outside – the Côte d'Or's answer to computer technology.

usually takes place about 18 months after the vintage and then, in theory, comes the long wait. Whites should in general be drunk at about five years, according to their maker, while the reds vary considerably.

In Alain Roumier's view the 1969 vintage is the best since he arrived at the Domaine in 1955. *"It was a very difficult vintage, but is superb and just starting to be ready to drink."* He is of the school that puts 1969 miles ahead of that other revered vintage 1971. Indeed he recommends his 1972s as more charming than 1971s. Those still trying to make up their minds about the controversial 1976 vintage might enjoy his word for it: *"hirsute."*

It may be that nearly thirty years of familiarity have bred, not contempt, but certainly irreverence for the things most worshipped in Burgundy, great wines and great tradition. He shows his few visitors (there is, quite understandably, no sign giving away the location of the property) round the fifteenth-century empty but grand living quarters that straddle the archway into the courtyard. Tramping up the pale stone spiral staircase he takes the steps two at a time, hurls open the door of the upper chamber and strides about, peremptorily swinging round the portraits of ancient de Vogüés on their venerable hooks so as to identify them by the label on the back.

There are several *"points chauds"* which Alain Roumier and the Comte presumably discuss heatedly over the lunch that often follows their monthly meetings. Alain Roumier would like to see the Domaine extended to include a few less grand vineyards. *"We could have a really good Second or Third Division team, why not?"* he gesticulates towards vineyards of plain Chambolle Musigny appellation.

The Count will have none of it. Not a vine will he contemplate below Premier Cru level. In his mind's eye, trusty manager Roumier doubtless thinks longingly of being able to satisfy just a few more orders – and of not having to run his bins down to the floor quite so soon after they are filled. And there may just be another idea in the back of his agile mind. If the company "Société d'Exploitation du Domaine" (the French are so literal) were to expand, it might be able to afford an auxiliary administrator who could plough through all that paper-work.

it is made in such small quantities." In a good year, he will make 10 hectolitres of Musigny Blanc, a "difficult" wine that wine lovers throughout the world will give their eye-teeth for. To its fans, Le Musigny Blanc, in the years in which it is produced, has the weight and finesse of the best Montrachets, a wine with great harmony and length. De Vogüé reds, of which Le Musigny is the apogee (but his Bonnes Mares can be superb), have an extraordinary fabric of flavours and, above all, enormous vivacity. There should be not the merest hint of the "soupiness" that can dog many a well-made red burgundy, but rather nuances of the most subtle and luxurious of *consommés.*

The beautifully-kept de Vogüé cellars house casks of all sizes, right down to 60-litre miniature barrels, so that there will be no waste, no matter how small an amount of an appellation is harvested. All wines go into wood, up to a third of which might be new, but much of which looks well-weathered as well as well-tended. Bottling

Domaine de la Romanée-Conti

The wines of the Domaine de la Romanée-Conti fetch auction-room prices rivalled only by those of that other superstar produced in very small quantity, Château Pétrus. For such wines there seems to be no shortage of buyers, usually American, prepared to spend the equivalent of the cost of a good overcoat on a bottle to keep themselves warm inside.

The quality and scarcity of the wines themselves have established this exceptionally high price level at the Domaine, but it is the inexhaustible co-owner Madame Bize-Leroy who is taking the major initiative in maintaining it. "Lalou" is one of French gastronomy's great characters, for all her slender years and even more slender frame, and she never fails to create a strong impression on everyone who meets her. Her partner in this famous wine enterprise is the quiet and scholarly Aubert de Villaine.

The casual visitor to the little village of Vosne-Romanée is unlikely to come across this blessed pair. The rather poky little courtyard around which are clustered the offices of the Domaine are difficult to find, even after determined inspection of the back streets. Besides, "we receive only by appointment," according to Mme Bize-Leroy, who adds with a slightly sad little sniff: *"We're always being visited, but they tend to be lovers of wine rather than big buyers."*

If you do gain an audience (and they are not *that* exclusive – there was the young couple from Oregon who arrived by bicycle, with no appointment, and with nowhere to stay, but showed such an intense love of her wines that Madame invited them back to stay with her), you will be received in the large airy office where the two owners try to meet with the full-time administrative staff two or three times a week. For two people entrusted with perhaps the world's most expensive vineyard, they are remarkably unreserved, and obviously keen to make a good impression on strangers. There is none of the languid approach of some of the Bordeaux chatelains who can seem almost embarrassed by the details of their great wines. At the Domaine they are eager to convince you of their achievements and attributes.

Lalou is a very persuasive lady. She is extremely forceful, though bird-like in features and frame, with fashionably close-cropped hair and couture clothes of a style rarely seen in the world's great wine cellars. For a typical day's inspection of the offices and cellars she will wear tight but chic trousers, a little Courrèges

"Lalou," Burgundy's most formidable female.

bomber-jacket perhaps, and high-heeled strappy sandals. One feels sure that Madame Bollinger and Veuve Clicquot would not have approved. Despite her striking looks, Mme Bize-Leroy is no dumb blonde. Bionic woman would be nearer the mark. Every weekend she goes rock-climbing with her farmer husband: Chamonix if the weather is good, locally if there is a lot of work to do. That most critical pair of French gastronomic critics Gault and Millau go into raptures about Lalou's knowledge of wine and her ability to match it with food (thanks partly to a little help from her friend Jean Troisgros). The big names in the wine world come flocking every year to an annual blind-tasting marathon she holds in her large farm-house just outside Meursault, at which she serves a devilish run of mystery glasses followed by a feast of her own devising and execution. Her daughter Perrine shows every sign of being as awesome an achiever, having a book of poetry published before she was 20, and knowing a great deal about wine herself.

Lalou's fulltime operation is directing the fortunes of the distinguished house of Leroy at Auxey-Duresses, and it is through this that she

Co-owner Aubert de Villaine, a mean winemaker on his own account.

Each precious bottle is counted then numbered on the label at Bouzeron, except for these specimen copies doled out to those who can't afford a proper one.

comes by her important role at the Domaine de la Romanée-Conti. Her beloved father Henri Leroy died at the end of the 1970s, and she now takes complete control of the Leroy wine enterprises, as well as inheriting an undisclosed share (50 per cent?) in the famous "DRC."

Aubert de Villaine is the perfect foil for this glamorous, vivacious woman. Quiet, serious but determined in a firmly polite sort of way, he has the air of a rather distinguished schoolmaster. He too has his own wine interests, although on a more modest scale, with a small family vineyard in the village of Bouzeron, of which he is mayor.

"We take all the decisions together," says Madame, *"though we don't always agree."* Even a very brief visit will reveal the constant small discords that enliven their working relationship. *"No, no, no, we average thirteen – no twelve – thousand bottles of Richebourg,"* is Madame's view. *"No, I think it's nearer fifteen,"* Aubert de Villaine will volunteer, and the point will be discussed, with great enjoyment and not a hint of acerbity, for up to five minutes.

The agreed statistics on the Domaine's enviable average annual output are given finally: 6,000 bottles of the fabulously-expensive Romanée-Conti; 24,000 bottles of La Tâche; a compromise of 13,000 bottles of Richebourg; 14,000 bottles of Grands Echézeaux; 17,500 bottles of Echézeaux; 20,000 bottles of

Romanée-St-Vivant sold under the Marey-Monge label; and a little bit of white wine of a very special appellation, 2,400 bottles of Le Montrachet. The areas the Domaine owns in each of these heady appellations can be calculated from the fact that Madame reckons 30 hectolitres per hectare is a pretty good yield.

Montrachet apart, all these vineyards are within a short walk of the cellars and on the gentle slopes above the village of Vosne-Romanée, though even Le Montrachet, much closer to Madame's own Leroy headquarters, is entirely administered from the Domaine's Côte de Nuits base. The Domaine is in the enviable position of being sole owner of the two most famous, and expensive, vineyards, La Tâche and Romanée-Conti itself. Along with the dramatically walled Clos de Vougeot just along the back-road through the extensive Echézeaux vineyard, these tiny plots of red clay and their gnarled vines that hardly reach waist-height must be the most-photographed vineyards in Burgundy.

There is no doubt that the Domaine's wines are different from almost any other bottle of red burgundy. "Sweet," "rich," "roasted," "ripe" and "velvety" are all terms that are used regularly to describe their concentrated, almost "Pinot-concentrate" flavour. Madame explains its quality by the fact that they take such care "right from the bottom." This starts with top quality rootstock (the Romanée-Conti vineyard was one of the last in France to be converted to American rootstock, so that there was a period between 1945 and 1952 when none was produced) and continues through extremely strict pruning. This is done by a team of formidable local women, the most formidable of whom is the wife of the winemaker, Madame André Noblet, who often takes sole charge of the Romanée-Conti vineyard herself.

Probably the single most distinctive characteristic of winemaking at the Domaine as compared with its neighbours is how late their vines are picked, anything from ten days to a month after the surrounding vineyards. The normal vintage dates in the Côte d'Or are relatively early, of course, and usually earlier than in Chablis, the Rhône or Bordeaux for instance. This means that, in an average year, the Domaine may start picking towards the end of the first week in October; but they remember picking La Tâche in the December snow back in 1965. They pick in ascending order of price of the end-result, and what they are after is the optimum combination

SOCIÉTÉ CIVILE DU DOMAINE DE LA ROMANÉE-CONTI

PROPRIÉTAIRE A VOSNE-ROMANÉE (COTE-D'OR) FRANCE

ROMANÉE-CONTI

APPELLATION ROMANÉE-CONTI CONTROLÉE

3.344 Bouteilles Récoltées

Nº FACTICE

ANNÉE 1979

LES ASSOCIÉS-GÉRANTS

Mise en bouteille au domaine

PRODUCT OF FRANCE

of health and ripeness in the grapes. While explaining this Madame will slip out her smart little black crocodile notebook and show you some lines from Papa that she has scribbled in the back to keep the Domaine on the straight and narrow:

Lorsqu'au cadron de l'année
Le cycle de la vigne va prendre fin
Chaque heure de soleil en plus
Fera le vin encore meilleur.

The picking process itself is fastidious ("*On pige,*" says Madame), and all but the healthiest grapes are rejected to allow for a fermentation that can often continue for as long as three weeks. At this point another unusual wine-making element comes into play: human flesh. The Domaine still believes in breaking up the red grapeskins by the application of bare feet, and there is one school of thought which attributes the wines' distinctive style at least in part to this bodily immersion technique. In the cellars across the backstreet from the offices, looking like any old farm building rather than the cradle of the world's most expensive wine, are blackened old crush vats for the reds, which have been trodden by many a Burgundian foot. The tiny amount of Chardonnay that is harvested from their rows in the Montrachet vineyard each year is pressed pneumatically and, since 1977, the must is fermented in temperature-controlled stainless steel.

This move to "freshen up" the Domaine's Montrachet, which some critics found just too heavy and even slightly oxidised in the past, has been the only significant change in methods at the Domaine under the present regime – and it should be remembered that this is a Domaine which has been under the same joint ownership for more than a century. All wines, red and white, go into new wood, mountain oak bought and treated by the Domaine itself for two to three years before being made up into casks. The precious wine is only put into its carefully-numbered bottles after at least 18 months and often two years in cask, usually along with a substantial dollop of *vin de presse* because tannin is needed for the long ageing periods prescribed by Madame. When bottled the wines are considerably paler than after ten or twenty years' ageing – a curious phenomenon that some think attributable to sulphur content at the bottling stage. Her father said, and now Madame says, that you should wait fifteen years at the very least for a traditional burgundy vinified properly, but – and this is the most interesting bit – you must wait even longer than this with indifferent vintages.

Most winemakers, in whatever wine region, content themselves with their greatest achievements in the better years, and accept the fact that nature occasionally puts them in their place by handing out a bad year when, however hard they try, they will never make a great wine. But this is not the view at the Domaine de la Romanée-Conti. There was a dreadful commotion in 1980 when a "wine authority" was unwise enough to cast aspersions in public on some of the Domaine's 1975s which are yet, in Madame's terms, in their infancy. Impartial teams of tasters were recruited; letters and refutations written; and above all much was said about the way in which the wines of "poor years" such as 1956 and 1954 developed after fifteen years and more. "*The 1975s will take a long time,*" we are assured, "*and even Le Montrachet 1965 is just starting.*"

With wines as much in demand as those of the Domaine, there is of course a problem: how to restrain all those proud owners from cracking open their bottles too early. And how to be sure they are stored in ideal conditions. A party of Californians brought some of their 1959s specially back across the Atlantic to try them alongside bottles of the same wines that had

DOMAINE DE LA ROMANEE-CONTI

Romanée-Conti

Les Echézeaux

Les Grands Echézeaux

Le Richebourg

Romanée-St-Vivant

Clos de Vougeot

La Tâche

Concoeur

Flagey-Echézeaux

N

1 mile *1·6 km*

Vosne-Romanée

Nuits-St-Georges

to Le Montrachet

Lalou's much-missed father, *left,* with André Noblet, the *"type énorme"* in charge of the cellars and Aubert de Villaine, in 1978.

rested *"sur place"* in the Domaine's unusually well-stocked cellars to check just how much of a bad deal they had – and went away delighted with how similar the "American" and "Burgundian" samples were. This must in part be due to the great weight of these wines, and indeed Madame reports that even in Australia they are not too *"fatigués par le jet lag."*

Current policy is to try to put the wines on the market a little bit later in their development (in order to minimise the possibility of hasty conclusions on the part of wine luminaries, perhaps). The 1978 vintage, for instance, much-acclaimed but fabulously-priced, was not sold much before 1982. In principle they sell in *tranches,* but the principle sometimes becomes blurred by demand, up to half of which has come from the United States.

Monsieur Noblet is, as he is described locally, *"un type énorme,"* a great rugby player in his youth, printer later, but persuaded back to the calling of his father by Lalou's father just after the war. He is a wonderfully bear-like character, with twinkling eyes and a keen appreciation of what is what. Born in the village itself, he now devotes his life to what goes on in the uncomfortably small underground cellars of the Domaine. An orderly but unspectacular cavern perhaps 10 by 15 yards houses all of a normal year's crop in casks from which honoured guests may taste, but should then carefully pour back what remains of their tasting sample. This is precious stuff.

There is no respectful silence, however. Madame Bize-Leroy and Monsieur Aubert de Villaine discuss each wine with excitement and conviction. Each glass is the subject of a dispute that each enjoys, with Noblet pronouncing slowly but deliberately somewhere towards the end. The wines have enormous richness, even when young, even at their most lowly level of Echézeaux, which has great liveliness and charm. Grands Echézeaux is a bit meatier, Romanée-St-Vivant almost gravelly in its texture when young and Richebourg is an aptly-named wine that cries out to be left alone throughout its youth. La Tâche and Romanée-Conti are very special. *"Someone wrote once that La Tâche is better than Romanée-Conti,"* says Madame crossly. *"This is stupid because they're so different. It's like saying Picasso is better than Chagall."* Some say La Tâche is feminine and Romanée-Conti masculine, an almost irresistible comparison in Burgundy. For André Noblet, La Tâche is *"une grande dame"*; you can keep it as long as Romanée-Conti, but it will be ready to drink sooner.

In the Domaine's blackened bottle-store there are all sorts of tantalising little blackboards hung over the bins on which are scribbled such evocative descriptions as "Tâche 1976" and "Rbg 1971." For Noblet, 1978 is the greatest vintage in all his years in and around this treasure trove.

André Noblet travels hardly at all outside

The main gate of the world's most famous Domaine, hidden in the backstreets of Vosne-Romanée.

his cellars, but the owners, especially the energetic Lalou, have travelled considerably. They both try to drink as widely as possible; and Aubert de Villaine, who is married to an American, has tried the wines of one of California's most-respected specialists in Burgundian grapes, Chalone. Madame's comment on a Chalone wine she's tasted: *"Oui – mais c'est chaud."* She is not convinced that Californians will ever produce top quality wine when they pick so early, but she has been impressed by Oregon and remembers an Eyrie Pinot 1970 that was *"intéressant,"* if *"assez léger."* She has vicariously paid her respects to Bordeaux too, via her daughter who has visited many a château there *"en travel."*

Those who come to pay their respects at this Burgundian temple are received with great courtesy and energy, and a handsome crimson and gold visitors' book carries a record of signatures and eulogies from all over the world, including great pages of Japanese characters. Perhaps their most famous visitor was Krushchev, but Madame has a wonderful story of how even he was unable to bend the rules of the Domaine. The Great Bear of Russia came to France and included in his itinerary was Dijon, where he was officially presented with all sorts of smart burgundy by his government hosts. These he firmly declined and demanded to be taken to the Domaine de la Romanée-Conti. Those who have read accounts of his meetings with others will know that Krushchev had a healthy acquisitive streak, but did not like to make the contribution to our capitalist system usually demanded in return. Today Madame tells the story of how he claimed his La Tâche was a present with much shocked shaking of her neat, pretty head, accompanied by comradely shakes from de Villaine and her secretary. *"Jamais, jamais, jamais,"* she exclaims. *"On ne donne jamais. C'est un principe. On sait qu'à Bordeaux c'est fait"* (more shaking). *"Mais ici, c'est pas avarice, c'est un principe."*

The principles behind the Domaine de la Romanée-Conti are clearly highly successful, and it is difficult to imagine anyone who could persuade those in charge to change.

Marquis de Laguiche

For some – Arlott and Fielden in *Burgundy Vines and Wines* for two – Le Montrachet is quite simply "the greatest dry white in the world." Alexandre Dumas took time off from his three musketeers to urge those lucky enough to taste Le Montrachet to approach it with bared head and bowed knee. And even that most well-educated of wine-lovers Hugh Johnson acknowledges it as "the greatest white burgundy."

This tiny, unprepossessing plot of vines covers less than eight slightly sloping hectares of limestone pressed up against the hills at the southern tip of the smart bit of the Côte d'Or, between the communes of Puligny-Montrachet, which faces slightly east, and Chassagne-Montrachet just round to the south. There is the odd semi-grand greystone arch in the wall round the vineyard, but in the main it instills little respect in the casual observer – at least in those who have not heeded Dumas.

To the thousands of growers in Burgundy, a few vines in Le Montrachet would represent the pinnacle of vineyard ownership, but only a handful of them are able to make this proud boast. Of these, the most important and the most respected is the Marquis de Laguiche. His two hectares are sufficient to be called *"une surface importante"* and all over the world his white and gold label is recognised as the very smartest Le Montrachet signature.

It is strange, therefore, at least to those of us outside the much-ramified life of the French landed gentry, that the Marquis himself does not take a greater interest in his property, so prized by oenophiles the world over. He is an utterly charming elderly military gentleman who spends much of his time and energy at the Château de Laguiche in Charolais beef country looking after the forests he has inherited. He also spends time in Paris, and travels abroad a good deal. Several times a year he makes his way to Beaune to visit the man who has been entrusted with the making, raising and selling of the wonderful wine which bears his name.

The arrangement whereby one of Beaune's most respected firms, Joseph Drouhin, has complete control of the Marquis' vines and wines stems from the years immediately after the Second World War, when Maurice Drouhin had become a close friend of the Marquis during his military service. Who better, then, to look after the fortunes of one of Burgundy's most respected wines than this second-generation head of one of Beaune's fastest-growing and most respected wine firms.

The current captain of the ship, Robert, hates to hear his family business Joseph Drouhin referred to as one of the local *négociants*, and cultivates assiduously the image of being *propriétaire-viticulteur*. Robert Drouhin, who is the man behind the Marquis de Laguiche Montrachet label today, is a very extraordinary man.

Robert Drouhin entered the family firm in 1957 when he was only 23 and is today one of the few "leaders" that Burgundy can be said to have. He may be good friends with fellow-giants Louis Latour and André Gagey of Louis Jadot; but his public "conversion" in 1976 to a new, or perhaps more accurately old, way of winemaking has not won him friends with the lesser men of his native region. He is a tall, chisel-featured man, with sculpted pale lips, a grey brush of a crewcut and a deliberate air. Far from impulsive or matey, he takes time to know and gives the impression of one much preoccupied with his own ideas and his own family of three sons and one daughter. It was a catastrophe that led him to a fundamental rethink about the methods that his century-old family house had been using. A devastating fire destroyed the new bottling plant he had built in 1973, along with enormous stocks, and he is the first to admit that Drouhin wines from the vintages 1973 to 1975 were uninspiring – largely because he could not keep full control through contract bottlers. *"It showed up all our weaknesses,"* he says, before admitting with a touching air of apology that he then commissioned a market research analysis which showed that consumers were disappointed in the trend towards red burgundy that was short on colour, flavour and longevity.

In 1976 Robert Drouhin worked out a new philosophy of winemaking which, through a return to traditional methods, has resulted in a Drouhin style of wines that have really satisfying

The thinking of Robert Drouhin, determined to marry the best of the old and the new, casts a new light over medieval Beaune, the *négociants'* capital of Burgundy.

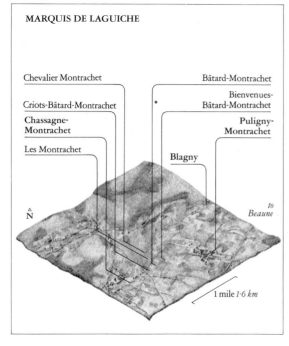

MARQUIS DE LAGUICHE

Chevalier Montrachet

Criots-Bâtard-Montrachet

Chassagne-Montrachet

Les Montrachet

Bâtard-Montrachet

Bienvenues-Bâtard-Montrachet

Puligny-Montrachet

Blagny

to Beaune

N

1 mile 1·6 km

Seasonal transformation in the Montrachet vineyard, still cultivated *à l'ancienne* for the Marquis de Laguiche, *left*, by the always immaculately dressed Robert Drouhin.

colour, more "texture" and greater ageing potential. Since the 1976 vintage white wines have been fermented at lower temperatures and reds have been fermented for up to 15 days in open oak vats no longer made in Burgundy, "instead of the all-too-frequent 5 to 7 days" as it says in the lavish booklet produced to celebrate Joseph Drouhin's centenary in 1980. This development alone would have been fine, but Robert Drouhin has been eloquent about these changes since – thereby niggling many of those who continue with the newer, easier methods.

This is not to say that Drouhin is a great showman. He is anxious to establish the fact that he has no desire to be a *vedette*; he wants to "disappear behind the wine itself." He has however felt sufficiently motivated to take a stand, indeed several stands, on behalf of his native region. When the first Gault Millau "Wine Olympics" were held, bringing less than glory to Burgundy, he staged a re-run, under rather tighter conditions, and established that Burgundy was not to be forgotten as a producer of top quality red and white wines. He is far from parochial, however. He is clearly fascinated by the American way of wine, and about Janet Trefethen whose Chardonnay did so well in both the first and second olympic trials he enthuses for instance: *"Elle est dynamite."* (pronounced, *naturellement,* "dean-a-meat").

Such is Robert Drouhin's lack of insularity that he has been keeping tabs on California for years and has many good friends there, including, inevitably, Bob Mondavi who, Drouhin claims, quite without malice, has copied not a few ideas from the amazing Drouhin cellars underneath the rue d'Enfer in the heart of the old town of Beaune. *"First of all he experimented with new casks. Then cool fermentation was the thing. Now skin contact is his great preoccupation,"* he says of his latest observations of Oakville from the Côte d'Or. *"I have some very good California wines in my cellar and I often show them to friends. But after one bottle I can often find that the taste is too much. They are very good at producing different tastes from technology, but they have not yet mastered the art of matching grapes to soils."* Despite this, Robert Drouhin is a fan of California Chardonnays, and has his eye open for the latest developments in Oregon in which he has great confidence for American counterparts to the great wines of Burgundy.

He finds the US his "most intriguing market

by far," and spends a considerable amount of time travelling around there, as often as possible accompanied by his Belgian wife Françoise. As one of his adoring staff put it: *"The US is his personal interest and he wants to manage it himself. In fact he wants to be everywhere and manage everyone himself. He doesn't want just to be in an armchair surrounded by secretaries; he wants to be in constant touch with everything that is going on in a viticultural and oenological sense."*

Robert Drouhin's interpretation of this sentiment might be: *"It is essential to have a high degree of personalisation behind each wine."* But for once, unusually for Burgundy, he is talking about the personality of the wine rather than that of its maker. The Drouhin way of winemaking is that *"you listen to what the wine wants rather than giving orders to the wine."* He and, in their different roles, his team try to emphasise the particular characteristics of the provenance and vintage of each wine, rather than put a "Drouhin gloss" on every bottle. This is no mean achievement for a firm which may be offering hundreds of different wines.

The combination of old and new is well illustrated by the original Drouhin cellars in the heart of Beaune on the one hand, and the new development at Chavet on the way out of Beaune towards the Marquis de Laguiche's vineyard (which is administered from here). The new cellars, whose second phase was completed in 1981, are not exactly romantic – indeed it is weird to see a group of traditional French workers, all royal blue and berets, chopping up vineyard stakes inside this ultra-modern, meticulously custom-designed building. Above ground are the man-high open wooden vats in which the reds are fermented, as well as the space-age shiny steel rotating fermenting vat, mounted on a horizontal axis, with which Robert Drouhin claims excellent results for long-lived Grand Cru reds of better vintages. Down below are low-lit, temperature- and humidity-controlled cellars, as tidy as a showhouse, for the fermentation of whites such as Le Montrachet in small oak. Drouhin's philosophy on oak is that treatment is much more important than provenance; and he accordingly buys his wood with great care *"from the mountains of France"* and gives it to Roger Raymond of Ladoix-Serrigny for breaking and drying.

Chavet is run under the eagle eye and imperious hand of female oenologist Laurence

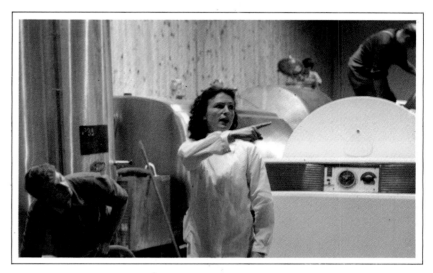

Jobard. Robert Drouhin could hardly prove his determination to move with the times more forcibly. There is a thoroughly modern laboratory there, which he claims comes up with exactly the same results as he would have predicted by instinct. *"It is dangerous to think you can master nature,"* he explains. Everything with Robert Drouhin is serious and carefully deliberated. *"If you become too sophisticated and listen only to what market research tells you, you will end up with a wine that is light, white and fruity. But wouldn't it be awful if there were nothing else in the world? At least with tech-*

Oenologist Laurence Jobard, much respected.

"The very smartest Le Montrachet signature," and all from two hectares.

nology we know what we are doing, but it is important to use it as a control only."

After fermentation (both alcoholic and *"le malo"*) at Chavet, the best wines are trundled into the centre of Beaune, perhaps three kilometres away, to develop in small oak in the medieval cellars under the main offices. This includes most of the Drouhin personal holdings of 28 hectares of land in the Côte d'Or, all Premier and Grand Cru, and some of the top wines from the newly-developed 30-hectare holding in Chablis all those miles to the north. (Robert Drouhin, for all the distance, is one of the few Chablis producers *sérieux*, and big, enough to continue to mature Grand Cru Chablis in oak.)

Red wines go into the low-ceilinged cellars of the old kings of France or the high-vaulted ones of the Church, but whites usually go into the fifteenth-century catacombs of the old Dukes of Burgundy, who must have been extremely short fellows. The Marquis de Laguiche Montrachet, and a little bit of that noble gentleman's Chassagne Montrachet, will rest here alongside Robert Drouhin's own darling white Beaune, Clos des Mouches, over the winter months. The temperature is naturally cool and the sediment falls without much external encouragement. These great whites are racked once in the winter and once in the spring, and fined with gelatine, while the reds are fined with the traditional eggwhite for which Robert Drouhin is a stickler. After eight or nine months, the wines return to Chavet for bottling, and then back to rue d'Enfer for careful insertion into one of the immaculate Drouhin bins, making a total of four journeys between old and new branches of the Drouhin enterprise.

This seems to have no ill-effect on the character of Le Montrachet as of Marquis de Laguiche out of Robert Drouhin. It has enormous stature and height, but no hint of the fatness evident in some of its imitators. This master winemaker has in recent vintages managed to weld together the elements of superbly ripe Chardonnay fruit, citrus-like acidity and very subtle oak to produce a wine that is already remarkable in its satin-textured complexity at two years. It is capable of developing even more over the next decade, as Robert Drouhin himself advises in his lavish and detailed chart showing each of the many wines he will make in a good year, together with details such as their ageing potential and the maximum permitted yield. No

appellation is more restrictive than that of Le Montrachet, in which no more than 30 hectolitres per hectare should be made in most years, and Robert Drouhin allows none of his other whites as long a recommended development period: all of twelve years.

This is in an ideal world of course. Drouhin do their best to hang on to their wines for as long as possible before releasing them to an avid connoisseur's wine market. Yet they have to admit that they are often to be found selling even a wine as great as Le Montrachet only two years after the vintage. They presumably just have to hope that sense prevails over cupidity. *Le cash flow* is as important in France as anywhere else in the world.

Robert remembers the 1959 vintage, two years after he joined the family firm, as being the most difficult for Le Montrachet. As it had done in the amazing 1947 vintage, the natural alcohol level reached 15°, two degrees above Montrachet's already manly average. For him, 1978 and 1979 have been some of the finest years for Le Montrachet more recently, and it is clear that the wine is lucky to have the strong concern and interest of a single individual such as him. He is proud of the fact that, in Burgundy, unlike Bordeaux, it is rare to find general managers subordinate to proprietors who are more figureheads than controllers. Robert Drouhin himself takes all the decisions about Le Montrachet.

The links between the Marquis de Laguiche and Drouhin are now closer than ever, since Robert has proved with what skill he can manage the Marquis' two-hectare patch in the top part towards Puligny, universally acknowledged as the best. He revels in the luxury of nurturing the largest single holding in this famous vineyard. *"We can select, you see,"* he says excitedly. *"If you have just one or two* pièces, *you can't really choose between the good and the best, but we are able to separate the different pressings and to reject those that are not up to our standards. In 1980, for instance, we sold off about 25 per cent of our production, which can be sold as Le Montrachet of course, but not as Marquis de Laguiche. And in 1975 we sold off all that we had."* What a sacrifice, when the average annual production is only 650 cases of this precious liquid gold.

Robert Drouhin is not a man to make compromises that would sacrifice quality. Despite criticism, he has shown himself determined to resist the trend to dispense with oak. He is almost alone in stressing the importance of a wine's credentials and origins in the taste. He pioneered the system of branding corks in detail so the consumer could be assured there was no inter-appellation skulduggery. He has worked on building up a completely new estate in what is, in relative terms anyway, foreign territory with success that is evident in every bottle of his chablis. He has withstood derision for his initiating role in the Beaujolais Nouveau phenomenon (for which he claims credit way back to 1959). Unlike many of his counterparts, he has no broker or *courtier* but knows the producers sufficiently well to be able to buy directly himself. As his booklet is keen to stress, with its glamorous pictures of a neatly-dressed Robert among the vines, he is most at home in the vineyard.

Although he admits to receiving many, many visitors, his slender austerity is way out of line with the standard Burgundian roistering image. One feels sure that he would never dig one of his guests in the ribs and urge "Let's crack another bottle." And when he is entertaining close friends in the Burgundian wine trade, he may even choose to serve claret as suitably "neutral ground." His wife Françoise's love of claret is attributed to her Belgian upbringing, and she is reputed to have a good collection in "her cellar." They both love Sancerre ("lots of fruit") and good, basic Alsace. *"When I write to my friend Hugel for wine,"* says Robert Drouhin, a great winemaker who has probably never made a sweet wine in his life, *"I don't ask for the rich wines they consider great, but for a Riesling of a light year, or for a Pinot Blanc."*

One can easily imagine that wine leaves him little time for any other interests (he is well-disciplined about his work in the office, cellars and vineyards). We see from the definitive booklet, however, that music is a passion, as with so many wine people. There he is in the music room next to the dining room, part of the sextet that is the tightly-knit and determined Drouhin family. Robert, of course, plays the most complicated instrument.

CHABLIS

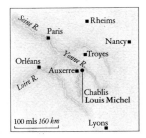

The best vineyards of Chablis slope sharply down into the tiny village whose name has been prostituted around the world.

To wine geographers around the world, Chablis fits neatly into Burgundy, making unique steely wines from Burgundy's great white gift to winemakers everywhere, the Chardonnay grape. The Chablisiens themselves, on the other hand, refer to "the Burgundians" with a certain amount of detached animosity. About half of all the wine produced in this pocket of northerly vineyards 60 miles from any Côte d'Or vine is bought by the big *négoçiants* of Beaune-and-around to be sold under their own labels. Many of the growers whose aim is to sell Chablis with a label showing a Chablis address feel that it is "the Burgundians" who upset the prices with their determination to have a wine from this outpost in the Yonne *département*. For the tiny but toothsome 1978 vintage, prices were pushed up to a level that even the most avaricious Chablisien admits were *"un peu excessifs."*

The fact that chablis is in such demand from *négoçiants* has benefited the Chablis wine trade enormously, however. After suffering considerably from phylloxera at the turn of the century, the vineyards of the small region dwindled, a trend exacerbated by the lure of nearby Paris for a new generation of potential vine-growers, the infertility of the soil, and its susceptibility to spring frosts. Those who had tasted great chablis, however, were unwilling to forget it and prices gradually rose to make vine-growing a more attractive activity – especially as fertilisers and a wide range of Heath Robinson-like anti-frost measures were developed. Such is world demand for real chablis (as opposed to that offered by the brothers Gallo and the like) that the Chablisiens have seen their vineyard area double in the last ten years; possibly, some think, to a level that is *"un peu excessif"* for the maintenance of quality.

Ripe Chardonnay grapes in Les Clos vineyard. They managed to escape the bane of Chablis, spring frosts.

Louis Michel

Chablis should never be a wine produced in great quantity, as any visitor can see. The village itself is tiny, meriting a single, unenthusiastic entry (for its only hotel) in the Michelin guide. Through it, by the old grey stone of the higgledy-piggledy cottages, meanders the narrow River Serein, its green highlights already suggesting the product of the vineyards it reflects. This is very agricultural country, the sort that would look quite at home on a packet of butter, and is far from any major centre of population. Most of it is fairly flat, but one crinkled slope across the Serein from the village is responsible for the best that it has to offer the world, Grand Cru Chablis, with Premier Cru vineyards around its outer flanks.

By the leafy riverbank, just opposite sites with names such as Vaudésir and Les Clos that are engraved on the hearts of fine wine enthusiasts around the world, are the premises of Louis Michel and his son Jean-Loup, who concentrate on the production and, importantly, distribution of their own top quality chablis. Louis Michel is not the best-known name of Chablis; to the energetic Jean-Jacques Moreau must go that honour (although most of his customers will be much more familiar with his blend of table wines from all over northern France, Moreau Blanc, than with his Grand Cru treats). Joseph Drouhin is another world-famous name which should be associated with really top-quality chablis, but he makes his in Beaune and this is described on page 100. The name Albert Pic and the associated (through winemaker Michel Remon) Régnard should also be known by any enthusiast for Chablis' best wines, just as René Dauvissat, William Fèvre and François Raveneau make some wonderful chablis on a rather smaller scale.

The story of the Michel family mirrors nicely the story of Chablis, however, and their apparent steps toward and faith in a secure future bodes well for those of us who wish to continue to enjoy the very best wines that the region can produce. Of almost 18 hectares of vineyard owned by the Michels, only two are in ordinary AC Chablis, and none are in the much more ordinary outlying Petit Chablis area. Their two hectares of Grand Cru vineyard are made up of parcels in Grenouilles, Vaudésir and Les Clos, and their 14 hectares of Premier Cru land fall in Vaillons (also sold as Séchets), Montmain, Fourchaume and Montée de Tonnerre. As is usual in Chablis, their vineyards are spread

The Michels' old pigeon tower overlooks the village *lavoir*. They have stayed with the land through thick and thin, and feel a little resentful of those who returned to vine-growing only since Chablis has become more profitable.

about, and have resulted from additions to the original vines worked by Louis' father in his spare time from working for one of the bigger concerns in the region when it was difficult for a peasant to sell his wines under his own label.

By the 1950s Louis Michel had started to market his own wines, and in 1968 his clean-cut son Jean-Loup started his own label to sell wines from the vineyards he had inherited from his grandfather. Nine years later, they decided to amalgamate their selling activities but each retain their own nine hectares of vineyard. Is this a matter of individual pride, then? *"Sure it is!"* smiles Jean-Loup without a moment's hesitation. Peasant pride is strong. Louis Michel himself admits that his fiercest critic by far is his son.

Ask for the Boulevard de Ferrières in Louis Michel's address in the town of Chablis and you will encounter blank shrugs. Ask for the man himself and you will be directed immediately, with a smile, to an absurdly pretty courtyard, all pink and red geranium windowboxes, around which live Monsieur and Madame Michel Senior and, in the old ivy-covered pigeon tower overlooking the leafy stream and village *lavoir*, Jean-Loup and his young wife. The women share the all-important bookkeeping, while the men occupy themselves in the bright new cellars beside and underneath this neat courtyard.

The price of chablis quadrupled between 1970 and 1978, which meant that even small peasant enterprises such as that of the Michels were able to re-invest in winemaking equipment. The Michels used their new *cuverie* for the first time on the 1980 vintage, not perhaps the most auspicious christening, but they must at least have been satisfied by their design. All has been meticulously thought out, with tanks fitting by centimetres under the roof, and gantries for ease of operation in the clean halls lined with pale wood in the style of a sauna. Just four men cover all the necessary jobs in the vineyard as well as in the cellar.

To the wine student, the vineyards of the Chablis region say "kimmeridgean clay." To the vine-grower there they say "devilishly difficult." On the steeply sloping best vineyards, the thin topsoil can easily be washed away and has had to be re-distributed. The land is so inhospitable to the vine that it needs substantial, though careful, fertilisation and treatment in between plantings. With this has come an increase in average yield from 25 to 50 hectolitres per hectare in the last 25 years. Most devilish of all, however, is the vineyards' susceptibility to severe frost just as the year's growth is starting. More than any other fine wine region, Chablis has been beset by this springtime hazard. The 1956 vintage was completely lost, but since then more effective ways of

1973, 1978 and 1979 are the vintages the Michels prize most.

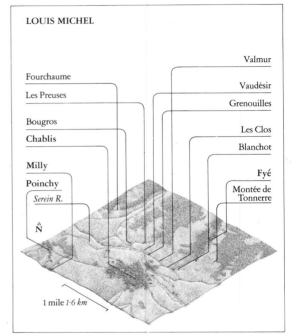

LOUIS MICHEL

Fourchaume
Les Preuses
Bougros
Chablis
Milly
Poinchy
Serein R.
N

Valmur
Vaudésir
Grenouilles
Les Clos
Blanchot
Fyé
Montée de Tonnerre

1 mile 1·6 km

combatting fatal shrivelling of the growth have been developed.

One of the most effective is the superficially primitive method of placing little heaters (called, of course, *chaufferettes*) in the vineyard. They warm the air around them sufficiently to disperse the danger. The other method, *aspersion*, is used widely in the more sophisticated climes of California, but requires a nearby source of water and some investment in reliable piping and pumps. The vines are continuously sprayed with water which, perversely, protects them with a layer of ice. The Michels cannot use this method with ease, but Jean-Loup regularly does duty on the town's rota of frost guards. He has to stay on alert all night whenever there is the slightest hint of danger, and the minute the temperature falls below zero he rings the siren at the Mairie to waken the *vignerons*. Pyjama-clad legs somnambulate through the vineyards lighting the *chaufferettes* and aspersing water where it can be aspersed.

Another unusual characteristic of the region is that it is planted with one variety only. Fifty years ago, perhaps as much as half the vineyard area was planted with the much less noble Sacy grape, but now Chardonnay alone is responsible for any wine carrying the name Chablis. There has been a sensible amount of work on selecting the right clones of Chardonnay for the region,

but the Michels have found that the rootstock can play an even more important part. They have to be careful to match early-ripening rootstock such as SO4 to vines which do not need to hang on for extra ripeness in the autumn vineyard. In a normal year Grand Cru vines will be picked last, and up here in France's chilliest still-wine region every minute of sunshine is so important that summer pruning is the rule – as, of course, is chaptalisation (though in 1976, nature robbed France's sugar trade of these important customers).

The vintage usually starts in the first week of October, ten or twelve days after their counterparts further north in Champagne who pick early to keep an even higher level of acidity than the 4 or 4.5 the Chablisiens need to give their wines that "green" tartness when young. A group of up to forty pickers swarm over the Michel vineyards to bring the whole crop in to their pneumatic press within a couple of weeks. Laroche, Fèvre, Deauvissat . . . Jean-Loup Michel can count other owners of such sophisticated equipment on the fingers of one hand. He and his father bought it back in 1970 when they were the second, after Testut, to take this expensive step.

At about the same time, they made that even more important jump: from wood into stainless steel and other inert materials for maturation.

This has been the single most obvious change in Chablis winemaking in the last decade or so, and only William Fèvre, François Raveneau and, in Beaune, Joseph Drouhin cling to the benefits of oak treatment for their best wines.

This wood *versus* stainless steel argument will run and run. Jean-Loup is the essence of frankness. He can evince all sorts of examples, often Californian, of Chardonnays which have been swamped by oak; he points out that oak for oak's sake can produce a stale, slightly artificial-tasting wine counter to the "fresh taste" that most wine-drinkers look for today; but he admits that, unlike producers on the Côte d'Or, they cannot command sufficiently high prices for their wines that would warrant the investment in and the upkeep of oak.

One can see how this reliable and hygienic material suits the Michel style. Both father and son agree that they want to produce wines that are, above all, *"très nets, très fins."* The ultra-clean, pure, flinty Chardonnay of the Michels, so unlike anything produced further south in Burgundy or elsewhere around the world, in its lean, aristocratic way, can last and develop over twenty years, but is rarely allowed to. Now that temperature-controlled stainless steel vats are used for fermentation, and the malo-lactic (so important to achieve in this high-acidity region) is supervised in a special controlled chamber, the

The Michels are unusual in the high proportion of vineyards they own in the heartland of the region, but have clearly like almost all their peers moved away from traditional techniques.

wines are bottled much sooner than they were in the days of wood. The polythene wraps are taken off the spotlessly clean bottling line during the summer months so that the vats can be emptied ready for the coming vintage. In an ordinary year, the Michels would counsel their customers to broach their Premiers Crus after about four years, and their Grands Crus perhaps just within a decade of the vintage – but they are well aware that most of the 85,000-odd bottles they sell each year are opened long before this.

In the equally pristine catacomb of cellars that form the Michels' shopfront, hospitality suite and tasting room combined, they perch their visitors on stools round the low, scrubbed *"rustique"* tasting table, carefully lining the wooden spittoons with a plastic bag, and placing a plate of the local puffy cheese *gougères* dead centre. Then, and only then, will they settle down to discuss with ingrained familiarity the nuances that differentiate their *crus:* Les Clos noticeably dry; Grenouilles strongly perfumed; Montée de Tonnerre firm and elegant.

What is fascinating for the outsider is how they manage to make such consistently good wine, on such a tiny scale, and so much in isolation. They admit that they don't exactly taste

around. Their staple drink is water, and they very rarely drink wines from outside the inner core of the Chablis vineyards. They may make the effort to put out something special, Domaine de Chevalier 1964 for instance, if visited by one of their favourite foreign agents, but make no pretence to be in any way cosmopolitan.

Even their methods of selling seem almost amateur, in the nicest possible way (and after all, who wants to be sold to professionally?). They, like other Chablis growers of repute, export about 80 per cent of what they produce, but had to be discovered by most of their agents abroad via the friendly proprietress of the old Cerf Volant in Auxerre.

Thanks to some rather dubious help along the way from the likes of Mountain White Chablis, Spanish Chablis and even Pink Chablis, the name Chablis is known throughout the world. Thanks to their uncompromising quality, the best Premiers Crus and Grands Crus (which take so much longer to show to advantage) appear ennobled on wine lists in the smartest establishments. The contrast between the expensive life-styles these wines wash down and the simple friendliness of the men who make them is one of the most marked in the wine world.

In the cellars below the tower the Michels have carefully refurbished a little tasting chamber in which they can entertain those who spot their discreet sales message hidden in the ivy.

RHONE

Despite the millions of tourists who hurtle through it each summer, the Rhône Valley and its wines tend to be overlooked. Only the most alert passengers on the Autoroute du Soleil even catch sight of the vineyards as they zoom along the east bank of the river from Lyons to Avignon.

This cavalier attitude to some of the world's most intriguing wines seems to be mirrored in the prices they command; the Rhône can offer some of the best value to wine-lovers today. From a year like 1976, considered a success in the Rhône, Burgundy and Bordeaux, the very top names of those two very different wine regions north and south Rhône can be found for the same price as a very ordinary bourgeois claret, and for very much less than any name from the Côte d'Or. At the top end of the scale, Rhône wines represent even greater value: Paul Jaboulet Aîné's Hermitage La Chapelle 1961, perhaps the greatest Rhône made since the war, costs less than a third of the price of a first growth claret from that great vintage. This is a comparatively recent phenomenon – Hermitage was classified with the greats only a century ago, and its worth acknowledged even in Bordeaux where those wines which had been "hermitaged" commanded higher prices than the much punier specimens that had to rely on the vineyards of the Gironde alone.

Visitors to the Rhône who wish to pay homage to its wines should stick to the much quieter road on the west bank as they leave the industrial wastes of Lyons behind them. Up here the vines are grown on frighteningly steep terraces, difficult to work and even more discouraging to those who persist with them in that the local appellations demand vine varieties that are naturally shy-bearing. Each of Côte Rôtie, Condrieu and Château Grillet can be great, but there is a danger that they will become extremely difficult to find.

A good Côte Rôtie, such as Les Jumelles from Jaboulet, La Rolande of Vidal-Fleury, La Mouline of Guigal or from a good individual grower like Jasmin, is magical. Although based on Syrah, the most important "noble" grape of the Rhône, a certain amount of the strange white Viognier is allowed, up to 20 per cent. This gives Côte Rôtie, when well done, an additional perfume and elegance that the all-Syrah reds from a little further south lack.

Such wines, however, can have you gasping to taste Viognier in its unadulterated state, as in the curious white wines of Condrieu and that unique single-property appellation within it, Château Grillet. This very low-yielding variety, found nowhere else, produces wines that really do have a haunting perfume which some call "may-blossom," some "apricots" and others everything in the hedgerow from cow parsley on. The best wines are dry but full-bodied and capable of interesting development over several decades. Some traditional locals turn out undated wines that can be too heavy with a sweetness that masks this exotic scent. Georges Vernay and Paul Multier at the Château du Rozay make some of the best Condrieu. Château Grillet, the smallest appellation in France (a fact known by all wine quiz enthusiasts), has its own

No training on wires for Rhône grapes, such as these grown in Châteauneuf's pebbly vineyards.

natural amphitheatre of vineyard, and a reputation for greatness that has not always been upheld in recent vintages.

Thirty miles south, on the opposite bank of the river, are the north Rhône's most famous vineyards, those responsible for the intense, long-lived, meaty red wines of Hermitage. These are wines that automatically command respect, though not always affection, from wine drinkers who are not prepared to wait for them to show their charms. The wines of Cornas, also based on Syrah, can last at least as long as Hermitage, although they are even less appreciated.

There are several fine producers based around Tain l'Hermitage, the small town in which most Hermitage and the lighter Crozes-Hermitage is made. Gérard Chave regularly

Châteauneuf was known for its Château des Papes, the papal summer residence.

walks off with Gold Medals at the Paris Fair. The houses of Chapoutier and Delas have good reputations. But it is Paul Jaboulet Aîné, and their second label Jaboulet Isnard to a lesser extent, that is responsible for a staggeringly wide range of well-made Rhône wines, and especially for their Hermitage La Chapelle that has continued to win acclaim from all who taste it. At Gault Millau's "Wine Olympics" in 1979, they waltzed off with first, second and third prizes – an achievement that can be queried in detail, but must be admired in principle.

The southern part of the Rhône is quite different. The valley flattens out, the soil changes from hard, granitic to a loose hotchpotch and the climate softens to raise minimum alcohol levels permitted from 10°, for Hermitage for example, to 12.5° for Châteauneuf.

Châteauneuf-du-Pape is the most famous wine of the southern Rhône, and justifiably so. It can be a rich, sturdy red with many layers of flavour. Sadly, however, it has become one of those appellations like Vouvray in which really great wine represents only a few per cent of total production, most of it being mediocre and worse. Ironically, in an area which gave birth to the Appellation Contrôlée system under the energetic Baron le Roy in the 1920s, with laws which are elastic enough to include up to thirteen different grape varieties and any number of different vinification techniques, the name seems to be in danger of becoming prostituted.

There are still a number of very *"sérieux"* estates making traditional wine built to last, not as long as Hermitage of course, but able to mature gently to something of real interest. These include the Domaine de Mont-Redon, Domaine de Beaucastel, Domaine du Vieux Télégraphe, Chante-Cigale and Château Fortia. But the Reynauds at Château Rayas, described below, have managed to produce something even more special – usually by ignoring all the rules.

Hermitage La Chapelle, Jaboulet

E ven if his wines were not some of the most consistently exciting made in France, Gérard Jaboulet would deserve a place in this book purely on the basis of his perceptive and comprehensive knowledge of the wines currently being made all around the world. Present him in London with an obscure pair of new releases from the Pacific North West and he will smile delightedly, announcing that he remembers one with affection from a tasting in Seattle and has a bottle of the other at his own cellar in Tain l'Hermitage. Passing lightly over some interesting new developments in the vineyards of China, he may then make a relevant and fascinating observation starting: *"I tasted a few days ago wines from Mexico, North Mexico, where Martell have 299 hectares of vineyards 1800 metres high. Not 300 hectares because then they'd have to pay too much tax . . ."*

The fact that, today, great wines of the Rhône are under-appreciated has stimulated Gérard's natural curiosity about what he is competing against in the world market-place; and he disseminates this extra-ordinary knowledge in a way that is not patronising, simply enthusiastic. The top proprietors of Bordeaux and Burgundy occupy a position that must seem unassailable; there is really no need for them to acquaint themselves with any wine produced outside their cellar door. Jaboulet wines still have to be sold rather than allocated, and to sell it helps to know what you are up against.

Of all candidates for inclusion in this book, only Christian Moueix was as interested as Gérard Jaboulet in the selection. Indeed Gérard threatened to turn the inquisitorial tables in his eagerness to discuss the relative merits of various California wineries. He spends at least two weeks a year in the United States. Through his importers Frederick Wildman, he has come to have great respect for Paul Draper at "Reedge," another very cosmopolitan winemaker. He has not so far been too impressed by the newer wine regions' attempts at making a Syrah, but thinks that examples have emerged from Ridge, Joseph Phelps and Zaca Mesa which vindicate his theory that Syrah, proper Gros Syrah, could do better in California than Zinfandel ever will. Petite Sirah, he thinks, may well be the Duriff as commonly believed in California, but points out that there has never been any Duriff grown in his area and knows of it only in Calabria in southern Italy.

It is hardly surprising that Gérard is so

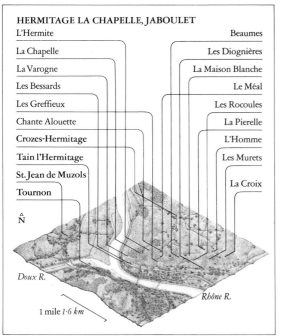

Not-so-discreet advertising below the Chapelle vineyard.

HERMITAGE LA CHAPELLE, JABOULET

L'Hermite
La Chapelle
La Varogne
Les Bessards
Les Greffieux
Chante Alouette
Crozes-Hermitage
Tain l'Hermitage
St. Jean de Muzols
Tournon

Beaumes
Les Diognières
La Maison Blanche
Le Méal
Les Rocoules
La Pierelle
L'Homme
Les Murets
La Croix

△
N

Doux R.

Rhône R.

1 mile *1·6 km*

Gérard Jaboulet – one of the world's widest-ranging palates?

enthusiastic about North America; it sounds as though he had some wonderful times there. There was his memorable visit to the famous wine connoisseur of Fort Worth *"wiss a yooge private cellar – phew!"* Here he found no fewer than thirty-seven different vintages of his pride and joy, Hermitage La Chapelle, including that of his birth year 1942, which was served as a surprise, after a trans-Atlantic call to his secretary, along with Château Haut-Brion 1942. This was the first time Gérard had tasted "his" wine. But it is in opinions rather than recollections that he is particularly valuable. He believes, for instance, that there is enormous potential for top quality wine in Spain, and rates particularly CUNE, to whom he has exported some Syrah cuttings whose progress should be worth watching.

Gérard Jaboulet may have drunk as widely as any man on this earth, but he certainly doesn't look as if he has, with his twinkling brown eyes and sturdy schoolboy looks. He fairly whizzes about the family firm's cellars below the famous La Chapelle vineyard in Tain, with short, eager steps in his capacity as *président directeur général*, which he took over from his father Louis when he retired in 1976. Louis still plays an important part, however, sitting on the national appellation committee INAO, and standing in for Gérard during the five or six months he spends travelling, usually in week-long doses. Brother Jacques specialises in the all-important vineyard work, as well as selecting the bought-in

Well, it *might* be ready for drinking by 1999...

grapes, which represent up to three-quarters of their production.

The firm was founded by the eponymous Paul Jaboulet in 1834. His daguerrotype portrait hangs in Gérard's tiny office. Over the years his name has become firmly connected in wine-lovers' minds and palates with a wide range of wines, from both north and south Rhône, of a quality that is always dependable and often awe-inspiring. Their Hermitage from La Chapelle vineyard is their most revered wine, and they are responsible for nearly a third of the 4,500 hecto-litres of Hermitage produced in an average year. They also turn out very impressive wines from that much more lowly appellation Crozes Hermitage, in which they are responsible for 3,000 of the 43,000 hectolitres these lower vineyards usually produce. *"Crozes-Hermitage Domaine de Thalabert is our little baby because it is much more problematical to produce really good wine from these vineyards than from Hermitage itself."* says Gérard.

Having such an extensive range of wines clearly keeps family morale, and activity, up to the necessary pitch. They make a Cornas from the vineyards south and across the river which, of all Rhône wines, Gérard thinks is wildly under-appreciated. As a "gamey" wine, he suggests it is a perfect partner for game. From the north there is St Joseph Le Grand Pompée and the magnificent Côte Rôtie Les Jumelles, a brilliant name for the much sought-after wine of the Côte Brune and the Côte Blonde. In line with the

The Hermitage hill above Tain, seen from Tournon, its twin town across the Rhône. The steeper vineyards' topsoil is almost completely eroded every year.

increasing disaffection for the low-yielding Viognier, Jaboulet include only about 6 per cent of these white grapes in the Syrah-based blend for this wine, even though 20 per cent is officially allowed.

In the southern Rhône where they have no vineyards, the family have built up excellent connections, and rely heavily on the assistance of energetic *courtiers* based in Vacqueyras and Châteauneuf. Even a simple Côtes-du-Rhône is a fine wine when sold under the elegant Jaboulet label. Their Gigondas can be superb, and their Châteauneuf-du-Pape Les Cèdres, with its 20 per cent dollop of "the" Jaboulet grape Syrah, provides an interesting contrast with the wines of Jacques Reynaud (see page 114), who Gérard indulgently admits is the king of Châteauneuf, for all his idiosyncrasies.

Jaboulet also produce a small proportion of white wines, notably Hermitage Le Chevalier de Stérimberg and Crozes Hermitage Mule Blanche from the strange local grapes Marsanne and Roussanne, which develop into weighty, rich, almost "gummy" wines. The days at the start of October, when the last of these grapes are brought in, heralds the final phase of ripening of the Syrah grapes planted in the famous La Chapelle vineyard. They will come in perhaps two weeks later, always the last to reach the fermentation vats in Tain.

Tain and Tournon form one of those conurbations like Buda and Pest which are split into two very different halves by an important river.

During the afternoon, Tournon on the right bank of the Rhône is in often-welcome shadow, while Tain, and the south-facing slopes of the granitic lump called Hermitage which it skirts, are bathed in sunshine. The steep Hermitage vineyards have been terraced, allowing strategic areas for the placing of incongruously commercial advertisements for their owners among the vines.

La Chapelle, generally acknowledged to produce the finest wines of this fine appellation, is made up of the best slope Le Méal, and one almost as good known as Les Bessards. A winding track leads up dizzily to a spot on this wild, heather-covered rock from which one can look down over the baked biscuity earth that, just, covers the vineyard to the rooftops of Tain; the snaking river; and the more industrial aspect of Tournon from which the river carries railway sounds with disconcerting clarity. This is the only important wine-producing point on the left bank of the Rhône – and what a point.

So worn is the topsoil, after one of the longest histories of wine production in France, that it has to be doggedly carried back up the slope after every vintage in the steepest parts of La Chapelle. No easy modern technique has been developed for this job, but helicopters have proved a boon for the task of spraying later in the year, as in that other steep-sided wine valley, the Mosel. At least there are no particularly troublesome climatological hazards in this and other Jaboulet areas (although Cornas can sometimes suffer from summer hail).

The lonely little ruined chapel, which few can think of as they savour Jaboulet's top Hermitage. The vineyards were still worked by mule in 1982, but Gérard has invented machinery that does the job more efficiently, if less picturesquely.

The vines look as though they could withstand anything. The gnarled black stumps look even older than the 70 years maximum age any La Chapelle vine has, and well past the 35-year average age. It is a combination of this maturity and their rigorous training and pruning that restricts the vines to a yield of between 25 and 30 hectolitres per hectare (and only 10 in 1961). As at Côte Rôtie, a very strict Single Guyot method is employed at La Chapelle, and the vineyards must be one of the most punishing to pick.

When the dark Syrah grapes reach the Jaboulet cellars in the backstreet below, Gérard destalks about 40 per cent of them but leaves the rest in whole bunches in order to keep acidity levels up – although in a year such as 1977 when there is considerable rot he will destalk more. In Bordeaux, incidentally, he thinks some properties run the risk of acidity levels that are too low by destalking too zealously.

He believes that fermentation temperature is vital to extract the best and most from this powerful, tannic grape and accordingly keeps the vats cooler than most of his Bordeaux counterparts, and never warmer than 26°C (79°F). Because of the character of Syrah, no *vin de presse* is added after the two-week fermentation, and the wine is put straight into small oak cooperage bought in Burgundy. Most reds at Jaboulet, and certainly Hermitage La Chapelle, spend eighteen months in cask. These have a life of three years for Jaboulet's most famous wine, and are therefore an important element in its flavour.

A wine as concentrated as Hermitage La Chapelle takes a full year to settle down after bottling (but no filtering), according to Gérard. With an average alcoholic strength of 13°, well above the legal minimum of 10°, and all that ripeness from being the last grapes picked, Hermitage La Chapelle needs to be left in peace for many a year. Sadly, much of it is drunk before the ten-year minimum Gérard would advise, and it must be heart-breaking for him to see how little of his wine lives to see its twentieth birthday when he reckons most of the better vintages are showing their best. The 1974, a lightish vintage, he has reserved to drink in the 1990s, for instance. Perhaps if this wine were more of an established commodity in the auction room, wine-lovers would be persuaded to pass it on when they couldn't afford to hang on until it reached maturity, but as Gérard himself points out a little ruefully, his wines fetch very unrewarding prices in the saleroom.

He feels that his beloved Cornas can last as long as Hermitage La Chapelle, and tells of tasting the 1962, another light vintage, at his local three-star restaurant Pic and finding, in 1981, that it was still very youthful. (It is hardly surprising that the Pic "home team" is his favourite, but he also has great respect for Chapel and the brothers Troisgros, while generously admitting that one can eat best in Switzerland.) He advises a wait of anything from six to ten years for his "little baby" Crozes-Hermitage Domaine de Thalabert, which seems a little more in keeping with today's rush to experience, and beat inflation.

Although Gérard is so keenly aware of current trends in the world in general and in the world of wine in particular, there is little sign that he has adapted methods at Jaboulet to accommodate them. He started work there on New Year's Day 1969, fresh from high-powered business and oenology studies at Montpellier, knowing that he "didn't want to change a thing." In fact the only major change in vinification at Jaboulet happened two years later when they began to ferment the white wines in stainless steel and at much lower temperatures than before. It shows

good north Rhône wine with at least ten years in bottle can be a tricky pair to distinguish. Great years such as 1961 and, in time, 1978 are the sort that develop this quality of intensity and great mouthfilling fruit of a sweetish, perhaps blackberry sort. With a yield of only nine hectolitres per hectare, this vintage is still almost black, like other, more recent great years such as 1966, 1969 and 1972. In 1977 acidity was high, and in 1975, unusually, it was simply too hot.

Gérard has the endearing, and surely correct, view that tasting is all. The visitor will be greeted by a flash of his bright smile: *"Now, first the most important thing. What do you want to taste?"* He is delightfully likely to add a vintage or two that you might not have dared specify, considers the selection carefully and adds perhaps *"un rosé pour nous amuser."*

He and his great friend Gérard Chave meet regularly for serious comparative tastings at which they will each submit five of their own wines and assess them "blind." Such friendliness between the "two greats" of a small appellation is a compliment to both of them.

As tasters, Gérard respects the British to a quite flattering extent, and admires the seriousness and skill he meets in London's Charing Cross Hotel every October at a tasting that has become *the* event of the British wine trade calendar. With the US and Switzerland, the British Isles provide most of Gérard's export customers, who buy 60 per cent of what he has to sell, a substantial yearly average of 1.5 million bottles.

England and Ireland are favourite stops on Gérard's busy itinerary, and the fact that he is a keen fly-fisher is not entirely unconnected with this. His excellent grasp of English, though presumably not his lovely accent, comes from a two-month stint at "a very bad school in Clapham" supplemented by student visits to Brighton and Dublin of which he has much rosier memories. It is difficult to see how anyone as jolly as Gérard Jaboulet could fail to have a good time wherever he goes. And today, when he spends most of the time with fellow wine-fanatics, he must find life, even when away from his family of daughters and equally musical wife Odile, really quite tolerable.

But where does he choose to go on holiday? Crete. Far away from anything to do with wine.

in the wines. The whites never go into wood and, according to a tradition established at Jaboulet before any other French producer considered it, are bottled in the spring with a little bit of carbon dioxide still in the wine. It dissipates through the cork but helps to keep these powerful wines fresh and flowery.

Louis and Gérard are currently engaged on a project to ameliorate their wines' reputation which has nothing to do with vinification techniques. Their aim is to have Hermitage La Chapelle recognised as a *premier cru*, a Rhône answer to the established Bordeaux and Burgundy phenomenon. Since there are three representatives from Burgundy and eleven from Bordeaux to just three from the Rhône on the INAO Committee concerned with such matters, they are not optimistic about their prospects.

In a way the Bordelais have more to fear in Gérard's wines than the Burgundians to the north. With age, their Hermitage, Côte Rôtie and Cornas can become very claret-like, indeed like very good claret. A good Pomerol and a

Château Rayas

The old family house is as isolated as the vineyards.

The choice of Château Rayas and its eccentric owner Jacques Reynaud as *the* top property in the southern Rhône should be questioned by no-one – except the thousands of wine enthusiasts who can never have heard of it. With an annual production of only 25,000 to 30,000 bottles, this isolated vineyard and ramshackle cellars constitute one of the smallest enterprises included in this collection of "greats." There is also Monsieur Reynaud's tendency, indeed determination, to hide his extremely powerful light under a bushel.

Those who have tasted his rich, almost herbal reds and curiously pungent whites rapidly develop an acquisitive feeling about them; but this is rarely encouraged by their maker, who does almost nothing to publicise, or even sell, his wines. There is the story of the bright young English wine merchant who was determined to add these sumptuous goodies to his list and set out to buy them while en route to the south of France. He duly wrote a series of letters in advance suggesting, advising and finally demanding a meeting on a set date, each without a word of reply. Undaunted, he turned up at the appointed time to find the entire property deserted. He spent nearly an hour stamping round the delapidated buildings and exploring the surrounding vineyards without finding any sign of his prospective supplier. Eventually, and with great reluctance and perplexity, he drove off along the lane leading away from the property, only to catch sight in his mirror of Monsieur Reynaud cautiously starting to heave himself up from out of the ditch where he had been sheltering from this potential new customer.

The wines themselves are considerably less reticent. The Reynaud tradition of cutting back yields to half those of their neighbours and keeping the wines in wood for up to five years results in an enormous impact on the senses. Unlike so many wines sold as Châteauneuf today, Château Rayas can still be enjoyed after twenty years, and is made only in those years when the quality is thought to warrant it. In other years, the wine that is produced on the Châteauneuf vineyards is sold under the second label, (Clos) Pignan, or perhaps even as Château de Fonsalette, their Côtes-du-Rhône property 15 miles to the north.

This cussed pursuit of quality and scant regard for cost-effectiveness is not something that Jacques Reynaud worries about for an instant, partly because cost-effectiveness as a concept does not mean anything to him. His job is to carry on the winemaking mission begun by his grandfather as an offshoot from a family of *notaires*, and inherited from his strong-minded father Louis who died on Ascension Day in 1980. Louis was a dogmatic innovator who is largely responsible for the style of Château Rayas and its associated wines. He had little time for officials and believed *"Appellation Contrôlée – c'est la garantie de la médiocrité!"* This resulted, for instance, in the somewhat arrogant description of his humble Côtes-du-Rhône as a "Premier Grand Cru" on labels produced in his lifetime.

His son prefers a quieter life, and Château de Fonsalette is today rather more modestly described. He lives alone in the shuttered farmhouse just down the hill from the cellars, occasionally visited by his much more cosmopolitan sister on leave from her orthopaedic clinic in Paris. There are presumably days when he says less than a dozen words, usually to the young *pied noir* who helps him in the cellar. As a result, his lips almost seem to be out of practice and make only the smallest of concessions to the need to move during speech. He is not therefore an easy man to understand.

But behind pebble glasses his eyes betray his passion for his wines. He must be nearer 60 than 50, but with his snub nose and compressed flexi-features, he looks more like a mischievous schoolboy.

There are no helpful signposts to Château Rayas. You must chart your way across the wild country above Châteauneuf to the north-east,

Jacques Reynaud, eccentric son of an eccentric father.

via signs to the well-groomed Vaudieu, and hope to hit upon the right track.

Around the cellars are 13 hectares of rough reddish vineyard, 11½ of them with black grapes hanging low and dusty from widely-spaced, untidy bushes. At 80 to 100 metres above the Mediterranean, Château Rayas is one of Châteauneuf's highest properties, but Monsieur Reynaud believes it is the aspect and constitution of the soil that play the most important part in making Château Rayas such a great wine. His beliefs are neatly contrary to common wine lore, but then one would expect nothing else from Louis' son. Both have been firmly of the opinion that top quality vineyards this far south should face north; the grapes do not go short of sunshine in Châteauneuf, the problem is to maximise their complexity. For this reason, the Reynaud philosophy flies in the face of the most widely-accepted truth about Châteauneuf: that the enormous flat stones in the vineyard play an important part by reflecting the sun's rays and storing up heat during the day for extra night radiation. Monsieur Reynaud is mighty proud of his land, precisely because it does *not* have these large day-storage heaters, but is made up of much finer soil, sand-based with lots of different elements in the sub-soil and small pebbles on the surface. This, you will be told, is *terrain fin*, and only it can produce *vins fins*.

When he moves on to describe the vines themselves, Monsieur Reynaud destroys a third commonly-held belief: that the best, longest-lived, most complex Châteauneufs are made from a mixture of different varieties, and especially some Syrah. Château Rayas is made from 100 per cent Grenache, the grape that is dismissed in most regions as being capable of some agreeable little rosés, but very little of real quality. So much for the thirteen red grape varieties permitted for Châteauneuf by the authorities.

"On n'est pas tout à fait d'accord avec les officiels," says Reynaud with nice understatement. He disapproves of the official line, which is to encourage plantings of Syrah, believing it not suited to the local terrain. He grows a little of it at Château de Fonsalette, and has experimented with another approved grape, Mourvèdre, but is disappointed by its ageing properties. Indeed the only other approved red grape variety which he would countenance is Cinsault, which underpinned good Châteauneuf in the days before phylloxera struck.

His white Châteauneuf, produced in tiny quantities, is made up of Grenache Blanc and Clairette, but he is experimenting with a bit of the (illegal) Chardonnay and Sauvignon Blanc at Fonsalette. The Sauvignon is perhaps not quite at home in such a hot climate, but the results with Chardonnay are impressive. A little bit of Fonsalette Pinot Noir was fermented in 1981, in addition to the Grenache and Syrah grown on the nine hectares of vineyard there, but at Rayas itself Grenache reigns in solitary splendour.

The vines are not notably ancient, being pulled up on average after thirty-five years, so this is not the explanation of Rayas's tiny yields

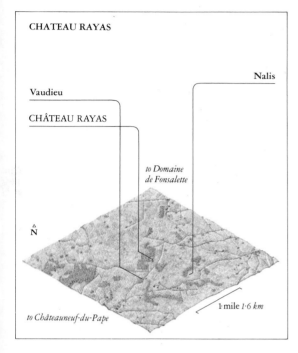

CHATEAU RAYAS

Vaudieu

CHÂTEAU RAYAS

Nalis

*to Domaine
de Fonsalette*

N

to Châteauneuf-du-Pape

1 mile 1·6 km

of between 10 and 25 hectolitres per hectare, in an appellation where up to 42 is permitted. The secret is in the pruning and training of the vines throughout their vigorous growing season. The appellation laws for Châteauneuf are of course unusual in several ways, one of which is that by law producers must practice *triage*, or sorting, and reject a certain proportion, up to 15 per cent, of each crop. It seems unlikely that Monsieur Reynaud is *complètement d'accord avec les officiels* over this one.

Châteauneuf's unusually high minimum alcohol level, 12.5°, presents him with no problems, however. His wines have a staggering average strength of 14.5°, although their mesh of different flavour elements covers this potency decorously. Monsieur Reynaud claims to have produced a Grenache that was 16° which everyone took for 13°. He achieves this strength by being the last to pick in the region, and usually leaving the sweet, juicy grapes on the vine until well into the first week of October. The red grapes are not de-stalked, and neither are those

Inside the cellars, *opposite*, there seems to have been little change for decades except for that modest new filling machine lurking in the shadows.

from Châteauneuf nor those brought down from Fonsalette; they are left to ferment for about eight days in the sultry bacteriological paradise of a Château Rayas enamel fermentation vat. Because quantities are relatively small, different grape varieties being kept separate almost to the time of bottling, excessive heat should never be a problem. This is a winery that would win no prizes from a sanitary inspector. Jacques Reynaud does his round from vat to vat, waving away the flies before poking at the bubbling froth with an old stick. He listens at the side of a cobwebby cask to see whether the fermentation inside is over. It is all very primitive and rustic, and said to be ever more so since his father's time.

Fonsalette is made in exactly the same way as the Châteauneuf wines although, as Monsieur Reynaud points out with a shrug, he can charge twice as much for Château Rayas. He keeps the reds and whites three or four years in cask usually – although he still had a couple of barrels of Fonsalette Grenache from the 1976 vintage unbottled at the end of 1981, when he was selling Château Rayas 1976 for 65 francs a bottle and Château de Fonsalette (presumably a little light on Grenache) for 35 francs.

The question of the provenance of these barrels is by now immaterial. They are ancient things, containing about 600 litres, covered with dust and the same sort of dubiously natural-looking material that modern opera sets seem to be made of. If you have managed to gain access to the cellars, then Reynaud *fils* will risk life and limb on a rickety old ladder to give you many tastes from these casks, probably from a strangely un-rustic Duralex *tastevin*, or perhaps from a wine glass with only half a base.

After *assemblage*, the painstaking task of bottling by hand starts. An ancient bottle-washer is put into action and the bottles are filled at a rate that would make today's technical directors wince. Labels are put on by hand whenever there's nothing better to do, the little triangular neck-labels carefully gummed and laid out top to tail on the work bench in the dark little office where a Western Union cable lies waiting to be opened.

The United States is often Monsieur Reynaud's biggest market, after French customers (mainly local but including some smart restaurants and Steven Spurrier in Paris) who take half of what he produces. There's Martin's Wine in San Francisco, Chadderton in New York and . . . whoever is it in Boston now?

CHATEAU RAYAS
CHATEAUNEUF-DU-PAPE

MIS EN BOUTEILLE AU CHÂTEAU

APPELLATION CHÂTEAUNEUF-DU-PAPE CONTRÔLÉE

PROPRIETAIRE
J. REYNAUD

75cl

CHÂTEAUNEUF DU PAPE
VAUCLUSE
FRANCE

Gérard Jaboulet's favourite Châteauneuf – and Jacques Reynaud will countenance no other.

Heaven knows how they found him. British importers O. W. Loeb managed it by their tried and tested method of asking at the local gastronomic temple, l'Auberge de Noves, where (according to Monsieur Reynaud's version) they compared Château Rayas with Domaine du Mont Redon one day over lunch and "were here within minutes."

But back to the "bottling line": whites are sold straight after bottling, while reds are left to develop further in bins behind the office for another two years or so. According to the man who should know, red Château Rayas (pronounced "rye-ass") should be drunk at any time between ten and twenty years after the vintage – quite a contrast to the average Châteauneuf today which can be enjoyed at four or five years. The best vintages he recalls as 1945, 1969 and 1971. The 1976 he admits is now quite drinkable (most other wines from this vintage and appellation started to fade in 1982), as are his 1974s. The 1974 Château de Fonsalette red tasted late in 1981 was certainly a revelation – *à point,* what one might hope for from a really good Châteauneuf of this year, and certainly well worthy of Louis' proud epithet. Château Rayas tasted at about the same time was not nearly ready, but rich, velvety, with masses of fruit and a scent of violets; to be broached into the second half of the 1980s.

The odd claret case-end in Jacques Reynaud's cellars betrays some knowledge of other French wines, but he has little time for serious exploration. Despite the fact that it is probably the only other wine region in the world where Grenache, as Garnacha, is taken seriously, Monsieur Reynaud had never heard of Rioja, for example. And in Hugh Johnson's classic *World Atlas of Wine*, Château Rayas is notable by its absence from the dozen top Châteauneuf labels which appear there. Monsieur Reynaud did not bother to comply with the publishers' request for a label or two, so unconcerned is he with the international context in which his wines are set.

He is not without local pride in his own produce, however. He makes a little Fonsalette rosé, and is most disgruntled that he is not allowed to make a Châteauneuf rosé as he knows he could make an extremely good one. Not many Châteauneuf producers could manage it of course, but he could.

And does he drink his own wine every night? *"On goûte un peu,"* he admits with a winning grin from ear to ear. Does he perhaps take a look at other Châteauneufs sometimes too? He is shocked, and then sly. *"Oh no – but I think the others drink mine though."*

Here is a man who is convinced that his wine is not Châteauneuf-du-Pape but Château Rayas.

LOIRE

The thought of a wine world without a Loire is a dismal one. Without the wines of this famous French river there would be many vital lacunae in the rollcall of invigorating dry whites, as well as sad gaps in the many other types of wine that the versatile Loire can turn its hand to. It is a fact, however, that most of the wines that the Loire is best at are not those to which the epithet "great" could be applied. There is in many years some extremely appetising Muscadet, with the tireless Marquis de Goulaine, Louis Métaireau, Château la Noë and the Château de la Galissonnière property being responsible for some of the most respected. But all of them make wines to be drunk within a couple of years of the vintage, to go with informal eating, or to precede grander bottles.

At the other, eastern, end of the Loire vineyards, Pouilly-Fumé and Sancerre seem more likely candidates for greatness. Wines such as those produced at the fairy-tale Château du Nozet by Patrick de Ladoucette achieve higher prices and enormous vogue. In Sancerre and Pouilly-sur-Loire there are many, especially local growers, as concerned as him to make clean, exciting wines from the Sauvignon grape.

There are the Loire reds, of course – and a good Bourgueil of an exceptional year can develop into something special – as well as a range of pink and a very creditable selection of sparkling wines. The greatest treasures however are to be found among the best of the white wines made from the Chenin Blanc grape which, though widely planted elsewhere, never manages to reach the same level of lusciousness as in small pockets of vineyards along the Loire.

Just south-west of Angers is the exceptional appellation Savennières, where older vintages of this dry wine, high in fruity acidity, have shown that it could hold its own among the greats. Awarded special status are La Coulée de Serrant and La Roche aux Moines, but some have been more impressed recently by the performance of a few of the small properties just a few miles up the Layon tributary in the Quarts de Chaume and Bonnezeaux appellations. In good years they will be blessed with "noble rot" to turn out wonderfully rich, golden wines that are worthy of being kept several decades after being bottled. A classic example of the importance of the micro-climate, this is an area that deserves much more attention – though some of the dull wines currently sold under the wider appellation Côteaux du Layon do not serve as good ambassadors.

Vouvray, however, must be the real catch-all appellation in the Loire. The worst wines sold under this name can be musty, semi-sweet, unbalanced liquids with acidity that swipes nastily at the gills just as they leave the mouth. The best, happily, are so good and, incidentally, so underpriced, that they demand inclusion in a book such as this. They range from still, through

pétillant to méthode champenoise sparkling, and from the boniest of bone dry, through all shades of lusciousness to downright dripping with unctuous richness.

Most producers have a shot at all styles, but perhaps the most impressive characteristic of any Vouvray (and the sweeter ones in particular) is its longevity. Alone among the wines along this river, characterised by a naturally high acidity level because of their latitude, the wines of

Some great bottles of red Loire wine are made – as here in Caslot's Bourgueil caves – but very little of it is designed for a long life.

The River Loire links a wider variety of wine areas than is found in any other region of France. Perhaps the noblest are the long-living Vouvrays, such as those made in Huet's limestone caves, *right*, although even here horizontal presses have now taken over.

Vouvray (and to a lesser extent those of Quarts de Chaume and Bonnezeaux) achieve a weight and complexity that gives the acidity something worth working to preserve, for well over half a century in many cases.

After the prosperous, scrubbed town of Tours, the tiny cluster of cottages built into the north bank of the Loire just to the east that is the village of Vouvray, provenance of all these vinous excitements, looks unlikely to say the least. The fact that the village is clearly far from prosperous, however, despite a newish *piscine* and *centre de sports*, might indicate to the canny wine-lover that prices of the local produce had not risen as they might have done. Vouvray is a worthwhile hunting ground. Most of the wine is sold as very ordinary stuff under the labels of merchants from all over France, and even further afield.

The name that is most readily associated with Vouvray of great quality and lasting power is not that of a Vouvray vine-grower at all. Marc Brédif is a *négoçiant* based between Vouvray and Tours at Rochecorbon and he shows what can be

done by skilful selection and blending to produce wines of all degrees of sweetness that can grow old extremely gracefully. This enterprise has been taken over by the dashing Baron de Ladoucette, and will doubtless continue to introduce wine-lovers all over the world to the proposition that Vouvray is to be treated with the same long-term respect as great claret, sauternes and Hermitage.

This collection is concerned primarily with those who produce grapes as well as wine, however, and there is still – despite the small rewards they receive – a small number of growers producing first class Vouvray, of which Foreau at Clos Naudin is one of the two most dependable.

It is impossible to ignore, however, the contribution to Vouvray and Touraine, and even perhaps to Loire wines as a whole, made over many decades by Gaston Huet of Haut Lieu.

Gaston Huet

Professional administrator Gaston Huet in his office with *"mon gendre,"* Noël Pinguet.

Gaston Huet, obliging, diminutive and bespectacled, must be the best-known inhabitant of Vouvray. To the cognoscenti among winelovers he is known as the producer of some of the most elegant and individual Vouvrays still available. To officials of the wine world he is known as the Loire representative on INAO, the official appellations committee. To other Loire *vignerons* he is valued as vice-president of the regional committee on Loire AC wines, and has been president of the CIVT, the Touraine wine growers and merchants organisation, since 1975. And to neighbours who may have nothing whatsoever to do with wine he is known as Conseiller Général of the department, and mayor of Vouvray since 1947, a year which he is pleased to point out was an extremely good vintage.

The most extraordinary, and to wine-lovers prized, aspect of Monsieur Huet's busy schedule is that he still manages to make such exceptional wine despite being *"pris"* almost every evening by some official dinner, a regular on the 6.40 dawn special to Paris for national meetings and a participant in missions which have taken him as far afield as Thailand and California. The secret lies in *"mon gendre,"* his daughter having been wise enough to marry Noël Pinguet who is slow-

ly bringing methods in his father-in-law's *caves* up-to-date.

Gaston Huet himself is clearly thrilled by this new influence and watches bemused as his son-in-law fusses over a brand new Bucher pneumatic press, wondering out loud whether it can really be as gentle as the old-fashioned vertical presses which they used till 1935. Noël Pinguet curses him affectionately as being *"méticuleux et maniac."*

"Méticuleux" he certainly is, in his official activities as much as those of his own business concern. Any visitor is taken automatically to Monsieur Huet's pride and joy, the Maison des Vins in Tours, beautifully reconstructed round a quiet courtyard in the shadow of the church. Here there is a wine museum, a *salle des fêtes* and all the administration for the wines of the Touraine. He may be a little shy at first with the visitor, but can be seen to relax delightedly when an official document is put in his hand. It may be an agenda that needs tidying up, or wines to be chosen for an official banquet: *"Ah oui, le gibier avec un Bourgueil, et du Gamay avec le pigeonneau . . ."*

In his rather battered Citroën Club, he will still be discussing official business, or giving a methodical and considered view on behalf of all the growers of the region. It can be difficult indeed to get a man used to making careful generic statements to talk only about himself and his wines – a fact which amuses him.

It may not be the business of those in Gaston Huet's position to blow their own trumpet, but with a property such as Le Haut-Lieu there is little need. The long, low house where Monsieur Huet lives and has his offices (unthinkable that these two functions should be separated) is any francophile's dream. At the heart of his neat vineyards is this little *manoir* with white shutters, dormer windows along the roof and rows of copper pans winking through the kitchen window. Inside, as bridge between living and official quarters, is Monsieur Huet's own office, very formal with Louis XV chairs, marble fireplace and ormolu clock, but all on a tiny scale. Through the crisp net curtains is a pretty, well-tended garden between the house and the famous Le Mont vineyard, and on the other side a courtyard with the only giant intrusion, ancient trees towering above the buildings and out of all proportion to the baby wild cyclamen in a carpet at their foot.

All around this idyllic spot are the 32 hectares of Huet vineyard, all AC Vouvray and all planted in Chenin Blanc. Chenin, or Pineau de la Loire as it is known locally, is one of those curious vines that winemakers in California and South Africa find so useful – but to produce wines quite unlike those made in this middle Loire homeland. Gaston Huet tasted quite a number of California Chenins when he visited there in 1975, but has not

The tiny chamber in which Huet sparkling wines are recorked is cut into the Vouvray cliffs overlooking the river and Montlouis.

been impressed by the efforts of these "newer" regions, and reckons the soil is the most important factor. Only in Anjou and Vouvray is Chenin Blanc taken seriously, he shakes his head.

The Huet vineyards lie on soil that in French is described as "*argilo-calcaire,*" which sounds so much more romantic than "clayey-limestone." The subsoil, into which are built the caves such as Gaston Huet's on the outskirts of the village a mile or so down the road from Le Haut-Lieu, is not, as often thought, chalk, but calcerous. Such complexity must play an important part in achieving the richness of top class Vouvray such as those made by Gaston Huet, but latitude is another important difference between these luxuriant Chenin Blanc vineyards and their "new world" counterparts. The Vouvray vintage rarely takes place before the end of October and is one of the latest in France. Unusually, white wines are harvested after red, and last considerably longer. Acidity is the key here. The "bite" that makes the Chenin Blanc a useful white wine grape in hotter areas gives Vouvray an exceptionally high level of acidity in the northerly Loire, even when harvested as late as this: usually between six and eight grams per litre, when most wines are nearer four. What is important in the vineyards above Vouvray is to hang on for as much ripeness in the grapes as possible.

This noble plan can be foiled by a phenomenon as prosaic as a flock of greedy starlings. In 1977, Gaston Huet lost 12,000 litres of wine to them and has accordingly imported one of those California "tic-tac" megaphone bird-scarers to safeguard subsequent crops. This represents one of the few concessions to modernity he has so far made in the vineyard. He feels strongly that chemical treatments should be kept to an absolute minimum and prefers to nurture his crop by physical means. The summer pruning is an important feature here, leaving the grapes on the high-trained leafy vines exposed to as much ripening sunshine as possible. The official maximum yield is 45 hectolitres per hectare, but he rarely manages more than 30, though he has had to move the uprooting age for vines down from 65 to 40 years for financial reasons.

Huet is rare in Vouvray for keeping the wines made on his different, extremely respectable vineyards separate right up to the time of consumption. They all face south, for maximum ripeness again, and Le Haut-Lieu, named after the Huet property itself, is particularly good

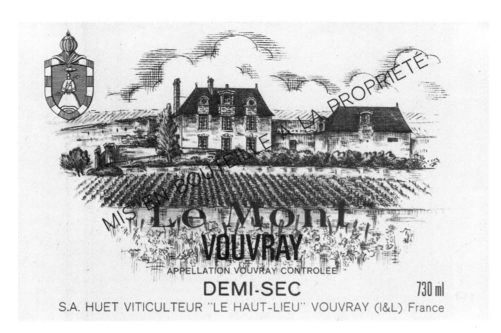

Long-lived Vouvrays like this, their richness belied by enormous acidity when young, are some of the world's most under-valued wines. Even this Demi Sec will last for 30 years.

for demi-sec Vouvray. Le Mont, in front of the house and sloping down towards the river, is the heart of the Vouvray appellation, near the rocks and producing a particularly low yield. Clos du Bourg is capable of producing round, supple wines, and some lovely Moelleux in good vintages, but Gaston Huet has recently substantially replanted this rocky vineyard, so we may have to wait a while to see its wines at their best. He tells the story of how twenty years ago the officials tried to decide which of these three vineyards was "the best" and found that the three wines they picked out as being superior to all other samples submitted were all from Huet.

The winemaking operation *chez* Huet, including his important sparkling wine activities, no longer takes place at Haut-Lieu but in their network of tufa caves on the outskirts of the village, a workplace known officially as *"en bas."* In the chill of November there is no problem achieving the slow, cool fermentation necessary for wines of quality with ageing potential, which is what Huet seeks. They may have to heat the cellars a little to get the fermentation going, and it often continues until well after New Year's Day. Monsieur Huet would like to ferment all his wines in oak but here, as all over the wine world, stainless steel continues its remorseless takeover – except that in the irregular shapes of these caves it can be difficult to accommodate something as orderly as a right-angle. Tanks are squeezed into apparently impossible crevices, looking much more out of place than the old hollows into which animals would be tied when the locals were sheltering from the flooding river down below. (M. Huet's caves open at one point on to a most spectacular view over the valley and the Montlouis appellation opposite, complete with a fig tree from which the courteous gentleman will offer ripe fruits to the visitor.)

Inside the caves is a flurry of activity in March, involving many of the fifteen workers employed at Gaston Huet, when the wines are popped into bottle. This hastiness is in order to lose not a gram of that precious life-preserving acidity. Malo-lactic fermentation is something to be avoided at all costs in Vouvray, and this applies to all qualities and levels of sweetness.

Vouvray is usually sold either as Sec, Demi Sec and Moelleux (roughly pronounced "Mwa-le") but, confusingly, there are no rules governing the last two descriptions, which probably

New stairway hewn in the Huet cellars in the 1960s.

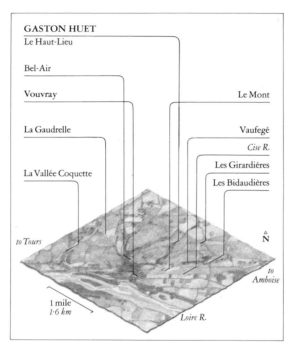

GASTON HUET
Le Haut-Lieu
Bel-Air
Vouvray
La Gaudrelle
La Vallée Coquette
Le Mont
Vaufegé
Cise R.
Les Girardiéres
Les Bidaudières
to Tours
△ N
to Amboise
1 mile
1·6 km
Loire R.

encompass most of Vouvray's most exciting wines. Wines that are Sec must contain less than five grams of sugar per litre in Vouvray, one gram more than the general EEC regulation on "dry" wines, presumably because there is all that acidity to counterbalance the sweetness. There are a number of Demi Sec wines from Vouvray which are difficult to distinguish from the officially dry ones, so overpowering is the acidity. Gaston Huet applies his own rigorous standards, however, and made a Demi Sec only twice, in 1980 and 1981, in the last six years.

For a Moelleux wine, one that is really golden, rich and develops a character that is almost reminiscent of burnt honey or, according to Monsieur Huet, wild cloves, very special conditions must be achieved. The grapes must be attacked by noble rot and allowed to concentrate under its influence in a prolonged autumn. Vintages which Monsieur Huet remembers with affection in this respect are 1976, 1973, 1971, 1970, 1969, 1964, 1962 and 1961. As elsewhere in northern Europe, 1976 was extraordinary, and two-thirds of all the wine produced by Monsieur Huet was Moelleux. Like their counterparts in Germany, *vignerons* in Vouvray are dictated to completely by the weather as to the style of wines they produce each year. It is possible to make small quantities of Moelleux wine in less

wonderful vintages, but this involves a time-consuming sorting process and is rarely practised today.

Monsieur Huet does not worry too much about the lack of Moelleux character in vintages since 1976; he believes in hanging on to his wines for years before selling them, and Moelleux wines can, after all, last for decades. He sells about 120,000 bottles of wine a year and keeps a staggering five years of wine in stock. In 1981 he was selling a 1965 Sec and a 1966 Moelleux – at the pitifully low price of only 27 francs a bottle. It makes him just a little cross to see Sauvignon-based wines, from further along the banks of the Loire, without a hope for the development over the next three decades, selling at the same price as his precious bottles. He is pleased, however, to see that the new generation in the Vouvray wine trade tend to have learned administration before technical matters. Watch out for an increase in Vouvray prices.

Gaston Huet reckons that even his Demi Sec wines can last 30 years and as for his Moelleux . . . well, he is still enjoying the 1921 and 1913, and an 1874 tasted recently was in excellent shape. That Sec 1965 that he is currently selling would still make an excellent aperitif. Demi Sec he recommends especially with creamy fish dishes, pastry-based entrées such as *vols-au-vent*, and the local delicacy called in Tours *"rillons."* Moelleux too, with its perfect harmony of acidity and richness, will do duty as a special apertif, as well as standing up wonderfully to *foie gras* and even strong cheeses.

He now finds himself in the invidious position of having to drink his own delicious wines every day, such a generous host is he, always opening up a new bottle for visitors. His mention in Hugh Johnson's *Wine Atlas* has made quite a difference to the number of people who have found their way up the backroads to Le Haut-Lieu. They come from as far afield as the Napa Valley, and Monsieur Huet was delighted to be able to return the compliment to, among others, Ric Forman – whose interest in rich Chenin-based wines must be purely disinterested. The carefully-treasured green and gold visitors' book at Haut-Lieu boasts signatures from Moscow, Tokyo and all sorts of exotic parts of the globe.

With all these remains (one hesitates to suggest there could ever be "dregs" of such nectar) of great Vouvray, Gaston Huet rarely has the chance to taste wines outside his own region. He does buy a little burgundy by exchange with his

friend the Marquis d'Angerville of Volnay, as well as a bit of claret from a friend in Libourne. Despite this obvious enthusiasm for "the classics," and although the California wines he was most impressed by were Cabernets, he regrets the worldwide spread of Cabernet Sauvignon and Chardonnay, thinking there is a danger in trying to make the same sort of wine in widely differing climates and conditions.

He is particularly interested in technical matters, and completed his agricultural studies way back in 1928. Vouvray has a flourishing sparkling wine trade, of which sales constitute 70 per cent of all AC Vouvray made. Gaston Huet increasingly finds his attention being focussed on still wines, however, which make up half of this production now. Of his sparkling wines, he makes half not *mousseux*, but *pétillant*, which he feels is "more Vouvray," just as he feels its

strength of character means these Chenin wines need a sugar content that puts them into the Sec rather than Brut bracket. He sells two qualities: basic, and Cuvée Reserve which some have mistaken for champagne, each at bargain prices.

For these wines as well as for his more long-lived still wines, Gaston Huet always has far more orders than stock with which he can fulfil them, which makes his prices seem even more generous. He sells about 20 per cent, all still wine, abroad, but clearly enjoys his chosen method of maintaining contact with French customers – at agricultural shows. He is often asked why he doesn't expand, and points out that he would then have to lose this personal selling; he would have to appoint a vineyard manager instead of being able to supervise everything himself; and besides, if he were to buy more land it would have to be from inferior vineyards.

Part of Le Haut Lieu – "any francophile's dream."

CHAMPAGNE

It would be inconceivable to exclude champagne from a book about great wine. Champagne is the wine-lover's luxury. It is an indulgence that we all agree is worth every penny. Almost every bottle produced is testimony to a great achievement: that of turning mainly black grapes grown at the northern limit of vine cultivation into an exhilarating, perfectly-judged mixture of crisp white wine with a steady stream of controlled bubbles to cheer us while we drink it.

As a wine region, Champagne is very special. Although it was one of the first to develop an enlightened and harmonious system of co-operation between the vine-growers and the *maisons* who produce most of the region's wine, the aura of the wine itself is at odds with the idea of the peasant *vigneron*. Despite the dramatic increase in the smallholder-turned-champagne-maker in order to supply weekending Parisians with their roadside bottles, champagne is still more at home in the gilded *salons* of Rheims and Epernay and its champagne mansions than in the tiny office-cum-sitting room of the *récoltant-manipulant*. This is not to say that there are not some extremely capable winemakers among the growers of Champagne; but one must understand that great champagne depends for its greatness on a large bank of stocks from which to assemble the blend, such as only an enterprise of some size can afford.

There is something very cosy about the social climate in Champagne. Christian de Billy of Pol Roger goes shooting with people from Lanson, Laurent-Perrier, Moët and Bollinger for instance; Madame herself was a Perrier-Jouët; and their children consort with the children of other champagne families, many of which have close links with that other aristocracy of luxury in the *haute couture* world.

The Champenois seem to have an almost limitless capacity for their singular local drink. Local doctors do not relate the resultant problems of digestion, but local dentists report a premature effacement of enamel in those who take their duties as citizens of Epernay and Rheims most seriously.

Of course there are now many different types of champagne to choose from. Champagne has always been blended and proud of it – a blend of different soils, different grapes and, originally, different vintages. The champagne drinker of the past had simply the choice of the individual house styles of each *maison*'s blend. The original skill of the winemaker lay in blending to maintain the consistency of this style.

The last century, however, saw the emergence of vintage-dated champagne designed to exhibit the characteristics of that particular year: the blanc de blancs champagne made of

Pinot vineyards at Cumières gently slope down towards the Marne.

Chardonnay grapes only; the cult of the single-village wine; and the "cuvée de prestige" or "de luxe cuvée" that represents the very best that house can do. There are a host of quite delicious wines that fall into this last category, of which Dom Pérignon is the best known and brilliant prototype designed by the Moët & Chandon people. They are also responsible for the very stylish Blanc de Blancs Dom Ruinart. Other special champagnes much in demand include Taittinger's Comtes de Champagne, another blanc de blancs, Heidsieck's Diamant Bleu and Perrier Jouët Belle Epoque, though there are tip-top blends sold in small quantities at the top end of the range of most *maisons*.

Among the *maisons* there are three who are able to command superior prices for their standard non vintage blends as well as for these special de luxe *cuvées*. Bollinger, Louis Roederer and Veuve Clicquot-Ponsardin have built up their reputations as first-class *maisons* over the last century so that their basic wines will usually be nominated among any champagne-lover's favourites. Bollinger's late-disgorged Tradition RD, Roederer's clear-glass Cristal and the elusive Veuve Clicquot Grande Dame are all wonderful wines in their own way too.

But there is one champagne house that aspires to such excellence in its non-vintage blend that it has lifted it up into the same price bracket as all these exclusive bottlings. The house of Krug occupies a very special position in Champagne.

Krug

The visitor to the Champagne region can hardly turn a corner without being confronted by large hoardings and man-high letters proclaiming the location of the many champagne cellars there. The one exception to this rule of grandiose self-publicity can (just) be seen at 5, rue Coquebert, a narrow street on the northern outskirts of Rheims where the curious might spot a discreet brass plaque engraved with the name Krug. Krug champagne is for the cognoscenti, as the Krug entrusted with selling it is proud to claim. *"You don't merely impress anyone with Krug, you share it. It's like meeting someone with the same unusual breed of dog as yourself, or finding someone in a shop buying the same book."*

Although the premises at 5, rue Coquebert may lack pretty tour guides, viewing platforms and recorded messages, one member of the family will probably be on hand to provide the ultimate in personalised visits. Paul Krug retired (officially) in 1977 and left his sons Henri and Rémi in charge as fifth-generation Krugs responsible for maintaining Champagne's most revered name. All three live with their wives around the courtyard (which has hardly changed in a hundred years) above the chilly tunnels of maturing champagne, each named after a previous member of this famous wine family.

Both fourth and fifth generations of the family agree that there was no family pressure on Henri and Rémi to join the firm, but with such opportunities there, and two very different characters available to tackle them, it must have seemed inevitable to all observers. When Paul was eventually asked at some press conference how long he had had his sons in the business, he shrugged and said *"Only since they were born."*

They are both in their early forties and Henri, the elder, is President and winemaker. Like his scientist wife, he has the calm, quizzical air of one used to turning thoughts about in the privacy of his own mind. While Henri will slip quietly into the back room they reserve for visitors, Rémi tears round the door and bounds in. Beneath his little black curls, his Yves St Laurent spectacles and his boyish smile he is a snappy dresser, with smartly casual suits and understated silk ties. Whereas Henri's territory is the vineyard, the cellar and the tasting room, Rémi has no limits. As one of the many literary works commissioned by the firm puts it, Rémi's job as sales chief is to *"krugiser la terre entière."* One week he may be in New York, the next in London, and the next perhaps in the Republic of

The traditional champagne press is programmed to give up only the best portion of the juice to great champagne such as Krug 1973.

Rémi and Henri Krug –
salesman and winemaker
respectively, although both
are firmly "Krugiste".

China on a gastro-
nomic voyage with his
chums among France's
top chefs. Doesn't
Henri resent always
being the stay-at-
home? Sitting quietly
in his office next to the
tasting room studying
a glass of Krug 1969,
he looks up, around
him and asks: *"But
this is a good job
too, no?"*

It is Henri's re-
fusal to change the
methods of his father
and grandfather that
makes Rémi's job so
much easier; there
is no shortage of
"unique selling
points" with Krug.
The family's decision
to seek the help of the
cognac firm Remy
Martin in international
marketing has doubt-
less eased the strain on
their finances con-
siderably, but seems to
have left them free to
go their own, very
"Krugiste" way.

Krug show every
sign of being the last to
stick entirely to the old practice of fermenting in
oak rather than stainless steel, and they regard
this as one of their cornerstones of quality.
Should they ever decide to follow all their competitors into *"inox"* they will have to do some
very skilful backtracking indeed. Rémi, on one
of his many loquacious walks around the cellars,
will make the point that for them, unlike the
Bordelais and the Californians, the first six
months determine 90 per cent of the quality of
the resultant wine. *"The story of how we get the
bubbles into our champagne is not nearly so important as our dear oak casks,"* he will say, pat-
ting one of them tenderly in the long hall that
makes up one side of the courtyard. In a good
year, it will be full of 200-litre barrels of fermenting wine. Space in this hall may mean quotas
from Seattle to Sydney eight years hence.

The Krugs have experimented with fermenting in stainless steel and found that the result is a
blander wine. *"It's not the effect of oak on the
taste of the wine,"* explains Henri, *"but the
combination of the wood and the volume of wine
that, through the temperature curve and resultant clarification, improves the material itself."*
They choose low-tannin oak from the Argonne,
which weathers to bluey-black casks that are as
lovingly sprinkled as a Florida lawn to get them
in shape for each vintage.

Krug's own vineyards at Le Mesnil-sur-
Oger on the Côte des Blancs and Ay, Bollinger's
home town, supply about 20 per cent of their
requirements for sales that amount to scarcely
half a million bottles a year. The freshly-picked
grapes are transported in unromantic grey plastic
crates, designed to minimise breakage of the
skins, to their press-house at Le Mesnil and the
must brought to join Krug's carefully-chosen
bought-in material in the cask hall.

The first sorting-out takes place towards the
end of November, when some casks of wine that
does not quite come up to scratch may be sold off
to other champagne houses. In a good year they
may simply sell off a couple of the less satisfactory casks at this point, but in poor quality
years such as 1967, 1968 and 1972 they may have
sold off almost one third of the newly-fermented
wines. *"You see, we don't have a regular non-
vintage blend to sop up wines that are not perfect
quality,"* Rémi explains patiently. *"We are only
concerned with the prestige market."*

With the wines still in cask, the second important tasting and selection process takes place
in the spring, when Henri decides on the crucial
blending of new wines and reserves (they keep
wines from vintages over the previous decade, in
stainless steel because they *don't* want them to
develop at this stage) to achieve the special Krug
harmony. Rémi, a keen musician himself, is long
on musical similes: *"We talk about music not
from Bonn or Salzburg, but by Mozart, just as
champagne bears the stamp not of geography but
of its maker."*

To make Krug Grande Cuvée, which com-
prises about 80 per cent of their output, Henri
will blend up to ten different vintages using perhaps fifty different base wines to make a wine
that has the rigour, the body, the finesse and the
ageing potential of Krug. It is not an easy champagne to appreciate. Inexperienced champagne-
drinkers often find it too austere, without
appreciating the body that underlies it. When the

Krugs launched their Grande Cuvée in place of Private Cuvée which, with its high proportion of Pinot Noir, had won a special place in the hearts of stalwarts throughout the world, there were dubious mutterings at first. But then it had been only a twinkle in Paul's eye nine years before and needed time to show what a beautiful thing it could become. Bottles of Private Cuvée may still be treasured as collectors hoard old coins, but the new currency of Grande Cuvée is now accepted as highly valuable tender in the world of wine, selling at about the same price as most of the prestige *cuvées* mentioned on page 126. The official story is that Grande Cuvée contains noticeably more Chardonnay than Private Cuvée, made possible by the acquisition of vineyards at Le Mesnil and desirable by a change in

taste towards rather lighter champagnes in us capricious consumers. *"You don't play Bach in the 1980s the same way you would have done in the 1930s, and yet Bach is still eternal."*

One of the other reasons given for the formulation of Grande Cuvée was to have a mainstream wine even more distinct from the full-bodied, apparently-eternal wine they make from single vintages which warrant it. The Krugs are by no means committed to this vintage-dated second string to their bow, however much customers in the United States and Britain may lap it up. (In late 1981 the Krugs had an urgent demand from a customer in the City of London – his Krug 1955 was getting low.)

A favourite saying of Paul's papa was: *"Krug 'cuvée' champagne is my baby. For vintage champagne I have to share the credit with*

God." Rémi points out that the vintage wine is not better than Grande Cuvée, just different. *"We could price the two at the same level, although in fact we tend to ask about 15 per cent more for the vintage wine because it is rarer. Mind you, we're talking here about the difference between the very expensive and the very, very expensive. Perhaps eventually even the English will see my point about Grande Cuvée,"* he adds wistfully.

After the crucial spring blending stage, the champagne process takes place. The *remuage*, all-important to get our Krug clear and bright, takes place about half way through the bottles' stay in the cool cellars beneath the courtyard. This stay is the longest in general application in any major champagne house – an average of six years' stock is stored down below, and vintage wines are often not released until about eight years after they were made, when stocks of their contemporaries from other, more hurried outfits are already exhausted. Krug's four *remueurs* each have their own patch and get to know just how bottles will behave if a little too near the door or light.

The swan-necked bottles are disgorged six months before shipment, and a small *dosage* of around one per cent is added. Krug has always

Vintage champagne is the work of God, but Grande Cuvée is the Krugs' own, "our darling baby."

The Krugs' courtier up to his eyes in work at their Le Mesnil vineyard, *left*. It could be fifteen years before the must from these grapes finally reaches the *remuage* stage, *below*.

been known as a dry champagne, even in the days when Tsarist courts demanded much stickier stuff. They still have old labels captioned "Extra Dry for Invalids;" and the only time in recent history they have made a sweeter wine was a special tiny parcel for their grandfather in his last years. *"As far as I see into the future, our wines will always be dry because they are mellow and round naturally. There is no variation at all in dosage for different markets. Krug is Krug and we expect Krug-lovers to come to us."* The only concession the Krugs are prepared to make to the needs of their different customers around the world is to put slightly stronger corks into those bottles destined for hot and very distant countries.

The powerhouse for the creation of Krug, year in and year out, is Henri's domain, the tasting room. The brothers may sit up on the white formica worktops, swinging their legs over the white tiled floor, just not banging their heads against the glass-fronted cupboard in which tasting glasses hang upside down ready to present hundreds of samples to the Krugs in the approved way. (They eschew the champagne *flûte* in all circumstances as it does not show the bouquet to advantage; the thin-stemmed, K-monogrammed glasses they have had made specially are nearer a tulip than a triangle in shape.)

Here Henri will study the Pinot Noir from different vineyards, base wines that will lose their blush when the second fermentation attracts the pigment into the resultant sediment. He looks carefully at different Chardonnays, not keen as a Krug to produce an all-Chardonnay Blanc de Blancs as so many of his counterparts have done. And he defends the importance of the oft-overlooked Pinot Meunier in the blend as a particularly fruity ingredient. *"Pinot Noir and Chardonnay are such monsters, they need to be tamed,"* he says, trying to describe to an outsider what has been learnt over five generations.

Both Henri and Rémi went to *lycée* in Rheims and then on to business school in Paris, but one gets the impression that what they learned at 5, rue Coquebert was of most use to them. It seems likely that among Henri's four sons there will be at least one keen to carry on making champagne. But it will be a very long time before either retires from his chosen work.

"I can't believe how much fun my work is," enthuses Rémi, although the observer would not share his incredulity. Mannequin-slim, he spends an inordinately high proportion of his working time in the world's best restaurants. He is very gastronomically-minded and what really thrills him is the latest news on Michelin stars and top chef's movements. For him Alain Chapel at Mionnay and Michel Guérard are masters. He loves to cook himself, and tries to experiment with his wine. As an aperitif he chooses Grande Cuvée, a vintage Krug (preferably the 1955, though the 1905 he celebrated his engagement with was quite passable) would introduce the main dish, with which he'd normally choose claret or red burgundy. But no messing about on the outer fringes of the Gironde for him; he buys wine on an exchange basis with worthies such as Baron Elie de Rothschild.

Rémi Krug is known the world over for his tireless promotion of the family name, and is not unaware of its value and prestige. He works constantly to persuade retailers and restaurateurs of the necessity to divide their champagnes not into vintage and non-vintage, but into "regular" and "prestige", and tells of a horrifying visit to a famous store once where he found his precious Krug slumming it among the non-vintage wines of "our dear colleagues" instead of languishing on the rather more salubrious shelves reserved for Dom Pérignon and the like. (Laurent Perrier's Grand Siècle is in the same undated but splendid state, and the advent of similar styles from Lanson and Pommery et Greno should make Rémi's job easier in the future.)

But most wine salesmen at least have a range to choose from, while the Krugs don't even allow themselves to venture into a Crémant (tried but not for the 1980s) or Côteaux Champenois (scorned, even though their still reserve wines taste considerably better than any Côteaux Champenois ever do) – and at present there is no addition to the range (unthinkable to *better* Grande Cuvée) other than the vintage wine. Surely Rémi tires of his daily round of Krug, Krug then more Krug? Not so. He does drink champagne from other houses (although only in the company of very close friends), but he can remember "only one or two times in my life when I have had to drink Krug when I didn't really want to." What a lucky man.

ALSACE

Poor old Alsace. Little-known abroad and scorned by most of the French, the wines of this thin strip of vineyards in the lee of the Vosges overlooking the German border span a range of qualities unappreciated by most of the world's wine lovers.

The French tend to look upon Alsace simply as a useful source of cheap Sylvaner to offer a cut above *vin de table* drinking. The hordes of German tourists who invade the region each weekend probably associate it with the milky *vin nouveau* they swig in the autumn and the piercing-clear new season's wine in spring. By rather better-educated wine drinkers throughout the world, Alsace is blessed for whistle-clean dry and fragrant Rieslings and Gewürztraminers that often provide the only safe choice on a dubious restaurant wine list.

But Alsace is capable of very much stronger stuff than this. Just as across the Rhine, with the same sort of grape varieties, ripeness is the key to great German wine, so it is with all of Alsace's higher levels of wine quality. Unlike Germany, however, there has been no rigid structure defining them – a fact which must have played a part in how under-appreciated they are. Nomenclature in Alsace tends to be a hotch-potch of words such as "Réserve," "Cuvée," "Traditionelle" and "Personnelle," awarded in different contexts and measures by different houses, often in letters almost too discreet for even the most diligent of label-students.

Small wonder then that the superior wines of Alsace have gone largely unmarked. But the late 1970s saw a much-needed agreement on legislation to sanction the very top wines of all: Vendange Tardive and, even richer, Sélection de Grains Nobles. The grapes must reach certain minimum levels of ripeness, measured as in Germany in degrees Oechsle. The Riesling, for instance, must in Alsace reach 95° to make a Vendange Tardive wine and 110° to make one of the very rare Sélections de Grains Nobles, while across the border in the Palatinate it needs 92° to be called an Auslese and 120° to reach the heady heights of Beerenauslese. The authorities, who are revered rather than feared in orderly, quality-conscious Alsace, must be given at least three days' notice of a grower's intention to pick such very special wines in order that they can tramp around the late autumn vineyards making sure the grapes are as ripe as is claimed. Further controls include inspection of each press-load and cask, as well as compulsory tasting of the wines.

The wonder of these wines, and those in the echelons immediately below them, is their life. They are extremely powerful, uncompromisingly straight wines when young, and have the potential for great longevity. As they go up the quality scale, they range from bone dry to more than 50 grams of residual sugar in a litre of Sélection de Grains Nobles wine from an exceptional year such as 1976. But even with a natural

sweetness equivalent to about a tablespoonful of sugar in each bottle, the wines are strong and steely in a way that puts them in a class apart from any other late-picked wines. Many of them can happily be drunk with the rich meat dishes of the region, flying high in the face of the most common wine-and-food rule of all.

Because their voices are so faint in the world of wine, the Alsace wine men tend to sing as a choir, which means that there is an attractive lack of rivalry among them – helped by the fact that some of the major houses are related by marriage in any case. It is sometimes said you must never

Despite a bit of gentle fertilisation, yields in Alsace vineyards are often kept to nearer 75 hectolitres per hectare than the 100 allowed by AC law.

Husseren-les-Châteaux –
south-facing plain can give
better wine than north-
facing slope in Alsace.

comment on the wines of one firm to another as you will almost certainly find yourself criticising your host's brother-in-law. This friendly spirit means that Alsace is much better organized than most wine regions in communal promotion, and eight of the bigger houses have joined together to form Les Grandes Maisons d'Alsace for joint promotions in Britain.

Because the region is relatively small, producing less than two per cent of France's total wine output, and has not yet managed to command very high prices for its wines (even 1976 Sélection de Grains Nobles wines could be found at under 120 francs a bottle in 1982), almost all firms are still family-owned, often by a family that has been in the business since the early seventeenth century. Most of them own some vineyards and buy in additional grapes, on long-term agreements, from owners of the tiny plots of vineyard that proliferate in this region where inheritances are still split between each heir. These small patches of vines are too small to make late-harvesting a viable proposition, either practically or financially, so Alsace is, unusually, a wine region in which "the cult of the small grower" is not strong. Most of the very best wines are made by a handful of the most punctilious houses, although (again unusually) some of the local co-operatives enjoy a fine reputation.

The two Dopffs of Riquewihr are effective ambassadors of the region, with Dopff au Moulin making some exciting wines at the top of the scale and Dopff et Irion responsible for clear-cut varietals (surely Alsace pioneered the concept of varietals?) named for individual vineyards. Both Louis Gisselbrecht and Schlumberger make some extremely good wines, but are less cosmopolitan.

For many, the Riesling from the Clos Ste Hune vineyard above Hunawihr, from Trimbach of Ribeauvillé, is the epitome of elegance in Alsace. The wines of Trimbach are irreproachably made to a recipe of great finesse. High in acidity and sometimes a little austere at first, they develop a character that locals, as they will, call feminine. Bernard Trimbach is responsible for the wines, and his charming master-of-*franglais* brother Hubert tells the world about them.

Marc Beyer does this job for his family firm Léon Beyer of Eguisheim, and must win the award for most dashing international representative of Alsace. His father Léon's wines are also characterized by handsome charm, being full-flavoured and broad in their appeal. In Gewürztraminers their Cuvée des Comtes d'Eguisheim regularly wins over those who had previously dismissed the variety as a blowsy trollop.

It was not difficult, however, to choose the single subject of this study. The firm Hugel et Fils have been making wine in Riquewihr since 1639 and, because of a determination to try for the very best from their own vineyards, and a willingness to invest in costly equipment before the rest, they are known throughout the world for the quality, richness and longevity of the wines at the top end of their range.

Hugel

The indefatigable Johnny Hugel tears round the narrow twisting lanes that dissect the vineyards above Riquewihr with the insouciance appropriate to one whose family have been entrenched there, making wine and the casks to put it in, for three and a half centuries.

Johnny is the middle one of the sons left by the much loved "Papa" Hugel when he died in 1980, three brothers who have, in that satisfactory way of so many French wine families, found a way of sharing out the work to their mutual satisfaction. Georgy is the oldest and looks after the purse-strings, the administration and sales in Paris and Belgium. André is the youngest, a youthful absent-minded-professor type in his early fifties, who scurries about in the regulation green Hugel boilersuit minding all forms of equipment, including the fleet of ancient trucks which have to fight their way through crowds averaging 20,000 visitors a day in season to the tiny walled town. Hugel's fifteenth-century cellars on the cobbled main street could not be more in the thick of it.

Like his brothers, and his mother renowned for her cooking, Johnny lives in the medieval town of Riquewihr; but he is probably the most cosmopolitan of the wine men of Alsace. He is responsible for the vineyards and for the vinification of the wines, but he is also Hugel's chief salesman and travels frequently in northern

Johnny Hugel, proud of the Sainte Catherine cask that has been in use since 1715, and proud of his wines that are yet to receive the recognition they deserve.

Hugel vineyards and, still in the huddled centre of Riquewihr, their original main cellars.

Europe and the United States.

Johnny is certainly keenly aware of the care needed to make good wine – the permanent crease-line between his deep-set eyes betrays that – but perhaps more importantly he is also aware of how his wines fit into context, both locally and worldwide. He adores the red wines of Bordeaux and still buys his clarets in London as a hangover from his first days selling in Britain. He has many friends there, and indeed it was Antonio Lopez at the Elizabeth restaurant in Oxford who introduced him to Hermitage La Chapelle 1961. He is slightly disillusioned with some Burgundy producers, but still admires the wines of de Vogüé enormously. He enthuses over great Hungarian Tokay (which is generous of him since he lead the campaign to save the use of the historic term Tokay d'Alsace for the Pinot Gris of Alsace in the face of misguided Eurocratic attempts to reserve it for Hungary).

Further afield he has been impressed by some of the Torres wines *("I have a couple of bottles of one of his unfiltered Viña Sols to give to my friends Louis Latour and Robert Drouhin")* as well as by a number of California winemakers, especially Walter Schug at Joseph Phelps. Philip Togni of Cuvaison, who once worked *chez* Hugel, showed Johnny round the back hills of the Napa, so that he is now convinced that's where the future for great, and subtle, California wine lies. He notes with a certain amount of relief that Alsace's most distinctive grape variety, Gewürztraminer, is safe from really elegant California imitation since it needs a wet June and July to precede two months of sunshine.

All this experience meant that Johnny Hugel was a natural candidate for the tasting team for the controversial Gault Millau "Wine Olympics," and for the "re-taste" organised by Robert Drouhin. (The Hugel wines did extremely well, although of course Johnny was not judging this section.) He is constantly organising banquets at which great wines of the world are compared by like-minded friends, all in the truest spirit of inquiry. He is exasperated by the average Frenchman's insularity concerning his national drink, and tells the story of how he was driven to lay on a far-too-special tasting for a visiting third-generation winemaker from Bordeaux, so patronising was he about the wines of Alsace. *"Alsace has always had enormous difficulty proving its identity,"* he bemoans. *"Even the Parisians don't know where it is."*

He also did cunning work in drawing up rules for Vendange Tardive wines so as to satisfy the all-important INAO (Appellation Contrôlée authorities). Hugel has been one of the few firms to give serious attention to these great wines of the region, so when in the late 1970s proper legislation was needed and it was the turn of Alsace to play host to the INAO convention, the Hugel family made sure the proceedings ended in their well-stocked cellars. The great 1921s and 1945s were poured. The Parisians, the Bordelais and the Burgundians were duly impressed – only to be told, isn't it a shame we're no longer allowed to sell these wines? Suitable regulations were duly drawn up.

Over this issue Johnny remained adamant that the terms Vendange Tardive and its even more glorious extension Sélection de Grains Nobles should be reserved for only the very best that Alsace could produce, and fought pressure to lower the minimum required must weights. With a similar fanaticism for quality he acted as Président of the first commission set up to delimit the special vineyards entitled to the new appellation, Alsace Grand Cru. There were problems with a plan as restricted as Monsieur Hugel's team suggested. *"I said publicly that I don't want to make Alsace another Chablis by downgrading everything,"* he says, describing the disbanding of his commission to make way for a team that was less restrictive.

The Hugels themselves own about 25 hectares of vineyard around Riquewihr, where the two most important sites are the steep, south-facing Schoenenbourg which, with its 40 feet of soil on a limestone and chalk base, is extremely good for Riesling and Muscat; and the gentler Sporen, whose heavier clayey slopes also catch maximum sunshine and are ideal for Gewürztraminer and Tokay. Only 5 per cent of their own grapes are of this exciting last variety, which

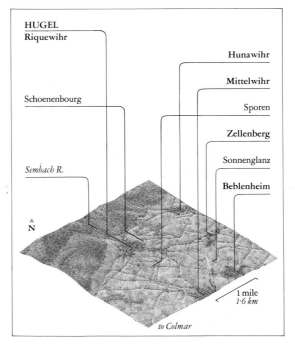

HUGEL
Riquewihr

Schoenenbourg

Sembach R.

N

Hunawihr

Mittelwihr

Sporen

Zellenberg

Sonnenglanz

Beblenheim

1 mile
1·6 km

to Colmar

Johnny Hugel admires for its longevity (he was delighted with the 1865 he drank on his fiftieth birthday) and likens to great Chardonnay when mature. They make a very little of their own Muscat (*"we drink it as an aperitif because we haven't yet found a food that goes well with it"*) and the rest of their vineyards are split equally between the two flagbearers of Alsace, the racy Riesling and the more galumphing Gewürztraminer.

The first *cuves* of grapes to be trundled up the village street to Hugel's almost impossibly tight receiving bay come from other growers' vineyards, however, which provide all of the firm's needs for their more basic wines. (Hugel, incidentally, are great proponents of Pinot Blanc rather than Sylvaner at this level.) At vintage time the cool air between the close-packed walls of Riquewihr's houses is heady with the smell of must, and there is, unless rain stops play, a crescendo of quality as the Hugels receive riper and riper grapes, carefully graded as they are weighed and examined. The most basic wines constitute well over half their output in a normal year. A notch above this is their Cuvée Tradition range, and quite noticeably more exciting is the Réserve Personnelle range on which they impose their own minimum quality and sugar levels. Even the most ungenerous vintage will usually produce some wine of Réserve Personnelle standard, but the rich Vendange Tardive wines are available in commercial quantities only every four or five years. Since the wonderful vintage of 1976, which Père Jean remembered as the best of his long life, only 1981 gave up a little. And the ultra-ripe grapes needed for Sélection de Grains Nobles appear even less frequently than this: there have been only nine Gewürztraminer "Hugel" Sélection de Grains Nobles since 1865.

The essence of winemaking in Alsace is, as they so proudly declare, to treat the grapes and resultant wine with as light a touch as possible. At Hugel this is particularly true. The grapes, never pumped and rarely even de-stemmed, are milled down into the presses through worn bronze rollers that must have been working when Johnny was born. Hugel was the first French firm to install a Vaslin press in 1958, and family folklore is that it was André who suggested they change the colour from dark green to today's pale yellow so as to make thorough cleaning a necessity. They say they find Willmes presses too hard and, further, insist on special stainless steel screws in their Vaslins because they avoid iron contamination and leave the must cleaner. In a typically efficient way they have worked out that the extra cost entailed by this is more than compensated for by the screws' longer life and what they save on must-cleaning treatments.

The must is settled in stainless steel tanks for up to twelve hours and then centrifuged before going, usually, to *wooden* casks of varying ages (their 1715 Ste. Caterine cask is reputedly the oldest still in use in the world) and varying capacities (very necessary when there may be so

Johnny's father Jean knew no vintage as great as the 1976 that produced this and other great dessert wines with unparalleled degrees of richness.

VENDANGE TARDIVE

SÉLECTIONNÉ PAR JEAN HUGEL

ALSACE
APPELLATION ALSACE CONTRÔLÉE

Fût 18

DEPUIS 1639

Sélection de Grains Nobles
TOKAY D'ALSACE "HUGEL"®

VENDANGE TARDIVE

700 ml e

MISE EN BOUTEILLE PAR HUGEL ET FILS·RIQUEWIHR·ALSACE·FRANCE

many different qualities of wine from the same vintage). With the 1981 vintage, however, André's young son Marc was allowed to experiment with a fermentation in stainless steel at about six degrees below the normal 20°C (68°F) in imitation of all he had seen, and been impressed by, on a trip to Australia in 1981. Johnny was convinced more by the need to let him test his hypothesis, that the aroma would be much more delicate, than by the hypothesis itself, but it will be fascinating to see how the likely next winemaker develops.

Wines are normally fermented right out, which usually takes between ten and twenty days, but took until July for some of the richest 1976s. Almost all wines, according to standard Johnny practice, spend some time in the large old, tartrate-lined casks, but they will normally try to get even great wines into bottle before the next vintage. It is an important tenet at Hugel that they never bottle and label at the same time, giving even the cheapest wines six months' rest and the Réserve Personnelle qualities up to two years. The 1976 Tokay d'Alsace "Hugel" Sélection de Grains Nobles, which Johnny thinks may be the greatest wine they ever produce, was not put on the market until 1982. Johnny says he likes his wines to have reached at least 80 per cent of their potential before putting them at the risk of consumption. This particular wine was picked at 135° Oechsle and the final wine has an alcoholic strength, like that year's greatest Gewürztraminer and the Vendange Tardive Riesling, of more than 13°. With the same sort of grapes, Palatinate winemakers turned out their Beerenauslesen with not much more than seven degrees of alcohol that year, demonstrating the fundamental differences in philosophy on either side of the Rhine. *"The Germans could produce wines like ours if they wouldn't sweeten them,"* is the somewhat peremptory way in which Johnny dismisses the everyday wines of Germany. *"Today our wines have almost more in common with Bergerac than Baden."* On the other hand, he generously maintains that the greatest white wine in the world is a Wehlener Sonnenuhr of a great year from J. J. Prüm.

At Hugel there is no shortage of family philosophies. There's the "Hugel way of bottling," which can be described as "water, water and more water." There's Johnny's famous explanation of the evils of over-fertilisation: *"You must never forget that the vine is a Mediterranean weed."* Or: *"A wine can never be better than the grapes which made it,"* with the coda on the inadvisability of over-oaking: *"I ought to try and make a Pinot Blanc with oak chips just to see how much Meursault I could get out of it."* Despite the fact that he seems to talk (and smoke) almost incessantly, Johnny Hugel is clearly a thinker, about food as well as about wine.

As a host, he is confident of his own wines, whether he is entertaining at the nearby l'Auberge de l'Ill (where he now represents the fourth generation of Hugels dining at the star-bedecked table of the fourth generation of Haeberlins) or putting some of his gastronomic theories to the test at home with his wife Simone. Although he seizes on any excuse to drink a good claret, he has demonstrated many a time how well his own wines go with main courses such as *gigot d'agneau* by offering guests the choice of, say, Château Montrose 1970 or his Tokay Vendange Tardive 1967. He also makes his more intimate friends eat the salad *with* the wine, and believes that a great wine will taste even greater with this notorious accompaniment. Cheese and wine as a combination he abhors, however. After years of experiment trying to match all sorts of wines with all sorts of cheeses, Johnny has given up on this well-known engagement on the basis that either battle or slaughter ensues.

Johnny will occasionally find time to fish, and likes to see as much as possible of his wife and daughters, in the white house next to Hugel's new underground cellars. One of his nieces has been drawing up official château boundaries in Bordeaux. Marc is studying under Johnny, his brother Étienne under André, and Georgy has his son Jean-Philippe following in his footsteps. It is all very neat, and the future of Hugel looks set fair into the next century.

They have been paid many compliments over the centuries, but one which pleased Johnny the most came from Ernesto Gallo who told him that his wines were the best he had tasted since he arrived in France – when Alsace was his last port of call. *"Every morning when I wake up,"* says this man who has no illusions about what makes the wine world tick, *"I give thanks to Mateus, Blue Nun and Gallo for what they do for us all."*

GERMANY

GERMANY

I t may seem futile to try to encapsulate all that is great about German wine in five short studies. Germany is capable of great, and indeed, unique, wines. Try as the viticultural testing stations might with their new crossings, almost all of Germany's finest wine is made from one grape, the Riesling. And try as the Australians, the Californians and the South Africans might, the Riesling achieves its most sublime in the northern climes of Germany, where it has to struggle right through to the end of October and sometimes later before it is properly ripe, thereby attracting all sorts of nuances and hints of this and that flavour that sing out individually when the wine is young, but in fine baroque harmony after they have been left alone for a while in bottle. For such a delicate style of wine, the Riesling takes on astonishing complexity over the years.

Because their methods tend to be so specifically geared to their cool climate and often extraordinary terrain, German winemakers are in general more isolated than the French. We go to worship but rarely to learn. There is simply no equivalent of the Rheingau or the Mosel anywhere else in the world. The tradition is that each is responsible for his own, unless he is a member of a co-operative in which case he may have his wine grapes fermented at one of the increasingly important Winzergenossenschaften. There is no buying-in or "trucking" grapes here. Send your mother-in-law up the hill for the grapes and get them into your own cellar as fast as possible.

Alcohol is one of the least-prized attributes of wine in Germany. Grapes will be graded according to their potential alcohol, but will rarely (though increasingly) be used to make a strong dry wine. What the German grower is looking for is a ripeness he will show off as fruitiness, balanced by refreshing acidity that will see the wine through many a year. Wines of top quality will never be chaptalised. But they may of course, much to the scorn of the French,

Picturesque, but expensive-to-work vineyards on the steep banks of the Mosel. "For some, a fine Mosel Auslese is the apogee of German winemaking."

have sweet unfermented grape must, Süss-reserve, added to enhance that peculiarly German quality of innocent and fragrant fruitiness.

This attractive quality is becoming noticeably more elusive, however, as an increasing number of German wines are made much drier, either *Trocken* or *Halbtrocken* (dry or half-dry). During the 1970s an enormous vogue for these wines developed within Germany itself, wines that can easily be drunk with food even when young; and it has reached such a point that some wine pundits even use the term "holy war" when describing the conflict between those for and against the new craze. Its advocates argue that Trocken wines are merely a reversion to the style of winemaking that was traditional when all German wines were fermented out to dryness, and methods for making *Süssreserve* "grape essence" were unknown. Its opponents maintain that the character of the fragrant Germanic grapes is best complemented with some residual sugar.

It will be fascinating to see whether these wines, sold under the somewhat hysterical slogan "Trocken ist In!," will wax or wane in Teutonic favour. So far they have not excited too much enthusiasm outside Germany; and by their most important foreign customers, the Americans, the British and the Japanese, it is the wonderful lusciousness of Beerenauslesen and Trockenbeerenauslesen that is most sought-after. These ultra-rich wines will always have a special place at the end of a meal along with the world's other great dessert wines from Sauternes, Tokay and Vouvray.

The greatness of Germany extends far further than this very rarefied sort of wine, and for many her sounder Spätlesen and most toothsome Auslesen represent the most useful treasure. There is something rather more versatile about wild flowers and honey than orchids and golden syrup. And such wines, provided they are well-made, can last for decades, gaining intriguing new flavours by the year.

For some, a fine Mosel Auslese is the apogee of German winemaking; and it is true that the Mosel is one of the few wine regions of the world where the very appearance of the countryside suggests to true wine connoisseurs the quality of the wines it produces. It is up in the reaches of the Saar and Ruwer valleys that this lightness, this almost steely quality, comes through most, and nowhere more than in wines from such enterprises as Egon Müller, von Schubert with the incredibly beautiful Maximin Grünhäuser label, and the "holy three," Bischöfliches Konvikt, Bischöfliches Priesterseminar and the Hohe Domkirche. And then in the heart of the Mosel valley proper there is perhaps the most famous German vineyard of all, the Bernkasteler Doktor, in which are two whose names adorn some of the very best Mosel wines, Dr Thanisch and the house of Deinhard. Just downstream from Bernkastel, almost within sight of this highly-favoured pocket handkerchief of a vineyard, is the base of perhaps the most revered name in the Mosel, J. J. Prüm.

The Rheingau is rather more classically German, representing a refinement of the sort of style of wine produced in other regions along the Rhine. These are fuller, rounder wines, many from ancient family estates and each showing a distinctly different character. One of the most famous of these is Schloss Vollrads, partly because of the extraordinary energy devoted to it and German wines in general by its present master, Graf Erwein Matuschka-Greiffenclau. There are others that have as enviable a track record, including Schloss Reinhartshausen and Schloss Schönborn. These are producing delicious wines at the moment, as are the hundreds of fine individual producers in the mould of Dr Weil, a newcomer to the Rheingau with not much more than a hundred years of experience.

The Nahe can occasionally lay claim to "greatness" in winemaking, with wines of great style coming from the cellars of those such as Paul Anheuser. Of the more southerly wine regions of Germany it is the Rheinpfalz or Palatinate that has such a distinctive and world-famous style of its own. Although in its outlying areas there is every new-fangled grape variety and wine-type, in the heart of the region around Deidesheim and Wachenheim are the "big three" Bs, producers von Buhl and, perhaps rather better known, Bassermann-Jordan and Bürklin-Wolf, who still concentrate on Riesling.

So many winemakers in Germany have something to offer. Those that follow achieve a consistency in their output that is admirable, as well as being fascinating characters in their own right.

State Cellars, Eltville

In Western Europe, Germany is unique in having the government turn its hand to producing wine on a commercial scale. Most major wine-producing countries have officially-backed research stations and oenological schools, but Germany's State Wine Domains are expected to make a profit from selling fine wine, as well as taking a lead in new techniques in the vineyard and cellar. The biggest of these, the Verwaltung der Staatsweingüter in Eltville, is responsible for many of the great names of the Rheingau – Steinberger, Erbacher Marcobrunn, Hochheimer Domdechaney, Rauenthaler Baiken – and is the largest individual wine estate in Germany. At its head is Dr Hans Ambrosi.

When Hans Ambrosi gets round to writing his autobiography, which he undoubtedly will, having already written well over twenty books and guides about German wines and eating-places, he might consider "The Reluctant Bureaucrat" as a possible title. "Administration I hate," he says cheerfully. "Having grown up in the vineyard I'm a practical man." Hardly what you would expect from the leader of Germany's major official wine enterprise.

For a start he is not even German. He was born, in 1925, in the middle of Rumania's hilly wine country and did not leave until he was 21. In 1981 he returned to his homeland for the

"Enfant terrible" Professor Dr Hans Ambrosi in the cloister.

first time, taking his own family on holiday there, only to find sheep and cows grazing on the old, untended vineyards, much to his fury. It is ironic that he should be so disgusted by the effects of state intervention there when he is such a leading light of the phenomenon as practised in West Germany.

With his solid wine background he came to Germany to study viticulture, which at that time meant a start in general agricultural studies in Stuttgart, before moving on to the rather more rarefied atmosphere at Geisenheim, Germany's world-famous wine research institute in the Rheingau. By a stroke of what he claims is luck, he chose as the subject of his doctorate a study of Germany's achievements in relation to the rest of the world in the field of clonal selection. Fortunately for the young research student, the results of this study were to show the Germans in a most flattering light: they were almost fifty years ahead of the French, and streets ahead of the only other two nations to take seriously this genetic sorting process in the vineyard, Austria and Luxembourg.

The vineyards of the Duke of Nassau which form the basis of the Eltville domain today were taken over by the Prussian government in 1866, just in time for phylloxera to strike. To set the necessary example to private vineyard owners, the Prussians instituted a thorough programme of plant selection, by checking hereditary background as well as by marking the best performers, so that in the early years of the twentieth century they had set up the world's first clonal selection process. Thanks to this zeal for health and efficiency in the vineyard, Hans Ambrosi was able to report in the early 1950s that Germany was way ahead of France, where clonal selection had only just been introduced and even today is ignored in many great wine regions (see Château Haut-Brion for an exception to this rule).

Although the French agree that vineyard hygiene is important, they are not at all enthusiastic about that second goal of clonal selection, higher yields. To the German vine-grower there is nothing shameful about producing 80 or 90 hectolitres of good wine from one hectare of vineyard, while his counterpart in Bordeaux or Burgundy may be limited by law to a yield of only 35 hectolitres and high-yielding vines are therefore of little use to him. Ambrosi argues that this derives from the French habit of equating quality with alcohol, whereas the Germans are looking for fruit and acidity and actually want to make light-bodied wines.

After leaving Geisenheim as something of a star, Hans Ambrosi went out as sole representative of German viticulture to the University of Stellenbosch in South Africa in 1955. "They didn't even know what I was talking about there," he remembers of his first attempts to introduce clonal selection on the Cape, "even though they would specially fly out a bull from England for animal breeding." He soon had them licked into shape, however, and taught table grafting extensively as a much less brutal and more effective alternative to the field grafting that was then practised.

While he was there he met his wife, and brought her back to her native Germany in 1966 having secured the important post of director at Eltville. She was later to bring him enormous added prestige by finding, on one of her frequent amateur archeological forays in the region, a Roman pruning knife that at last proved that viticulture is as old in Dr Ambrosi's Rheingau as in the Rheinpfalz and Mosel.

Dr Ambrosi has thrown himself into his task with such a degree of dynamism, ingenuity and sheer commercial acumen that the ancient walls and traditional slopes in his charge can hardly comprehend it all. To achieve as much as he has, must take a strong streak of ambition, but he is happiest when playing the downtrodden iconoclast. *"We are just civil servants, you know. We get the same money whatever we do,"* he will say with his special miserable look, which can change in an instant to one filled with mischief, as when adding: *"I have a lot of trouble with the authorities. Some of the high-ups think I am too informal, but in my researches I learned to think uncomplicatedly and so I am naturally very direct."*

Although he is still fascinated by research, one of the latest projects being to ensure that by trellising all vines can benefit from a high leaf wall so as to maximise ripening (*"the Swiss showed how important this is in cool climates, but look at the Burgundians who continue to train low and even snip off the young shoots . . ."*), he does not see his chief responsibilities in either the vineyard or the cellar. *"With all the sophisticated information and help available on wine production now, you have to be a fool not to get a clean wine into a bottle. But to sell it for a high price, that's much more of a problem."* As trend-setter in Germany's wine world, Ambrosi sees it as his responsibility to lead the way towards more realistic prices and marketing. In his large and impersonal bureaucrat's office he has neat, carefully-updated graphs showing that over the last few years the prices of German wine have failed to keep pace with the increase in the cost of producing it. *"In recent years,"* he could say in 1981, *"we have been lucky with some relatively big vintages, but now it is necessary to increase our prices a little, which means we have to promote our wines."* He admires Graf Matuschka's efforts in this direction (as described on page 145), and must feel they represent one of the few manifestations of ingenuity in the Rheingau

recently which have not emanated from himself.

Hans Ambrosi must have been very persuasive with his Ministerial masters to introduce his series of ingenious schemes to inject new life into the estates he administers and the way their wines are sold. Among these the Kloster Eberbach, a breathtaking old Cistercian monastery built in the twelfth century in the gentle wooded foothills of the Taunus Mountains and inherited by the Staatsweingüter, has played a major part. He is eager to re-energise the building and make it "less of a mausoleum." Certainly when one considers the energy generated by its occupants in the past, it is painful to see the deserted monks'

The twelfth-century Cistercian monastery Kloster Eberbach, transformed into education and sales centre.

More Cistercian
construction work, *above,*
the wall round the famous
Steinberger vineyard,
Germany's answer to Clos
de Vougeot, and, *right,*
experimental plantings
above Kloster Eberbach.

dormitory and empty vaulted chambers.

Now, thanks to Ambrosi's fertile imagination, the abbey comes alive on all sorts of
occasions throughout the year. In 1971 he instituted the annual wine fair at which young wines
from all over the Rheingau are shown to the
German wine trade in dizzying numbers. Under
the medieval arches, efficient pourers administer
tier upon tier of bottles, samples of the hundreds
of wines available for sale here. Ambrosi is proud
that this, a little like the Hospices de Beaune
auction in Burgundy each November although
with fixed prices and less tedious, is seen as a
price-indicator for the merchants who come each
April. As for himself, he reckons to have decided
on his own prices by the beginning of January. *"I
have to for my export customers, you see. If you
delay they just lose interest. In fact, I have
learned to tell the quality of a vintage even from
the grapes as they hang on the vine. And even
earlier than that, you can forecast quantity by
putting a bud under a microscope. We were the
first to sell so early."*

Another bright idea was dreamed up in 1973
by Ambrosi together with the irrepressible Professor Helmut Becker of Geisenheim (a sort of
freewheeling Ambrosi), Bernhard Breuer and
Hans Jochim Guntrum, and it has had even
wider-reaching effects. The German Wine
Academy, an English-language intensive course
in German wine lore, is now held about six times
a year. Kloster Eberbach provides the setting for
many of the lectures as well as for the candlelit
farewell dinner in the refectory, at which

Ambrosi quizzes each student before presenting
beautifully-engraved certificates as evidence of
their having taken part in this brilliant public
relations exercise. There are now well over 1,500
"graduates," many of them American as the
course is popular with GIs stationed across the
Rhine from the precious slopes of the Rheingau.
Ambrosi has since taken the instruction idea
afloat, with wine seminars aboard a Rhine cruiser
that stops off at all likely wine points.

The scheme on which he is currently engaged involves revitalising the old "Cabinet"
cellar of Kloster Eberbach, which he reckons to
have proved gave rise to the familiar German
wine term Kabinett. He plans to store 100,000
bottles of the very best wines of the very best
years from the state vineyards there. He will be
persuasive indeed if he can cajole the authorities
into allowing him to use the (retracted) term
Cabinet officially. We shall see.

He has no shortage of great wines to store
away in his treasure trove. Within his empire are
six estates, west to east along the Rhine at Assmannshausen, Rüdesheim, the Steinberg/Hat-
tenheim vineyards, Rauenthal, Hochheim and
Bensheim/Heppenheim in the Hessische Bergstrasse. Unusually for Germany, the 193-hectare
estate produces a sizeable quantity of (light) red
wine thanks to the Assmannshausen speciality,
and almost 10 per cent of the total vineyard is
planted in Spätburgunder or Pinot Noir. Riesling accounts for about three-quarters of the
state vines, however, and produces wonderfully
rich, firm Rheingau classics from the vineyards
on the gentle south-facing slopes.

Ambrosi's most famous site is the Steinberger vineyard, all of a neat walled piece just
below the road to Kloster Eberbach. Comparisons with that other plot of famous vines walled

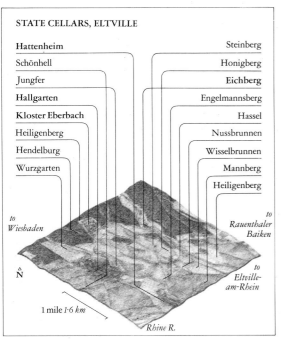

STATE CELLARS, ELTVILLE

Hattenheim	Steinberg
Schönhell	Honigberg
Jungfer	Eichberg
Hallgarten	Engelmannsberg
Kloster Eberbach	Hassel
Heiligenberg	Nussbrunnen
Hendelburg	Wisselbrunnen
Wurzgarten	Mannberg
	Heiligenberg

to Wiesbaden

to Rauenthaler Baiken

N

to Eltville-am-Rhein

1 mile 1·6 km

Rhine R.

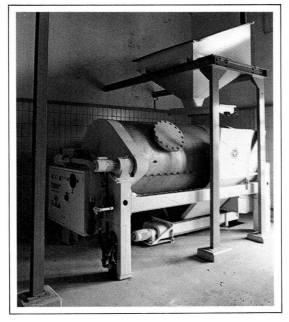

After crushing in the airtight press, *above left*, the wine is held in the stainless steel tanks, *above*, for short periods, given a few months in the traditional oak lurking in the wings.

by the Cistercians at Clos Vougeot are inevitable, and Dr Ambrosi is clearly envious of all the high jinks they get up to at the bigger Burgundy site. Steinberger encompasses 32 hectares (as compared with about 50 at Clos Vougeot) and is managed meticulously by Franz Zweifler, as is necessary for such an easily-identifiable vineyard. Some weeds are allowed to grow between the rows, but only to promote the aeration discouraged by tractor work, so visitors should not be shocked.

Grapes from here, and all vineyards except those at Assmannshausen and in the Bergstrasse, go to the cellars in Eltville at which Dr Ambrosi is based, to be crushed as rapidly as possible. The contrast between the romantic and traditional as suggested by Kloster Eberbach and the starkly functional cellars at Eltville (56-62 Schwalbacher Strasse) is salutary. At Eltville Georg Retzel looks after everything in a most workmanlike fashion. Willmes tank presses are covered with an outer steel cylinder to keep the whole process as anaerobic as possible. Dr Ambrosi's favourite descriptive word for wines is "racy," and his staff are clearly in agreement that everything possible must be done to keep this term appropriate.

One of the great problems is the large number of different wines made in every vintage, with several qualities from so many different vineyards. There are accordingly tanks of all sizes, down to tiny stainless steel ones that look like front-loading washing machines. These await the aftermath of a sufficiently warm summer and autumn to fill them with Beerenauslesen or even Trockenbeerenauslesen. Because of the part of the State Cellars' function which Ambrosi likens to that of a "model farm," each batch of wine produced is subject to rigorous tests and examinations so that, as well as producing wine for consumption, the domain is effectively producing wine for researchers too.

Underneath the workmanlike offices and attached winemaking areas (complete with Coca Cola machine) is an extraordinary modern,

Georg Retzel, *far right*, "dean of the Eltville cathedral of wine," housing more than 750,000 bottles of wine such as this.

temperature-controlled wine warehouse. Seven pallets high, are 780,000 bottles of state wine, all packed in the rather menacing cartons stamped with the black Prussian eagle (on which Ambrosi is not too keen). The warehouse was excavated and completed in 1976 and is uncannily quiet. Only the gentle whirr of the single forklift truck disturbs the silence of what Ambrosi calls this "cathedral" of wine, with Herr Retzel as dean.

He is left largely to his own devices, but Ambrosi is particularly involved with his own technique for making the much sought-after Eiswein. Unlike some other producers, such as Graf Matuschka of Schloss Vollrads, Dr Ambrosi is very enthusiastic about this additional frill on Germany's wine habit, calling it "one of my great enthusiasms." After trying out various methods, including putting a whole truckload of grapes in the cold room overnight, he has developed a method whereby the grapes are specially trained to grow between 2 feet 6 inches and 3 feet above the ground, and can easily be covered by plastic bags to concentrate the juice and prolong their life on the vine, right through to the frosts of December and January.

His is an unorthodox view. He purposely chooses the healthiest grapes that are not affected by noble rot, which he argues has a weakening effect, and that his Eiswein therefore lasts better than most Beerenauslese. *"Eiswein is still not accepted, and is thought of generally as a parvenu of a wine. But for me the ultimate gauge is the auction prices, and they provide the answer that Eiswein is very fine indeed."* To repeat, Hans Ambrosi has no qualms about commerce.

Wines of Spätlese quality and above receive a little time in wood and may well not be bottled for a couple of years. Dr Ambrosi would like to see the bottling and labelling carried out up the road at Kloster Eberbach, and is very distressed that his precious black wine fungus that has lined the walls of the cellars there is now starting to peel off because there are no longer sufficient wine organisms in the atmosphere. This must be one of the subjects he continually raises at those monthly meetings with "the authorities."

With much travelling and many friends around the world, Dr Ambrosi has an impressive wine cellar of his own, containing a wider range of wines than is usually found in Germany. He does not allow that there are any really good Rieslings made outside Germany, however. Yes, he knows the ultra-ripe richness of Gunter Brözel's Edelkeur made at Nederburg on the Cape; but really, when you're talking at this level, it is surely the man who is more important than the grapes, is it not?

Schloss Vollrads

Erwein Graf Matuschka-Greiffenclau is one of the most extraordinary young men in the wine world today. For most people, the challenge of being a twenty-seventh-generation proprietor of a top Rheingau property in need of restoration and renovation would have been quite enough to keep them occupied since taking over in 1977. For the tall, dark count this was not nearly enough. After all, there is a handful of others throughout the wine world who could claim a similar sort of background. Graf Matuschka wanted to do something really different.

His training had been in the law and economics, but he was recalled to the somewhat dilapidated family home and wine estate in 1965 when it became clear that his elder brother would prefer a career in radio and television journalism to one at Schloss Vollrads. This was not a particularly happy time, however, for although his father preferred politics to serious work on the estate (which was at last possible in the way that it never had been when the family's stand against Hitler counted), Erwein was supposed to stick to bookkeeping rather than tackle the more challenging work himself. Before long he was sales manager for a German Sekt firm, and so good at

it that he was offered a three-year contract to be responsible for Olivetti's sales in Germany.

When he eventually settled back into the massive eighteenth-century family Schloss above Winkel on the Rhine, he naturally looked around for the sort of "opening in the market" that his previous training had taught him to find. Graf Matuschka looked at how German wines were drunk and compared it with the role of wine in the more southerly European countries. He noticed that in countries such as West Germany, where per capita consumption was less than 20 litres a year, wine would not normally be drunk with meals. This led him to question the habits of generations and to formulate the view that they were misguided, and that German wines could be extremely good with food, thereby doubling (at least) their potential popularity. *"You see, our German wines can be much less complicated than many other wines with food,"* he explains. *"Even white burgundy can be very heavy, with too much alcohol and glycerine to be really comfortable with food, which is usually high in fats and so on anyway. People all over the world are leading more sedentary lives, and they seek good health even more. They have to be able to drive after drinking. Everywhere you look, people are turning to lighter food and drink. In Japan, they are turning away from the traditional saké. In the US there is the strong trend away from spirits to wine. In France they have turned to* nouvelle cuisine, *and here in Germany we are eating much lighter foods than we did, say, in the 1930s. The high acidity in our wines breaks down fats efficiently, and does a quite different job to French wines."*

He accordingly launched, and continues, an almost solo but extremely effective worldwide campaign to persuade wine-drinkers to drink German wines with their meals, by means of extremely practical, and often delicious, demonstration. The grandest of these have the grandest of names. At a Lukullische

For Graf Matuschka German wines must be seen to be at home on the dining table.

SCHLOSS VOLLRADS

RHEINGAU
1979er KABINETT
blausilber · Riesling
Qualitätswein mit Prädikat

Verband
deutscher
Prädikatswein-
Versteigerer

Unsere Mitglieder
besitzen Lagen
von Weltruf!

Vereinigung
Rheingauer
Weingüter e.V.

Erzeugerabfüllung
Graf Matuschka-
Greiffenclau
Oestrich-Winkel
Rheingau

Deutschland
A.P.Nr.

27074 002 80
e 750 ml

Weinprobe, over a meal of up to six (small, light) courses, Graf Matuschka will demonstrate how different wines taste with different foods, and how well the German wines he selects complement them.

The first of these, for an invited and gastronomically influential audience, took place on November 15, 1978, just over a year after he took over at Schloss Vollrads, and was held like so many of them within the awesome gilded dark blue walls of the castle's grandest dining room. Today, groups can book one of these sessions for themselves, and frequently do. Graf Matuschka has already convinced many of his countrymen of his revolutionary ideas, and almost all the wine he sells within Germany is either Trocken or Halbtrocken and specifically designed to be drunk with meals.

Foreigners have been a little more difficult to win over (only 35 per cent of his wines exported are dry), but the Graf continues to organise Lukullische Weinproben for gourmets around the world. In 1980 he preached in eleven cities throughout the United States, in London and, showing extreme daring, in Paris. In 1981 it was the turn of Oslo, Japan and Holland. His audience in London was the most difficult to convince, apparently. Even the Parisians showed more enthusiasm – but that may have been because he realised he would have to wheel out the big guns for such a chauvinistic stronghold, and accordingly treated them to an 1862 which quite took even Gallic breath away.

It would of course be easy to conclude from the energetic Graf's efforts that he is principally motivated by commercial considerations and the likely effect on sales of his own wines. He admits that many people leave his feasts with the firm resolution to try out more Schloss Vollrads wines. His campaigning has also resulted in at least sixty of Germany's top restaurants listing Schloss Vollrads. He points out, however, that the ultimate effect of his activities, if successful, will be to increase the consumption and prestige of good German wines in general.

His plans gained definition as a result of some International Food Organisation research which showed that we all have a maximum capacity for liquids, and that therefore wine is competing against all other beverages and will only be chosen in situations in which it can be shown to give sufficient pleasure or benefit to compensate for its extra cost. *"Only with food does wine have a special place,"* claims Graf

Matuschka. *"As with all beverages, it is the acidity that is the most important thing for 'the fresh-up.' It is important though that the acidity is not too aggressive, which is why our Halbtrocken wines are usually best-suited to food. Trocken wines are normally too dry and the acidity is too apparent. It is important to balance the sweetness in the food, such as the apparent sweetness that most sauces, vegetables, and meats such as liver have, with the amount of sweetness in the wine."*

Towards the end of the London Lucullan wine tasting he gave a short but learned speech on his efforts to find wines to go with fruits such as apples, pears, rhubarb and passion fruit, only to be asked, somewhat sardonically, whether he had managed to find a wine that went with that culinary fad the kiwi fruit. *"On the kiwi fruit, we are working"* was the solemn and preoccupied reply. It can be tough when you have to view every mouthful as necessary research. Graf Matuschka also admits that he has little time to cook himself, although he is extremely curious about the way the dishes he tastes are prepared. His official feasts at the Schloss are prepared by the chef from a nearby "one-star" restaurant, but he has recently given himself the chance to take a much more active role in the world of solids as well as liquids by opening, first, a casual country inn for visitors to his magnificent wine estate, and then in 1981 a fully-fledged restaurant in Winkel. The Graues Haus is the "oldest stone living-house in Germany," in direct translation of course, and housed what was presumably the more humble Greiffenclau family in the twelfth century.

It is clear from the hallowed position occupied by the Michelin guide in Graf Matuschka's otherwise unadorned Mercedes that it is his bible. He claims that with the Graues Haus he is not aiming for rosettes, however, but simply sticking to local country cooking as a complement to good Rheingau wines. He may be mistaken in supposing lime-spiked finger bowls are commonplace in the homes of his neighbours, but no matter. There is the chance here to eat well and imaginatively while drinking from a range of 120 local wines (mainly from the smaller estates and only one from Schloss Vollrads) presented in almost bewildering detail on the sixteen-inch-square wine list. From this unwieldy document visitors may learn more than most amateur geologists about the substrata of the Taunus mountains, and as much as the Graf

Opposite, the moated tower in which Matuschka snatches the odd moment to study the family archives, in between making wines such as this fresh, dry Riesling designed to be drunk with food.

himself about the rules on what to drink with fresh as opposed to smoked salmon. (Such a dedicated and concerned host is Graf Matuschka that he will telephone the efficient manageress Fräulein Schick in the middle of her night off to provide a sound translation for English guests of some obscure game on the menu.)

He eats out almost every night, but luckily has the physique that can take such treatment. His great height was imported into the family by his mother, the Countess Clara, who still lives with him in the vast living quarters that comprise a large portion of the country baroque pile that skirts the courtyard and gardens. Unlike the equally impressive Kloster Eberbach just a few miles east, Schloss Vollrads is most certainly a home. With its long approach up through the vineyards it is very imposing indeed, and is still an important winemaking site.

Indeed there is so much space under the 7,400 square yards of tiles above the outbuildings of the Schloss that Graf Matuschka has now added another vineyard to his empire, and from the 1980 vintage has crushed the grapes from the 15-hectare Fürst Löwenstein estate just over the hill between Schloss Vollrads and the village of Hattenheim. Graf Matuschka is delighted by the twenty-year agreement which gives him much more wine to sell, about 500,000 bottles in all each year, and adds a range of wines from heavier sandy loam that mature faster than the taut, lean, aristocratic wines produced on Schloss Vollrads' 47 hectares of lime and loess. (He adds nonchalantly that there would even be room to add a third property – such are the advantages of inheriting an estate designed to house all its workers.)

Graf Matuschka has also inherited a tradition of selling all the wines simply as Schloss Vollrads, with no individual vineyard attribution. He is well aware that his own family's wines are characterised by a noticeably high level of acidity, and that many of them need quite a time before they develop their inherent potential. Even lightish vintages can blossom into succulence after many years in bottle, and he evinces some of his 1963s and 1972s to make this point.

Almost all of the wines at Schloss Vollrads are 100 per cent Riesling, and an increasing proportion of them are either Trocken or Halbtrocken. As he points out, it is much more difficult to make a good dry wine than one in which the sweetness can be used to mask a slight fault. What he is after is a sort of steely purity, a taste

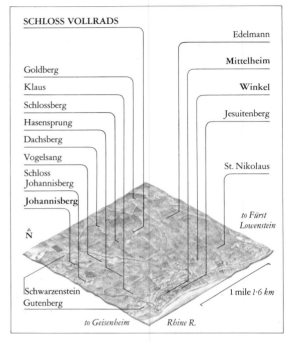

that is very fresh and racy, whatever the wine's age, and thanks to his extremely sympathetic young winemaker he usually manages to achieve this. Georg Senft was identified as the right man, when Graf Matuschka was interviewing the dozen possible candidates, by his reply to the test question: *"What do you do once the wine has fermented and is put into cask?"* The correct answer was: *"I sleep and let the wine get on with its own development."*

Senft had trained in Austria and studied in Franconia, so was already experienced with "dry" wines. He also shares the Graf's desire to do as little as possible to the wine. All cleaning treatments are applied before fermentation so as to allow the bouquet to develop without interference. There is room for all wines to spend a few weeks in wood at Schloss Vollrads (though by no means total reliance on oak as at some of the more traditional estates). The main purpose of this short spell in the barrel is to precipitate the tartrates as naturally as possible.

Bottling time must be a particularly nerve-wracking one at Schloss Vollrads, for the ingenious Graf has devised a complicated labelling and capsuling code whereby combinations of colours denote different degrees of sweetness and quality. To quote from his explanatory leaflet: *"Dry wines carry a silver strip neck-label stating Trocken. In addition their capsules have two silver bands and the main labels a silver frame.''* It was Hugh Johnson who suggested wine-lovers take a course in shipping signals before attempting to familiarise themselves with the Schloss Vollrads system.

The Graf is at least extremely generous with the printed material describing his wares, and supplies advice on keeping possibilities in general. Many other German wine producers must be amazed to read his advice that even his Qualitätswein (ordinary QbA) can last up to six years. He suggests Spätlesen be drunk between six and ten years, Auslesen between ten and fifteen, and some of the rich wines the estate produced in 1975 and 1976 may last more than thirty years.

By a quirk of nature, the Graf had still not had the chance to make a "real" Spätlese since his first vintage in 1977 in the first five years of his reign. Older hands may speculate that he will shift the focus of his attentions a little away from dry wines once given the opportunity to make really rich Schloss Vollrads, but he gives every impression of great determination. His forecast is that by 1986 almost all the wine produced in Germany will be dry. As a proprietor he is unusual in combining great personal involvement in his estate's produce with a willingness to delegate. He says somewhat ruefully that it was his Olivetti days that taught him the value to employees of delegation, and today he acts "as a ghost." He puts each slice of vineyard in the personal charge of an estate worker, and claims to have the lowest number of men per acre of any estate in Germany, and some of the happiest.

However sceptical some observers may be about the Graf's theories and dry forecasts, no one can deny the enormous amount that he has achieved in such a short time. The estate was in need of a generation prepared to make a major contribution to its fabric, and a very good job he has made of it. (His younger brother works for the official wine organisation in Mainz, thereby bridging the gap between the family's two major interests.)

The interior of the castle is now in very grand condition, although Graf Matuschka points out sternly that every room has to earn its keep, as reception centre or setting for one of his Lucullan evenings. In the lofty salon hung with ancient portraits and decorated with huge flower arrangements, the Graf will entertain guests to wine tastings, but always with a lesson in mind.

Inside the Schloss, "every room has to earn its keep."

Schloss Vollrads, in the heart of the Rheingau's tourist country.

ski enthusiast) he confesses to a great respect for the Rieslings of Alsace and, unusually, Luxembourg. Perhaps the Luxembourg love is not so strange; these wines have something of the raciness of his own. He also greatly admires some of the California Johannisberg Rieslings – notably Chateau St Jean and Joseph Phelps, and has no hesitation in drooling over top-flight claret. Lynch-Bages, Pichon Lalande and Cantemerle are slightly lower-ranking favourites.

He is perplexed and saddened by the indifference to his finest wines he finds in Britain, especially in view of the fact that the price differential between the best and the worst Germany has to offer is so much less than its counterpart for the Britons' love, claret. His most faithful customers are in the United States, but his second biggest following outside Germany is in Japan. His 1981 visit there, during which he advocated the combination of his style of wine with raw fish and their sort of soya-poached meats, has clearly borne fruit. (He found himself preaching at the same time as Paul Bocuse was spreading the nouvelle-cuisine-with-French-wine gospel to the Japanese.)

He has become an international figure in the wine world, as all those Japanese signatures in the visitors' book at Vollrads bear witness, not to mention his many-striped postbag, as likely as not containing a parcel labelled "A Bit of Louisiana for Graf Matuschka," or some such.

He works hard not only at his own estate's reputation, but also at that of great German wine in general, being president of an organisation with an unbelievably cumbersome name that represents the German (self-elected) equivalent of Bordeaux's *crus classés* – all this as well as being consultant to a big American computer firm.

Although his approach to selling wine is so innovative, Graf Matuschka is fascinated by the traditions that have produced him. In the romantic medieval moated tower that dominates Schloss Vollrads he is occasionally to be found studying the family archives, which go back only as far as 1630 admittedly, but still give some insight and, of course, useful background for his theories. He has been particularly delighted by the discovery that, in the Middle Ages, wine was prescribed as a much healthier alternative to water by everyone from the doctor to the priest.

There is no question of simply assessing and appreciating each wine on its own merits. You must compare, see how this wine tastes after that, as opposed to after a bit of bread. See? See how the food makes the difference? Within minutes he is likely to be discussing just exactly what proportion of vinegar should be allowed into a salad dressing for wines of different quality levels. And with what sorts of oil. The man is unstoppable. The spice of life for him is to assess the impact of different wines and foods on his senses. He once took part in a tasting sponsored by a glass manufacturer which proved that people could not recognise the same wine served in four different sorts of glasses. (He continues to use traditional Rohmers for tastings.) And he is always comparing the wines of other producers and other countries.

Very sportingly (but then he is a great sportsman – veteran of the Winkel football team, ex-racing driver, ice hockey player, handball and

Von Bassermann-Jordan

It is perhaps appropriate that the man at the head of the Rheinpfalz's only "all-wood" wine enterprise is also distinguished as an art historian. His solid eighteenth century house is a showcase for the *objets*, paintings and furniture he has either inherited or acquired. The labyrinth of cellars below has a wine-related antique, or even archeological, find at every turn. It is hardly surprising that this is one of the last bastions of oak in Germany.

Ludwig von Bassermann-Jordan is amused by the preoccupation of his many American visitors with the exact type of oak used in his cellars. He remains faithful to wood as the ideal fermenting and storing material for its physical properties. The exchange of air and wood may allow more evaporation than the stainless steel used by his neighbours, but gives a gentleness of pace to his careful winemaking process. The oak, which may come from Germany, Yugoslavia or France, is chemically treated after being made up in order to denude it of flavour, and is shaped into the ideal oval-faced form which is better for the deposit of yeast cells than circular-faced barrels, and allows more wine to be stored per square metre of cellar space. All of these barrels at Bassermann-Jordan have up to 2500-litre capacity, and if well treated they can last up to eighty years.

From wine press to bottle, Bassermann-

Jordan wines are in contact only with wood and Dr Bassermann-Jordan acknowledges it is worthwhile continuing this costly indulgence only if the quality of the "raw material" warrants it. What he means is that he has only the best grapes, from the best local sites. In 1981 94 per cent of his enviably-placed 65 hectares of vines were planted with Riesling, and by 1986 he intends to increase this to 100 per cent. Not that he

Ludwig von Bassermann-Jordan in the vineyards above Forst such as produced the Auslese treasure, *below*.

Aus dem Rheinpfalz Weingüte Deidesheim Geh-Rat Dr. v. Basser- mann-Jordan

SON VITE VITA

1976er Forster Ungeheuer
Riesling Auslese

Qualitätswein mit Prädikat
Erzeugerabfüllung, A.P. Nr. 5 106 064 19 77

Germany's best wine library is just a few feet above her most fascinating wine museum, containing vintages from 1706.

thinks ill of the many new crossings that proliferate in the Rheinpflaz in less favoured sites, but his customers "prefer Riesling." And who can blame them, once they have tasted the firm, spicy style of the Bassermann-Jordan range. They are the most important owners of that jewel of the region, the Forster Jesuitengarten vineyard, which many visitors may be surprised to see is now planted to the "high culture" system with 1½ metres between rows so that tractors can easily work the neat and gently sloping rows. This is a long way from the Mosel!

Although they have been vineyard owners since 1718, the Jordan family are relative parvenus in comparison with the great age of the

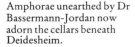

Amphorae unearthed by Dr Bassermann-Jordan now adorn the cellars beneath Deidesheim.

original property of which there were records in 1250. With such a background it was not so extraordinary that Ludwig's father was to become Germany's foremost wine historian, writing the definitive history and many other books about the grape in Germany. The German Agricultural Society has established the Friedrich von Bassermann-Jordan medal for those who make exceptional contributions in the same field.

Ludwig developed his interest in art history and archeology while studying at Freiburg university in the 1950s, and the interests of the two generations have dove-tailed nicely. In a cluster of little chambers in the garden is one of the best wine libraries in Germany, smelling of dust and damp paper. The shelves are crammed with an assortment of volumes of all ages and

provenances. Down below is an equally, perhaps more, impressive library of wine bottles, with vintages from 1706 and every vintage since 1880, making 10,000 bottles in all.

A tour of the cellars with Dr Bassermann-Jordan and his very pretty wife is fascinating – the Doktor supplies information about the wines and antiquities, Frau B-J about exactly whose house you are under at any point. They both travel abroad extensively, and have a very educated view of how their wines fit into the wine spectrum. They particularly enjoyed a visit to California in 1980, where they found Cabernets they thought could be compared with the best Bordeaux has to offer, but were relieved to observe that the Johannisberg Rieslings present no enormous threat to their own wines yet.

Dr Bassermann-Jordan has great respect for the intelligence and ingenuity of California's winemakers, however, one of his most admired being the Geisenheim-trained Walter Schug at Joseph Phelps. He is frequently visited by Americans, and *"could talk for hours"* with them about the minute problems of winemaking, so refreshing does he find the native American frankness. Like so many Europeans, he enjoys the constant discovery, resulting from a totally free exchange of views, that problems are usually not so localised after all.

Things may not be quite so cosy round the bottle of Auslese on the silver salver in the elegant pale blue drawing room with guests from just across the Rhine in Alsace. There is a fundamental divergence of views on either side of the river. *"The French are always more interested in alcohol; in Germany no one would buy a wine just because of its strength."* This is how Dr Bassermann-Jordan replies to Johnny Hugel's assertion that the Germans make their wines unaccountably sweet. He points out that of course the rainfall in Rheinpfalz is only half that of Alsace, which does play an important part.

And Trocken wines? *"You see, we never were members of the 'sweet wine party,' and so since the Trocken wine fashion we have not had to become members of the 'dry wine party.' We*

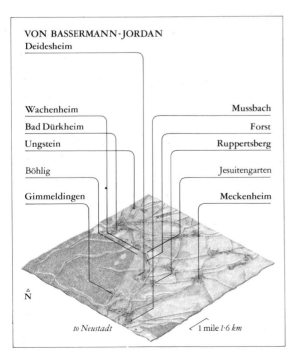

VON BASSERMANN-JORDAN
Deidesheim

Wachenheim

Mussbach

Bad Dürkheim

Forst

Ungstein

Ruppertsberg

Böhlig

Jesuitengarten

Gimmeldingen

Meckenheim

N

to Neustadt

1 mile 1·6 km

are not fashion-followers. We simply like fresh wines that have had a bit of time *to develop before bottling so that they are able to last."* This is official Bassermann-Jordan policy, which results in a summer bottling after several months in wood.

Tall, white-haired and smartly-dressed, Dr Bassermann-Jordan is cosmopolitan in his wine-drinking tastes, admitting without shame that in winter he switches over to good burgundy and claret with meals. He allows that the French make the best reds, but has doubts about whites. He will countenance good *old* sauternes with pleasure, however.

Vineyards in Rheinpfalz such as these between Forst and the Mittelhaardt slope only gradually.

Bürklin-Wolf

The big three Bs of the Rheinpfalz – Bassermann-Jordan, Bürklin-Wolf and von Buhl – are all extremely friendly. They may like to stake their territorial claims, as anyone who wanders around the gently-sloping vineyards of the Mittelhaardt, studded with the three companies' emblems, can see, but relations between them are excellent. Ludwig Bassermann-Jordan even spent part of his training period up in the next village, Wachenheim, under the great Dr Bürklin-Wolf.

This much-loved man, perhaps the most energetic Pfalz pioneer, died in 1979; but the firm, the largest privately-owned estate in Germany, continues to turn out wonderfully earthy, almost chewable wines under the direction of his lively widow and the much-respected winemaker Georg Raquet.

With about 100 hectares of vineyard, Bürklin-Wolf is about the same size as a large Bordeaux château – Yquem? – but is concerned with a much wider range of wines. They are not nearly as single-minded about Riesling as their friends in Deidesheim, with about 25 hectares planted in Müller-Thurgau, Gewürztraminer, Scheurebe, Weissburgunder and Ehrenfelser. Their vineyards are around Wachenheim, Forst, Deidesheim and Ruppertsberg, the heart, as they proudly point out, of the Mittelhaardt. The immaculately-groomed Bürklin-Wolf vineyards stand out proudly among those of some of their less meticulous neighbours. Strict pruning is necessary for quality, admonishes Frau Bürklin-Wolf. And careful weeding is needed in this relatively dry area so that every ounce of moisture goes to nourish the vine, adds Herr Raquet (who is immaculately groomed himself).

Herr Raquet is from a wine region with rather less prestige, the Rheinhessen, but augmented his credentials by training at Geisenheim and started at Bürklin-Wolf in 1966. Today he lives in a modern house overlooking the Böhlig vineyard facing (ideally) south-east from Wachenheim, and is in charge of one of the wine world's most impressive combinations of the old and the new. This is perhaps epitomised by the somewhat curious sight of the thirteenth-century cellars full of stainless steel tanks. It is not, as Frau Bürklin-Wolf hastens to point out, an attempt to compromise quality, but simply that "we work in a very modern way." They take their responsibilities as educators very seriously and usually have some ten trainees with them for a year's apprenticeship. Their policy is to buy the newest machines possible, but only if they help to improve quality. Their presses are the latest thing to be seen at the agricultural shows. They have their own special *tracteur-enjambeur* that can work two rows at once. They have their own nursery where they can select only the best clones.

Frau Bürklin-Wolf is a charming and thoughtful hostess – more immaculate grooming and archly raised eyebrows – so one can easily forgive just a touch of arrogance in this Berliner. *"We know our wines of Auslese quality and above are the best in the world,"* she says calmly – and after enjoying one of her beautifully-arranged tastings you are sufficiently disarmed to accept this statement as the very least she could claim.

The twin forces behind the Rheinpfalz's most famous house: winemaker Georg Raquet and Dr Bürklin-Wolf's widow.

Such a wine will spend the *shortest* time in wood at Bürklin-Wolf.

The intricate German wine law demands minimum must weights for Rheinpfalz Riesling Kabinett, Spätlese and Auslese wines of 73°, 85° and 92° Oechsle. Bürklin-Wolf set themselves their own minima of 78°, 88° and 100° respectively, and suffer no commercial disaster as their local climate is so warm – the warmest in Germany, they claim. They also make the ultimate commercial sacrifice in poor years of selling off up to 30 per cent of their wine to be sold under labels that will not put the reputation of Bürklin-Wolf at risk. This means that as much as 300,000 litres of their wine may be discarded as not coming up to their particular scratch.

Partly because they depend less heavily on Riesling, Bürklin-Wolf are not so wood-fanatical as von Bassermann-Jordan. They have a large oak capacity and use it carefully. *"It is not true that white wines are better the longer they are kept in wood,"* points out Frau Bürklin-Wolf. *"We want our wines to have a fruity freshness. We will ferment in oak in those years which are high in acidity to help correct this, and will usually keep our better wines for a time in wood. The Beerenauslese wines and Trockenbeerenauslese wines stay the shortest time in wood because they are put into the smallest barrels, and the latest any wine is bottled is usually just before the next vintage."* She and Herr Raquet leave the crucial decision as to when to bottle each wine to the cellarmaster Adolf Knorr, whose family has had only five generations of experience with Bürklin-Wolf. His young son Fritz, luckily for the future of the enterprise, is not a rebellious type.

Herr Raquet looks very much the business-man, and it is easy to forget the vital role he plays in making the wines he sells. Selling is not a difficult business here, of course. There is never a shortage of customers for the million or so bottles they produce every year. As much as thirty per cent of them are snapped up by private customers, many of whom sweep into the court-yard themselves to have their Mercedes or BMW loaded to the gunwales with their prized bottles.

They receive about five thousand visitors a year, and are well geared-up to welcome them with stables converted into a large tasting room,

"Direct sales" are an important part of business here.

complete with Italian Renaissance altar at one end, to remind them perhaps of how transient are physical things such as Deutschmarks and how immortal the pleasure given by great wine. The

BURKLIN WOLF
Wachenheim

Bad Dürkheim
Deidesheim
Ungstein
Gimmeldingen
Mussbach

Forst
Ruppertsberg
Mandelgarten

Meckenheim

N

1 mile
1·6 km

Fritz and Adolf Knorr, fifth and sixth generation winemakers in the cellars where, *below*, Herr Raquet inspects one of his well preserved veterans.

late Doktor used to say that the number of Deutschmarks you paid for a bottle would be the number of years you should wait before drinking it. Thanks to Germany's remarkably low rate of inflation, his adage has remained quite accurate. His widow and Herr Raquet will be drinking their 1971 Spätlesen and Auslesen during the next five years, but have tales of much older bottles that are still in awe-inspiring condition.

The United States is the firm's most enthusiastic export customer and Frau Bürklin-Wolf accordingly packed Herr Raquet off there in 1980. He was thrilled to meet so many knowledgeable collectors and connoisseurs of his wines there, but disappointed to see how ignorant the general American public were of any but the cheapest wines Germany has to offer. Frau Bürklin-Wolf feels *"we are very international and it is important to travel – though of course most people come and see us."* She seems to be managing excellently, from her luxurious house on the outskirts of the village. Her 21-year-old daughter Bettina is currently following in Herr Raquet's footsteps at Geisenheim, and Frau Bürklin-Wolf hopes eventually to hand over the business and house to this extremely lucky girl.

J J Prüm

The Mosel, or Moselle as French-speakers and traditional English-speakers call it, has everyone reaching for superlatives. To the tourist, the narrow winding valley with sunlight bouncing off the sparkling river on to neat little houses clustered round the foot of impossibly steep vineyards is pretty in a crisp, sharply-defined way as nowhere else. Any serious wine lover, on the other hand, values the valley for wines which have the sort of refreshing elegance found in no other wine region. the Riesling grape is now grown all over the world, but only in the Mosel is it reared in such a cool climate and with such experience that it produces wines which are high in fruity vigour and yet low in alcohol so that they can be drunk at times when any other wine would seem too much.

Of all the names savoured and swapped by enthusiasts for these wines (and almost every wine-lover finds himself a Mosel-fan in the end), J. J. Prüm's is the most revered. Indeed, so great is this family firm's reputation around the world that the reality of the premises in Wehlen, a quiet village just downstream of Bernkastel and its tourist-traps, comes as an enormous surprise. The word enormous is perhaps inappropriate here. The tiny village houses almost a dozen wine firms which use the name Prüm, even though they may not have been related to the great "J. J." for six generations. To mark their existence is just one modest plaque, in the traditional greeny-grey slate of the Mosel, on the gatepost of the tiny enterprise named after Johann Josef Prüm, grandfather of the present incumbent Dr Manfred Prüm.

If you wander by mistake round the back of the solid stone house that was built on the banks of the river in the early days of this century, you will be amazed by the farmyard feel of this world-famous property. There is no grand modern equipment, nor even a carefully-preserved rusticity; merely the air of a family-run small-holding whose motto might well be "make do and mend." Five minutes with the enthusiastic and jolly Manfred Prüm, however, dispels any fears as to the seriousness and quality of the enterprise. If there has not been great investment in technical trappings, it is because he is convinced there is no need. This is a small firm, employing only about 15 workers to produce less than 100,000 litres most years, all of them made by the academic Dr Prüm himself.

The extraordinary topography of the Mosel valley, which loops back on itself every few

miles, means that extremely personal supervision of vineyards as well as winemaking is quite possible for Dr Prüm. From his homely salon, with green brocade walls and art deco furniture inherited from two generations back, he can see at least half of his 13½ hectares of vineyard across the river. It was this combination of Prüm ingenuity and Mosel geography that was responsible for the famous sundials above the vineyards of Wehlen and Zeltingen, installed by Jodocus Prüm in the middle of the nineteenth century as an efficient substitute for providing each vineyard worker (and there were many more in those days) with his own timepiece. They remain as easily visible, locally useful and confusingly similar today.

The vineyards over which Dr Prüm presides remain remarkably similar to those of his grandfather and encompass some of the finest, most desirable land in Germany. Plots in this ultra-traditional area are tiny, some of them being perhaps only 50 square metres and reachable only on foot. The Prüm holding in the wonderful Wehlener Sonnenuhr vineyard just across the river from the house and cellars, four whole hectares, is enviably extensive in an area where even half a hectare is thought of as a fair size, and land prices are quoted per square metre rather than per hectare. In the rare instances when some vineyard land actually comes on to the market,

Eighty years ago the Prüms were able to tack on this solid stone house to their humbler white-painted origins just visible on the right.

In the famous Wehlener Sonnenuhr vineyard, villagers who have worked the steep vines all their lives, and the sundial, installed by Manfred Prüm's forebear to act as timepiece – and give the vineyard its name.

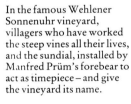

prices of as much as 100 Deutschmarks per square metre (which effectively means per vine) are not uncommon – and this is before the enormous cost of working these inhospitable vineyards is taken into account. Almost all of the Prüm vineyards are officially classified as "steep," which sometimes means at an angle of more than 45 degrees.

There is no chance of using the new sophisticated vineyard machinery here, although the simple winch system is invaluable on slopes like this. Helicopter spraying is being developed, which must make sense, but in general the old traditions are seen as absolute rules by vine-workers whose attitudes have hardly changed in two generations.

The thoughtful Dr Prüm shakes his head a little over his neighbours' resistance to change. *Flurbereinigung*, the official scheme to rationalise vineyard holdings and geography, has cut little ground around Wehlen, either metaphorically or literally. The locals cannot believe that, even subsidised, the expense would be worthwhile, and prefer to stick to their small traditional plots. Thanks to a rather more open-minded attitude in his father, Dr Manfred Prüm benefits from vineyard holdings that are quite well concentrated. He keeps in close contact with his vines and vineyard workers, and most of them are to be found just over the slender Wehlen bridge and a minute or two's dizzy ascent up the vineyard road, built only in 1959.

The vineyard workers have usually had quite a time to get used to working on the steep,

slatey soil being, typically, women in their forties from the village below. There was even one born in 1894 who was still making her determined way up the slope through the vines during the 1981 harvest. Dr Prüm worries that there is as yet little sign that younger people are interested in this difficult vineyard work, although the visitor surprised by the blare of a transistor in the middle of this rampant rusticity might think otherwise.

Manfred Prüm himself had little chance of a rebellious youth. Born in Trier and brought up on the family property in Wehlen, he was frequently called upon to help out in the vineyards and cellars before setting off on a legal career. He was just in the middle of his qualifying exams in 1969 when his father Sebastian died. A family conference was hastily convened and it was decided that Manfred and the youngest brother Wolfgang should take over the family wine business, while the other two brothers continued in fields which have them today in banking and high-powered industry respectively. Although this is an enterprise producing a relatively small amount of wine, there is nothing peasant-like about the Prüms or their wines.

Dr Prüm is a less-travelled man than he appears. As he points out: "*I do like to ski, but really holidays are hardly necessary if you live in the Mosel. To have bad weather on holiday is depressing, but here we can work if there is bad weather. And if there is good weather we can pack up the girls in the car and take them to the beautiful Hunsrück hills for the afternoon. I really have too much work to do here to travel on business, and besides we have all the important visitors coming to us."*

He reckons that if he has two visitors in a week, then that's a busy week. No coach parties here please. Instead he will welcome only old friends or friends of friends into his light, bright hall, lined with florid vine-covered art nouveau tiles and hung with hunting horns and antlers. He likes nothing more than a visit from an equally well-informed and intelligent Californian winemaker (Robert Mondavi is his favourite so far), so that they can settle down for what Dr Prüm rates as *"a really impressive conversation – I don't like monologues, I like dialogues."* He is flattered by the fact that someone using such sophisticated techniques as Mondavi should be so fascinated by what goes on in Manfred Prüm's backyard, but admits *"it is understandable because we have gradually developed a very strong tradition in our very special climate and topology with the great Riesling that we know very well."*

In addition to his 4 hectares in Wehlener Sonnenuhr, including the very best Wirtspitz part Dr Prüm has 2½ in Graacher Himmelreich and a hectare in Zeltinger Sonnenuhr, as well as two hectares around Bernkastel and a total of 4 hectares on the left bank of the river mainly around Wehlen. This means that the majority of his vines face south-south-west, a situation with which he is extremely happy. As far north as this, it is the ripening process which is crucial, and Dr Prüm argues that, since photosynthesis needs warmth as well as light, afternoon sunshine is much more valuable than sunshine in the early morning, when there is often fog anyway (which lifts naturally and does not need the morning sun to "burn it off"). Vineyards that face south-south-west are therefore in an ideal position from which to benefit from the sunshine from late morning until late afternoon. The best quality wines come from the lower slopes, but mainly because temperatures are gentler here rather than because of that popular tourist explanation about the sun being reflected off the surface of the river. The highest vineyards here are a dizzy 200 metres above the river, but the best wines come from less than 100 metres up.

It is important on these slopes that the vines get as much drying air around them as possible, so they are all trained on their own poles, rather than being trellised as in the Rheingau. Besides, training vines along wires at 45 degrees would

present its own problems. Viticulture here is painstaking and painful. It is difficult to imagine a temperament more suited to this sort of work than that of the rural German. In some parts even the practice of replacing vines plant by plant is continued, and these gnarled stumps, whose very existence on such gradients seems to defy gravity, are usually pulled up after about 50 years, having managed to provide an astonishing average of 90 hectolitres per hectare (though locally yield is usually measured in bottles per square metre).

All but 5 per cent of Dr Prüm's vines are Riesling, Riesling of the traditional type still found only in the Mosel, the Rheingau and parts of the Nahe. Yes, the wines of the Rheingau and Alsace can be good, allows Dr Prüm, but they are not typical of *the* Riesling. The small area that is not planted in Riesling is used to cultivate varieties such as Optima which, in very lean years, will be added to bolster up the Oechsle level and cut back the acidity in some of the greenest wines. (There is now not a single Müller-Thurgau vine on Prüm property.) Acidity is what makes great wines of the Mosel so wonderful, and so extraordinarily long-lived, but in some years there can be too much of this good thing. In years such as 1980, even producers such as Prüm may deacidify with chalk, although Manfred prefers to do what he did to

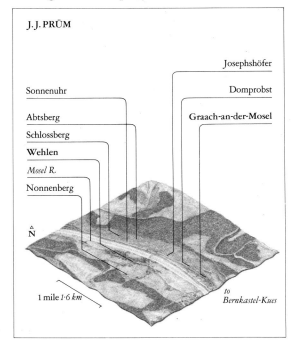

J.J. PRÜM

Josephshöfer

Sonnenuhr

Domprobst

Abtsberg

Graach-an-der-Mosel

Schlossberg

Wehlen

Mosel R.

Nonnenberg

N

1 mile 1·6 km

to Bernkastel-Kues

"Our 1971 Kabinetts are now at their peak," but a bottle of 1921 Kabinett was also "in excellent condition" at sixty.

some of his 1979s, to leave them to soften by bottling them only after the next vintage.

The four rooms that house the winemaking activities of J. J. Prüm are not the domain of expediency, nor are they of any technological wizardry. There is an old centrifuge with which the must is cleared before fermentation. There is even a filter, with all of a dozen filter sheets in it. But the visitor will look in vain for the flashy smile of a stainless steel tank. Those in search of signs of technical progress have to content themselves with a few fibreglass tanks, in which the fermentation usually takes place for about a week (though there was the famous 1959 Trockenbeerenauslese that was still fermenting slowly well into 1961). Almost all the wines go into Dr Prüm's round, typically Mosel barrels at some point in order to stabilise them before bottling cask by cask. The bottling procedure itself is wonderfully primitive, with trays of up-ended bottles wheeled over to one corner of the cellars for a sulphur rinse before being filled. (The quiet is music to the ears of any bottling-hall veteran.) There is little need for treatments of any sort, and the average winter temperature of only 5°C (41°F) is sufficiently low to clarify most wines.

Dr Prüm's wines have the reputation of being some of the longest-lived in the Mosel, and

this applies at quality levels even as modest as Kabinett. "*Because we are very cautious in our winemaking, and try not to work too much on our young wines, they will last to a great age. We like our Kabinetts to be opened no less than five years after the vintage. Our 1971 Kabinetts are now at their peak, for example, but they will stay in such good condition for some years to come. Last Sunday I opened a bottle of 1921 Kabinett which was in excellent condition.*" With one of the finest wine libraries in the Mosel in his cellars, Manfred Prüm is well-placed to make such pronouncements. He advises anyone with stocks

The Prüm labels and the view from the Sonnenuhr vineyard, *opposite top*, show the same dizzy scene. Dr Manfred Prüm, *opposite below*, has no wish to leave it, even for holidays.

Verband Deutscher

Prädikatswein-
Versteigerer e. V.

Erzeugerabfüllung
Weingut
Joh.Jos.Prüm
Wehlen/Mosel

Mosel — Saar — Ruwer

Qualitätswein
mit Prädikat

Amtliche Prüfungs-Nr.
2 576 511 - 4 76

Joh.Jos.Prüm

1975er
Wehlener Sonnenuhr
Auslese

The locals are proud and stubborn. *Flurbereinigung* has cut little ground round Wehlen.

reached higher Oechsle levels to make a considerable quantity of extremely good Spätlese, as well as producing the richer Predicates the grapes were crying out for. This year matched the two other greats of the century, 1949 and 1921. As Michael Broadbent says in his *Great Vintage Wine Book*: "One expects perfection from 'J.J.' in a perfect year."

Since 1972 he has been bottling his lesser wines, of QbA quality, under the label Dr M. Prüm, and these can be good buys for those who are not able to wait for their pleasures. Under this label and, to a lesser extent even under the main J. J. Prüm label, he is now producing some Trocken and Halbtrocken wines in QbA, Kabinett and Spätlese qualities. One gets the feeling that he is moving with the increasingly dry times in Germany only with reluctance. He admits that Trocken presents "a difficult concept" and feels it will only ever represent a small proportion of the output of such elite firms as his own. Like any self-respecting German winemaker however, he is not slow to point out that it gives them the opportunity to make many different qualities of wine from the same vineyard and the same vintage – unlike their French counterparts.

He may even choose a Halbtrocken himself occasionally as a thirst-quencher, or even with some fish dishes. The Prüm family, which most lunchtimes includes Manfred's mamma, must eat a lot of fish, for it is the perfect foil for their light, elegant wines. He confesses that, just occasionally, he will serve a good claret with something like venison (though an older Auslese without too much residual sugar can be delicious, mind you), but is wary of this dangerous practice. When you are used to wines with about nine degrees of alcohol, 11° or 12° must seem like the drink of the devil.

His favourite times are spent at home, inspecting, comparing and enjoying Prüm wines with friends or family. *"Our wines with their low alcohol are very good for the evening, and very good for young people. In our house we drink wine more by itself than with food. We sit around together and we laugh a lot."* With such assets, it should be easy to be happy. The only trouble with Manfred's resolution to leave his beautiful valley as seldom as possible is that he has little opportunity to see how happy he makes others.

of one of his Kabinett wines to keep a bottle for twenty years and see how it develops that wonderfully heady, almost "petrol" old Riesling nose without losing its freshness. And anyone lucky enough to have some of his 1976 Beerenauslesen should be restrained from even thinking about it much before the end of the century.

Although 1975 was so satisfactory because there was a good-sized crop as well as a good quality one, 1976 has so far been the most exciting vintage in Manfred Prüm's reign because Edelfäule, noble rot, was so prevalent, producing these greats which we must not even think about. He did, incidentally, use a lot of the grapes which

ITALY

In most years Italy is the most prolific wine producer in the world. Wine, its production and consumption, is an integral part of life in every corner of the country. Two millennia ago this land was the source of all knowledge about wine. Thousands of different wines are made there, so why are so few of them singled out here?

It is worth remembering that twenty years ago Italy exported hardly any of her wine production at all, and yet today she is responsible for well over half total wine imports into the United States and supplies every embryonic British wine drinker with the Soave and Valpolicella on which to cut his teeth. This is how dramatically Italian wine producers at the lower end of the quality scale tailored their product to suit the tastes of non-Italians. A similar process at the top end has not yet taken place.

This book is about great wine, wine that can be considered great in all corners of the wine-consuming world. Specialist Italian winemakers have been relatively isolated from what has been happening outside Italy. They have continued to make the sort of wines Italians have traditionally liked and respected – reds that have been toughened by long years of ageing in ancient barrels, often bitter and rarely with any great fruit. As Marchese Piero Antinori, whose family have been making wine from their Florence base since 1385 but who has taken a good look around the wine world, admits: *"Italy is an island in terms of wine appreciation."* This makes it difficult to recommend some of Italy's most respected wines to non-Italians, even though their makers have performed spectacularly well in the traditional mould.

Nowadays Italian white wines can be clean and refreshing, and there are some recent experiments with Chardonnay grown in cooler micro-climates; but most of Italy, even more than

Italy's mouthwatering vineyard scenery, as here in her exciting Piedmont region.

Spain, is too hot for the production of really fine white wine designed to grow old gracefully. Her strength is in full-bodied reds, but even for them the cooler pockets of vineyard have to be sought out if the aim is to produce wines that are fascinating as well as robust. In a country so far south, this means that the best vineyards have to have a certain altitude, which is why Piedmont in the north-west and Tuscany in the central Appenines provide the most rewarding hunting ground for wines of quality, now supplemented by the Alpine foothills in the north-east where an increasingly interesting range of wines is being made.

A trend which shows every sign of changing the taste of both wine and wine-drinkers in Italy has its roots up here in the north-east – that of importing grape varieties from elsewhere to a land still almost exclusively dependent on its own native grapes. Pinots Bianco, Grigio and Nero, Cabernets of both sorts, Renano Riesling and Sauvignon are now commonplace products of Friuli-Venezia Giulia, all closely related to their translations into French or German. And there are now pockets of Cabernet and Chardonnay being cultivated, sometimes still only experimentally, all over Italy, along with the very slow evolution of winemaking techniques which will eventually make a much higher proportion of better quality Italian wine accessible to foreign palates.

It would surely be very sad indeed if Italian winemakers were simply to turn out facsimile French wines, however, for Italy has its own stamp of grapes and soils to offer the world. While wines such as Sassicaia, the pseudo-claret from the coast near Livorno, Venegazzu and Costozza, can provide great drinking enjoyment, they do not seem very closely linked to Italy's wine heritage.

A direct legacy of the past are the Barolo and Barbaresco of Piedmont, concentrated, almost dank wines that take hours, sometimes days, to soften and round out after the bottle is opened. Tradition requires that the wines are made from the intense, black Nebbiolo which, like most of Italy's commonly-grown grapes, is little known outside the country. This is a variety which is capable of the most exciting fan of flavours. There are violets and even perhaps the local truffles in the bouquet of a really fine aged

Nebbiolo such as the wines of Gaja of Barbaresco and Ceretto, Pio Cesare, Cordero, the two Conternos, Franco Fiorina and Ratti of the Barolo region. But with their minimum alcohol level of 13° and a mandatory two but often more years in large oak, many Barolo wines can be brutes. Lovable brutes, but brutes all the same.

The wines of Tuscany tend in general to be rather softer, though here again the wine most in demand in Italy, the Brunello di Montalcino of Biondi-Santi, is difficult for those who like to drink rather than chew their wine to appreciate it. Italian law dictates that it spend a minimum of four years in wood – a great deal to ask even of a grape as concentrated as the Sangiovese Grosso, or Brunello.

Some of the best Chiantis have for long represented the most accessible red wine drinking to non-Italians. The wines of the beautiful hills of Tuscany are capable of taking on intriguing nuances of flavour when well-made and carefully-aged. Some older vintages of the Chianti Classico of Badia a Coltibuono are available for inspection in this regard and can be rewarding wines. This is the territory of the small estate, often attached to a small hilltop castle of enormous appeal to those of us congenitally prey to the lure of olive groves, cypress trees and Renaissance architecture. There are so many wine producers, within the Chianti Classico consorzio and without, that it is difficult to single out names, though those privately owned rarely disappoint in the bracket of good medium quality wine, albeit of a distinctly rustic sort.

For decades the wines of Carmignano, just north-west of the Chianti zone, have hinted at the potential of adding a little bit of Cabernet (Uva Francesca) to the prescribed Chianti mix of Italian red and white grape varieties. The theme has been developed by the most remarkable winemaker in Italy today, Piero Antinori, with his Tignanello – a wine that commands prices several times higher than even the best Chianti, by improving upon the Chianti recipe. His argument is that Italy is capable of making stunning wines provided her winemakers will accept the fact that tradition alone may not always make the best wine.

Things are changing at last, however, and a future version of this book will probably have a much enlarged Italian collection.

Tignanello

The dashing Marchese Piero Antinori commands his family's wine empire from a tall, stone-vaulted chamber in the Palazzo Antinori, a fifteenth-century palace in the Piazza Antinori, Florence – an address that rightly suggests a certain historical standing. The antithesis of parvenus, the Antinoris, like the Greiffenclau clan of Schloss Vollrads, have winemaking origins that pre-date those of the third oldest wine house in this book, Hugel of Alsace, by more than 250 years. When Giovanni, son of a Renaissance Piero Antinori, entered the Florence Vintners Guild in 1385, he would have been welcomed and respected as a member of what was already an influential silk and banking family of that wonderful city.

Over the centuries the family's wine interests have developed so that today it is with wine that the name Antinori is most readily associated, with one of the most consistent ranges of what Tuscan vineyards have to offer and some special "creations" that have earned Piero's reputation as Italy's most innovative wine producer. With one of their two big estates, Santa Cristina, bang in the middle of the Chianti region (the other being Castello della Sala just outside Orvieto) Antinori's fortunes depend heavily on Italy's best-known wine, but Piero continues to battle with the Chianti authorities about just how the wine should be made – and has proved with his Tignanello that the region is capable of producing not just good but great red wine.

"We think that chianti is produced with the wrong formula, so we began at the end of the 1960s" (when he must have been barely 30) "to experiment with similar but different wines, made without the traditional mistakes. When Baron Ricasoli invented the well-known chianti formula, reds made then were terribly hard – because the stems were always included and they didn't know what

malo-lactic was – so that they might well have needed white grapes to soften the wine. But in those days it was just a little Malvasia, not Trebbiano. Then in the last hundred years all the peasants found out how easy and productive it was to grow Trebbiano vines so that when the DOC laws were formulated, the authorities just had to include Trebbiano as an alternative to Malvasia because it was a fact in the vineyards.

"In our opinion this was already a mistake. Fifteen years ago we said there should be white chianti too because this would solve the white grape surplus. But now there is so much Trebbiano planted in our region that, although we use the legal minimum, ten per cent, in our chiantis, other people are tempted to use the full 30 per cent allowance of white grapes – and it's simply nonsense to make red wine with 30 per cent Trebbiano. It's so light and so acid. This has led to people making use of the 15 per cent southern Italian musts they are allowed to add, and now we find many, many chiantis which really don't have the proper character of the region.

"So we set out to produce the best wine we could from about 100 per cent Sangiovese grapes grown here. Mind you, the Sangiovese vines have to be very carefully selected. When in the mid-1960s everyone started to increase plantings in the Chianti Zone (which went up five-fold in only a few years then), many of them bought grafted roots with the wrong clones and the quality suffered – a big mistake for Chianti. We took a great deal of trouble with this.

"And we also wanted to improve the vinification system so we studied malo-lactic fermentation, something that was almost unknown in Italy then, and found that it was very important for this area's wines – though not easy because it's so cool and because the pH of our wines is so low. In the past the governo was used to induce malo-lactic, usually unwittingly, but for a wine as 'serious' as our prototype Tignanello, governo is hardly suitable. So we try to control the malo-lactic and complete it by the end of the year, which is already something very unusual for Italy.

"Lastly, and most importantly, we have completely changed the philosophy of ageing. Not big old barrels for a long time, but small, new wood for a much shorter time. After many visits to Bordeaux and consultations with Professor Peynaud, we became convinced it could work and indeed found that it produced much better quality; and so, now that we also understand the *importance of bottle-ageing, we keep Tignanello in small oak casks between one and a half and two years and then in bottle a further one to four years. So you see the origin of Tignanello has been to make something better than chianti in the Chianti region, using local grapes."*

The Marchese is not simply being a cussed spoilsport. He is clearly deeply concerned about the reputation and future of his native region, stimulated by what he has been able to observe on his travels outside it. For although the Antinori family has its roots so deeply embedded in the Tuscan soil, the present generation of Piero and his younger brother Lodovico, who looks after the United States market, have a high proportion of American blood coursing through their veins; and a cosmopolitan outlook was fostered at an early age by the English nanny regime, to be followed by education abroad. It is wholly consistent with the family's traditions of concern for the long term that Piero should be taking such a stand on the wines of Chianti. His father Niccolo (who is "retired" but still visits the office every day) developed the company in both human and physical resources by an almost patriarchal approach to his employees, many of whom have been with Antinori all their working lives, and by overseeing a programme of continuous reinvestment.

The development of Tignanello, now one of Italy's most respected and expensive wines, needed some cash; but more importantly it needed perseverance and the confidence to withstand setbacks and criticism by other winemakers throughout Tuscany, one of Italy's most conservative regions.

The first numbered bottle of Tignanello to be offered to the sceptical Italian public was dated 1971, made only with Sangiovese and the concentrated local Canaiolo, and aged in small French oak – a completely new sort of wine for Tuscany, and even for Italy. Between this vintage and the next one thought worthy of the Tignanello label, 1975, the technical staff at Antinori, headed by the energetic Dr Giacomo Tachis, experimented with different types of oak and different mixes of grapes. They finally decided to phase out Canaiolo for this untypical wine of the region because it seemed to do nothing to improve quality. But early success with blending Cabernet Sauvignon with Sangiovese convinced them that this "French grape" had something worthwhile to offer the wine, and now it constitutes about ten per cent of the blend.

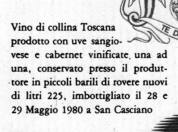

TIGNANELLO

1978

Vino di collina Toscana prodotto con uve sangiovese e cabernet vinificate, una ad una, conservato presso il produttore in piccoli barili di rovere nuovi di litri 225, imbottigliato il 28 e 29 Maggio 1980 a San Casciano

750 ml ℮
12,5 % vol.

Val di Pesa dai Marchesi Lodovico e Piero Antinori di Firenze (R.I.382/FI) e successivamente adagiato in fresche cantine sotterranee per un ulteriore riposo in bottiglia prima della spedizione.

VINO DA TAVOLA DELLA VAL DI PESA
MARCHESI L. e P. ANTINORI S.p.A. - FIRENZE
ITALIA

"What we were trying to do in all these efforts was to prove to other producers and to the committee that the law is an ass and should be changed. We hold out strong hopes that we've convinced a lot of people and that the regulations will be changed to allow 0-10 instead of 10-30 per cent white grapes; and we'd also like to see 0-10 per cent 'free' grapes, giving the flexibility to add Cabernet or Merlot for those producers prepared to take the trouble to produce top quality wine. If this is the result then the Tignanello experiment will have proved something and therefore had a good result. But even without the laws of 1963, we would still have made a Tignanello."

Tignanello, which to those who have not tasted it may simply represent an expensive way to flout authority, but to those who have enjoyed it suggests exciting new possibilities for one of the world's most alluring wine regions, gets its name from the small patch of vineyards on which the vines are grown. On the Santa Cristina estate that produces Antinori's best chianti is a gently curving slope of vineyards running round from south- to west-facing by an old farmhouse that at one time probably belonged to a family called Tignanello. The vines, predominantly Sangiovese but supplemented by a bit of Cabernet Sauvignon, are trained high on wires to produce

A breakthrough for Italy: small cooperage and even a dash of Cabernet Sauvignon. But still only a table wine. No D.O.C. for those who play with the rules.

The rolling hills of Tuscany Chianti Classico country are quite high enough to keep the Tignanello vines sufficiently cool.

Fermentation, in stainless steel, takes about twelve days, the must kept in constant contact with the skins. Indeed, in a line-up of Italian wines Tignanello stands out for the concentration of its colour – partly because there are no white grapes in the blend, partly a result of skin contact and partly because of the barrel-ageing policy. After racking, the malo-lactic fermentation usually takes place by the end of December and the wine is then put into small new Slovenian oak of standard 225-litre "Bordeaux" size. Dr Tachis is a great proponent of a new philosophy of oak ageing in Italy, preaching that wine should be "mature but not aged." Most of his theories are backed by his experiences with Tignanello and Sassicaia, the all-Cabernet wine made under Antinori auspices on the Tuscan coast. He is a shy man, still in his forties (" but Tignanello has turned my hair white") and considered by the Antinori staff as "our magician." Born in Alba in the heart of Barolo country, he came to Antinori via Emiglia-Romagna, *"but I feel very much at home in Bordeaux, which is good for both Tignanello and Sassicaia."*

Under Dr Tachis' supervision, Antinori were the first to use *barriques*; and he remembers how *"everyone thought we were crazy,"* noting with a trace of quite excusable satisfaction that *"now everyone seems to be copying us."* They tried Limousin oak, but that gave a very pronounced French character and Piero, surely quite rightly, is anxious to minimise possible accusations of merely counterfeiting France in Italy. Slovenian oak, traditional for chianti, was more suitable in this respect and as the firm already had good contacts with a Yugoslavian supplier, all that was then required was to teach Italian coopers to make small barrels. Now Antinori are well into a routine in which the Tignanello *barriques* are used for their first two years, scraped before use for a third, and then used for their Villa Antinori Chianti Riserva.

Great emphasis is put on ageing at Antinori. The bottles are kept for at least a year and often longer before being labelled prior to despatch. The Tignanello label is to the Italian wine trade what Ridge labels were to the trade in California in the 1960s. All the information is there: how it was made (though there was a bit of a slip-up, specifying Canaiolo instead of Cabernet for the 1977!); the exact bottling date; ripeness of the grapes when picked; total acidity of the grapes; alcoholic strength; average temperature during fermentation; duration of the fermentation;

luxuriantly leafy plants up to 1½ metres apart, planted in wide rows 2½ metres apart on the calcerous soil. The small rocks in this land form a terrain that is known locally as *galestrino*, a name that has inspired Antinori and a handful of other chianti producers to name a remarkably crisp, dry Tuscan white Galestro, an attempt to use the Trebbiano in a more suitable way than merely lightening the local red wine.

As anyone who has visited Tuscany outside high summer knows, the rolling hills are comparatively high, 300 to 400 metres above sea level in the case of the Tignanello vineyards, and can be quite cool enough to provide a micro-climate designed for quality. A nearby lake and its feeding streams provide natural underground drainage and, although sprinkling is not allowed in Italy, the Antinoris have done everything possible to ensure that Tignanello vines enjoy the most auspicious situation. A young whizz kid, Paolo Fenocchio, is in charge of the 600-hectare Santa Cristina vineyard, of which Tignanello is the most carefully-nurtured product. In the cool depths of the shuttered country villa on the Santa Cristina estate are ancient and impressively blackened mouldy cellars; but it is in the more modern winery buildings next door that Tignanello is made, before being shipped to the firm's San Casciano plant to be aged in temperature-controlled cellars.

post-malo-lactic acidity (usually high); time in cask and bottle; and first despatch date. It comes as no surprise to learn that 60 per cent of Tignanello is exported and sells best on the other side of the Atlantic, to the world's most inquisitive wine buyers.

Not that there are enormous quantities for sale. Little more than 120,000 bottles (sold as 20,000 six-bottle cases, so precious is this wine) are produced, and then only in years such as 1971, 1975, 1977, 1978 and 1981. Total production of the much less Italian Sassicaia is two and a half times this but both are sold at about twice the price even of Antinori's Riserva chianti, about 8,000 lire in 1982. There is no shortage of takers even at this price, very high for a young "Vino da Tavola" in Italy; but Dr Tachis admits *"Tignanello does not necessarily sell to the traditional chianti drinker."* The wine not only looks more concentrated than chianti, it tastes it. The Cabernet's influence can be sensed, but the predominant flavour is one of the scented, powerful Sangiovese grape, which matures a little faster than Cabernet and is given extra definition by its

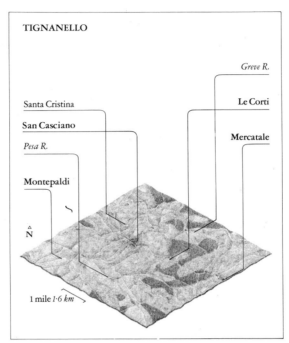

Picking and unusually well-tended oak in vineyards and cellars at Antinori.

At the Palazzo Antinori, in the Piazza Antinori, named after a family that has been famous in Florence since the fourteenth century.

confinement in small oak. Tignanello from a vintage such as 1978 is a wine to keep, perhaps until 1988, while 1977 produced a much lighter, softer wine. Dr Tachis' favourite was 1975: *"great balance, rich in colour and flavour; the 1971 was perhaps a bit too aggressive."*

The Marchese feels uneasy about France and its potential influence on the wines he could make. *"It's frustrating for us because we have the oldest viticulture in the world and yet after so many centuries when we want to make really top quality wine we find ourselves turning to French or German grape varieties. We tried 100 per cent Cabernet and the results were very, very good, but they weren't Italian. We have very few of our own grapes suitable for exceptional wines: Nebbiolo yes, Sangiovese in certain conditions, and Moscato in its category.*

"We have also tried to produce top quality outstanding white wine using Italian grapes but so far without success. We've planted 12 hectares of Chardonnay at our Orvieto estate and a bit of

Sauvignon, and I am very excited to see what will happen. I'm very confident, because we are using small barrels again to extract maximum flavour. When we tried small barrels for Malvasia and Vernaccia it was not, in truth, a great success. Please don't think I am against Italian wines. I think Barolo can be a fantastic wine, so long as it isn't allowed to get tired. Pio Cesare 1971 is marvellous, for instance.

"When I get a little tired here, I go to California, which is so stimulating. Every time I go there – and I have been many, many times – I come back wanting to try something new. It is extraordinary how much they have learned in such a short time. I find them much more inspiring than the French. They have a mentality very similar to ours and we have frequent exchanges with their university at Davis."

Unusually for an Italian, Piero Antinori drinks widely, from all over the world, and tries to keep abreast of developments everywhere so that he can apply any newly-learned principles. His certificate from the great Bordeaux wine fraternity, the Commanderie du Bontemps de Médoc et Graves, may hang in his office, but California is clearly his chief source of new ideas. A favourite story at Antinori is that of a visit of Piero's old friend Robert Mondavi and his team from the Napa Valley. A great banquet was given to welcome the Californian visitors and at the end of it Robert Mondavi stood and toasted his host saying, "You know Piero, I have always thought of you as the Robert Mondavi of Italy, and I mean that as a compliment!" Piero smiled and admitted, quite truthfully, that he himself had been known to observe to his staff that he saw Robert Mondavi as the Piero Antinori of California – mutual admiration of the truest sort.

There seems to be little danger for the 600-year-old firm, provided they can stave off take-over bids. It certainly looks as though the next generation has wine aspirations: Piero's eldest daughter Albiera had already made her own wine, from her own grapes and with her own label, before her fourteenth birthday.

It will be fascinating to watch the evolution of the wine regulations in Central Italy. Who knows, perhaps one day Tignanello, one of Italy's great wine achievements, will be entitled to a grander name than "table wine."

SPAIN

SPAIN

Age is an agreed virtue for vines everywhere. The bush method of non-training is a Spanish speciality, as here at Vega Sicilia where wires are seen as a dangerous intervention with God's goodness.

Spain has more land planted with vines than any other country in the world, but only quite recently has she started exporting the top quality wines she is capable of producing from some pockets of this land. Some may be surprised to find as many as three contenders for the title "great" from a country that is still largely associated with the most basic wines. What is so attractive about Spain's best wines, however, in contrast for instance to many of those the Italians regard as their best, is that they are so easily appreciated by wine-drinkers far outside their region, or even country, of origin.

Wines from the wild woolly hills of Rioja, Spain's only established quality wine region, were the success story of the 1970s. Once thirsty Americans and Britons had discovered how much easy, warm, oaky flavour they could buy for a fraction of the cost of a bottle of classed-growth claret, they boosted rioja exports tenfold.

Of course rioja varies in quality almost as much as claret does (not *quite* as much, for no rioja can reach the dizzy heights of complexity in a first growth of a fine year), and there are some very poor bottles indeed. To produce really exciting wine, rather than a loose-textured mixture of oak (oak essence has been offered even to the most scrupulous Rioja *bodegas*) and sweet berries, it is necessary to start with good grapes – a concept that a surprising number of *bodegas* ignore – and these should be a well-judged blend from the Rioja Alta and Alavesa rather than the jammy Baja sort. Tempranillo should play an important part and the addition of white grapes, though common, does not usually contribute to making a "serious" red wine. Careful tempera-

Barricas and the American oak of which they are made are the key to the flavour of great red rioja such as CUNE make with such impressive consistency.

seem to have stagnated somewhat, just as Lopez de Heredia is perhaps a little too traditional, as anyone who has fought their way through their cobwebs can testify. Muga and La Rioja Alta both enjoy excellent reputations, quite rightly, but they are dwarfed (almost literally as they are neighbours) by CUNE, who produce more top quality rioja than any other *bodega*. Their wines of Reserva and Gran Reserva level often represent 15 per cent of their total output, and in a wine region where taxes are calculated on quality, it is CUNE who pay the highest taxes.

Miguel Torres based in the Penedes mountains west of Barcelona is highly unusual. The dramatic results he has achieved stem directly from adapting French methods, and vines, to local conditions. His carefully-kept vineyards are, for example, some of the very few in the whole of Spain where the concept of training along wires is understood and practised. (It is even forbidden in Rioja.) Every year he makes some new exciting wine, of a sort that those who knew Spain's wines a decade ago would have thought impossible, but he still feels as though he is working in a vacuum. Within Penedes he has no rival, among makers of still wine, for he is the only producer prepared to work at getting the best out of the ground as well as the cellar.

The most famous, and expensive, wine within Spain (though little-known outside) is made in even more isolation. Vega Sicilia is curious in many respects, a bizarre hangover from a precursor of Miguel Torres still making truly exciting wine by disobeying all the rules. That a wine for which people happily pay a thousand pesetas and more for a bottle is technically able only to call itself a *vino de mesa* or "household wine," seems absurd. This highlights the embryonic state of Spain's quality designation system, with only Rioja having detailed, perhaps too detailed, arrangements for classification of different wines.

What each of these three makers of world-class wines share is altitude. Spain gets so much sunshine that it is only by countering this with mountain cool that the growing season can be sufficiently extended to produce complex wines. Each of CUNE, Torres and Vega Sicilia, in their different ways, are capable of making red wines that should make the most Francophile wine-lover sit up and take note.

ture-controlled fermentation should then be followed by meticulous cellarwork. It is part of the rioja tradition that several years are spent in small American oak *barricas*. The amount of flavour they impart to the wine must be carefully controlled and the all-important racking should be done so as not to expose the wine to too much air. Then bottling, and some time spent maturing the wine in bottle. (It is an attractive feature of the Spanish winemaker that the custom is to offer a wine only when it is ready for drinking. Let us hope this withstands the rapid rise in interest rates in Spain.)

There have been some interesting new developments in Rioja, with massive new *bodegas* built from scratch, the sherry people Domecq actually putting money into vineyards too. Olarra and its dramatic building have impressed many, and Marques de Caceres has made great some very good wine by following closely the original Bordeaux model. Of the traditional houses, it was "the two Marquesses," Riscal and Murrieta, that were best known abroad, but they

Torres

When Miguel Torres was an oenology student in Dijon in 1959, he suffered from his French classmates' stereotyped view of the Spaniard as an impoverished and ignorant peasant. Twenty years later he had the satisfaction of seeing the first vintage of his special baby Gran Coronas Black Label triumph over such French jewels as Château Latour 1970 and Château La Mission-Haut-Brion 1961 in Gault Millau's famous ''Wine Olympics,'' at which the judging panel included two Spaniards and twenty-seven Frenchmen.

Miguels Junior and Senior – both great individualists. Miguel Junior has brought unheard of innovations to Spanish viticulture and winemaking.

Miguel Torres has got where he has by being the very opposite of chauvinist, by seeing the enormous potential for importing the best of other wine regions to his own, the Penedes in Catalonia, in the green hills due west of Barcelona. But things did not always go smoothly. For a start, Miguel was not particularly interested in the family wine and brandy business, which had its origins in the seventeenth century. Even when he got to college in Barcelona, he was much more interested in chemistry and biology than in anything more closely related to the family business. When he was 18, in 1959, it seemed clear, however, that his elder brother was to be allowed to indulge his fascination for plastics (he is now heavily involved with Torres, chiefly importing spirits) and Miguel was expected to be groomed for a life of winemaking. He agreed to accept the place his father had found for him at Dijon, but more because he looked forward to the much freer social climate there than the one he left behind in Franco's Spain.

In fact it took all of the two years he spent in Dijon, interspersed with stints in Epernay, Bordeaux, Beaune and Cognac, to get the young Torres interested in wine at all. There was simply too much else to do, even if as foreigners he and his great friend Chilean Alejandro Parot were rather outcast by the natives. Luckily, the grape got to them in the end, and in the final exams Miguel managed to come out top.

At this time, Torres was a relatively small, old-fashioned firm selling perhaps 20,000 cases a year, and depending heavily on its brandy business (which even today continues to operate side by side with the wine business without all the official physical separation required by most other governments). Miguel gritted his teeth and quietly began to instal the beginnings of a proper lab in the firm's headquarters in the small town of Vilafranca, an interest that continues to this day.

Within a year of returning from Dijon, in 1962, he got permission to try out some of the viticultural lessons he had learned, on a single hectare of vineyard where he planted rows of imported vines on an experimental basis. At this point Torres, like most of the Penedes wine producers, relied almost exclusively on local small-holders for their grapes and owned only 10 hectares of vines themselves. But Miguel, the first Torres to show much interest in the vineyard, reckoned that it was essential to control their wines right from the rootstock up, and that there was a natural limit to quality if they continued to rely solely on local grape varieties, however well they were handled.

While these new cuttings were being nurtured through their first years by the young Miguel, the firm took another important step towards improving the quality of its wines: they fermented wine themselves for the first time in 1963. Miguel knew from the education his father had been wise enough to insist on that temperature control would be vital, but difficult in the warmth of a Vilafranca September, and accordingly he hired a cellar up in the mountains in which he painstakingly, and somewhat defiantly in the face of family criticism, fermented in small oak barrels.

Miguel himself admits that some of the criticism was justified. Just before he was called up into the army he blended a batch of the firm's staple white, Viña Sol, tasted it and, against tradition, insisted on bottling it straight away to avoid the possibility of oxidation. His father came to visit him after his third week in the army, rather ominously bearing a case of this batch of Viña Sol, to show his headstrong son a nice crop of sediment in the bottom of each bottle. Because he had failed to wait a day or so for the yeast cells to settle, Miguel had the shame of causing 40,000 bottles of wine to be re-bottled.

Miguel experimented impatiently with imported cuttings and with different rootstocks.

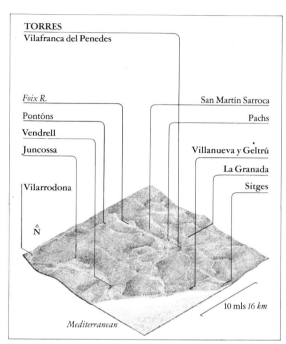

He knew that either careful clonal selection or the development of new and suitable *vitis vinifera* varieties could also improve the quality of his wines, but these methods are even less suitable for a young man in a hurry than the established vine that takes a mere three or four years to show its paces in new surroundings. His particular problem was to establish vineyards capable of producing fine red grapes. As this is such an important sparkling wine region, with San Sadurni de Noya just six miles north-east of Vilafranca being Spain's *"champaña"* capital, there was no shortage of good local white grapes when Miguel started his work in the early 1960s. Red grapes were hardly grown, however, representing only 10 per cent of the total planted vineyard (although now this proportion has risen to 25 per cent, largely thanks to Miguel having shown just what could be achieved). By the early 1970s, it had been established that very creditable Pinot Noir and Cabernet Sauvignon could be produced from the middle Penedes region, especially if properly trained on wires, a practice most local growers still regard with a mixture of amusement and incomprehension.

The Penedes, rising quite steeply from the Mediterranean coast, is divided into three viticultural zones, which Miguel with his extremely cosmopolitan outlook on wine life automatically describes in terms of California's carefully-

Pruning for training wires is a new technique in Spanish vineyards and Torres have had to persevere to transform vineyards from the scene on the right.

charted Regions. The high Penedes is the most westerly, has vineyards up to 800 metres high and is Region I. The middle Penedes around 250 metres and centred on Vilafranca is Region II, and the low Penedes veers towards Region III as it slopes down to the coast. Miguel Torres is almost alone in the Penedes, indeed almost alone in Spain, in the importance he attaches to vineyard siting.

Miguel's single overwhelming aim was to show the world that his native region, sometimes written Panadés but pronounced in Catalonian "Penner-dez," is able to produce wines of real quality. His father had seen the importance of having a superior or Reserva sort of wine and sold Gran Coronas, which was Torres' mainstay red Coronas, made from a blend of local grapes, given additional age. It was Miguel Junior, however, who introduced the world-beating, if easily-confusable, Gran Coronas Black Label, the wine of which he has been most proud so far. With this he introduced the concept of selection. *"With Black Label we want to keep quantities very small, four or five thousand cases at most, like a small château. The grapes always come from the same small 10-hectare patch in the middle Penedes which gives us about 50 hectolitres per hectare."* The proportion of Cabernet Sauvignon in this blend is steadily increasing, and is likely to end up at no more than 90 per cent, supplemented by the local Ull de Llebre (hare's eye) which is not unlike the Tempranillo

of Rioja.

The famous 1970 was Miguel's first Black Label shown to the world, but since then there have been blends labelled 1971, 1973 and 1975, their signature being very full, ripe Cabernet aroma, backed by a rigorous framework. It was notable that in Gault Millau's "olympics," this wine was rated highest of all by their team of professional oenologist-technicians. It has the same concentration of flavour as a great claret, but is rather softer, partly because of climate and partly because Torres use only American oak. Black Label is put into new oak for its first six months, and then older casks for up to two years. *"We tried French oak,"* says Miguel, *"but Spaniards are much more used to the taste of American oak; it's two-thirds the price of French; and it's much easier to work with."* They continue trade links forged centuries ago by importing 300-litre barrels from the United States, using them for five or six years for wine and then putting them to good use for brandy ageing later.

Miguel has continued to experiment with all sorts of imported grape varieties since his first one-hectare nursery. Torres now control 400 hectares of vines, mainly in the middle and high Penedes. The latest acquisition is a plot bought by Miguel himself that is fifteen miles outside the Penedes region, and it will be interesting to see how he persuades the authorities he can sell these wines. He has had many a disagreement with officialdom, and has even written a book, *Vino*

Español, which he describes as a polemic, critical of the current Spanish wine scene and pointing out the opportunities for Spain now that temperature control can be combined with its even and dependable climate.

The firm's holdings include two large estates up in the mountains, where snow has been known in the vineyard, at Poblet and Pontons (they may be good at choosing sites, but not at choosing easily-distinguishable names). Here, after experiments lower down, Miguel is now producing some fine Chardonnay, Riesling and even Gewürztraminer and Muscat d'Alsace. Further down towards Vilafranca, at a height of perhaps 250 metres, are 40 hectares of Torres vines around their remarkable brandy ageing cellars at Sant Marti where Pinot has adapted particularly well.

Also in the Central Penedes, they have 100 hectares just to the west of Vilafranca at Pachs-Penedes where Miguel now lives with his German wife Waltraud (Walla), his two teenage daughters and his young son called, of course, Miguel. At Pachs is Torres' major winemaking enterprise, a large functional shed full of stainless steel tanks and complete with a bank of horizontal presses. It would win no prizes for cosmetic appeal, but represents great fastidiousness by Spanish winemaking standards. By 1970 Torres had introduced stainless steel temperature-controlled fermentation for all their wines, and, with their sparkling neighbours Codorniu, they were the first to introduce such extravagance in Spain.

Miguel saw that it was important to keep his casks of maturing wine in proper low-temperature conditions. There were no cool cellars available, so he simply constructed them, part excavating, part building afresh, so that in the middle of the countryside an enormous pit has been hollowed out into which two enormous man-made cellars were built, in 1975 and 1981.

From 1972, when the Pachs operation got under way, there was a noticeable increase in quality; but the great thing about Torres is that there continue to be new excitements. Miguel is anxious to stress that he will never dispense with local grape varieties. They buy in 50 per cent of their needs from local growers, all of whom supply traditional grapes such as the crisp white Parellada, the Grenache-like Garnacha, the Carignan-like Cariñena as well as the totally Spanish reds Ull de Llebre and Monastrell. Miguel's stated aim with imported varieties is not imitation but improvement.

Viña Sol has become almost synonymous in Spanish for fresh, dry white wine. Seen in bars and restaurants throughout the country, and increasingly in the United States and Britain, it is made from 100 per cent Parellada, and is designed for early drinking. Sangredetoro (called Tres Torres in Britain because we apparently couldn't stomach another Bull's Blood) is a full, very warm blend of Garnacha and Cariñena that is relatively high in alcohol and matures fast. Coronas is mainly Ull de Llebre, given a year's oak ageing. It is, although Miguel would doubtless baulk at the comparison, the most rioja-like of the Torres range, with lower alcohol and good keeping qualities.

These are all good value, but perhaps more interesting are the "newcomers": Pinot-Noir-based Viña Magdala; Riesling-based Viña Waltraud in honour of Señora Torres; and Viña Esmeralda which is a delicate blend of Gewürztraminer and Muscat d'Alsace. Miguel has to pick the Gewürz very early, sometimes in the second week of August, to keep its flavour. Miguel continues to try to improve his Pinot Noir, but achieved impressive results with his 1974, when it was still called Santa Digna. Riesling is being moved ever higher for greater raciness. Merlot has been tried on a small scale with great success. He has failed to make anything of Chenin Blanc, but is working even on Petite Sirah. Experiments continue in the cellars as well

The wine with which Miguel Junior has won most acclaim – notably when the 1970 vintage "beat" French greats at the Paris "wine olympics".

as the vineyard, with the Torres three-strong team of oenologists, one of whom worked with the family's great pal Robert Mondavi.

The cream of each crop is sold with the prefix "Gran." Gran Viña Sol now has some Chardonnay in the blend and promises to get better and better (a sample of straight Chardonnay grown on Torres vineyards was stunning). Gran Viña Sol Green Label is Parellada given bite by 30 per cent Sauvignon and is bottled unfiltered and unrefined. It is indeed rich, but it would be interesting to see what would happen if Chardonnay were substituted for the Sauvignon. Special reds are Gran Coronas, which has twenty months in oak, at least three years in bottle, and a steadily increasing proportion of Cabernet Sauvignon. Then at the top of the tree is Gran Coronas Black Label.

At the time of writing, two of the latest Torres developments were the production of a fast-fermented Tempranillo/Ull de Llebre *à la beaujolaise*; and the emergence of Santa Digna wines from the new Torres operation in Chile, set up by Miguel's old Dijon classmate Alejandro Parot at Curico, 120 miles south of Santiago. But doubtless, even in the time this book takes to print, there will be new adventures of Miguel's devising.

Miguel has enormous energy, and exhausts his agents abroad when he visits them, as he often does. He has so far found the time to write four books. "*Well, what else is there to do on Sundays?*" In addition to these, he issues regular

New techniques, as in temperature-controlled fermentation for Torres white Viña Sol, are matched by a healthy regard for traditions that go back to the days of the press shown below.

newsletters in English with his sister Marimar, who is in charge of selling Torres wines in the United States, their most important export market where they sell well over a million bottles a year.

Miguel has spent quite a bit of time in the United States and this has clearly played a part in shaping his philosophy of wine. He sees a great similarity between the Penedes and the Napa Valley. Both are subject to the gentle influence of the sea, have mild summers and vintages that do not vary enormously. Soil is mixed, with clay, limestone and chalk in the case of Penedes. Both are at an exciting stage of their development. Miguel feels that, now that he has the best grape varieties, and vinification can be controlled, his future could be as exciting as that of California's best.

France has little hold on him. When in France, he will choose an Alsace (because he knows the houses there and feels safe) or a known château, but his favourite non-Torres wines come from Australia, New Zealand and California – all countries where winemakers have struggled in just the way he has.

CUNE

uis Vallejo is president and chairman of the Compañia Vinicola del Norte de España (usually and understandably shortened to CUNE, pronounced "coonay"). He is quite unlike either the manic innovator Miguel Torres or the competent manager of traditions at Vega Sicilia. As head of Rioja's only *bodega* that combines size with a reputation built up over more than a century, he is naturally a man of some urbanity and sophistication.

With his distinguished mop of silvery hair, hooded eyes, and open smiling countenance, he has the air of a conductor, or perhaps one of Covent Garden's better-heeled patrons. His Hermès tie and hand-made shirts do, it is true, look just a little incongruous in the sprawling CUNE *bodega* in Haro which he visits every week from the family base in Bilbao. The cook-house-keeper Pilão plays a very important part in the life of the *bodega* and spoils him, as they say, something rotten. Indeed, his first question to a visitor is likely to be "*What do you want to eat tomorrow?*" Pilão likes to be able to show off a bit. We settled on a first course of potatoes with the chorizo so admired by Paul Bocuse when he came to cook for CUNE's centenary celebrations in 1979.

CUNE, selling about 300,000 cases of rioja a year, is still family-owned, with the Vallejo family, through Luis' grandmother, the chief shareholders. The family have fingers in several pies, of which wine is not the most important, and this gives Luis a certain detachment, and reticence about his own role. This is not to say that he does not know a great deal about wine. His cousin Victor, based in Madrid, is the biggest shareholder and plays the role of kid brother in the enterprise. He is big in Firestone, Spain, but refuses to drink Firestone California wines when at their headquarters in Akron, Ohio.

It is Luis who really runs the show in Haro. He is a respected figure in the Rioja region, which has over the last few years seen all sorts of different, and often powerful, characters come and in some cases go. There has been no shortage of capital influx into this, Spain's top quality wine region; and new *bodegas* sprang up in the 1970s in some cases rather faster than new vines (a significant fact). Just outside Logroño, the region's capital, a prison-like edifice has been built recently as a *bodega* with a "Se Vende" sign outside, and the area is studded with other new building projects.

Workers at CUNE must feel almost smugly

Luis Vallejo, in charge of CUNE and much more besides.

secure in the ancient *bodega* in the chief town of the Rioja Alta, cheek by jowl with other well-established and respected houses such as Muga, La Rioja Alta and Lopez de Heredia. Only the Bilbao-Barcelona railway line disturbs the calm in the insulated old barns and converted biscuit factory that house CUNE's winemaking operations.

CUNE was one of the founder powers in the all-important Consejo Regulador which decides the rules governing the production and labelling of rioja wines; but divergences have since arisen between the interests of the new but often giant companies and outfits such as CUNE whose reputation is stronger than any recent rulings of the Consejo. The Vallejo family has been likened to the Bulmers of England, who dominate the cider trade from Hereford and have built up their business very slowly but very surely with no hint of any underhand practices.

Although the CUNE business was started as a provider of export wines for blending, their name as a producer of first-class rioja has been built in Spain. All the top restaurants there make sure they have one or two best wines from CUNE at the top of their wine list. It was only in the mid-1970s that CUNE started to export, and today shipments to their two most important export markets, the United States and Britain, account for less than 10 per cent of their total sales. CUNE are a very Spanish company.

Luis Vallejo himself admits that to a large extent it has been the top wines of CUNE, their Reservas and Gran Reservas which constitute a particularly high proportion of their output, that have built their enviable reputation within Spain. Even their basic red, however, the CUNE 3° which is bottled three years after the vintage, has won praise in high quarters.

What distinguishes CUNE's wines from most other reds of the Rioja region is their balance. In a CUNE bottle, the vanilla flavour of oak is always kept in balance by the excitement of good, pure fruit quality. Their two most-loved reds are the Gran Reserva versions of their Imperial, in the Bordeaux bottle, and Viña Real (meaning Royal) in the Burgundy shape. Luis himself is more of an Imperial man, and recommends fifteen years as the age at which his Gran Reservas reach their peak. The 1964 Gran Reservas tasted in 1981 were wonderful. There is much more colour and intensity of flavour in aged CUNE wines than in most riojas of the same vintage. Both of these were a deep rich blackish-tawny, the Viña Real having a bit more colour and alcohol. The Imperial had scent, elegance and a dry finish. The Viña Real was equally

well-balanced, perhaps very slightly coarser, but had a most seductive bouquet of violets. By any standards, CUNE Gran Reservas are very fine wines, often without that tell-tale overlay of American oak that makes many riojas so easily identifiable.

Because wood ageing plays such an important part in Rioja, many producers have taken this as an excuse not to pay too much attention to the quality of fruit (and often wine) they put into their *barricas*. Not so CUNE. Like many other *bodegas*, about 50 per cent of their raw material is bought in (there are other well-known *bodegas* where not a drop of wine is fermented on the premises; it is all done by budgets and barrels). They own all of 380 hectares of good vineyard land themselves, and control a further 220 under close agreements with local farmers. All their own land is in the two best and complimentary sub-regions Rioja Alta, mainly around Haro and Rioja Alavesa to the north of the River Ebro.

The CUNE vineyards are looked after by Jose Madrazo, and this is an exciting time for him. He can now see the fruits of a policy designed to maximise the quality of grapes that go into CUNE wine, which include instituting a system in 1976 whereby growers were recompensed for the quality as well as the quantity of the grapes they sold, the first of its kind in Rioja.

Viña Real and, slightly more austere, Imperial (*right*, by CUNE's ancient sales ledgers) are the bodega's flagships of quality – and 1970 was a tiptop vintage, or *cosecha*.

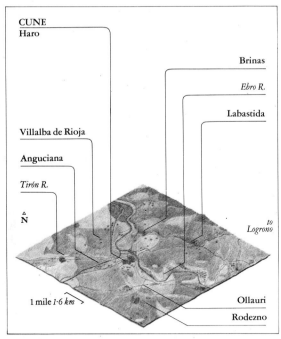

CUNE
Haro
Brinas
Ebro R.
Labastida
Villalba de Rioja
Anguciana
Tirón R.
N
*to
Logroño*
1 mile *1·6 km*
Ollauri
Rodezno

The company has recently taken over a small farm at Laserna, between Logroño and Laguardia in the Rioja Alavesa, where they are producing wine under the Contino label, chiefly because they feel they could not expand the main CUNE business without causing a drop in quality. The company is also pioneering experimentation with French grape varieties (shades of Torres) in Rioja. They have about a hectare each of Chardonnay, Sauvignon and Cabernet Sauvignon, which produced their first crop in 1981.

Tempranillo is the basic red grape from which top quality rioja is made, supplemented by about 25 per cent of Garnacha in most CUNE wines – although the proportion of the faster-maturing Garnacha will be higher in their cheaper blends and much higher in the wines they buy in from the hotter Rioja Baja. The Rioja Alta is much cooler and rises in the west so that vineyards around Haro, less than 20 miles from Logroño in the east of the Rioja Alta, can ripen up to twenty-five days later. The Rioja wine-makers place much more emphasis on the provenance of grapes than on the grape variety. Ask for a glass of Tempranillo in a Haro bar and you will meet some very blank looks. This is partly because the soils of the Alavesa region and the Alta regions are so different (with the Baja region being even more distinct, if less distinguished). In the Alta the soil is red and clayey, while that of the Alavesa is yellow and alluvial. Because the winding river provides the dividing line, even very close bits of Alta and Alavesa can produce wines of a very different character.

Alta wines tend to have more acidity and tannin, while those of the Alavesa are fruitier, rounder (if they have not been sharpened up by the increasingly common practice of adding surplus white grapes) and develop rather faster. Viña Real usually contains about two-thirds Alavesa grapes to one-third Alta; the other way round for the rather more austere Imperial.

As elsewhere in Spain, low bushes are the rule here – in fact wires are banned from the vineyards of the rugged Rioja region with its forbidding blue-grey mountains to the north. Vines are usually pulled up after about thirty-five years, but there are still plots of vines that have simply been abandoned by farmers in the era when grapes were not such an economical crop. Even in the early 1970s grapes could be bought for as little as four pesetas a kilo, but by 1980 farmers could expect up to 30 pesetas – still a modest amount by most French standards.

Although some vineyard owners have started to plant vines 2½ metres apart to allow modern machinery in between, this remains a relatively primitive region. CUNE still receive some grapes by donkey. Luis Vallejo may complain that the big companies have forced land prices up to a million pesetas a hectare, but this is still half the price being asked for good land in the Penedes region to the east. The common theory is that average yields in Spain are low, but could be increased dramatically (thereby upsetting the world's wine market) if only they learned to be efficient in the vineyard. According to Luis Vallejo, their average yield of 35 hecto-litres per hectare is about the most they can hope for. They already use preventative sprays extensively, but irrigation is not permitted and their climate is surprisingly ungenerous.

The vintage usually gets underway towards the end of October, but takes up to a month so that CUNE's concrete fermenting vats can sometimes be used for as many as three different batches of grapes. The grapes are kept separate by region, but will usually already be mixed by grape variety. When they reach the big *bodega* in Haro, or the auxiliary one in Elciego in the Alavesa, they enter the province of Basilio Izquirdo, a young oenologist who came to CUNE from that rather undistinguished wine region La Mancha, via an impeccable Bordeaux training. He was taken on in 1973 on the recommendation of Professor Peynaud, nicely illustrating how open-minded are the CUNE policies. He is able to drop, without affectation, the names of wine-makers at, for instance, Châteaux La Mission-Haut-Brion and Pétrus, each of these sharing the characteristics respectively of earthiness and

CUNE's oenologist Basilio Izquirdo is, unusually, Bordeaux-trained.

intense fruitiness with CUNE's best red wines. Basilio visits his Bordeaux friends every year, and clearly has a keen sense of where good rioja fits into the international landscape. *"Of course things are very different here,"* he allows. *"We don't have* négoçiants, *for instance, and we can produce much larger quantities. But my job is to copy the best and most appropriate aspects of Bordeaux. It is good to have the chance to do the small things so well."*

After a temperature-controlled fermentation lasting between seven days for basic wines and up to three weeks for wines that will eventually be Gran Reservas, the different *cuves* are classified according to what sort of wine it is thought they will be best for. By June these types will be fully blended and will be ready to go into the American oak *barricas* that are so important in the Rioja region. New oak is bought regularly, but there is no cachet in this for American oak is so aggressive when new. The policy, which may help to explain the extreme oakiness of some of the traditional white riojas, including CUNE's very popular Monopole, is to "break the new oak in" on the poor, defenceless whites. Reds will normally spend one year in big oak casks and then up to four in *barrica*.

They are experimenting now with the new no-oak white trend in their Lanceros wine, and even the classic Monopole gets less than the traditional two years in oak nowadays. As in most conscientious Rioja *bodegas*, there is increasing emphasis on the importance of time in bottle at the expense of years in wood for reds – though it must be said that in 1981 there was still a wine destined to be Imperial Gran Reserva 1976 in wood. It was sweet and noble and quite surprisingly lively, although tannin was very evident. This was partly because the better wines get a little bit of press wine and a small proportion of stalks retained in the fermenting vat.

CUNE keep stocks of an average of nearly five years' sales, an impressive statistic in a region where maturity is at such a premium. Luis Vallejo is saddened by recent developments within the Consejo which equate the designations Reserva and Gran Reserva simply with age, rather than involving the concept of quality. CUNE produce an Imperial Gran Reserva only in years which they think justify it, which in the 1970s excluded 1971, 1972, 1974, 1977 and 1979, for instance, despite what publicity handouts may say about the consistency of vintages in Rioja. Luis Vallejo reckons that, of the vintages he has seen, 1970, 1964 and perhaps 1952 are the best.

He is lucky to be able to speak with authority about older vintages of his wines. In a small private cellar just to the left of the entrance to that part of the *bodega* where some of the older casks are stacked, charged with wines in their final stages before bottling, is a collection of ancient bottles, perhaps rivalled only by what is left of the old Paternina cellar at Ollauri. Luis Vallejo is rather casual about this cache. No, he's not sure which is the oldest bottle. An 1888 perhaps? He knows there's some 1910 and 1911, and yes he'd be delighted to open a bottle of 1928 to compare with a wine from another *bodega* being sold as a 1928 by the enterprising wine merchant in Haro's main square. He was pleased to see the vigour in the CUNE 1928, but not surprised to see how much better and more scrupulous than the other it was. This comparative tasting was merely a further confirmation of the confidence in the family firm that is ingrained if you are a Vallejo.

Vega Sicilia

ike Château Rayas, Vega Sicilia is a great wine of which many a well-educated connoisseur will never have heard. What makes Spain's most sought-after wine so extraordinary however is that it is made in such splendid isolation.

It is even quite difficult to describe the location of Finca Vega Sicilia, so far is it from any known Spanish wine region. This thousand-hectare farm is way up in the high valley of the river Duero (Douro in Portugal) about 25 miles east of Valladolid. A century ago vines were quite common in this wide green valley, but as communications became easier the local farmers gave up in favour of crops that were more profitable in the harsh climate – all except for Vega Sicilia and the co-operative at the village of Peñafiel 10 miles up the road that is responsible for some robust reds.

Within Spain, the rich red Vega Sicilia can command the most amazing prices. One wine collector paid 190,000 pesetas for a bottle of the 1920 vintage; and a gang sold old Vega Sicilia bottles filled with inferior wine with a fake label in a swindle discovered in 1980. In its 120 years the *bodega* has certainly had its genuine local imitators, but they have not been able to sustain the same vigour in the vineyard and patience in the cellar that has made Vega Sicilia what it is.

It was started by a Señor Lecanda in 1864 with some imported vine cuttings from Bordeaux, and it continues to combine that wine region's influence with ultra-Spanish techniques. Don Jesus Anadon has been in charge since 1950. A lunch in Peñafiel's restaurant (one whole grilled baby lamb served to every four diners) or an evening in Valladolid with Señor Anadon is an education in how popular one man can be; every minute he has to get up to shake some new acquaintance by the hand, or pause to acknowledge the enthusiastic greeting of someone across the room.

It is hardly surprising that he commands such respect. He is at the helm of an enterprise capable of producing wine that won over that Great British connoisseur Winston Churchill; that earned acclaim from the French when King Juan Carlos served it to Giscard d'Estaing; and that has to be rationed to satisfy only about one-quarter of the orders for it. He was initially an agricultural engineer, with a particular interest in genetics, but was seconded to Vega Sicilia when his employers took over this already-estimable *bodega*. When the property was bought by the Czech-Venezuelan family

Vega Sicilia, Spain's most treasured red wine, is made in splendid, intensely agricultural, isolation high up in sheep-farming country.

VINO FINO
DE MESA
Elaborado con uvas: Cabernet Sauvignon, Malbec, Merlot, tinto fino y albillo

VEGA-SICILIA
COSECHA 1964   "UNICO"

Medalla de Oro y Gran Diploma de Honor
Feria de Navidad de Madrid de 1927
Medalla de Oro y Gran Diploma de Honor
Exposición Hotelera de Barcelona de 1927
Gran Premio de Honor
Exposición Internacional de Barcelona 1929-30

R. Sanidad n.° 30.1.500/VA - N.° embotellador 2342 - Contenido 75 Cl. - Grado alcohólico 13,5°

Esta cosecha se ha escogido para ser embotellada este año y consta de 96.000 botellas.

El número de esta botella es el   Nº   69379

BODEGAS VEGA SICILIA, S. A.
El Presidente

VALBUENA DE DUERO (Valladolid) España

1981

Neumann in 1964, they made Señor Anadon an offer too generous to refuse, in deference to his vivacious and *soignée* wife and family of seven children.

Their eldest son Javier is their fifth child and now a student who *may* take over from his father, who is already talking about the 1970 vintage of Vega Sicilia (which will not be sold until the mid-1980s) being his swansong. Señor Anadon's brief over the last thirty years has been to maintain the traditional "artisan" methods in the *bodega*, while increasing the amount of wine available. When the Neumanns (who are not wine-drinkers themselves and drink what Señor Anadon calls "rum and firewater") took over, annual production was only about 25,000 bottles. In 1980 it had risen to the slightly more realistic 125,000-bottle level, and the plan is to reach the dizzy heights of 200,000 bottles by 1985. This involves planting every available square metre of hillside, and constructing a completely new cellar in the chalk cliffs that bound the vineyard area, *"just like my friend Torres."*

Señor Anadon lives a simple life, as a pillar of Valladolid society. By 6.30 every morning he is up. By 7.30 he is at mass. By 8.30 he is taking an active part in the city's café politics. Not for him the heady world of international winemaking

The genial Jesus Anadon – "a simple life, as a pillar of Valladolid society."

and wine-study. When he was given sole responsibility in 1964, by a Neumann of exactly the same age as himself, he made one very thorough trip to Bordeaux. A good snoop round châteaux which included Latour, Margaux and Chasse-Spleen, and he reckoned he learned enough to keep Vega Sicilia going for another few decades. Today he drinks very little non-Spanish wine, choosing water when he doesn't have to entertain, usually Vega Sicilia preceded by its younger version Valbuena when he does, and has somehow found time to develop a respect for riojas from Lopez Heredia, CUNE and Marques de Murrieta as well as for the Torres range, particularly Gran Coronas and Viña Esmeralda.

Even this selection of favourites, which many a British or American wine-lover might match, is relatively cosmopolitan for a Spaniard.

The fact that a certain amount of mystery surrounds Spain's most expensive wine is not surprising. Not only is it produced in very limited quantity and in geographical isolation, but even its makers themselves have been somewhat confused by what is growing in their vineyards. One might have expected Señor Anadon's passion for genetics to have inflamed an interest in ampelography some time ago, but it was not until the early 1970s that they dug out some old documents which gave some clues as to exactly what was planted in their very mixed patches of vines.

Señor Anadon's young oenologist Mariano Garcia is, like all thirty vineyard workers and ten *bodega* workers, a local man. He is fired by the pride that comes of being involved with the region's most treasured product. According to him, about half of the total vineyard of 120 hectares is planted with a Spanish grape with the illuminating local name of Tinto Fino, or Tinto Aragones. This is closely related to the Tempranillo of Rioja, he thinks, but has developed its own character here and is capable of nice high sugar levels. Cabernet Sauvignon, or Bordeos Tinto as the locals call it, represents up to 30 per cent. The white Albillo accounts for perhaps 5 per cent and gives additional acidity to the blend, although this seems to have little effect on its dense, almost black colour. The rest of the vineyard is divided between those Bordeaux red vines Merlot and Malbec. Malbec is being increased at the expense of Cabernet as it shows a better aptitude in coping with the well-drained alluvial soil and the extraordinarily harsh climate.

The Vega Sicilia vineyards warm up towards midday, but frosts in both spring and winter are the biggest problem these tough vines have to face. In 1971 the entire crop was lost. When Señor Anadon introduced his own "mini-meteo" to chart the rainfall that is so important in this very arid region, he found he had to blend in anti-freeze with the ink. The *bodega*'s altitude of 765 metres plays a very important part here – hardly a new problem, but Señor Anadon has not yet developed any anti-frost techniques other than fervent prayer.

The growth is always very late, way behind that in the temperate vineyards of Bordeaux far to the north, and the vintage rarely starts before the end of October. These vines, planted out and given five years before they are expected to produce wine on the "survival of the fittest" principle, develop deep, strong roots essential to battle against winter cold; and they are all grafted on to American rootstock just to be on the safe side.

All the mature vines look incredibly ancient, even though Señor Anadon says he grubs them up after fifty years. Like tough, gnarled old peasants, they are planted in widely-spaced traditional low bushes on the gently un-

dulating vineyards that skirt little pine-clad hillocks. Much against what you feel is his better judgement, Señor Anadon has planted an experimental 3-hectare patch with vines trained on wires, but says he is not hopeful of the results. The uncharitable climate, the difficult terrain . . . and he likes the vines to be low enough to benefit from radiated daytime heat during the night.

It is difficult to argue with him when he has been turning out such wonderful wine all these years. One of the factors must be the tiny yield of

usually less than 20 hectolitres per hectare which results from leaving only three or four buds on each vine after pruning. The lack of rain, and the prohibition (respected here) of irrigation must also play a part in concentrating the flavour to its amazing density.

Lack of sunshine, despite the late spring, is no problem in the ripening period, and indeed the vineyard slopes are north-facing, so careless are they about this commodity which is so treasured further north. Mariano Garcia thinks this angle is a factor in determining the aroma and flavour in the grapes he has brought in every autumn, across the single-track railway that dissects the vineyards to the *bodega* itself.

This long, low pale building is beautifully kept and has a most unusual extension, a long, rather decrepit aqueduct trailing across the fertile valley into the distance. On the other side of the *bodega* is the tall house, shut up for most of the year but occupied by the Neumanns when they visit their Spanish property in the summer.

But it is in the cellars beneath the central *bodega* that all the most important things happen at Vega Sicilia. Even as the grapes are brought in there is careful selection. Will this batch make Vega Sicilia, or is it more suited to Valbuena (sold at both three and five years old), or must it be part of the 12 per cent that has to be sent, much against Señor Anadon's wishes, to the government distillery? Valbuena tends to be made from those vines which either get least sun or are youngest.

All grapes are destalked and put into work-manlike epoxy resin tiled vats, very thick to retain the heat of fermentation, and left to ferment at a stately pace for up to twenty days. Señor Anadon finds it very funny that visiting Bordelais always ask how he manages for temperature control. Autumn is as cold as spring up here, and the fermentation never reaches a temperature much more than 28°C (82°F). No press wine is added, which makes Vega Sicilia's longevity all the more amazing. It spends months in large American oak vats to allow malo-lactic fermentation to take place before being consigned to small American oak *barricas* for more years than any other wine in this book. It is worth noting that rigorous selection is practised at this point and the whole vintage may be rejected, as has happened three times in Señor Anadon's reign.

Five high, the *barricas* are stacked in beautifully-kept cellars, towards the end being racked,

Oenologist Mariano Garcia works, like all the staff, fired by local pride.

The Vega Sicilia vineyards, currently being extended, look an unlikely source of vinous greatness.

that have spent many a year in wood, will marvel at the care that must go into retaining life and fruit over the years in Vega Sicilia's wines – although with wines as "hand-crafted" as this, there is inevitable bottle variation.

It is a point of great pride with Señor Anadon that he, unlike the Bordelais, puts his wines on the market only when they are actually ready to drink. There has been an increase over the years in the amount of bottle-age given, and today Vega Sicilia is almost always at least ten years old before it is sold. In 1981, the 1967 vintage was the youngest wine available, and the 1960 had not yet even been offered.

Talking to Señor Anadon about his international sales program is hilarious. So small are the quantities of wine available that he measures each country's allocation literally in cases. There are 100 cases for Britain, a generous 200 for the United States, 120 for his oldest customer in Puerto Rico, and of course 10 for Señor Neumann to give to his friends in Venezuela.

When selling merely means allocating, there is little need for a sophisticated label, which may explain the antiquated innocence of the style of labels for Valbuena and Vega Sicilia. Valbuena usually carries the vintage date as well as the age when it was bottled. The numbered Vega Sicilia labels carry a facsimile of the signature of "El Presidente" (Neumann, not Anadon) and sport the word "Unico" because, as Señor Anadon points out with great pride, there is no other Spanish wine like it.

This must be the most isolated fine-wine property in Europe. Señor Anadon has done a wonderful job, but because of the small amount made even he has not had the chance to taste many old vintages of his wine, which gives every indication of being capable of up to a century's ageing. He once tasted a 1917, and can report that with age Vega Sicilia will not leave a sediment but may start to stain the bottle.

It is that sort of wine. Best vintages in the Anadon period have been 1948, 1959, 1961, 1964 and 1970, but every vintage is marked by great richness, being almost gamey and with a slightly sweet concentration of flavour. A colour so deep it is almost black is backed by lots of alcohol (usually 13°) and a dry, very intense finish. This wine deserves a wider range of fans – or perhaps we should just keep it to ourselves!

with extreme care and risking only a tube rather than pouring, only once a year in the winter chill. Vega Sicilia proper will usually be in small oak for at least four years, up to two of them in new barrels. Five- and three-year-old Valbuena (which together represent about two-thirds of total production) are in oak for only two years, but it does put attitudes here into perspective when one considers that even this period, accorded to the *bodega*'s lighter blends, would be regarded as an absolute maximum in Bordeaux. Those who have chewed over Barolo, or "hunted the flavour" in a rioja, or other wines

CALIFORNIA

CALIFORNIA

Over the last decade California has proved itself the most exciting wine region in the world. Even as recently as 1975 it might have been difficult to defend its right to a place in this book. Today there can be no serious wine enthusiast who is still unaware that the West Coast is producing wines that can hold their own with the best that Europe has to offer. Of course they are different, which can make relative assessment a difficult exercise. The California winemaker may look to Pauillac and Puligny for inspiration, but California has its own flavour to give the wine-drinking world: a richness, a sunniness, an exuberance that makes the wines easier to appreciate when young. Hence those sensational comparative tastings at which California "beats" France.

Winemakers in Europe have had centuries of experience on which to draw. Their counterparts in California have been trying to cram the acquisition of an equivalent amount of knowledge into a tiny fraction of the time, and have succeeded to an extraordinary extent, thanks to a very sophisticated level of technological back-up. The world-famous (o)enology faculty at Davis and its equivalent at Fresno have done much to disseminate information, and are acknowledged even by the French to have raced ahead of their own wine research institutes in many respects. The Californians have benefitted equally from their native enthusiasm, and from the availability of money. Many is the fortune, acquired in another commercial field, which has allowed someone to develop his thesis that California can produce some of the finest wine in the world, unhampered by tiresome budgetary constraints.

In one important respect Californians still have a lot to learn. The role that soil plays in the making of wine has always been played down by California authorities, in startling contrast to the reverence which the French *vigneron* accords his patch of earth, and it is taking time to identify the pockets of West Coast vineyard most suited to each varietal. The approach through most of the 1970s seemed to be to plant the most cultivable land, the valley floors in Napa and Sonoma for instance, and then compensate for any deficiencies or disasters by all manner of technical high jinks: adding soil nutrients, using huge propeller wind machines or spray techniques to prevent frost damage, irrigation to compensate for dry weather, night picking to avoid the blistering noon heat, or even T-grafting one varietal over to another more suitable (or more fashionable) one. The Californians, unlike the French, are prepared to experiment. They are also prepared to admit their mistakes. Brix maturity levels at picking are edging down, while fermentation temperatures nudge towards the rather less glacial European norm.

So far, in the best-known areas for top quality wine, there have been particularly impressive results from Cabernet Sauvignon grown

in the central Napa Valley and from some Chardonnays grown in northern Sonoma, but it will be fascinating to see how California's top vineyards are geographically distributed in twenty years' time. Growers are starting to redevelop the hillsides in established areas and to find cool pockets of land in newer wine territory. Promising vineyards are now emerging all along the West Coast – from the Santa Barbara hinterland in the south up through Oregon to Washington State in the north.

Geography still plays a relatively minor role

in California's fulsome labelling. An appellation system is being devised, but so far it is fairly crude, taking into account only large general regions rather than hinting at any special quality by virtue of location. This is hardly surprising in view of the state's short history of wine production, this time around at least. Grapes are often "trucked" from growers many miles from the winery in any case. The most common practice, as in Australia, South Africa and other emerging wine countries, is to name the wine after the chief varietal in them, which must comprise 75 per cent of the blend by state law and is often 100 per cent.

Of the seventy or so varietals planted, the two which have helped to hoist California's wine flag so high have been Cabernet Sauvignon and Chardonnay, a fact that has not escaped the notice of makers of fine claret and white burgundy. The trend towards planting a small proportion of the Bordeaux blending grapes Cabernet Franc and Merlot continues, and Merlot is beginning to establish itself as a varietal in its own right. It has been with Johannisberg or

Hillside sites are being explored as at Joseph Phelps, *left*, as an alternative to the Napa Valley's characteristic flat plantings, *right*.

White Riesling, the California cousin of the great Riesling of Germany, that the greatest progress has been made in very recent years, although the wines will always be rather heavier than their European counterparts when grown in California sunshine. Great Pinot Noir produced in this climate has been elusive, but each vintage brings more exciting results; and now there are experiments with Late Harvest Semillon/ Sauvignon Blanc blends in the sauternes mould, and with Syrah in attempts inspired by Hermitage and Côte Rôtie. Whatever it takes to make great wine, the Californians will eventually try out, although the industry suffers from worshipping the god of fashion more assiduously than that of aptitude. If the customer wants Blanc de Cabernet, then give him one – a pale pink, carbon-bleached version of this great red wine grape.

Hype is an important word in the California wine industry, and some producers seem to have taken rather too keenly to heart the theory that you can sell anything so long as you charge enough for it. They do say that you can sell the first 2,000 cases of any new release, for curious, wine-fanatical San Francisco doctors and Los Angeles lawyers exist in about this number. But you may well have difficulty selling the second 2,000 cases. It takes just one favourable outcome from a tasting attended by a handful of wine writers for a winery's reputation to be made, for the next three months at least. In an industry as new as this, there are bound to be inconsistencies, some of them quite unconnected with the efforts of the winemaker. As the president of

Chateau St Jean, a winery that has established its solid reputation remarkably quickly, points out: *"It's time to take stock and look at the other elements. You have to be prepared to invest heavily for consistent quality."*

All this investment has to be paid for, and in a market that is so short of really top wine that most new releases have to be allocated rather than sold, prices are not low. The most sought-after varietals from the most respected wineries tend to cost only a little less than imported wines of similar pedigree, though those prepared to dally with a varietal such as Zinfandel, California's native spicy rich red, can pick up bargains.

Prejudice and snobbery may exist among some California wine consumers, but it is almost unknown among the producers. As one would expect of the most laid-back state, the style of the wine people is very informal. Jeans, cut-offs,

Wine is for the people, and their licence plates.

beards, broad grins and T-shirts are the order of the day. There may be isolated attempts at the "elegance" of entertaining in France (the most ambitious being in Jordan's grand dining room), but there is rarely even a hint of the rigid formality that governs behaviour on the other side of the Atlantic. Winemakers hold rock concerts in their grounds, welcome new recruits to their trade from Hollywood, put wine names on their car licence plates and stickers all over the winery buildings.

But hand in hand with this carefree atmosphere is a certain fanaticism. When the American decides he is "into wine," the thirst for knowledge as well as for liquid is impossible to underestimate. Everyone wants to know the most intricate technical details about how the wine they are drinking was made, which has led to a proliferation of high-powered newsletters, and to labels that are so informative they border on the ridiculous. Dave Bennion (all California winemakers seem to be called Dave, Steve, Bill or Phil), who pioneered illuminating labelling at Ridge, admits that the thing has got out of hand. *"They're even including the Brix as well as the alcohol on the totally dry wines,"* he smiles.

The shape of the California industry is changing almost daily, with the reputations of many of the newer "boutique" wineries being made and broken all the time. The California Wine Institute, the official body that represents the interests of the state's wineries and issues such unlikely posters as one urging "Employees must wash hands with soap and water before returning to work," has been doubling its membership every three years. In such a youthful and changing structure there is no authorised ranking, no counterpart to official classifications of quality in Europe, and it was not easy to pick out just four winemakers specially concerned with the very highest realms of achievement. It seemed fair to restrict the choice to those establishments with a proven record of consistent success, leaving the next few years for a fair assessment of some of the new "buzz" names. The final selection covers a fair geographical range as well as highlighting those varietals which have been most successful in California.

Chateau St Jean's white wines, and particularly Chardonnays, have won friends all over the world and influenced people throughout the wineries of California. Robert Mondavi deserves a place in this book more than any other winemaker in the world for his interest in great wine and its makers everywhere, although the quality of his Reserve Cabernets also fully justifies his inclusion. Just across the Napa Valley, Joseph Phelps Vineyards with a German winemaker produce wines of dazzling consistency. And, south of San Francisco at last, Ridge Vineyards are responsible for reviving a winery and customs from pre-Prohibition days, melding them with a healthy respect for and understanding of, great claret, and producing extremely "serious" Zinfandel, as well as elegant Cabernet.

It was tempting to include several smaller enterprises. Chalone had been a strong candidate for the Chardonnay position. But its splendid wines are so difficult to locate that any further eulogy might have led only to frustration, particularly for readers on the far side of the Atlantic. The same argument applied to wineries such as Stony Hill and Mayacamas, both of which have produced some very fine wines. Almost every winemaker in California aspires to greatness in some way, which is a refreshing change from the lackadaisical approach of some European winemakers. No account of great California wine is complete without mention of the idiosyncratic Joe Heitz, to a certain extent the daddy of them all, whose Cabernet Martha's Vineyard is one of California's most distinctive wines. Then there is Beaulieu Vineyards (BV), whose Georges de Latour Private Reserve Cabernets provide one of the longest records of great winemaking in the state. BV is now in the hands of a giant corporation.

Wineries such as Chateau Montelena, Freemark Abbey and Trefethen, whose names appear at the top of the comparative tastings now, may have to wait a decade before they convince the most sceptical traditionalists of their worth. The big question with all that California has to offer the wine lover is "Will it last and develop?" The wines are inspiring and charming in youth and usually drunk by their very early middle age. We must hope for opportunities to see whether in later life they develop the finesse and complexity to justify their claim to match the very best Europe has to offer.

Robert Mondavi

Now in his late sixties but with the vitality and curiosity of a five-year-old, Mondavi has always been a keen traveller. While working for his father at the Charles Krug winery, making wines aimed at the American mass market, he took a good snoop around Europe's most respected wine producers, particularly those in Bordeaux, and became convinced that the Napa Valley in northern California was capable of giving the world wine as fine as any. Today there can be few countries where wine is taken seriously which have not been visited extensively by Mondavi.

His main aim in all this travelling, however, is to learn. He will pack his winemaking team into a minibus and drive them round the Médoc, visiting all the best properties there to help them get the best out of their Cabernets back home. Then he will trundle them off to the Rheingau to pick up a few tips on Late Harvest Rieslings.

Luckily for the future of California's best-known winery, Robert's two sons are eminently capable of looking after things back home. Mike is President in charge of marketing and planning and Tim is winemaker, delighted to be corralled in the winery, tinkering with each aspect of the winemaking and trying to improve on every vintage.

Although heavily influenced by their father's travels, the Mondavis' is very far from a copy-cat operation. They have been formidable innovators themselves. Since the winery started in 1966, each vintage has brought the opportunity to test a wide range of new techniques. In Bordeaux the Château de Pez 1970 experiment of making a cask of each component *cépage* to provide insight into the standard claret blend was an isolated and daring exercise. At Mondavi there are three full-time research workers whose sole job is to compare small test samples of wine. Every single facet of the winemaking operation will be tested, right down to the individual barrel staves. Tim admits that in some respects the winery is like a giant school chemistry set, *"and boy, do I like to play with it;"* but the aim always is to inch nearer perfection.

There are those who feel that Mondavi should stop fiddling about and settle down, and indeed Robert himself feels that by now he is almost there with his Cabernet Sauvignon. So confident is he of its quality that he horrified fellow winemakers in the autumn of 1979 when he released his Reserve Cabernet Sauvignon 1974 at $30 a bottle. But he reckoned even then it was

A sudden downpour just before the grapes are ready to pick can make all the difference between a vintage that is great and one that is diluted and poor. In such circumstances top French winemakers tend to shrug their shoulders and accept the rain as an act of God. Not Mondavi. His reaction is to hire a fleet of helicopters to hover above the vines to dry them out. That really is style, the style of a man determined to make great wine. As he says himself: *"I want to belong in the company of the fine wine people of the world and I'll stop at nothing to do it. What interests me is excelling."*

worth every cent, and so – significantly for more cosmopolitan wine lovers – did Baron Philippe de Rothschild who the next year signed up a joint venture with Mondavi to produce a Napa Valley Cabernet to be put on the market at the same price as his precious Bordeaux first growth, Château Mouton-Rothschild. If ever a single event gave the Golden State credibility in the eyes of the chauvinist French, it was this.

Mondavi would doubtless be the first to admit that, of all his wines, his Cabernets have been the most consistently success-ful; and it is a tenet of Mondavi philosophy that the land round the winery, just north of Oakville on the "vibrant" western side of the Valley, is a prime site for this revered varietal. Mon-davi's Cabernets are dark, rich wines with the power one would expect from one born Italian, and attempts at subtlety that only such a Francophile would make. Any doubts on this last facet of Robert Mondavi's character would be dispelled by the most cursory in-spection of the cheeses

served, before dessert of course, by Bob and his vivacious second wife Margrit at the frequent and stylish feasts held in the spectacular recep-tion room – in full view of successive troops of envious tourists. This room is probably the only one in which the luxury item, Robert Mondavi Reserve Cabernet, is regularly incorporated into salad dressing.

The impressive long, low building has been used to good effect as a "logo" for the winery and is one of the most popular stop-offs on any visit to the wine country. When the much-esteemed architect Cliff May was called in to

design the Robert Mondavi Winery in 1966 his brief was to create the first new winery of any size to be built in the Napa Valley since Pro-hibition. The structural design makes it impos-sible for the visitor to imagine any other than the carefree California spirit prevailing in the breezy whitewashed arcades that connect the different parts of the winery. The wide arch with its roughcut tower and view through to the vines somehow sums up the informal yet totally com-mitted attitude to wine here. It would be as un-thinkable to find such a building in the Médoc as it would have been to find a replica of Château

Part of the winery, a design "unthinkable in the Médoc."

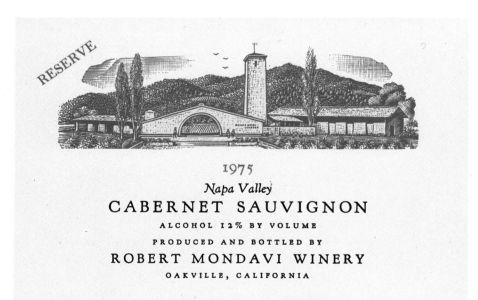

RESERVE

1975

Napa Valley
CABERNET SAUVIGNON
ALCOHOL 12% BY VOLUME
PRODUCED AND BOTTLED BY
ROBERT MONDAVI WINERY
OAKVILLE, CALIFORNIA

ROBERT MONDAVI WINERY

Sugarloaf Ridge
State Park
Napa R.
St.Helena
Silverado Trail

Joseph Phelps
Oakville
Conn Creek
Heitz Cellars
Lake Hennessey

N

5 mls 8 km

The 1974 Reserve Cabernet won headlines for its price tag, but this 1975 won converts to California quality all over the world.

Ducru-Beaucaillou in the Alexander Valley – until an oil fortune was put into building the Jordan Winery, that is.

Even more unthinkable to a Bordeaux château-owner is the gift shop at the entrance, albeit very stylish but complete with souvenir corkscrews, monogrammed glasses, sweat shirts and the lot. Imagine Château Lafite's horror at such a thought, compounded by their indignation at the US-produced T-shirts which give every American the possibility of emblazoning a blown-up version of that stately property's label all over their chests. But Robert Mondavi is nothing if not a PR man and confidently urges visitors in one of his many leaflets *"to enjoy the friendly atmosphere which pervades our winery premises."* The friendly atmosphere is fanned by exceptionally well-briefed public relations staff. All this frothy topping needs a solid base, of course, and Bob Mondavi would have been rumbled long before now if what went on in the more workmanlike section of the winery did not justify all the noise he makes.

More perhaps than for any other winery, it is impossible to give an up-to-date picture, for things change at whirlwind speed here. In the spring of 1982, let us say, they had 800 bearing acres, of which 685 formed the largest vineyard contiguous to any Napa winery, with a further 300 coming into production fast. They believe that their To-kalon vineyard by the winery and the Oak Knoll site on the other side of the valley

near Joseph Phelps are near-perfect for Cabernet Sauvignon and Sauvignon Blanc respectively. Tim, long, thin and as loquacious as his father, is proudest of these two varietals, *"though our Chardonnay and Pinot Noir are getting better all the time."*

Charting the history of the Robert Mondavi winery necessarily involves steering a course from one focus of intense concentration to another. In early 1982 the chief preoccupation was with finding the perfect moment to pick each varietal for optimum balance of sugar and acidity, for although Mondavi Senior is aiming at increasing specialisation the winery still produces a wide range of different varietals. These are all grown in slightly different micro-climates,

T-shirts available at the winery shop. Cheaper, but will they last as long as the 1975 Cab?

the factor which Mondavi, unlike his friends in France, believes is infinitely more important than soil composition. He admits good drainage as a vital ingredient, and while safety from frosts and other extremes of weather is desirable, he more often than not has the equipment to avert meteorological disaster (those helicopters, for instance).

Whether they are from Mondavi's own vineyards, which supply almost half the winery's requirements, or bought in, grapes that arrive at the constantly-expanding receiving bay of the Robert Mondavi Winery can, like patients arriving at a brand new hospital, expect treatment by the very latest methods and equipment. Everything that money can buy and experience requires is installed at Oakville. New presses have been bought only to be discarded a year later for something just a little better. There are regiments of stainless steel fermenting tanks, each computer-controlled to maintain the temperature at exactly the agreed level. Robert Mondavi is no braggard. He happily tells the story against himself of how when he first met André Gagey of Louis Jadot in Burgundy, he was convinced he would ruin his own California wines by fermenting as high as 88°F (33°C), but now he admits ruefully to having come round to his way of thinking. Mondavi, as usual, was one of the first Californians to warm up his thinking on fermentation. *"If we allow rather higher temperatures we can get away from simple fruit to*

rather more complexity. We don't know exactly what complexity is, but we're trying." This explains his policy of allowing reds to reach the high eighties and some of the whites to go above 60°F (16°C).

Another field in which the Mondavi team has led is that tricky question of stem retention. Way back at the crusher/destemmer there is a special by-pass system that allows them to vary the proportion of stems left in contact with the must from zero up to as high as three-quarters for some batches of Pinot Noir. Skin contact is another variable, and various formulae are applied here as a result of assiduous study of small samples from previous vintages. (All over one section of the winery, a series of demi-johns and small containers of all sorts bubble away to provide data for future undertakings.)

To the European visitor, a tour of the Mondavi winery can be baffling. Huge portions of the equipment are unrecognisable to those raised in more traditional climes. There are the serried ranks of roto-fermentors, programmed to allow a certain length of skin contact for each varietal-vintage combination. Chardonnay grapes, about 50 per cent of the total, and about 10 per cent of the total Sauvignon Blanc production, are left in the roto-tanks for up to 16 hours and then transferred to small oak cooperage for a fermentation that may even reach 75°F (24°C) towards the end.

All other varietals are fermented in stainless steel using a technique met in the European sec-

Mechanical harvesting at dusk or later can get grapes to the winery at safe, cool temperatures. Getting the ripeness at picking exactly right is a current preoccupation at Mondavi.

tion of this book only *chez* Moueix, that of injecting bacteria to ensure that the malo-lactic fermentation occurs just after alcoholic fermentation. *"I never skipped a year at Pétrus,"* says Bob Mondavi proudly, admitting that was where he saw how important stem retention could be. Tim, an ex-Davis graduate like Christian Moueix of Château Pétrus, is now in charge of the lab where this "malo" technique was developed. *"We couldn't go to a book for advice because all the books said 'Don't do it, the volatile acidity will go up.' Well the VA did increase slightly, but only slightly, and we're happy with it, not because we are for acid reduction, but because it makes for more stable wines."* Tim was the most reluctant family member to get involved with his father's famous winery – their sister Marcie looks after sales on the East Coast – but is now clearly hooked; and his smiling, youthful sincerity bears witness to what Robert reports is enormous dedication. What could be an extremely tricky handover seems to be going quite well. Tim acknowledges that it was his father who developed the wines' style, *"and my job is to see that the style evolves. If my father feels we should go another way, I have plenty of chances to convince him of how I feel. He's never told me what has to happen, though he may manage to convince me."* Just one example of this process is the Mondavi Petite Sirah. Robert argues it should go; Tim says it should stay. We can watch to see whether father convinces son.

One of Tim's recent preoccupations has been oak. There was a time when the winery's Oakville address could seem almost too apt, but the most thorough Mondavi research program of any so far has looked in detail at exactly what was needed to give each varietal just enough of the right sort of wood ageing to enhance rather than swamp its flavour. With painstaking care they looked into the advantages of treating wood with steam rather than fire, the relative merits of Limousin and Nevers oak, and the benefits of different intensities of charring or "toast." *"I firmly believe now that, in decreasing order of importance, are the character of each individual wine, then the method of coopering, including the degree of toast, and only then the origin of the oak."* So now they go for "fire only" heavyish toast casks for Pinot Noir and Chardonnay grapes to give them a vaguely smokey character, and light toast barrels for the Bordelais grape varieties Cabernet and Sauvignon Blanc. Tim could not help feeling just a little smug when they told him at the top Bordeaux cooper Demptos that their local university had conducted just the same experiments, a full two years after the Mondavis.

All this work has resulted in a complicated routine for the workers in the giant cask hall,

There's no shortage of scientific wizardry at Mondavi, but when it comes down to it, the noses have it.

No expense has been spared on getting exactly the right sort of oak (usually brand new) for each varietal, later tasted at the revolving tasting table in a session that can last four hours.

many of whom are highly qualified and here for the kudos of having the words Robert and Mondavi in close conjunction on their resumé. Chardonnays remain here for between seven and twelve months, and Cabernets usually between eighteen and twenty-six, with one batch receiving the treatment for a "probably excessive" thirty-three months.

The "regular" Cabernet Sauvignon releases from the winery often contain as many as fifty different components, and even the small quantity of the special Reserve Cabernets may be blended from twenty-five ingredients, not necessarily from any particular vineyards, but those judged best qualified to typify both that vintage and superlative quality. The major decisions in this blending process are made at a circular table on a swivel base next to the lab. A normal session

at this table, which can and usually does accommodate about fifty different wine samples, consists of four hours of concentrated tasting; and the really important decisions about Robert Mondavi wines tend to be made in the tiny alcove in which it is located, hard by the computer that churns out data on the temperature curve of each tank, optimal ripeness of grape varieties at harvest time, and almost anything else you could wish for.

Robert Mondavi has demonstrated, however, that the future of a wine can be dictated by factors which have nothing whatever to do with what goes on in the winery, or even the vineyard. If ever a winemaker can take credit for reversing the popularity and fortunes of a single grape variety, it must be Mondavi with what he did for Sauvignon Blanc. Until he got going on it, this

Robert, Tim, Michael and Margrit Mondavi. Entertaining – and how – is another of the winery's important functions.

varietal was relatively neglected by the American wine drinker. He drank it with enthusiasm, even a little reverence, if it came from France under the label Pouilly-Fumé, but the name Sauvignon meant little to him. So Robert Mondavi slowly fermented it, gave it barrel-age and started to sell his Sauvignon as a wine called Fumé Blanc and has not looked back since, except to throw the occasional glance over his shoulder at the rest of the California wine industry following in his footsteps.

Another example of his commercial acumen was the speed with which he picked up on the growing consumer demand for products that were "natural" in some suitably convincing respect. Hence his "unfiltered, unfined" wines, the first of this new breed on the market, designed for those who want to chew their wine, sometimes quite literally. Mondavi not only looks around to see what wines the Napa Valley can best produce, but keeps a keen eye on what his customers want to drink. If they want wholemeal wine, he'll give it to them. If they want less alcoholic wines, ditto. Mondavi was one of the prime movers in getting an exemption clause added to California wine law which had officially countenanced as wine only those liquids containing at least 10 per cent alcohol.

It is said that he got going on this project with even more force than usual, spurred on by a tank full of Late Harvest Johannisberg Riesling they harvested in 1977 with 43 per cent sugar, a ripeness they had never encountered before. The Pacific Telephone Company made a good deal of money that day as Mondavi frantically called his friends in Germany to find out what to do.

The Robert Mondavi Table Wine story provides another example of his looking to the market place as well as the vineyards; and although it has absolutely nothing to do with the making of his great wines, he would presumably be only too delighted by any parallel that might be drawn between his move into the lower end of the wine spectrum and that of his partner Baron Philippe's Mouton-Cadet.

Ironically, Robert Mondavi's move back into the coolest northern part of the San Joaquin Valley that supplies about 80 per cent of California's wine, brings him full circle, just a short hop from the Acampo winery bought by his father Cesare back in the 1930s when he was trying to build up a wine business for his children to inherit. When Bob Mondavi set out to create a winery *his* sons could inherit, he was already 53 and setting up on his own in controversial circumstances, having split acrimoniously from the Charles Krug winemaking operation run by the rest of his family. Jockeying with lawsuits and maintaining an untarnished image as a new top quality winemaker cannot have been easy, but Mondavi seems to have got away with it. Whether a normal person, with only half his energy, could have done it is open to question.

When he finally succeeded in getting his share of the Charles Krug spoils, Robert was able to buy out the Rainier of Seattle interest so vital in the early years, and now the business is all in the family. There is a strong family streak throughout the whole team at Oakville, which Mondavi and Margrit do their best to foster. The girl at the gift shop is able to report, for instance, that her mom's been pickin' for Mr Mondavi since the beginning. *"He's a swell guy to work for, you know,"* she confides, adding with a giggle, *"and he's kinda cute too."*

He is not a tall man, although his features are quite frighteningly strong. A big nose and mouth are set firmly above a powerful jawline, presumably great assets for his tireless tasting activities. He talks almost non-stop, the gangster-like rasp punctuated by hoarse squeaks when he gets particularly excited. But he is not issuing threats, he is making promises: promises that this year's wines will be even better than the last; that California is "coming of age;" that his new operation with the Mouton people will be even more exciting than ever for all of them.

Everyone who has met both Robert Mondavi and Baron Philippe can see how pre-ordained it was that they should be working together. *"We met and liked each other,"* says Mondavi simply. *"I think we've got a lot in common. What's exciting about it for me is that there is a man who has done more for Bordeaux in the last twenty-five years than anyone else. And he thought: 'They're different in California, but they belong.' Gee, of course we're different. We're six thousand miles away."* This is no PR stunt by Mondavi either, but a genuine fifty-fifty operation, for which approval was granted only after extensive meetings between Lucien Sionneau and Tim Mondavi. Wine is the point here, and the venture was launched with 2,000 cases of what they reckon is Napa's finest Cabernet Sauvignon from the 1979 vintage. There may be 7,000 cases a year eventually, as well as the venture's own winery in addition to its own vineyard, just across the St Helena Highway from the Robert Mondavi Winery. This seems highly desirable for such a sought-after vinous treasure, currently languishing in an unceremonious stack of barrels in one corner of the Mondavi cask hall and referred to there simply as "the joint venture wine."

With the many delegations of visitors from Europe, Robert Mondavi first does all he can to greet them personally, even if it means stepping straight off a plane to do it, and secondly puts out with characteristic generosity what he reckons are the European counterparts for comparison. For the visitor who is interested, he is quite prepared to open up a bottle of Château Latour 1976 to taste alongside his Reserve Cabernet, and then to open up a Lafite if the Latour turns out to be disappointing. He is usually happy with the results.

"I'd just like to say this," he might say after such a tasting, a favourite prelude that assures him of his audience's rapt attention. *"All that is happening now is just reconfirming to me what I always felt years ago. People everywhere know and believe that we belong in company with the finest wines in the world."*

Night-picking gets the grapes to the winery in ultra-cool condition.

To taste his Reserve Cabernet Sauvignon 1975 is to taste the results of thousands of man-hours' intensive search for excellence, drawing on the best the world has to offer a winemaker with enough energy, money and sheer nosiness to scour it.

Chateau St Jean

Richard Arrowood, "winemaster" at Chateau St Jean in Sonoma County, likes nothing more than a good snoop around the cellars of those credited with making the finest wines of Europe. His European tour in the spring of 1981 included an intense session with Alexandre de Lur-Saluces, for example, during which he worked out how experience and techniques at Château d'Yquem might help him with a brand-new little project to produce a Late Harvest Semillon. As someone determined on perfection, he naturally goes to the top for the answers. *"The free and open exchange of information between wine people, even competitors, thrills and astounds me,"* he says. *"I think ours must be the most open industry in the world – apart from medicine of course, but that's not involved with production."*

This is not to imply that he always gets the best end of the deal, however, or that he owes his undoubted success merely to culling other winemakers' ideas. He is proud of the fact that on a recent visit to Burgundy he spent two hours taking notes from Robert Drouhin, who then turned the tables for a five-hour session. *"I think the US has done in maybe five years what other more traditional wine countries took a century to do,"* he says, adding coolly, *"the French shouldn't panic, but the California renaissance might make them think about their techniques more."* He has noted with amusement top French producers move at last from hand pumps to piston pumps, for instance, when Californians moved from piston pumps to centrifugal pumps two decades ago.

If Dick Arrowood sounds intensely self-assured, it is partly because he rather encourages that image, and mainly because he can afford to. In an astonishingly short time Chateau St Jean has built up an impressive reputation in California for exemplary white wines, with its best Chardonnays having few peers as consistent, and its Late Harvest Johannisberg Rieslings rivalled only by those made by Joseph Phelps Vineyards.

The winery was founded way back in 1974, just north of Kenwood in Sonoma's Valley of the Moon, in country looking considerably more fertile than its name might suggest, pushed up against the lower slopes of the Sugarloaf Ridge. The winery's efficient handouts describe the buildings themselves as "a bit of Europe," "a unique, turreted and towered chateau of Mediterranean arched elegance in which are created world-class wines that have become a legend in their own time." In fact the buildings are about as European as the English muffin, found in every American diner but never in England, and perhaps conform more to the American dream of the Mediterranean than to the reality. There is immaculate ochre stucco (an echo of the even newer Jordan winery up the road), ornate colonnades, a "visitors' tower" from which self-guided tours start, and scrupulously manicured gardens complete with landscaped waterfall and ornamental pond. *"We view the visit to the Chateau as a very unique experience, and the basic design has been set up specifically for visitors,"* explains the winery's president Allan Hemphill, safe from any of them in his 500 square-foot, five-inch pile office on the first floor.

Visitors to Chateau St Jean are indeed treated well, and signs of genuine thirst for knowledge rather than inebriation are rewarded by some of California's best-trained staff in the Tasting Room ("Shirt and Shoes Required"). Hemphill explains how they choose to allocate their "four or five different levels of hospitality," and expands on the importance of making a visit to Chateau St Jean match up to the quality of their wines. As Dick says: *"It would be like preparing a gourmet dinner and then serving it with paper napkins and plastic cutlery otherwise. Sure we get Joe Sixpack too, but visitors to Sonoma tend to be a bit more serious than those Napa tourists and we believe in giving them something to get their teeth into."* This includes a newsletter of daunting technical depth, accurately reflecting the interests and preoccupations of

Dick Arrowood himself sees in every load of grapes during the crush. "It's good for the mind and the body."

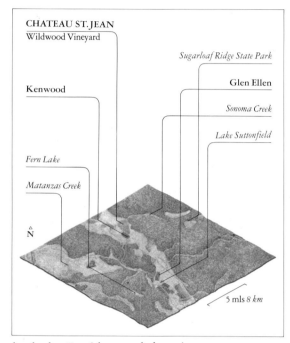

CHATEAU ST.JEAN
Wildwood Vineyard

Sugarloaf Ridge State Park

Kenwood

Glen Ellen

Sonoma Creek

Lake Suttonfield

Fern Lake

Matanzas Creek

N

5 mls 8 km

both the President and the winemaster.

The appetite of the trio who founded the winery for fine wine production was whetted during their travels to Europe. Robert and Ed Merzoian, now in their fifties, are members of a highly successful farming family in the Central Valley and were joined in this exciting wine project by their brother-in-law Ken Sheffield, based in San Francisco and now a crony of Dick Arrowood over many a bottle of fine European or rival California wine. The winery is named, confusingly for Europeans, after Ed's wife and Ken's sister Jean, rather than a French male. Yes, maybe it should therefore have been Chateau Ste Jean; that was a bit of an oversight, admits Arrowood.

The most distinctive characteristic of the winery's policy has its roots in the founding family's experiences of European wines. Ignoring the common California practice of labelling wines simply by varietal and general geographical provenance, such as "Napa" or "North Coast," they decided to opt entirely for individual vineyard designations. *"The French and the Germans don't have a monopoly on those kinda wines, you know,"* admonishes their bright young winemaster. This was not a new concept in California in the mid-1970s – Ridge had established themselves on the basis of their vineyard-designated reds – but Chateau St Jean

became the very first West Coast winery of any size to be designed specifically for such wines, and in this case almost exclusively white wines.

"At first people saw it as a sort of artsy-craftsy marketing ploy," Dick Arrowood recalls. *"They thought we were just trying to make ourselves seem special by appearing to offer a range of different Chardonnays from the same vintage and roughly the same region, but we've certainly proved ourselves now, being one of the wineries that has been around a little longer than the rest."*

Those who have enjoyed Chateau St Jean's Chardonnays from the Robert Young vineyard up in the Alexander Valley, and learned from comparing them with those from the Wildwood vineyard just to the south of Chateau St Jean itself, will agree that the winery's policy, finicky and complicated for winemaker and consumer alike, has paid off. Life is difficult enough for Côte d'Or burgundy fans who can resort to maps and appellations of the Côte d'Or that have been established for decades and sometimes centuries. For California connoisseurs, trying to chart their way round this tiny plot in Sonoma named after the grower versus that other one in the Santa Cruz mountains named for an old oak tree, things are even more complicated. *"Yeah, it is difficult,"* admits the articulate Allan Hemphill (who gave Arrowood his first job at Korbel sparkling wine cellars), *"and perhaps the winery is running ahead of consumer knowledge. The newsletter can help of course. What tends to happen in the educational process is that a customer finds a name that he likes. Then he finds out roughly where it comes from. Then he may get interested in the vineyard and the growers themselves, which is why we're tending to make personalities out of the people we buy our grapes from. I must admit honestly that only a very small proportion of our customers are into this, but it is accelerating rapidly."*

Will there come a day when the vineyards of California are as carefully, lovingly and uncontentiously mapped out as those of France and Germany? *"It will be interesting to see what happens,"* allows Hemphill, *"because there really are only a few vineyards recognised as capable of producing vineyard-designated wine of a consistent quality. We've seen some names come out and all the wine writers have praised them, and then the next year the wine is atrocious."*

The model in California is of course very much more Burgundian than Bordelais, as there

1975

Chateau St. Jean

ALEXANDER VALLEY

Chardonnay

ROBERT YOUNG VINEYARDS

PRODUCED AND BOTTLED BY
CHATEAU ST. JEAN · KENWOOD, SONOMA VALLEY, CALIFORNIA
BONDED WINERY NO. 4710 · ALCOHOL 13.9% BY VOLUME

is a well-established tradition of buying in from vine-growers who do not usually produce wine themselves. Only the tiniest wineries provide 100 per cent of their own grapes; at Chateau St Jean there will probably never be more than 30 per cent of their requirements from their 80 planted acres around the winery and a further 40 near Windsor at La Petite Etoile. The winery has already specified more than a dozen vineyards on the labels of its varietals, but Hemphill stresses that this is a highly selective process. *"We research the vineyard in great detail first, working a minimum of three years with them before assigning names."* And what sort of contract do they eventually enter into with a selected grower? *"A very expensive one,"* he laughs. *"We effectively go into partnership so that we can plan for the long term."* This involves guaranteeing prices for the grapes which may be well above market prices, in exchange for control over varietals and vineyard techniques. *"We try to stay away from 'the market,'"* says the president of "the Chateau" (pronounced "sher-*toe*"), with just a shade of self-satisfaction. *"The grape market is a psychological one to a great extent. It can have enormous ups and downs that have nothing to do with anything other than a very slight shortage or a tiny glut. Our aim is to have long-term plans, and to get away from the traditional adversary relationship between us as producers and our growers."*

Chateau St Jean have adopted a pricing policy that means they can afford to reward their growers suitably, and with Chardonnays such as the Robert Young selling at $25 a bottle and their best sweet Johannisberg Rieslings twice as much as this, they are comfortably in the top bracket of wine prices. The visitor to the sumptuous premises might be forgiven for thinking the winery had some appeal as a tax loss, but according to Hemphill it crept into the black on its own account after only five years of operation, when most Californians look forward hopefully to making a profit perhaps after ten or twelve years. *"If you worry about wine quality first, you find magic things can happen."*

The man behind this wine quality (*"we pay him a million dollars a year, you know"*) is a fanatic, and proud of it. He likes to be described as "intense" and is at pains to establish himself as something of a tyrant in the winery. One feels that the Protestant work ethic burned strong and unflickering in at least this soul while the rest of his contemporaries surrendered to the fashion-

able laid-back life-style of the West Coast in the late 1960s and early 1970s. At this time he was doing graduate work at Fresno in fermentation science and making his mark in a career that took in Korbel, United Vintners and Sonoma Vineyards where the first vintage, 1974, of wines under the Chateau St Jean label was made. His 1974 Auslese-rich Johannisberg Riesling put the winery on a pedestal, and subsequent Chardonnays managed to reinforce this stature.

He is proud of, but unsatisfied with, all aspects of his operation. Unimpressed by outside acclaim, he is in constant pursuit of the perfect wine. *"Hopefully, I'll never make a wine I think is perfect, so I've got a job for life."* Everything is part of this relentless search, each grapeload and bottle examined with an objectivity rarely found in Europe. About half of the vineyards around the Chateau are on the steep hillsides, for instance, on the land that Europeans reckon Californians should have planted all along. Here

At Chateau St Jean, *opposite*, the vineyard name is all – and Robert Young's wines are more sought-after than most.

Shades of Disneyland at "the Chateau" which nuzzles up against the Sugarloaf Ridge in Jack London's Valley of the Moon.

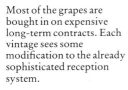
Most of the grapes are bought in on expensive long-term contracts. Each vintage sees some modification to the already sophisticated reception system.

there are, most unusually for California, vines planted up to a thousand feet above sea level – Chardonnay and Sauvignon Blanc especially. Three years ago, Arrowood admits he would have said that these vineyards produced wine of noticeably better quality than their counterparts on the valley floor, not so flat in Sonoma as in Napa. Now he's not so sure. *"I've found some very interesting fruit quality from the valley floor recently."* He is of course particularly proud of the Johannisberg Riesling they buy from Robert Young and Belle Terre, where the Russian River fogs have so far brought him some botrytised grapes every year.

During vintage time his adrenalin flows at torrential speed. *"I crush every load myself, I like to get a feel for the quality of every batch. I'll probably work a sixteen- or seventeen-hour day then, but it's good for the mind and the body, especially my weight."* He also plays tennis and skis, but basically reckons that wine and then trout fishing are his two major hobbies.

He is particularly proud of his Willmes membrane tank press (*"Phelps had one, but mine is the only all-stainless"*) which gives him high quality juice in good quantity with low phenolics, in quantities up to 100 tons a day. The vast outside press and the imposing quartet of holding tanks above it can get hot in the late California summer and the press is blanketed in carbon dioxide to prevent oxidation of the must. Inside is one of the strangest sights in any California winery: there is the customarily impres-

sive bank of gleaming stainless steel tanks for settling and fermenting, except that at Chateau St Jean they are tiny, to accommodate the produce of all those individual vineyards. A dozen of them hold less than 500 gallons or 20 hectolitres, and even the biggest holds no more than 3,500 gallons or 155 hectolitres.

Most fermentation takes place in stainless

Chateau St Jean is king of the small lot. Even the biggest of these gleaming stainless steel fermenters is only 3,500 gallons – tiny by California standards.

steel, except for that of some of the Chardonnay (which makes up almost 60 per cent of the Chateau's total production, planned never to exceed 100,000 cases). Dick Arrowood was surprised by the outcome of his experiments to compare the results of all-stainless, all-oak and stainless-finished-off-with-oak fermentations. He was expecting the third method to yield the best results, but may have to admit that all-oak fermentation seems best for Chardonnay. This is partly, he believes, because some oak extractives are soluble only at very low alcohol levels, so can be incorporated into the flavour of the wine only if it is fermented in his small French oak cooperage. He had thought he would lose some of the important grape aromas if there were no stainless fermented component, but now he's not so sure.

In the cask room, stacked five-high with barrels on perilous-looking gantries, he is fermenting three-quarters of his Chardonnay in casks that range from brand-new to four years old, and at temperatures that creep up from 40°F (4°C) to as high sometimes as 67°F (19°C). After a three-week fermentation they are racked out of cask and either clarified naturally or centrifuged and put back into cask for four to six months. The bottling line at this predominantly white wine establishment (Cabernet and Pinot have been cut down to represent only about one per cent of total production) is one of the most advanced, in terms of hygiene if not speed, in the world, and Dick Arrowood can then safely rest his bottles for about a year in the case of indi-

vidual vineyard Chardonnay, before releasing them, or rather allocating them, to the winery's avid customers. For several reasons he may feel more confident about the stability of his wines than most. *"Wine is* not *a living thing,"* he says testily. *"It's organic and changeable, but unless there's micro-biological spoilage, it can only change as a result of external influences."*

Sauvignon Blanc, Pinot Blanc and the reds go into oak for some ageing too, and about one-third of Sauvignon Blanc production is fermented in oak. Wines that are not given wood-ageing tend to be given about four to five months in bottle before leaving the winery, and they may well be ready to drink at that point.

Dick Arrowood believes that his finest Chardonnays are best drunk at between five and ten years, and reports that his first Chateau St Jean vintages are holding out well. Few consumers get the chance to put this to the test, although one suspects that there are cellars all over the United States harbouring small quantities of his wines to savour in the future. At the winery they are keeping more and more wine back for "the library."

Dick Arrowood strolls easily around his workplace, where the visitor is assailed equally by the strong vanillin smell of oak and the high volume of the piped music everywhere ("Allan won't let me play hard rock"). *"Our Chardonnays are built to last. They are high in acid and high in alcohol – maybe a little too high in alcohol in a vintage like 1979 when we had 14.5°. I'm looking for an average of about 13°, and you know white burgundy can reach that level too. Chardonnay needs to be mature when picked; otherwise there's none of that oily butteriness. We try to average 24 Brix because we want maximum fruit without too much alcohol."* Try tackling him about the possibility of cooler areas to achieve equal complexity with a little less alcohol and you will be reprimanded with the argument that *"you can't get away from the fact that the climate here is more Mediterranean than Burgundian. At least we don't have to chaptalise every year, and the vintages are much, much more dependable than they are in Burgundy. Provided a wine has sufficient acidity, it can take high alcohol levels of 13° or so."*

His 1980 Robert Young Chardonnay, just 13.9°, when tasted early in 1982 was of course very youthful, but showed enormous class on the nose. There was something very streamlined about this wine, almost a steeliness that is seldom found in the walloping whites of California. It seems unlikely that Arrowood could ever produce a wine that lacked fruit, and every vintage he makes seems to get just a little nearer his goal of perfection. He is convinced that Sonoma and the Alexander Valley have the best potential for top class Chardonnay, because there are more pockets of ideal micro-climate and the sort of soils to which it adapts best. *"We like well-drained gravelly soil for Chardonnay, and a high mineral content is good too. I haven't yet worked out the connection between the soil and the sort of minerally taste we like. Maybe it comes not from the roots but from the dust on the grapes themselves. We can't detect the minerals in the wines analytically, but there does seem to be something there."*

Here is something else that will preoccupy Arrowood for a couple of years, and perhaps help him in his single-minded program of constant refinement. But what happens if he ever gets bored? He may eventually, having another thirty years of working life ahead, run out of aspects with which to tinker. Simple, he says. If he ever feels that coming on, he'll simply be up and off for another snoop around Europe.

The singleminded young Arrowood produces whites almost exclusively in a wide range served at the winery's tasting room by some of California's best-trained staff.

Joseph Phelps

Joseph Phelps is one of those rare men who had a dream, managed to achieve it, and seems very content indeed with the results. As a highly successful Colorado construction engineer "big in bridges," he was hired to build the new Souverain winery at Geyserville and quickly fell prey to the charms of the wine country life and terrain. Like many others before and since, he found that the undulating Silverado Trail down the east side of the Napa Valley is as pretty as it sounds and one glade in particular caught his attention.

In 1973 this gentle, deliberate, and now much-respected outsider had acquired the 670-acre cattle ranch just off the Taplin Road next to Joe Heitz. It is typical of Phelps' thoughtful approach that he still feels guilty about changing the function of the property (even today referred to as "the ranch"), and has to keep reminding himself that the cattle weren't paying their way anyway. No one could accuse the man of desecrating the landscape. About his simple and solid pair of redwood barns, joined by a creeper-hung bridge giving exciting contrasts between light and deep shade, he admits "*I probably put more of myself into this building than any other.*" The

Joseph Phelps at work in the lab of the winery he dreamed of building.

design makes the most of the winery's view over the entire valley and of the hillside behind with its knolls and clumps of live oaks so characteristic of the Napa. The atmosphere throughout is one of calm, self-assured progress, suggested by the confidence of the beams and angled glass.

"We know we're putting ourselves fair and square in the sights of those who accuse anyone who's tackling more than two varietals of being a dilettante," says the man whose name can appear on as many as eighteen different labels in some vintages. But the extraordinary thing about this wide range of wines is how uniformly good they are. It is difficult to pick out one varietal in which they excel in comparison with their others, but they are inevitably associated closely with Johannisberg Rieslings, partly because this is the only Napa winery with an unbroken record of producing a botrytised version since 1975 (a long time in California wine history), but substantially because of the winemaker here.

Walter Schug was born and brought up at the State Wine Domain at Assmannshausen, that funny little red wine enclave at the western end of the Rheingau, and, of course, studied at Geisenheim. He came West to learn in 1959 and was talent-spotted by the perceptive Joe Phelps when the time came to design and operate his new winery. With a slight German accent still and a fairly frequent visitor to his homeland "for family and equipment – but not techniques," Walter Schug is a natural focus for all German visitors to the Napa Valley. It is not surprising to find that he is the most respected California winemaker in Germany, but his solid track record is fully acknowledged on the West Coast as well. He was an important speaker at the first international symposium of the Masters of Wine at Oxford in 1982.

His grey bushy hair suggests a maturity at odds with his direct, clear, pale eyes and youthfully trim figure, distorted only by the outcrop of a walkie-talkie on one hip and a huge bunch of keys on the other. He spends a great deal of time in the vineyard, and radio waves form an important part of communications here. But the base for major decision-making is in that bridge, which contains a well-equipped laboratory and the light, well-designed offices of the winemaker and his boss. Joseph Phelps, with an interest in speciality food shops, is now much more concerned with edibles and drinkables than constructibles, and he is no absentee landlord on his dream site.

One hundred and seventy-five of the 670 acres are now planted with vines and these have over the years been supplemented for the sake of versatility by additional land acquired and grapes bought in. It was initially intended as a red wine ranch, but things have not quite worked out that way. As Walter Schug says, *"we're not ashamed of trying new things here, and then admitting we were wrong if necessary."* Phelps and Schug are the first to admit that there is a long way to go in matching specific sites with the most suitable varietal, and already on this property first planted only in 1974 there are bare patches where they have decided to rip out the vines and start again. Schug's patron is even more ruefully down-to-earth about the work to be done on siting. *"We know half of what we ought to know and we've only acted on half of that."*

Walter Schug, California's most consistently versatile winemaker?

At Joseph Phelps they have
an almost "European"
attitude to hillside plantings.

In the late 1970s two important steps were
taken. Joseph Phelps with a partner bought the
Stanton Ranch near Yountville to provide each
of them with about 50 acres of cooler land particularly good for whites. And, perhaps more
importantly for the long-term, Phelps began to
develop vineyards on the hillsides sloping behind
the winery. They now have about 70 acres that
can technically be called mountain site, although
much of the land in the immediate vicinity of the
winery has almost identical conditions. With
names like Big Hill and Alpine Meadow, these
new plots have added much greater flexibility to
the Phelps range, for they have fully utilised the
different directions in which the various knoll-
sides face.

They can now successfully produce
Gewurztraminer on the ranch, for instance, and

half of their 16 acres of the varietal are in a low
dip on a bit of north-facing mountainside where
acid is high and the pH is low. They are hoping to
repeat 1977's success with a Late Harvest
Gewurz, but the standard wine consists of a
blend between the two different styles produced
on the hillsides and at Yountville. Half of their 40
acres of Chardonnay are now also on hillside
vineyards too, planted on south-east facing
slopes for morning sun.

The second most important white grape
variety planted by Phelps is their famous Johannisberg Riesling, half of the 30 acres on low land
near the winery and half at Yountville which
comes bang in the middle of heat summation
zone Region I, as opposed to the Region II
characteristics of the home ranch. The two vineyards again produce two very different styles,
but Walter Schug guards against letting the
acidity fall too low in the warmer zone by picking very early indeed. He aims for only about 19°
Brix in grapes that are destined for his Early
Harvest Johannisberg Riesling, and was even
picking early in the second week of August in the
precocious harvest of 1981.

The aim, typically California, is to harvest
grapes like Riesling at night or first thing to keep
them fresh. Schug eschews skin contact and
presses his aromatic varietals as fast as possible,
being a great believer in adding all the press juice
immediately. In very hot years he may even add
tartaric acid, forbidden in Europe but perfectly
acceptable in California, Australia and South
Africa and a great help to Schug's Rieslings when
the pH is higher than 3.5, both in terms of
flavour and ease of handling the resulting wine.

Riesling is the only variety that is *not*
planted on the hillsides, at least experimentally,
at Phelps, thus putting paid to any neat analogies
with the Mosel. In Germany the most important
factor is summer rain, according to the ex-
Geisenheim student, and if he were to plant his
Riesling on the hillsides the yield would be very
low and the grapes might develop a "papery"
taste. Much better to cultivate this humidity-
loving varietal in lower, damp conditions – just
like those by the river near the Phelps homestead
just half a mile downhill into the valley from the
winery. Or, even better for botrytis, at Yountville where humidity is provided by its proximity
to San Francisco Bay and "the acids aren't burnt
off."

Only Chateau St Jean can rival Joseph
Phelps' record of botrytised Johannisberg Ries-

lings, and certainly the best wines from each winery are enormously impressive in their youth. Joseph Phelps produced one picked at an amazing 48° Brix in 1978, residual sugar 30 per cent, and one almost as rich in 1976. All sceptics, and indeed Messrs Phelps and Schug themselves, are hanging on to see how they prove themselves over the years. So far they have demonstrated great purity of botrytised Riesling flavour, perhaps not as delicate as their German counterparts, but apparently very well-balanced. They lack the burnt, slightly flat quality in some other attempts. Half-bottles are the order of the vintage here, sensibly, but even these tenths are released at about $20 each from the winery.

Walter Schug has always been able to rely on natural botrytis and feels innately antipathetic toward the artificially-cultivated spores method developed by certain other wineries. Like Chateau St Jean, they may experiment with a little botrytised Semillon on their five-acre plot of this Bordeaux varietal, grown not to produce a single-varietal wine, but to *"fill out the middle body of Sauvignon Blanc."* Walter Schug insists that his job is to produce great wine, not a great varietal, and therefore steers clear of the *"aggressively grassy character"* of unblended Sauvignon. About 10 per cent Semillon nicely rounds out the flavour, as both Mondavi and Arrowood have found, but Schug further refines his offering by taking care not to give it too much rich oak character.

"I'm a great believer in the importance of the size of oak as well as the type and the time spent in it," he says. Joseph Phelps Vineyards is unusual in the amount of intermediate-sized oak they have – a clear heritage from the Rhineland – and Schug gives his Sauvignon/Semillon blend six months here and Gewurztraminer perhaps half that. All wines, red and white, are fermented in stainless steel, except for the barrel-fermented Chardonnay. Chardonnay then gets about six months in small French oak cooperage, and most red wines between one and two years.

Five acres of Scheurebe is Walter Schug's new venture. He bottles it as a varietal only if it reaches Late Harvest richness, for he feels only then does it present itself as a wine with sufficient class to capture newcomers to the variety; but results so far have been good, considerably better than many rather coarser versions from Germany.

They have given up for the moment on the final white varietal they would like to add to the

SELECTED LATE HARVEST
Napa Valley
Johannisberg Riesling

1979
Joseph Phelps Vineyards

Alcohol 9.6% by volume   Residual Sugar 16.8% by weight
Grapes harvested at Stanton Vineyard at 34.5% sugar by weight
Produced and bottled by Joseph Phelps Vineyards, St. Helena, California

range, Viognier. Joseph Phelps is no mean connoisseur of fine European wines. He is an assiduous customer of Sotheby's and Christie's wine sales, and was introduced in his Boulder days to the greats of the northern Rhône. He may be a claret man now but has never lost his respect for and interest in the fruits of the Viognier and Syrah grapes. Davis have tried to get him and several others suitably healthy cuttings but have failed so far. Once they do get their hands on some budwood, their enthusiasm could double the amount of Viognier wine available in the world within only a few years!

When Joseph Phelps submitted a similar request for Syrah cuttings to Davis they told him to look out his window. Professor Olmo had also been a great fan of this Hermitage grape and had persuaded Christian Brothers to plant it on the plot near their new circular fermentation facility at St Helena, now the most obvious landmark in the panorama from the Phelps ranch. Phelps and Schug were delighted to find such a treasure under their noses and, deciding that they would take the cuttings even though they weren't virus-free, produced in 1974 the first commercially-available vintage of Syrah in California since the nineteenth century.

They are still not completely satisfied with their Syrah – *"it has a tendency to get pruney if we pick too late"* – but it is improving each year.

Schug's Rheingau origins are betrayed in Late Harvest Rieslings of unusual finesse for this side of the Atlantic.

Unusually, they are much more enthusiastic about their 18-acre plot of Syrah than about their 15 acres of Pinot Noir, and are fermenting a third of the Rhône grape by whole berry fermentation (or *macération carbonique*) techniques to improve complexity, and sometimes "lighten" their Syrah with a bit of Chenin Blanc.

"We're still tinkering with it," smiles Joseph Phelps, who firmly believes there will be a noticeable improvement in quality when the Syrah vines planted on the hillside start showing their form. They are waiting to see how their new Pinot Noir plantings at carefully chosen elevations *"to avoid high noon scalding"* will perform too.

For a winery like Joseph Phelps Vineyards, the costs of planting and developing a hillside vineyard are not substantially greater than costs on the valley floor. They save on frost protection and soil fumigation, both *de rigueur* on the flat, two mile-wide Napa backbone; and the land tends to be cheaper in the first place – perhaps $10,000 an acre as opposed to $20,000 for un-planted valley land and up to $30,000 for an acre of developed valley vineyard. Phelps' valley yields are kept unusually low, averaging little more than three tons an acre (about 40 hectolitres per hectare), by strict pruning and sometimes an additional summer thinning, so that the naturally lower hillside yields come as no great economic disadvantage to them. In any case, as Joe Phelps himself points out, *"it's not the yield in tons per acre that's important, but the pounds of fruit per vine – a basic fact we in the industry tend to lose sight of."*

Like all but a few California winemakers, he is still ambivalent about the qualitative advantages of hillside vineyards. This was the land the pioneers planted. Then the new generation felt they could do just as well, with much less effort, on the valley floor, and Phelps feels they may well be right. *Even Gewurztraminer can do well in the valley if it's cool enough. The hillsides give you automatically well-drained and aerated soil, but the alluvial deposits on the flat mean that most of the valley is well-drained too. There are swampy patches, and you have to know where they are."* Walter Schug is pretty enthusiastic about his new higher vineyards and interrupts here, waving towards the mountains he can see from his desk saying: *"We've planted about 70 acres on the hillsides, but there are probably another 30 we could plant."* "*Wooah!*" moans the man who would have to pay for the new

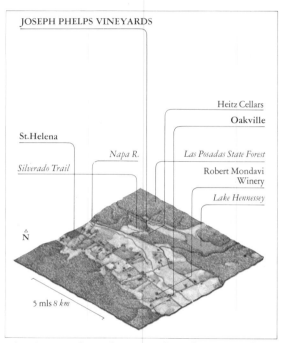

plantings. Schug shrugs and smiles. *"It's there, boss."*

Those of Phelps' 38 acres of Cabernet that are planted on the hillside are doing particularly well, on south-west-facing slopes, the sort of angle they are trying out for some of their 21 acres of Zinfandel too. They have a little bit of Cabernet Franc for blending, but buy in what Merlot is sold under the elegant JPV label, usually blended into one of their much-respected Cabernets. These have the charm of California's climate, but backed by definite structure that suggests they will last, if given the chance, rather better than some of the more fulsome West Coast Cabernets. Eisele and Backus are two special Cabernets much in demand, as is their Insignia, the *crème de la crème* of their red wine, usually Cabernet-based. It seems extraordinary to the outsider that one man, raised on curious almost-rosés in Germany, should be able to turn his hand so successfully to so many different styles.

Walter Schug is far from a prima donna, however; he is simply immersed in the process of maximising wine quality (and to keep him busy on Sundays he now has his own winery, Schug Cellars at Calistoga). He has purposely increased the temperatures he's aiming for during fermentation: reds from 80°F to 85°F and whites up from around 50°F to as high as 65°F in some

Schug, seen *left* testing the Brix level in beautifully healthy Cabernet Sauvignon, is a firm believer in the total inclusion of all juice from this special tank membrane press for his whites. See its twin on page 143.

Another German legacy – the medium-sized oval casks add a unique dimension to Phelps Sauvignon Blanc and Gewurztraminer.

cases. The emergence of the hillside sites with all their different facings and maturing times has turned the winery upside down and, now producing about 50,000 cases a year, the original building is at bursting point. The pressing capacity has been expanded, and in 1982 Schug was impatiently awaiting the results of trials in Germany of rotary fermentors for whites as well as reds. He is very proud of keeping in the forefront of developments in new equipment and reckons, rightly, that the plant at his disposal is infinitely "more advanced" than he would have had had he stayed in Europe.

After looking in detail at his red wine fermentations, carefully jacketed to keep them between 70° and 82°F, he has instituted a sophisticated system whereby the must is pumped rapidly over the floating cap of skins (which may be nearly 20°F hotter) two or three times a day. *"It is here that the winemaker exercises the biggest influence over the future harmony and quality of the wine. All too often prudent methods fall victim to work overload, manpower and equipment shortages."*

At regular tastings in the lab the Phelps team meet and exchange views on various options on different wines, leaning back on the wooden benches, crossing their denim or cord-covered legs and expressing their views in that confident yet relaxed California way. Bruce Neyers is in charge of sales and may volunteer: *"Late Harvest Riesling sells real well . . . You ain't got none? Well, just thought you'd like a little vantage point from the back seat."* They have no need to pull in customers. They sell on allocation mainly, holding back more and more of their better wines until they feel they are nearer maturity. For the first few years of the winery's existence they hoarded their youthful reds – and found themselves saddled with the reputation of being "a white wine winery" until the quality of their Cabernets forced a rethink. Today, they release even their whites too late for all the "new release" tastings because their style is relatively late-developing – but seem to manage quite well without public fanfare. *"We're low-key in our presentation,"* murmurs Joseph Phelps, and he looks pretty happy about it.

Winery workers dine in the "hospitality room"-cum-cask-hall.

Ridge

R idge is quite unlike the other California wineries in this book, and proud of it. Not for the boys up on Monte Bello Ridge a lavish architect-designed complex complete with the latest high tech in winemaking innovations and public relations. They are perfectly happy with their apparently hillbilly encampment of giddily-angled wooden barns. In their winery methods they are more interested in going backwards in time than forwards.

The winery's spectacular position more than two thousand feet above the Pacific Ocean, which laps the shoreline just 15 miles to the west, must have something to do with this confidently insouciant attitude. The winery's cosily domestic address, 17100 Monte Bello Road, Cupertino, does nothing to warn the visitor that he will have to wind for nearly five miles round the meanest of hairpin bends on the most basic of roads, much given to ice in winter and subsidence in stormy weather, up from the valley floor to the south of Palo Alto onto the top of the Santa Cruz Mountains. It seems perverse enough to site a dwelling here, let alone a fully-fledged winery to which grape trucks must commute from over 200 miles away during the crush. On a clear day they can see the sprawl of San Francisco with Mount Tamalpais in the background, ships on the ocean on one side of the ridge and the valley floor on the other. From this semi-industrial flatland floats up the roar of Mammon, but at the winery the only sounds are birdsong and the odd yelp of a winery worker. "Monte Bello" indeed, though Ridge is just three quarters of a mile from the San Andreas Fault. This is hardly the sort of location one would expect for a winery project built entirely from scratch.

The story of Ridge depends a great deal on historical accident. The winery was built as the Monte Bello winery and a start made on the surrounding Cabernet Sauvignon vineyards in 1880 and, as Schoonmaker noted, this area had established a fine reputation for "claret" by the time of Prohibition. The winery survived this, and the 1906 earthquake, and was still around in the late 1950s when four scientists from the Stanford Research Institute just 20 miles away were looking for a site on which to realise their dream of producing a little wine at weekends. With great luck they met the previous owner just as he wanted to sell, and by 1967 one of them, tall, bearded, quiet and quizzical David Bennion, had left academia to work there full time.

Ridge's first winemaker, David Bennion.

Vines so high they're way above the clouds.

Throughout the 1960s the winery was producing less than 6,000 gallons but was gaining acclaim for its distinctive "hand-tooled" wines. By 1969 the consortium decided that further growth was inevitable and so was a fully-fledged winemaker;

but the man chosen, Paul Draper, gracefully acknowledges that *"Dave's 1962 and 1964 were really great Cabernets."*

Even today this respected winery is owned by a group of private individuals, all of whom know each other and take the important financial decisions together. *"We really are trying to make the finest wine not just in California but in the world,"* says Paul Draper, *"so we told them they could make more money elsewhere. Luckily it turned out to be profitable within ten years, which is great, but I really don't know of any other group that works together so well – partly because they're all so bright, I suppose. We must have about four Nobel Prize winners."*

Bordeauxphile Paul Draper in the office inspired by a visit to Lafite, and, *below*, dwarfed by Rioja-like stacks of surprisingly ancient casks, not from Bordeaux.

David Bennion is now President and responsible for this successful financial side, although he is hardly typical of the American Corporate Man, being so laid back he is almost horizontal. He makes his way up to the winery several times a week, but the day-to-day winemaking decisions are now all in the hands of the jovial Paul Draper.

Paul Draper's reverence for tradition and his admiration of France's finest wines has undoubtedly played an important part in shaping Ridge's house style, one of the most individual in California. For some years they have laboured under the label of being producers of "big wines," but more attentive students note the intensity and range of so many different flavours rather than outright size. The wines lack the fatness, the sometimes aggressively ripe overtones, of some of California's more overblown reds, and Paul Draper would be delighted if you were to draw parallels between his Monte Bello 1977 Cabernet Sauvignon (put on the market at a cool $40 a bottle) and Château Latour. *"If I talk about first growths a lot it's because that is where we are aiming, and if I talk about Latour especially, it's because that's the one I admire most and drink most often. Bordeaux produces*

the finest wines in the world and it's therefore a good measure against which to see whether we get the same finesse and complexity." Draper has lined up on his desk a bottle each of the 1970 vintage of Latour, Mouton and Ridge, the last showing up rather well against the competition when last tasted, he thinks. *"I was introduced to fine wine back East and, since I didn't get married till I was 39, I've been able to afford a pretty good cellar."* He keeps up his interest in Europe via the written and spoken word too, and likes nothing more than a good bit of international wine gossip.

The other major factor determining the unique quality of Ridge's wines, all red but for a few barrels of Chardonnay grown and sold at the winery, is the location of their vineyards. When Chateau St Jean decided to pioneer vineyard designation for white wines, they were providing a counterpart to what had been Ridge policy for some time. Paul Draper is proud of the character of the individual plots of vines in which they specialise, and keen to keep their wines separate whenever the quality justifies it.

The vineyard of which they must be most proud is the 50-acre plot of very mature vines, almost all Cabernet, around the winery at Monte Bello. Up to a height of 2,600 feet these gnarled stumps, a relatively rare sight in California, flourish in the clear air way above the inversion level for a growing season considerably longer than the state average. During the vintage here, always in October even in the 1981 season that was so short everywhere else, shareholders and some of the oldest customers make their perilous way up to pick, two o'clock being picnic time up here on the ridge on October Saturdays. All is just as Paul Draper wants it here, except that he would like to add a little Petit Verdot to the four or five acres of Merlot that soften the Monte Bello Cabernet.

Monte Bello is still the only vineyard that Ridge actually owns, but when Paul Draper was taken on and given the brief to extend the winery's production from 6,000 gallons to nearer the 100,000 gallons produced today he started to look around for some more really fine Cabernet Sauvignon vineyard. *"Trouble was that high quality Cabernet was very rare and what there was was all tied up, but we did find patches of very old Zinfandel planted up in the mountains producing just one or two tons per acre, but super quality from very old vines. So although Cabernet Sauvignon has always been our prime aim,* *we decided to work on top quality Zinfandel too. We've proved that our low-yield Zinfandels are at least as good as most of the Cabernet Sauvignon available."* Low yields are very much a tenet of Ridge philosophy and they expect to average about two tons an acre when some of the less quality-conscious wineries *"might make more than six tons an acre – that's the trouble with our appellation system, 'Napa' includes everything, right down to the* palus." Paul Draper must be the only Californian who uses such a cosmopolitan word to describe the Napa River mud flats.

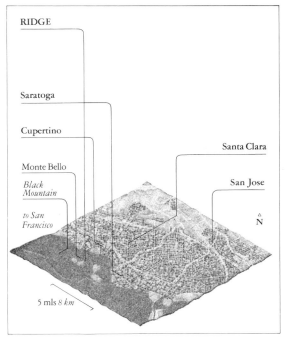

During the 1970s then, Ridge got themselves a name for their high quality Zinfandel – with justification, for they were the first to treat California's very own "mystery grape" seriously. This is not to say that they have managed to evolve one distinct style for the varietal. Even spread over Ridge's five or six major Zin locations, the grape manages to be tantalisingly indefinable, producing a lean, polished, elegant wine when grown at York Creek up in Napa, and a quite different one with concentration and tannic austerity at the Shenandoah vineyard in the Sierra foothills.

York Creek, on the slopes of Spring Mountain, is perhaps the nearest thing Ridge have to a "number two" vineyard. It is owned by Paul

79 Zinfandel, York Creek, bottled May 1981
The differing soils and exposures of the several Zinfandel blocks at York Creek and the Petite Sirah in the one mixed block seem to be major contributors to the unusual complexity of these wines. In addition, the mountain location protects the vineyard from the extremes of heat in the valley below and assures greater quality. This beautifully balanced wine combines an earthy character with the varietal spice and the oak of small cooperage aging. Although it should be excellent tasting this fall, it will develop more fully with three or four years of bottle age.   PD (5/81)

Begun in 1959, Ridge was one of the first of today's chateau-size California wineries, that is, those that attempt only the highest quality at the quantity levels of the classified chateaux (up to 40,000 cases). All the wines are aged in small oak cooperage with the majority receiving no cellar treatment other than racking. Located above 2300 feet on Monte Bello Ridge in the Santa Cruz Mountains, our winery and main vineyards overlook San Francisco Bay. For information on ordering wines or visiting us for tasting, please send a note or call (408) 867-3233.   DRB (1/80)

PRODUCT OF CALIFORNIA, U.S.A.

NET CONTENTS
750ML

RIDGE
CALIFORNIA
ZINFANDEL
YORK CREEK
1979

SPRING MOUNTAIN, 88% ZINFANDEL, 12% PETITE SIRAH
FOOTHILLS, NAPA COUNTY   ALCOHOL 13.5% BY VOLUME
PRODUCED AND BOTTLED BY RIDGE VINEYARDS, BW 4488
17100 MONTE BELLO RD, BOX A-I, CUPERTINO, CALIFORNIA

Ridge's Monte Bello Cabernet fetches their highest prices, but "serious" Zinfandels like this set them apart from the crowd.

Draper's great friend Fritz Maytag, producer among other things of fine Maytag Blue cheese from Iowa. Ridge take most of the production from this 100-acre vineyard at an unusually high 1,600 feet. The Cabernet York Creek they make contains between 5 and 10 per cent Merlot, on Monte Bello lines, while the York Creek Zinfandel has up to 15 per cent Petite Sirah blended in. Paul Draper is a great fan of Petite Sirah, bemoans its being unfashionable and argues that a good Zin needs the backbone of a bit of Petite Sirah if it is to last two decades. Just along from the York Creek vineyard is Draper's crony Ric Forman, who shares his enthusiasm for traditional techniques.

More long-term Zinfandel agreements have been made with growers on the Shenandoah and Fiddletown vineyards in the Sierra foothills, Paso Robles down the coast and the Geyserville, Sonoma site in the middle of which was constructed Souverain's enormous winery. The less concentrated wine from the Paso Robles vine-

yard might go to make up a San Luis Obispo County Zin, while Shenandoah and Fiddletown's light wine might end up being sold as Amador County. So of the 40,000 to 45,000 cases now produced by Ridge each year, a suitable maximum it is thought by that brainy committee, slightly more than half is unusually refined Zinfandel, 2,000 cases is the 100 per cent York Creek Petite Sirah about which Draper is so enthusiastic, and the rest is beautifully-fashioned Cabernet.

Most Europeans would be absolutely horrified by the prospect of receiving their raw material from so wide a geographical area. The Paso Robles vineyard is well over 200 miles from Amador County – about the same distance as Bordeaux from Beaune, say. And that is before the grape trucks have started the climb up Monte Bello Road. Paul Draper is very proud of Ridge's trucking system. Unlike many California wineries whose first direct contact with their growers each vintage is at the weighing machine,

Ridge resolutely insist on trucking their own grapes. *"All of our guys, even some of our top people here, hold truck licences, and at vintage time they drop everything and take to the road. We go out early every morning with three-foot gondolas to be trailed through the vineyard to stop premature crushing on the journey. The grapes are in by noon and crushed here, after a journey that lasts 3½ hours at the most, later that day probably, and never later than early the following morning. If we had rot it would be a problem, but here in California we're very lucky and it rarely affects more than 5 per cent of the grapes, and then only every fifth year or so. Distance is nothing because we're in control. We have far more control over our fruit quality here than many a winery on the valley floor, because we actually oversee them when they're picking."*

It is the ramshackle winery, not the vineyard, that really thrills Paul Draper, however, and he gives the impression of a man beatifically happy when talking and tasting wine, leaning on one of his beloved American oak casks. It is strange that the winery perhaps closest to Bordeaux in its heart, soul and aspirations should be one of the few top quality California producers *not* to have joined in the clamour for barrels from France's top *tonneliers*. This is out of neither cussedness nor meanness, but the result of Draper's analysis of experiments at Ridge and some of the ancient wine textbooks he loves to study. He has unearthed a detailed comparison of different oaks by Bordeaux winemakers that pre-dates Robert Mondavi's researches in this area by about seven decades. The three most successful were found to be Baltic oaks, no longer obtainable after the ravages of two world wars; fourth best was American; fifth Bosnian; and only sixth was the French oak then used by the Bordelais. *"There's more tight cooperage oak grown in the United States than anywhere else in the world,"* maintains Draper with pride, *"but what is really important is how you treat your wood – much more than where it comes from."* Ridge wines bear out this thesis. After up to two years in the carefully air- not kiln-dried American oak from which most of Ridge's barrels are made, the wines have none of that obvious, "hot," vanilla flavour so evident in wines that have spent time in less carefully-treated American oak. This may partly be because Ridge uses its barrels for some time. Some of the casks are ten years old, but Paul Draper claims there are still oak extractives there. Cabernet

Sauvignon goes into at least 50 per cent of older oak, but with their high-pressure water system the Spanish-speaking vineyard workers at Ridge blast out the tartrates thoroughly each year.

"Low yield vines make much more difference to the flavour of the resultant wine than the sort of oak you use. If a wine is hand-made and the yields are low, there should be no more difference between our Monte Bello Cabernet and a Pauillac than, say, between a St Estèphe and a Graves," Paul Draper claims. The 1980 Monte Bello when tasted in cask early in 1982 was certainly pure claret, however much one tries to resist such comparisons. Dry, complex,

Draper designed this tube himself – and then found it in a nineteenth-century Bordeaux catalogue.

fine, it had all the elements one would hope to find in a great red bordeaux at this stage in its development.

For Paul Draper tradition is all. He was thrilled when he found his own design of specially-angled metal racking tube in an old Bordeaux catalogue of winemaking equipment. (He would also find its twin if he ventured to Vega Sicilia in Spain, also heavily influenced by the Bordeaux of a hundred years ago.)

He was even more delighted by a visit from Guigal of Côte Rôtie, during which the Frenchman took one look at the perforated metal submerged cap fermentation grids used at Ridge, and shrieked with excitement that just such a thing had been used in his father's time and he had been experimenting with one in France for years. *"He said they had to dispense with the grid when they installed stainless steel tanks, but I built our grids specially so they'd fit in, in three panels, and I'm convinced the submerged cap has a lot to do with our wines' individuality. No other winery here since Prohibition has used grids like ours, though one or two are now trying."* Paul Draper's turn for excitement now, as he leads the visitor up a rickety staircase to the sprawling attic above the winery, looking like a scrap metal merchant's treasure trove.

When it comes to either primary or malolactic fermentation, he wants to leave everything to happen as naturally as possible. Yes, they do have some commercially cultured yeast on hand for those rare occasions when a tank just will not start fermenting, but they much prefer to use the yeasts that occur naturally on the grapeskins. *"It's fundamental in great French and Italian wine, and we're small enough to control it, so why interfere? I truly think it makes a difference. Just like introducing special bacteria to encourage the malo-lactic. I don't want to have something powerful and new like that in our winery until I'm really convinced it's a good thing. Once here, it would completely take over, and I'm an old conservative as far as bacteriological processes go.*

"With our size, we can afford to make totally natural wines. Whether they're better or not is a subjective judgement. Europeans would say they were. If people pick out our wines and say 'Ah yes, that's Ridge,' then maybe it's a factor. I think there's a great danger in getting a very clean and simple wine if you try to take great steps to make your fermentation too clean and simple. We're not trying to convert sugar into alcohol in the most efficient way. We think there's a place for at least one winery to carry on the pre-Prohibition methods of California."

Ridge specialities include the new gravity draining system for these fermentors and, gravity at work again, powerful water-cleaning of the barrels in the underground cellars.

The folksy touch.

Ancient vines give Paul
Draper's wines their special
character.

Paul Draper does not have formal training in oenology and has doubts about the tasting experience of some who have, but is lucky to be able to draw on more than twenty years' intensive study of some of the world's finest. Since 1969, his first vintage at Ridge made in conjunction with David Bennion, he has built up experience of California winemaking of an unusual length. At Ridge they are proud of the fact that their early-1960s start puts them in the pre-Heitz era, preceded only by Stony Hill and Hanzell performing in the same arena, producing small quantities of very fine wine.

Just ahead of the Mondavis in realising the importance of oak treatment, Draper reckons he now has the answer to the ideal alcohol levels to aim at: between 11.5° and 12.9° for Cabernet and around 13° for Zinfandel because it produces such a large berry. This puts Ridge wines,

especially their Cabernets, a good degree less alcoholic than most of their peers. So much for the not uncommon accusation of being "too big."

After up to two years in bottle they are put on the market, with a single case upper limit on orders of their most expensive wines, and instructions to keep tight hold of both bottle and cork for at least ten and ideally twenty years. They are proud of the fact that their wines are set for a longer life when bottled than their equivalents at Robert Mondavi (of whom Draper is a great admirer) or Beaulieu Vineyards. Their pride and joy was a blind tasting of Latour and Monte Bello they put on for New York wine writers. They all thought the Ridge wines more backward, and were dumbfounded when they failed to spot that the wines were not all from a single winery.

AUSTRALIA

AUSTRALIA

It comes as a surprise to those who cling to the traditional hearty, beer-swilling image of the Australian to find out how important wine is to him. Beer is giving way to wine so that per capita wine consumption in Australia is twice that in Britain and well ahead even of that other up-and-coming wine producer, the United States. An important factor in the popularity of wine in the last decade has been its price: a litre of wine can be bought for less than a litre of beer, or sometimes even Coke. And the technological expertise of winemakers in Australia's answer to France's Languedoc-Roussillon region, the vast, hot, irrigated areas along the Murray and Murrumbidgee Rivers, means that the quality for the price is perhaps the most stunning in the world.

There is still much more work to be done at the top end of the quality scale, however. The vine has been cultivated in Australia ever since the arrival of the first settlers, who took the precaution of picking up vine cuttings as they rounded the Cape of Good Hope, but only a very small proportion of today's vines are planted in the areas most suitable for them. The Californians have tended to compensate for this elementary mistake by the simple expedient of a huge investment of money. Few Australian winemakers have such resources at their disposal. Even for the very finest wines, prices are still comparatively low – in 1981, a 1977 Cabernet from the new St Hubert's Winery was the most expensive red on current release, retailing at A$16 a bottle. The "connoisseurs' market" in Australia is not so well-developed as in the United States – yet.

The Hunter Valley provides Australia's most famous concentration of wineries, wines that cry out for ageing, and hot air.

Fairly few Australian wine drinkers have any experience of fine non-Australian wine, and even many of the oenology students turned out by Roseworthy and Wagga Wagga (the down-under Davis and Fresno) will be taught that the most important job is to eliminate any wine fault, rather than being shown by exposure to a wide variety of different wine styles what creative options may be available. If Australia imports only 3 per cent of what she consumes, she exports an even smaller proportion, which means that Australia's fine wine secrets tend to remain secrets from the rest of the world.

If the outsider is woefully ignorant of the best Australian wines, this is hardly the case with Australia's wine lovers. It is perhaps the very fact that wine appreciation is relatively new that makes them so avid for guidance on what is best. Australian wine magazines organise comparative tastings on a scale more grandiose than any of their equivalents elsewhere. Their readers take to heart their counsel almost as faithfully as they do the results of the all-important State Wine Shows. "Successful" wines are sold under labels festooned in medals won throughout the continent, from Perth to Brisbane. There may be no official ranking of wine properties in Australia, but there is no lack of very specific rating of individual wines.

The reason that such a ranking of properties, like the *grand cru* system, would be spurious is the same as in California, only more so. The location of most wineries bears only a tenuous relationship to the provenance of their grapes. Trucking is an even more important feature of the grape industry in Australia than in California. Longer distances are involved, and con-

servation of fresh grapes by refrigeration or the luridly-named "brimstone process" until the winery is ready to ferment them is a perfectly acceptable part of winemaking practice. Petaluma (page 233) is a good example of this phenomenon. All but the very smallest enterprises still try to offer a range of different wines that bear little relation to what their area is best-equipped to produce.

Coonawarra and its suitability for Cabernet Sauvignon was one of the first area/varietal combinations to be identified. Wynn's and Redman make particularly inspiring examples. Much more accessible, but still in the state of South Australia, are the Eden and Clare Valleys, both higher than the Barossa, and making a name for their delicate Rhine Rieslings. Gramp's Orlando and Smith's Yalumba here show that even big companies can produce very fine wines, although this lesson is particularly apparent in Penfolds Grange Hermitage (the story of Australia's red giant starts on page 229) and in the classic mature Rhine Rieslings of Leo Buring, the South Australian subsidiary of the giant Lindeman. Lindemans also deserve enormous respect for the great aged Hunter Valley wines they release under typically complicated "Bin numbers." Australian wine lovers have to be numerate to find their way around Bin number This and Paddock That, but the effort is repaid at least in these great Hunter Semillons and Shiraz that have spent some time in bottle. The Hunter is Australia's Napa Valley, the first area in which quality was achieved by a number of highly motivated individuals, among whom Dr Max Lake of Lake's Folly was a pioneer. Tyrrell's (page 226) can boast a century-old tradition, but more recently "The" Rothbury Estate and "The" Robson Vineyard have also earned their definite articles.

In the state of Victoria, Chateau Tahbilk established just such an individualistic reputation, which is now being rebuilt; but some of the newcomers are particularly exciting. Balgownie,

Taltarni and Tisdall are all winning medals and then respect. Up in the far north-east of the state the family firm Brown Bros, thanks to prolonging the Australian gospel of low-temperature fermentation over months rather than weeks, is making some very fragrant whites and well-constructed reds. Near them Australia's hugely under-appreciated assets, the Liqueur Muscats of Rutherglen, are produced and mature to their unctuous richness and concentration. But perhaps the most exciting recent wine discovery in Victoria has been the potential of the Yarra Valley on the outskirts of the state capital Melbourne, where some excellent Pinot Noir is made.

Some see Australia's newest wine regions, the Margaret River and Mount Barker areas in the south-western tip of the country, as those with the greatest potential. Cape Mentelle has done well so far with concentrated reds, and Leeuwin can even boast a Mondavi as consultant winemaker in the making of their aromatic whites; but it is still too early to judge ultimate quality. What this illustrates, however, is what enormous areas must remain untapped by the vine-grower.

It is impossible to underestimate the size of Australia. Until the mid-1970s, vines tended to be cultivated where it was most convenient rather than most suitable. Perhaps by the end of this century the wine map will look quite different. Tasmania with its much cooler climate will probably assume much more importance, and all sorts of exciting pockets with the right micro-climate will have been sought out.

With wine as well as with any other aspect of Australian life, there are no qualms about "trucking" over huge distances. The country's most famous wine source is said to be Sheppard's Creek, named after the biggest road hauliers.

Tyrrell's

Late in 1979 there was a call from the *Melbourne Herald* to the old white clapboard homestead that is the headquarters of one of Australia's oldest wine families which told them they had won international recognition at last. The Tyrrells had no clue that their 1976 Pinot Noir had even been submitted in the Paris "Wine Olympics," and indeed Bruce Tyrrell's first reaction was *"Gault and Millau, who are they? French bastards would they be?"* They soon became aware however of the full impact of coming top of the Pinot Noir class, "beating" a Clos de Vougeot 1969 and other offerings from Burgundy. Celebrations were well under way before anyone remembered that the wine had been rejected by Australian wine judges as "not having any Pinot character."

Bruce's father and third-generation winemaker Murray Tyrrell is a wine judge himself and one of the industry's most prominent characters, rivalled only by his chum Len Evans and Dr Max Lake for the number of entries against his name in the index of any book on

The famous Murray Tyrrell and his son Bruce, with typically red Hunter soil and atypically serious expressions.

Australian wine. His craggy face, forthright opinions and willingness to express them loud and clear make him unforgettable. His son observes: *"I've never been able to work out why my father and Len Evans bother to use the telephone when they both holler so loudly down it at each other."*

It is no accident that these three famous wine men all have their winemaking base in the Hunter Valley, just an hour's flight north-east of Sydney. Those closer to other wine regions sometimes complain that the Hunter makes just 1 per cent of all Australian wine, but at least 50

per cent of the noise about it. Its uncompromisingly difficult and distinctive characteristics seem to have attracted just the sort of men to deal with them. It is probably the world's hottest wine region with high aspirations to quality (so hot that some winemakers add Trebbiano to sharpen up their reds), and its curious volcanic soil over a limestone base puts its own very definite stamp on the ungrafted vines, giving rise to one of our more original tasting terms, "sweaty saddle."

Murray Tyrrell feels his responsibilities as a Hunter man keenly, having taken over in 1959 from his Uncle Dan who made his first Hunter Valley wine in 1883. *"I consider the Hunter has so much to offer in general terms of winemaking that the distinctive style and special quality of the area should always be maintained."* He may have doubled production in his time and brought the family's own vine acreage up to 110, but in the rough and ready winery buildings topped by romantic corrugated iron, he sticks to the original family philosophy that earth floors keep casks damp and wine maturation optimal. Everything looks very Heath Robinson in the tightly-packed sheds, with hosepipe "brine lines" looping from cask to cask, doing their bit to keep things as cool as possible. When it gets very hot, they even spray the winery roof – with icy water.

When you have got tradition in a country like Australia, you tend to flaunt it. At Tyrrell's they still use a brace of hand presses. *"They're not that much slower and we think we can get more good juice per ton from 'em,"* says Bruce with conviction, adding about a much newer, neighbouring winery, which Murray co-founded, that *"we once bet Rothbury we could crush more than half they could using all their modern equipment. We did 14 tons to their 23. Tyrrell's is the only Hunter winery still using hand presses – and that's why my father is patron of the local rugby club: so we can get all the young studs out here and keep 'em fit."*

It comes as no surprise to learn that Bruce commuted by horse in his schooldays, nor that the family manage 800 head of cattle as well as all this fancy wine. Everything is rough, ready, but very effective. In the offices in the old homestead a computer sits oddly in Uncle Dan's old bedroom, the open windows do spittoon duty, and fine lungs substitute for an intercom. *"'Ere, the PM's on the line. Wants a dozen Pinot Noir '76"* was audible proof of Malcolm Fraser's interest in wine during a visit in 1981.

Even the tasting room is little more than a lean-to. Visitors may be slightly distracted by the shrieks of tourists fuelled by Blackberry Nip next door and the steady stream of winery workers helping themselves to the vacuum-wrapped giant bricks of cheddar in the fridge in the corner; but when going through the Tyrrell's range one is likely to be impressed by the clean winemaking style, particularly evident in their whites. Semillon is *the* white grape of the Hunter, where it is confusingly known as Riesling, and Tyrrell's Vat 1 Semillons have great attack and vibrancy; and, like all good Hunter Semillons, they are built to last, and last. It is with Vat 47 Chardonnays that Tyrrell's have really made their mark recently, however. With their almost-green tinge these lemon-coloured wines manage to combine raciness with richness. Some might argue they develop a little quickly, but their tendency to hurtle towards middle-age, albeit an exciting one, is being checked.

The family is enthusiastic about "imported" wines, drinking "as much as we can get hold of," and especially so about burgundies. They were some of the first to grow Pinot, and the first in the Hunter to experiment with Chardonnay, which Bruce describes as *"a bugger of a thing to grow – we have to literally send men through the vineyard pulling individual leaves off."* They started in 1970 with a "Pinot Riesling" (Chardonnay/Semillon blend) and had nearly 15 acres of prized Chardonnay vines in 1981 when the varietal was in enormous demand throughout Australia. In the Hunter it tends to yield about 2½ tons per acre, slightly more than most red vines do, but Bruce claims to have seen some less quality-conscious producers in Australia's irrigated vineland getting yields of up to 20 after really enthusiastic watering. Even quality-conscious growers often water two or three times a year – a horrifying concept to a Burgundian, but then so is chaptalisation to an Australian. Climate determines which moral stance is taken by winemakers.

There certainly seems to be little sacrifice of character in these Tyrrell Chardonnays – although the all-pervasive Hunter soil adds its mark to the grape's own. Murray Tyrrell's suspicion is that, as the vines mature, the wine they produce will become more distinctively Hunter and less distinctly Chardonnay; but there was no shortage of Chardonnay fruit on the 1978 and 1979 Vat 47 wines. All Tyrrell

Vintage 1977 - Vat 47

TYRRELL'S WINES

HUNTER RIVER.

NIL MAGNUM NISI BONUM

D2404

PINOT CHARDONNAY

Tyrrells Vineyards Pty. Ltd.
Wine Growers, Pokolbin, N.S.W.

PRODUCE OF AUSTRALIA

750 ml

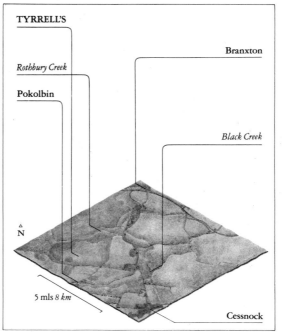

TYRRELL'S

Rothbury Creek

Pokolbin

Branxton

Black Creek

Cessnock

N

5 mls 8 km

Pioneers of Chardonnay, Tyrrells reserve "Vat 47" for their best.

Chardonnays are fermented and aged in French oak (*"as in Burgundy, one never ferments right out in a hogshead"*), in casks treated either by one of the cooperage firms that remain in Adelaide, or by an old man who visits them in his holidays from another strong family firm of the Hunter, the McWilliams. Chardonnays are given

The Tyrrells are also working hard in their Pinot Noir vineyard for a wine that's a great favourite with "the PM," Malcolm Fraser.

about ten months in oak, considerably longer than most vintages of Semillon, and then put into white burgundy bottles specially imported from France.

They may import things physical from Europe, but Bruce at least, now sales director of the family fortunes, would not readily admit to importing inspiration. *"I've been to California a couple of times and I think it's great. I just wish we had the money they have there. But I think people like us, the New Zealanders and the South Africans are all working together and swapping what we learn rather than using the traditions of Europe."*

The whole family (including sister Anne, now married to Victorian winemaker John Ellis of Tisdall) is proud of the story of how Murray, during a visit to a Bollinger press-house, threw off his jacket, rolled up his sleeves, took up a pitchfork and showed them how it was done. After all, the Tyrrell's have winemaking traditions as old as many a French wine dynasty.

Penfolds Grange Hermitage

The history of Australia's most famous red is the strangest, and one of the shortest, in this book – and provides a good illustration of the difficulties of establishing wine quality in a country with as few yardsticks as Australia.

Penfolds is an enormous company, with interests throughout the country's wine regions and a range that includes such delicacies as Penfolds Sparkling Tiffany and Penfolds VO Invalid Port. Its most treasured product, however, is Penfolds Grange Hermitage, a wine conceived by someone who began his career with them as messenger boy and brass polisher, and who continued to make Grange in secret when a company directive ordered production to cease, such criticism did it meet at the outset.

After 49 years with Penfolds, Max Schubert is retired now, but the licence plate MES 000 is often to be seen in the car park of "the Company's" winery at Nuriootpa in the Barossa Valley, for he continues to act as their senior South Australia man. He is a native of the state's best-known wine valley and, like so many of Barossa's inhabitants, of German stock. There is nothing remotely Germanic about his baby, Grange Hermitage, however. Like the not totally dissimilar intense reds of Vega Sicilia in Spain and Chateau Musar in Lebanon, it owes its inspiration to Bordeaux.

Max Schubert had worked his way up in the pre-war years, and shown such aptitude in Penfolds' developing technical side that several times

the chairman tried to get him released from wartime service. Max at the time was somewhere between Egypt and Benghazi, keeping his tastebuds in trim on standard issue *vino da tavola* and arak. During the late 1940s, he continued to impress. And so won over by a special range of sherries was the then chairman Mrs Gladys Penfold Hyland that in 1949 he became the first non-family man to be sent "O.S." (overseas) to study winemaking.

The energetic Christian Cruse was his Bordeaux host and mentor during Max Schubert's stay, and made sure that he tasted some of the best that Bordeaux had to offer. *"Each time I visited his home at Château Rausan-Ségla, he brought forth wines the like of which I hadn't seen before. I was amazed at the weight in these young reds, and it set me thinking that we could probably produce something like it because our wines are very big too."* All the way back to Australia, Penfolds' most prized employee considered how best he was going to achieve Médoc concentration from the raw materials available to him back home. *"We would have loved to have used the same varieties as in Bordeaux, but they simply weren't available in commercial quantity then. The only Cabernet Sauvignon I knew was in our own vineyards, but we only had a few acres. So we decided to go with our native Shiraz, and after careful vineyard surveys I decided on two sites: about 80 acres round the old Magill winery 600 feet up in the foothills on the outskirts*

The original Grange Hermitage vineyard at Magill is almost encroached upon by the city of Adelaide.

Penfolds

Grange Hermitage

BIN 95

VINTAGE 1975   BOTTLED 1976

SHOW AWARDS:
     Gold Medal Brisbane Show 1976, Class 16
     Gold Medal Adelaide Show 1980, Class 18
     Silver Medal Melbourne Show 1976, Class 24
     Silver Medal Sydney Show 1977, Class 14

Since 1952 successive vintages have been awarded
     27 Trophies   68 Silver Medals
     125 Gold Medals   40 Bronze Medals
             5 Championships

Grange Hermitage is generally recognised as Australia's finest red wine. This great wine was developed by Mr. Max Schubert commencing with the 1952 vintage. Grange is made from selected hermitage grapes grown at the Grange Vineyard, Magill, in the foothills of Adelaide, South Australia and the Kalimna Vineyard, Barossa Valley, South Australia. Matured in small oak casks prior to bottling, Grange Hermitage will improve with additional bottle maturation. During bottle maturation, it may throw a slight crust or deposit — it is therefore recommended that the wine be decanted prior to serving.

Bottled by PENFOLDS WINES PTY. LTD.
Adelaide

F/10068   WINE MADE IN AUSTRALIA   750 ml

Max Schubert and his wonderfully craggy face – a result of all that opprobium when Grange Hermitage was first launched?

of Adelaide, and an area in Morphett Vale to the south of the city that has now given way to housing. Today we rely on Magill for about 40 per cent of the grapes for Grange, and get most of the rest, including a little Cabernet sometimes, from our Kalimna vineyard, which is much better than most Barossa sites because it's relatively high and the soil is poor sandy loam. The yield there is only about 1⅓ tons per acre, while at Magill with its average vine age of 30 years we're getting no more than three – and that's taking no positive steps to keep yields down."

In those days most Australian reds were big and blowsy at first, and tended to fade rapidly into rather graceless middle age. Max Schubert's specific aim was to make *"an Australian red wine capable of staying alive for a minimum of twenty years and comparable to those produced in Bordeaux,"* so he knew that good quality fruit was not enough. He would have to put into practice the lessons he had learned about controlled fermentation and maximum skin contact, and employed an ingenious submerged cap headboard for the first vintage in 1951. Equally important was his use of (just five) new untreated oak hogsheads for maturation, using a standard well-seasoned 1,000-gallon cask usually used for Australian "dry reds" in those days as control.

The results he found thrilling. *"After twelve months, both wines were crystal clear, with superb dark, full, rich colour and body, but there the similarity ended. The experimental wine was*

bigger in all respects. The raw wood was not so apparent, but the fruit characteristics had become pronounced and defined, with more than a faint suggestion of cranberry. It was almost as if the new wood had acted as a catalyst to release previously unsuspected flavours and aromas from the Shiraz grape." He continued the refinement of the wine over the next few years, delighted by each new vintage and the wine's progress in bottle.

By 1956, *"the time appeared to be ripe to remove the wraps and allow other people to see and evaluate this wondrous thing."* This wondrous thing even got itself a name, "Grange" from the name of the original cottage built by the Penfolds on the Magill vineyard, and "Hermitage" partly because "Grange Claret" did not sound quite right ("Claret" being Australian for "red"), and partly because of what Max Schubert, good South Australian, calls darkly "the New South Wales factor," the firm's headquarters being in Sydney and Hermitage being NSW for Shiraz.

The Sydney high-ups called for sample bottles from each of the vintages from 1951 to 1956 and presented them to "top management," important wine people and close friends to assess the value of their investment in all that wine lying idle in the underground cellars at Magill. *"The result was disastrous,"* recalls the man responsible. *"Simply no-one liked Grange Hermitage."* Even after he and his chief South

Australian patron Jeffrey Penfold Hyland had hawked the wine around wine and food societies and wine tasting groups such as Australia's Beefsteak and Burgundy Clubs, the result was the same. Max Schubert can still remember every insult, of which "tastes of crushed ants" and "would make a good anaesthetic for my girlfriend" rankled particularly.

Just before the 1957 vintage, he received an order to cease production. Why tie up thousands of dollars in a wine no-one liked? Much less one that was "harmful to the Company image as a whole?" Luckily for future generations of Australian wine drinkers, Jeffrey Penfold Hyland could see some inkling of what Max Schubert was about, and encouraged him to continue to make Grange, albeit on a limited scale and without the important ingredient of new hogsheads, through the vintages of 1957 to 1960. Then the directors, encouraged by the more favourable reception Grange was now receiving after it had had a few more years in bottle, gave their official okay and allocation of funds to resume production.

Since that time, Grange's *réclame* has developed to a level of intensity particularly apt for this style of wine – so much so that Len Evans in his definitive *Complete Book of Australian Wine* refers to "Grangeomania" as an established Australian phenomenon, noting the obsessive nature of those who collect bottles of this wine, and its taste of "raspberries, strawberries, violets, truffles and old boots." Only ten to fifteen thousand cases of it are produced each year, and it is released, about six years after the vintage, at prices that seem positively cheap to the non-Australian, but which are the highest commanded in the bargain wine market there. Winning medals in the state wine shows is the way to win the respect of Australia's wine drinkers, and in this field over the years Grange's performance has been unparalleled. The incongruously drab magenta and grey label on each vintage lists its greatest triumphs prior to release; and these continue, for when they put the 1955 vintage into the Canberra Open Claret competition in 1980 it waltzed off with the top award "even though we've pensioned that vintage off now." Its style is so distinctive that wine judges tend to recognise it straightaway and almost instinctively trot out nineteen points (points are all in Australian wine assessment).

"We've often wondered why others don't try to make wines nearer to Grange Hermitage in

The "tank farm" gives some idea of Penfolds' range.

style," muses Max Schubert, who has trained many a winemaker who has gone on, with intimate experience of the Grange technique, to another winery. *"There should be quite a few who could attempt it, but of course it does require a fair economic investment."* The Grange of today, occasionally supplemented by grapes bought in from outside Kalimna and Magill (now surrounded by Adelaide suburban dwellings), is fermented for twelve days in stainless steel with a

The Kalimna vineyard in Barossa is the other major source of Shiraz, and sometimes Cabernet Sauvignon, grapes for "Grange".

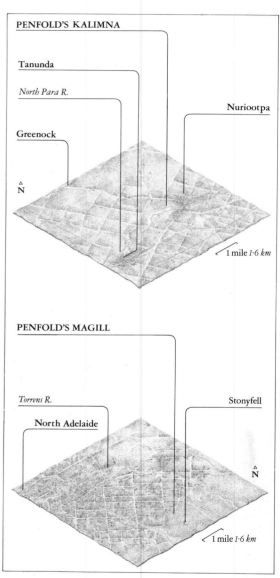

headboard and constant pumping over to get maximum extraction from the fruit. In some years, tannic acid may be added afterwards, unthinkable in Europe but quite legal in Australia (and California), and presumably a practice that can only be indulged in successfully with a wine of enormous character. After eighteen months in oak – American in preference to French because "our aggressive young fruit needs it" – the wine is put into bottle; but for all its vigour and richness, it is not over-alcoholic, usually about 12.5°, considerably less than most California reds, and presumably partly as a result of the vineyards' altitude. As Schubert says, *"what we've done is harnessed Australian ripeness. Grange is first and foremost an Australian wine."*

It is interesting to note however that, given the chance to create a Grange in the 1980s, Max Schubert would probably choose to fashion it from Cabernet. Back in 1950, he elected to use Shiraz for reasons of expediency rather than character, and now despite this he claims he compares Grange to the best clarets, "not Australian wines, and never the Hermitage of France."

Still a lively type, and a very snappy dresser, with his pencil-thin moustache and slicked-down hair, he does have the air of a conjuror about him. He has handed over day-to-day responsibility for Grange to a team of skilled technicians, but still fantasises about creating a new wine, *"the exact opposite of Grange – more elegance, from the classic Bordeaux mix grown somewhere very cool. If I could, I'd go to Tasmania, or round Canberra perhaps . . ."*

Petaluma

To wine writers like James Halliday, Brian Croser is "Australia's most talented young winemaker." To Croser's students at the improbably named Wagga Wagga school of oenology he is known as "the guru." And to some rival winemakers he is "our young Turk." That one individual could have made quite such an impact on Australian winemaking is remarkable. That he should have managed it before he was 30 among those as difficult to impress as Australians is almost unbelievable. It would be easy, in the reflected glory of his first releases of Chardonnay, Traminer and Rhine Riesling from the 1977 and 1978 vintages, to have developed certain prima donna characteristics himself – and it is true that Croser has the reputation of never returning a call. He sees himself, however, in very prosaic terms: *"In Australia there are attempts to glamorise wine and to develop the cult of the personality, but the winemaker is really only a quality control officer. A good winemaker is simply a good technical operator with*

the perception to make the correct decisions about how to treat high quality fruit, and these are all very small, subtle decisions."

It was not until he was looking for a practical application for his interest in biochemistry while studying agricultural science at the University of Adelaide that Brian Croser became involved with wine. His father had been a grazier in the Clare Valley, on land which is now covered with vines making first class Rhine Riesling, even though such an esoteric crop would have been unthinkable in the 1950s and 1960s, when Australian for wine was something sweet, red and heavy.

To earn money during vacations Croser started off on traditional agricultural lines, *"but every week I spent on cattle stations in the Northern Territory confirmed my desire to be in the wine trade."* Holiday jobs in South Australia wineries followed and Croser graduated from Adelaide covered in glory and with an offer, from the eminently respectable family firm of

Brian Croser, Australia's young turk, with his distinctly unglamorous winery behind.

Hardy's, not just of a job but of sending him for a stint to the young winemakers' Mecca, the school of oenology at Davis, California. He earned his passage by managing not to tread on the toes of Hardy's established winemakers at their Mile End premises.

Fifteen months of Master's Program under Amerine, Berg, Cleaver, Olmo, Singleton and Winkler during 1972-73 sent Brian and his multi-talented wife Ann back to Australia with ideas that still differentiate his wines from the rest. He admits that the most important principle he learned in California was that the grape variety and where it is grown is more important than how it is made into wine. It crystallised for him the realisation that to a large extent the Australian wine industry has been moulded by viticultural convenience. Technically, its wine-makers are at least as fine as their Californian counterparts – as they have to be, for most vine-yards are in climatologically unsuitable regions – but the business of finding the perfect spot for each grape variety has only just begun.

It was not until early 1975 that the impatient Croser could start to put his new principles into practice, on his promotion from assistant to head winemaker at Hardy's. By the end of the year he had turned round the methods of production to his satisfaction, and then become deeply dis-satisfied. *"I could see myself running three wineries, but completely deskbound. I made the fundamental decision then that I wanted to stay at grassroots level and teach."*

Luckily for a whole generation of Austra-lian wine graduates, he decided to leave Hardy's to set up a new oenology course at Wagga's Riverina College. This gave him the chance of formulating an exact philosophy which he calls quite simply "The Best Way to Make Wine" with the benefit of both academic and practical experience behind him. His course was built around thirty "axioms." The first is that fruit quality is the most important parameter deter-mining the quality of wine made from it, an extension of Davis's basic legacy. Secondly, *"fruit flavour is the single most important com-ponent. Sugar, acid, tannin and pH can all be manipulated, but the one thing the winemaker is powerless to inject into his blend is the flavour of healthy grapes."* (There *has* been work on developing "essence of Rhine Riesling" but, happily, the grape has proved itself more com-plex than hickory smoke and apple blossom for the flavourologists.)

Fruit and its importance continue as the basic theme of his axioms, as can be tasted in the intensity of the wines he makes. Fruit flavour is the backbone of all wines, argues Croser, and the nuances that come from yeast or wood or bottle ageing are simply methods of increasing com-plexity, building up interest around the essential raw material. It is hardly surprising to find that Croser's favourite Chardonnays come from Cali-fornia rather than the more restrained *climats* of the Côte d'Or. *"A lot of white burgundies may be superb in some senses, but you can't taste the grape off the vine, and that to me is part of good winemaking. They're too austere and don't have that luscious passion fruit/melon/bordering on ripe fig aroma. I like a mixture of fruit salad and wood."* Brian Croser is a great fan of Char-donnays made by his Davis contemporary Zelma Long, both at Simi and at Long Vineyards. He admits that such blockbusters can sometimes be too big to be good with food, but his philosophy is that of the purist, *"My concept of fine wine quality belongs not on the dining table but at the tasting table,"* he says sternly. *"A good Char-donnay can be consumed at almost any time by people who are seriously interested in wine; it's a bit like a table sherry."*

Croser was an exacting teacher, but he ad-mits that he is happiest, and most stimulated, when teaching and exposed to new and enquiring minds. His ideal is to combine academic and practical aspects of winemaking. While setting up the Riverina course, he established a small winery for the students to put into practice all those axioms. The "College" label has since established itself as one of Australia's most interesting (and award-bedecked); and compara-tive tastings of similar grapes and vintages under this and Brian Croser's own label are most in-structive. Croser seems to let rip when making wine for himself.

Petaluma began life as a hurried session round the Croser kitchen table after a party, his farewell to Hardy's. His lawyer insisted on leav-ing with a name for Croser's new personal wine-making enterprise, and Ann suggested the name of this small town in Sonoma County, California – because it sounded pretty (and possibly Aboriginal) rather than because it is known as the wrist-wrestling capital of America. Grapes are not yet grown there, although Croser believes the Californians may find ways to compensate for its low temperatures.

The first two commercial vintages of Petaluma, 1977 and 1978, were made at the College winery at Wagga Wagga, from grapes chosen with enormous care from the range that Australia's grape growers had to offer. Brian Croser's very first Petaluma wine was made at Griffith from late harvest Rhine Riesling grapes tracked down at the Mitchelton winery outside Melbourne.

Petaluma was assured of a brilliant future when that first Traminer carried off no fewer than three gold medals at the wine shows that are so important in guiding consumer demand in Australia. This started a rapid path to stardom for Brian Croser, which means that he is now an eminent and highly critical show judge himself and therefore declines to submit his Petaluma releases in the shows (where they would in any case be competing with so many wines to which he had acted as consultant that it would be additionally embarrassing).

Petaluma, the roving winery, finally found itself a permanent home when towards the end of 1978 Croser found himself once more heading towards a life of bureaucracy. The committees were starting to figure more than the classroom in his life at "Wagga" and he confessed to his old friend and mentor Len Evans his desire to put down roots for Petaluma. In less time than it took to down a glass, Croser, Evans and his partner had the whole thing worked out. Croser was finally going to get to build a winery for himself, instead of for the other people for whom he had advised, and it was to be in the cool heights of the Adelaide Hills which he had always reckoned would produce more sophisticated fruit than any other area. While he developed new vineyards here, terra almost incognita to other winemakers, he would buy fruit from vineyards in Clare and Coonawarra in which Evans was involved. Energetic Western Australian Denis Horgan of Leeuwin Estate has now taken a stake at Petaluma.

It was a perfect plan, just so long as Croser could get his unglamorous winery into shape in the four months before the 1979 vintage (in February and March in the southern hemisphere). The result was a 20 metres by 20 metres corrugated iron shed which makes up for what it lacks in aesthetic appeal in the sophistication of its equipment. There is one of those beasts still relatively rare in Australia, a Willmes press. Everything is eminently chillable, of course, although this is rather less vital up here in one of the country's highest wineries. Brian Croser de-

signed his own fermentors with a traditional headboard system to allow the grapeskin cap to be fully submerged during fermentation, which takes place at around a low, low 10°C (50°F) for red and between 8°C (46°F) and 15°C (59°F) for whites and lasts for up to four weeks for reds and Chardonnays, and up to 10 weeks for Rhine Riesling. For such a relatively small winery (producing 8,000 cases in 1980), there is a remarkably sophisticated laboratory, in which the complicated analysis of wine samples is considerably easier than the making of a cup of coffee. But then Croser is pretty fussy about his coffee, and the operation involved rather more than the simple addition of hot water to a powder.

The winery is being extended to make room for the planned eventual production of 8,000 cases of Rhine Riesling, 6,000 cases of Chardonnay and 8,000 cases of red wine, largely Cabernet. The plan is that eventually the Chardonnay will come from the little hidden valley around the winery below a winding mountain road near the village of Piccadilly. Initially the grapes were being brought partly from Cowra to the west of Sydney and partly from Coonawarra, from vineyards closely allied to the Katnook operation. Croser's strictures mean that both sources have "built-in obsolescence" because they're too hot for him. (Wines made under other labels from these vineyards have been winning awards consistently throughout Australia.) But Croser wants an even longer growing season and points happily to the fact that his vineyards will always be about five degrees cooler than Adelaide eight miles down the hill, as well as

Croser and his old classmate Jane Hogarth, who is now research director for this intensely technical enterprise.

PETALUMA

1980 RHINE RIESLING

750ml

PRODUCE OF AUSTRALIA BOTTLED AT PICCADILLY SA

Note that "Bottled at." Croser buys his grapes from hundreds of miles around the winery up in the Adelaide hills.

enjoying double the city's rainfall, about 45 inches a year. There will be no need for irrigation here, unusually for Australia's vineyards. *"This is the only place in South Australia that's as cool as Tasmania,"* he says. *"Mind you, I'm going to set up a meteorological station of our own, I don't trust the official one."*

The aim is to draw Cabernet from its acknowledged Australian home, Coonawarra, and Rhine Riesling from the mature, ultra-cool vineyards in the Clare Valley, famous for its delicate whites. All *crème de la crème* stuff. Chardonnay is still so new to Australia that it has not established its perfect spot, but doubtless the Petaluma site will be a strong candidate. Until all these planned vines start bearing, however, Croser has to dash about the continent checking up on fruit quality as it develops. During vintage time he regularly drives a thousand miles a week. What is so impressive and intriguing to those brought up on the European tenet that geography determines all, is that Croser manages to make such harmonious, integrated and complex wines from a blend of grapes which may be grown five hundred miles apart. The use of a local cool store for fruit growers has played an important part here in keeping freshly picked grapes as though freshly picked for days before fermentation. This man breaks all the rules.

Reds will probably be pure Cabernet ulti-

mately, although there is 20 per cent Shiraz in the 1980 vintage, and they will spend between 12 and 18 months in Limousin and Nevers oak (Chardonnay goes into Limousin for a year usually). Croser and his partner Tony Jordan, who together own a winemaking consultancy business, Oenotec, have also had great fun making small quantities of a port, reported to be divine but still under wraps like the intense, aristocratic reds. They are designed for consumption only after five years or so – again unusual for Australian reds, but Croser expects them to keep on developing for a further ten.

His Rhine Riesling is again intense, noticeably richer than a German wine, and more elegant and vibrant than most California counterparts. He feels strongly that the Californians take a rather cavalier attitude towards their Rieslings, while the Australians have always treated the variety with the respect it has to command in such a warm climate. His model for this variety is J. J. Prüm, no less, and he reckons his 1980 Clare Valley version is his best attempt (at any wine) so far. The Chardonnay, put into specially imported white burgundy bottles, is one of those massive, built-to-last wines which needs perhaps five years to start to show what it has to offer. There is burnt toast, some oak and of course Croser's favourite fruit salad on the nose.

To many, Croser's life must look ideal. He lives a couple of minutes' walk from the winery in his recently-extended house with Ann and three young daughters, and sees it as essential continually to taste great wines from all over the world, especially Europe, to compare with what is sitting in his own casks and bottles and vats. With a simple snack lunch, the visitor might well be treated to a 1945 claret after the palate-freshening champagne – French, of course.

But someone as singleminded and determined as Croser will never be satisfied. He has already made wine in California and Bordeaux, and has fine sherry and his own "champagne" as two secret goals – all this while waiting for the vineyards of the moon to conquer.

INDEX

Acknowledgements

"Research" seems far too laborious a word to describe the wonderful time I have had compiling this book. All the more feeble of me not to have had the idea for such an enterprise myself, for it has provided me with an entrée to the world's most exciting wine properties. The credit for it must go to my very good friend Caradoc King who deserves to benefit by more than ten per cent for it. I also owe enormous thanks to the wine people mentioned in this book. They have all been extremely helpful, courteous, hospitable and tolerant. The official bodies representing wine interests on a generic level were equally long-suffering, particularly Food and Wine from France, Club Expression, the Wines from Germany Information Service, Vinos de España, the Rioja Wine Information Centre and the Australian Wine Board. As always, the British wine trade has shown itself almost incredibly kind to this wine writer, and I would like particularly to thank Doug Endersby, Helen Thomson and Parry de Winton.

Jancis Robinson

Photographic credits
Numerals refer to page numbers (abbreviations: t, top; c, centre; b, bottom; r, right; l, left).
Bob Davis 223, 224, 225, 226, 233, 235. Patrick Eagar 7, 15, 77, 102, 131, 132. Jean-Paul Ferrero 9bl, 228, 229, 230, 231. Judy Goldhill 137, 138, 140, 142, 143, 144, 145, 146, 149, 150, 151, 152, 153, 154, 155, 156, 157, 158, 160, 161, 162. K. Kerth 163. Michael Kuh 9tc, 9cl, 9cr, 83, 86, 91, 94, 98, 141, 171, 172, 174, 176, 178, 179, 180, 182, 183, 184, 185, 186. Colin Maher 9tl, 10, 30t, 36, 59tl, 62, 85, 119, 120tr, 126, 133. Edward Piper 9tr, 16, 18, 20, 22, 23, 24, 25b, 26, 27, 28, 30b, 31, 32, 33t, 38, 39, 40, 42, 43, 44, 45, 47, 49, 50, 51, 53tl, 53tr, 53br, 54, 56, 58, 59tr, 59br, 63, 65, 66, 68, 70, 71, 72, 74, 75, 76, 78, 80, 81, 82, 87, 88, 89, 90, 92, 95, 97, 99, 101, 103, 105, 106, 107, 108, 110, 111, 114, 115, 116, 121, 122, 123, 125, 127, 129. Roger Pring 190b. David Russell 164. Tessa Traeger title page, 9c, 33b. Nik Wheeler 6, 9bc, 9br, 187, 188, 189, 190tl, 190tr, 192, 193, 194, 195, 196, 197, 198, 199, 200, 202, 203, 204, 205, 206, 207, 208, 209, 210, 213, 214, 215, 216, 219, 220, 221, 222. Jon Wyand 25t, 53bl, 55, 109, 120tl, 128, 134, 169. The photographs on page 61 are reproduced by courtesy of M. Delon and those on pages 166, 168 and 170 by courtesy of the Marchese Piero Antinori.
Illustrations
Sharon Finmark 77, 96. Dinah Lone 17, 18, 29, 32, 40, 58, 60, 65, 69tl, 73, 84, 102, 107, 119, 124, 126, 132, 139, 143, 153, 156, 159, 165, 169, 173, 175, 188, 217, 224, 232. David Mallott 34-5. Janos Marffy 48, 51, 181, 194tr, 201, 212. Andrew Popkiewicz 86, 93, 104tr, 109, 117, 135, 227br. The publishers are grateful to Nicholas Faith for assistance in the preparation of the map on pages 34-5.